MW01006748

WILLIAM FAULKNER
— DAY BY DAY —

WILLIAM FAULKNER DAY BY DAY

CARL ROLLYSON

UNIVERSITY PRESS OF MISSISSIPPI / JACKSON

The University Press of Mississippi is the scholarly publishing agency of the Mississippi Institutions of Higher Learning: Alcorn State University, Delta State University, Jackson State University, Mississippi State University, Mississippi University for Women, Mississippi Valley State University, University of Mississippi, and University of Southern Mississippi.

Designed by Peter D. Halverson

www.upress.state.ms.us
The University Press of Mississippi is a member of the Association of University Presses.

Manufactured in the United States of America

First printing 2022
∞

Library of Congress Cataloging-in-Publication Data

Names: Rollyson, Carl E. (Carl Edmund), author.
Title: William Faulkner day by day / Carl Rollyson.
Description: Jackson : University Press of Mississippi, [2022] | Includes bibliographical references and index.
Identifiers: LCCN 2022019447 (print) | LCCN 2022019448 (ebook) | ISBN 9781496835017 (hardback) | ISBN 9781496842879 (epub) | ISBN 9781496842886 (epub) | ISBN 9781496842893 (pdf) | ISBN 9781496842909 (pdf)
Subjects: LCSH: Faulkner, William, 1897–1962. | Authors, American—20th century—Biography. | Novelists, American—20th century—Biography. | LCGFT: Biographies.
Classification: LCC PS3511.A86 Z9623 2022 (print) | LCC PS3511.A86 (ebook) | DDC 813/.52 [B]—dc23/eng/20220525
LC record available at https://lccn.loc.gov/2022019447
LC ebook record available at https://lccn.loc.gov/2022019448

British Library Cataloging-in-Publication Data available

Nature doesn't disdain what lives only for a day.
It pours the whole of itself into each moment.

—TOM STOPPARD, *SHIPWRECK*

In Memory of M. Thomas Inge

CONTENTS

WILLIAM FAULKNER
— DAY BY DAY —

INTRODUCTION

TO NEVER DEVIATE FROM CHRONOLOGY IN A BIOGRAPHY, I WROTE IN *The Life of William Faulkner*, is to say that a life is just one damn thing after another. Flashbacks, flash forwards, and digressions are necessary in biography as much as they are in Faulkner's fiction, in order to understand the dynamics of characters and events. And yet biographical narratives, because they are designed as stories, inevitably discard many precious details and the feel of what it is like to live day by day. So this book is an effort to recover the diurnal Faulkner, to write in the present tense about past events as if they are happening now. And where there are still gaps, where I cannot account for certain days, perhaps other researchers will come along to fill some of those voids, prodded by what I have included or overlooked. This work builds on Michel Gresset's *A Faulkner Chronology*, but his work is concerned with the "main events in the *writer's* life," whereas I am concerned with the whole man—including every detail I can recover. The modernist prejudice against biography, against looking at every aspect of a writer's life, has to be countered by John Keats's declaration: "Does Shelley go on telling Strange Stories of the Death of Kings? Tell him there are strange Stories of the death of poets." And before Keats, Samuel Johnson: "The heroes of literary as well as civil history have been very often no less remarkable for what they have suffered than for what they have achieved."

My approach is inspired by Jay Leyda's *Melville Log*, that bedrock of Melville biography. Leyda wanted to establish a groundwork for the biographies yet to come. Although Faulkner has many biographers, there is no reason to suppose that others will not appear in this and the next millennium so long as this world and its literature survives.

For each entry, except for the obvious facts, I have noted in curly brackets {} the source for the entry. In many cases, entries have, or could have, multiple sources—primary and secondary. I have not tried to trace all the sources for each entry. The entries are extracts, not the whole document, letter, or incident.

This book is for Faulkner readers of all kinds with a wide variety of interests in the man and his work. The entries are suitable for dipping into and can be read in a minute or an hour, by the bedside or propped against another book or other suitable support during a meal. It is difficult to read several Faulkner biographies side by side, but this book, by ranging over several sources, stimulates several points of comparison between biographies and other sources.

What holds true for another book of this kind, *Marilyn Monroe Day by Day*, also holds true for this one. It is for anyone who delights in savoring all aspects of becoming and being a self. One of the chief virtues of these books is that they do not force their subjects to conform to any one biographical narrative. Reading about Faulkner day by day yields many different Faulkners and perhaps suggests new angles and perspectives.

ABBREVIATIONS

AB: André Bleikasten: *William Faulkner: A Life through Novels*
B1: Joseph Blotner, *Faulkner*, volume 1 (1974)
B2: Joseph Blotner, *Faulkner*, volume 2 (1974)
B3: Joseph Blotner, *Faulkner: A Biography* (1984)
BH1: Louis Daniel Brodsky and Robert W. Hamblin, *Faulkner: The Brodsky Collection, Volume I*
BH2: Louis Daniel Brodsky and Robert W. Hamblin, *Faulkner: The Brodsky Collection, Volume II: Letters*
BH3: Louis Daniel Brodsky and Robert W. Hamblin, *Faulkner: A Comprehensive Guide to the Brodsky Collection, Volume III: The De Gaulle Story*
BH4: Louis Daniel Brodsky and Robert W. Hamblin, ed, *Faulkner: A Comprehensive Guide to the Brodsky Collection, Volume IV: Battle Cry: A Screenplay by William Faulkner*
BH5: Louis Daniel Brodsky and Robert W. Hamblin, *Faulkner: A Comprehensive Guide to the Brodsky Collection, Volume V: Manuscripts and Documents*
CCP: Carvel Collins Papers, Harry R. Ransom Humanities Research Center, University of Texas at Austin
CFS: Joseph Blotner Papers, Center for Faulkner Studies, Southeast Missouri State University
CR1: Carl Rollyson, *The Life of William Faulkner*, volume 1
CR2: Carl Rollyson, *The Life of William Faulkner*, volume 2
CWF: M. Thomas Inge, ed., *Conversations with William Faulkner*
DM: David Minter, *William Faulkner: His Life and Work*
DSF: Dean Swift Faulkner, *Dean Swift Faulkner: A Biographical Study*, University of Mississippi master's thesis, 1975
EPP: Carvel Collins, ed., *Early Prose and Poetry*
ESPL: *Essays, Speeches, and Public Letters*
FC: Malcolm Cowley, *The Faulkner-Cowley File*
FF: Bruce Kawin, *Faulkner and Film*
FK: Frederick Karl, *William Faulkner: American Writer*
FU: Frederick L. Gwynn and Joseph L. Blotner, ed., *Faulkner in the University*
FW: Floyd C. Watkins Papers, Stuart A. Rose Manuscript, Archives, and Rare Book Library, Emory University
HHP: Howard Hawks Papers, Brigham Young University Library.
JB: John Bassett, ed., *William Faulkner: The Critical Heritage*

JP: Jay Parini, *One Matchless Time: A Life of William Faulkner*
JW: Joel Williamson, *William Faulkner and Southern History*
LC: James B. Meriwether, *The Literary Career of William Faulkner*
LG: James B. Meriwether and Michael Millgate, ed., *Lion in the Garden: Interviews with William Faulkner 1926–1962*
MC: *Man Collecting, an Exhibition in the University of Virginia Library honoring Linton Reynolds Massey (1900–1974)*
MFP: Malcolm Franklin Papers, University of South Carolina, Irvin Department of Rare Books and Special Collections.
MG: Michel Gresset, *A Faulkner Chronology*
MGM: Bruce Kawin, ed., *Faulkner's MGM Screenplays*
NF: Nicholas Fargnoli, ed. *William Faulkner: A Literary Companion*
NOS: Carvel Collins, ed., *New Orleans Sketches*
NYPL: Berg Collection, New York Public Library
PD: Falkner/Faulkner Family Collection, University Archives- Special Collections, William Patterson University
PW: Philip Weinstein, *Becoming Faulkner*
RHR: Random House Records, Rare Book and Manuscript Library, Columbia University
RO: Sally Stone Trotter, *Rowan Oak Collector's Edition: A History of the William Faulkner Home*
SL: Joseph Blotner, ed., *Selected Letters of William Faulkner*
SO: Stephen B. Oates, *William Faulkner: The Man and the Artist*
SS: Susan Snell, *Phil Stone of Oxford*
TCF: Sarah Gleeson-White, ed., *William Faulkner at Twentieth Century-Fox: The Annotated Screenplays*
TH: James G.Watson, ed., *Thinking of Home: William Faulkner's Letters to his Mother and Father 1918–1925*
UM: Paul Flowers Collection, University of Mississippi, Department of Archives and Special Collections
USC: Warner Brothers Archives, University of Southern California School of Cinematic Arts
USWF: Joseph Blotner, ed., *Uncollected Stories of William Faulkner*
WC: William B. Wisdom Collection, Tulane University Library
WF: William Faulkner
WFC: M. Thomas Inge, ed. *William Faulkner: The Contemporary Reviews*
WFH: Stefan Solomon, *William Faulkner in Hollywood: Screenwriting for the Studios*
WFJW: Lisa C. Hickman, *William Faulkner and Joan Williams*
WFO: James W. Webb and A. Wigfall Green, *William Faulkner of Oxford*

PRINCIPAL PERSONAGES

Aldridge, Leslie. A journalist, she met WF in Princeton and brought him home to her husband, literary critic John Aldridge. WF engaged in flirtation in person and by letter with Leslie Aldridge.

Anderson, Elizabeth Prall (1884–1976). Employed WF in a New York bookstore and later, after she married Sherwood Anderson, put WF up in New Orleans and facilitated his introduction to the city.

Anderson, Sherwood (1876–1941). Author of the acclaimed *Winesburg Ohio* and resident of New Orleans when WF arrived in 1925. Anderson was instrumental in fostering WF's career, drawing the attention of publisher Horace Liveright, who published WF's first novel, *Soldiers' Pay* (1926).

Bacher, William (1897–1965). A Warner Bros. producer who worked with WF on *Battle Cry* and encouraged him to write a script that eventually became *A Fable*.

Barr, Caroline (1855–1940). Born in slavery, she became a Faulkner family retainer who raised all three of the Falkner boys and WF's daughter Jill. Aspects of Barr are rendered in the portrayal of Aunt Mollie in *Go Down, Moses* (1942).

Bezzerides, A. I. ("Buzz" 1908–2007). A screenwriter who became WF's friend and collaborator with whom WF sometimes stayed while in Hollywood.

Blotner, Joseph (1923–2012). WF's authorized biographer and a faculty member at the University of Virginia while WF was writer in residence.

Braithwaite, William Stanley (1878–1962). An African American editor of several influential poetry anthologies, one of which included WF's poetry.

Brown, Calvin, Jr. (1909–1989. Son of Ole Miss professor, Calvin Jr. grew up with WF, who was an older friend and mentor.

Brown, Calvin S., Sr. (1866–1945). A professor at the University of Mississippi who encouraged WF's writing of poetry.

Brown, Maud (1877–1968). Wife of Calvin S. Brown, Sr. WF wrote *The Wishing Tree*, a story for her ailing daughter Margaret, who died in 1928.

Bryant, William ("Will") Clarence (1863–1939). Along with his wife, Sallie Bailey, Bryant was owner of the Bailey place, formerly the Sheegog place, and renamed Rowan Oak when WF purchased the property. Bryant took a deep interest in WF's work, and WF reciprocated by writing letters about his novels and stories and revealing in the process an abiding respect for Bryant and the gentlemanly code of doing business.

Buckner, Robert (1906–1989). A University of Virginia graduate, screenwriter, and producer at Warner Bros. who worked closely with WF.

Butler, Charles ("Charlie") Edward (1848–?). Father of Maud Falkner and Oxford sheriff and tax collector who absconded with the town's funds, purportedly taking with him an octoroon mistress.

Butler, Leila Swift (1849–1907). Maud Falkner's mother and WF's grandmother, a.k.a Damuddy, the name used by the Compson children in *The Sound and the Fury.* She fashioned toys for her grandson Billy and was endowed with an esthetic sensibility shared by her daughter Maud.

Carpenter, Meta (1908–1994). A script supervisor for director Howard Hawks when WF met her in December 1935. They carried on a sporadic fifteen-year love affair, which she wrote about in *A Loving Gentleman: The Love Story of William Faulkner and Meta Carpenter* (1976).

Cerf, Bennett (1898–1971). The head of Random House, Cerf courted WF for his list, and WF became a Random House author in 1936, when the firm bought out Harrison Smith. Cerf remained a staunch supporter of WF's work and did everything in his power to keep WF happy as a Random House author.

Collins, Carvel (1912–1990). Began researching WF's life in the late 1940s, becoming an important WF critic and friend of WF's friends and family, although Joseph Blotner, close to both Estelle and WF, became the authorized biographer. Collins continued to do research on a biography until his death, leaving behind a huge collection of material deposited at the Harry R. Ransom Humanities Research Center at the University of Texas at Austin.

Commins, Dorothy (1888–1991). Wife of Saxe Commins, who befriended both William and Estelle Faulkner, often hosting their stays in Princeton. Estelle corresponded frequently with Dorothy.

Commins, Saxe (1898–1958). Random House editor devoted to WF's work and also to looking after the author on his visits to New York and Princeton.

Cowley, Malcolm (1898–1989). Critic and editor of *The Portable Faulkner*, a significant influence in the WF revival in the late 1940s leading to the awarding of the Nobel Prize. WF stayed in Cowley's home, and the critic had several opportunities to observe WF in public and private.

Cullen, John B. (1895–1969). WF grew up with the Cullen family in school and on hunting expeditions. John B. Cullen wrote about the Nelse Patton lynching in *Old Times in the Faulkner Country* and about his friendship with WF.

Devine, Eric James ("Jim"). A lifelong friend of WF who often socialized and drank with him in New York City.

Falkner, Alabama Leroy. *See* McLean, Alabama Leroy.

Falkner, John Wesley Thompson (1848–1922). Son of Colonel William C. Falkner and grandfather of WF. A banker, railroad owner, repository of Falkner family lore, and the model for old Bayard Sartoris in *Flags in the Dust.*

Falkner, John Wesley Thompson, Jr. (1882–1962). WF's uncle (brother of his father, Murry). Called Judge Falkner, he campaigned unsuccessfully for public office—in one instance with his nephew William.

Falkner, Maud (1871–1960). WF's mother. Like her mother, she gravitated to art, especially painting, and encouraged her son's artistic ambitions and later defended his writing. She was the only Falkner family member that WF confided in.

Falkner, Murry (1870–1932). WF's father. A disappointed man who never found his vocation after his father sold the family railroad. He disparaged his son's writing and yet contributed significantly to WF's financial support. Murry figures in the character of Maury, Lucius Priest's father, in *The Reivers.*

Falkner, Murry ("Jack") (1899–1975). WF's brother, a World War I veteran, FBI agent, and author of *The Falkners of Mississippi: A Memoir* (1967).

Falkner, Colonel William Clark (1825–1889). WF's great-grandfather, a lawyer, businessman, Civil War officer, railroad tycoon, novelist, and poet, prone to violence but also to many public benefactions, including the support of education for African Americans. He serves as the model for Colonel John Sartoris shot down, as the old colonel was, by a business rival.

Faulkner, Alabama (January 11–20, 1931). William and Estelle's Faulkner's daughter. Her death had a profound impact on their marriage.

Faulkner, Dean Swift (1907–1935). WF's youngest brother, a pilot whose plane crash haunted WF, who had encouraged the career of his favorite.

Faulkner, Jill (1933–2008). WF's daughter, to whom he wrote frequently while he was away, especially in Hollywood.

Faulkner, Jimmy (1923–2001). John Faulkner's son and WF's nephew. WF was closer to Jimmy than to John.

Faulkner, John ("Johncy") (1901–1963). WF's brother, who adopted the "u" his brother added to the family name. John ran Greenfield Farm, owned by his brother, and published novels and a memoir, *My Brother Bill* (1963).

Faulkner, Lida Estelle Oldham (1896–1972). Daughter of Lemuel and Lida Oldham and WF's childhood sweetheart. She married him after divorcing her first husband, Cornell Franklin. The marriage was fraught with acrimony, exacerbated by the alcoholism of wife and husband, and yet the union endured to WF's dying day and seemed to strengthen in his final years.

Ford, Ruth (1911–2009). An Ole Miss student and then an actress devoted to *Requiem for a Nun* in its play form written, WF said, so she could star in it. WF and Ford often saw one another in New York.

Franklin, Cornell (1892–1959). Estelle Oldham's first husband, an attorney and government official, considered a good catch by the Oldham family, who rejected WF as Estelle's suitor because of his poor prospects. But the Franklin marriage, marked by excessive drinking and adultery, failed in the Far East, where Franklin served as an assistant attorney general and judge, and where Estelle Oldham set some of her stories.

Franklin, Gloria. Malcolm Franklin's first wife and a caustic critic of WF.

Franklin, Malcolm (1923–1977). Son of Cornell Franklin and WF's stepson. Malcolm spent much more time with his stepfather than his father and wrote about his close relationship with WF in *Bitterweeds.*

Franklin (Fielden), Victoria ("Cho-Cho") (1919–1968). Daughter of Cornell Franklin and Estelle Oldham, she became WF's responsibility after he married Estelle. As a child, she was especially close to WF. He dedicated a copy of *The Wishing Tree* to her.

Haas, Robert (1890–1964). Co-founder of Smith and Haas (1932–1936) and a vice-president at Random House. WF corresponded frequently with Haas, relying on his advice and seeking his financial and editorial support.

Hawks, Howard (1896–1977). Hollywood director and frequent collaborator with WF on several films. Their work together spanned more than twenty years.

Howorth, Lucy Somerville (1895–1997). Law student at Ole Miss, a member of the Marionettes drama group and a keen observer of WF.

Jonsson, Else (1912–1996). Wife of Thorston Jonsson (1910–1950), a reporter who interviewed WF in 1946 and predicted he would win the Nobel Prize. WF met Else Jonsson in Stockholm during his visit to receive the Nobel Prize. They became close friends and lovers, sharing time together on WF's trips to Europe and writing to one another for the rest of his life.

Klopfer, Donald. (1902–1986). Co-founder with Bennett Cerf of Random House and a staunch supporter of WF's work.

Linscott, Robert (1886–1964). A veteran Random House editor who worked closely with WF on several books and socialized with him as well.

Liveright, Horace (1884–1933). Sherwood Anderson's publisher who published *Soldiers' Pay*. Liveright has an impressive list of authors including Eugene O'Neill, Ernest Hemingway, and Theodore Dreiser.

Marx, Sam (1902–1992). Head of the MGM story department when WF arrived at the studio in 1932. Marx gave WF assignments and supervised his work.

McLean, Alabama Leroy ("Aunt Bama") (1874–1968). William C. Falkner's daughter, and the repository of stories about the colonel passed on to her great-nephew, WF, who treated her with profound respect and as an authority in the family.

Ober, Harold (1881–1959). WF's agent for much of his career, Ober handled selling his fiction and did much to support his client during tough times.

Odiorne, William (1880–1957). A photographer WF met in Paris in 1925. They become friends, Odiorne photographed WF, and they corresponded after WF returned to the United States.

Oldham, Lemuel (1870–1945). Father of Lida Estelle Oldham. He opposed her marriage to WF but later relied on WF's financial support.

Omlie, Vernon (1895–1936). Barnstormer and professional pilot, he taught WF to fly and accompanied WF to the air show in New Orleans, which became the setting for *Pylon* (1935).

Prall, Elizabeth. *See* Anderson, Elizabeth Prall.

Silver, James W. (1907–1988). Southern historian and friend of WF who visited Rowan Oak often and worked with WF on civil rights issues.

Smith, Harrison ("Hal") (1904–1975). Editor at Harcourt Brace, convinced the firm to publish *Sartoris*, and then established his own firm with British publisher Jonathan Cape. Cape and Smith published *The Sound and the Fury* (1929), *As I Lay Dying* (1930), and *Sanctuary* (1931). The partnership with Cape ended, and Smith and Robert Haas formed the firm of Smith and Haas, publishing *Light in August* (1932), *These Thirteen* (1933), *Doctor Martino and Other Stories* (1934), and *Pylon* (1935) until Random House purchased Smith and Haas and published *Absalom, Absalom!* (1936). Smith remained WF's lifelong friend, and Random House, his lifelong publisher.

Spratling, William (1900–1967). Artist in New Orleans who befriended WF, roomed with him, and accompanied him to Europe. They collaborated on a book, *Sherwood Anderson and Other Famous Creoles* (1926).

Starr, Hubert (1892–1972). A friend of Phil Stone, who met WF at Yale in 1918 and became a lifelong friend, hosting WF in California and corresponding with WF over several decades.

Stein, Jean (1934–2017). She met WF while in St. Moritz with Howard Hawks, working on *Land of the Pharaohs*. They became romantically involved, and she interviewed him for *The Paris Review*. He was devastated over her plans to marry.

Stone, Phil (1893–1967). A practicing attorney in Oxford, the young WF's mentor and promoter and one of the models for Gavin Stevens and Horace Benbow.

Summers, Jill Faulkner. *See* Faulkner, Jill.

Trilling, Steve (1902–1964). Warner Bros. executive, second-in-command to Jack L. Warner. Trilling made sure the terms of WF's contract were strictly enforced and resisted all efforts by those who reported to him to improve WF's employment.

Wasson, Ben (1899–1982). From Greenville, Mississippi, he met WF on the Ole Miss campus and invited him to join a theater group, the Marionettes. Wasson later served as WF's agent and remained his lifelong friend. His memoir, *Count 'No Count: Flashbacks to Faulkner*, was published in 1983.

Wells, Dean Faulkner (1936–2011). the daughter of Dean Swift Faulkner, WF's youngest brother. She grew up in the environs of Rowan Oak, supported by her uncle. She wrote *Every Day by the Sun: A Memoir of the Faulkners of Mississippi*.

Wiley, Bell Irvin (1906–1980). Historian and frequent visitor to Rowan Oak who corresponded with WF.

Williams, Joan (1928–2004). A young writer who visited WF at Rowan Oak and later became romantically involved with him. She wrote a novel about their affair, *The Wintering* (1971), and a memoir included in *Remembering Joan Williams* (2015).

Young, Stark (1881–1963). Critic, novelist, and playwright, a Mississippian and friend of Phil Stone who took an interest in WF, inviting the aspiring poet to New York City and providing a temporary place to stay while the young man acclimated to the urban environment and secured employment in a bookstore.

TIMELINE

1817

Mississippi is admitted to the Union.

1825

July 6: William Clark Falkner, "the old Colonel," is born near Knoxville, Tennessee, on the same day that his great-grandson, William Cuthbert Faulkner, will die.

1832

October 22: King Ishtehotopah and Chief Tishomingo sign the Treaty of Pontotoc, ceding six million acres of Chickasaw land to the United States. {B1, MG}

1835

The Chickasaw begin their migration to Oklahoma.

1836

Lafayette County, Mississippi is established, with Oxford as its county seat. {MG}

April 2: Charles George Butler (Maud Falkner's grandfather) becomes the first sheriff of Lafayette County and also its surveyor. {JW}

1837

William Clark Falkner, age twelve, accompanies his family to Missouri. {JW}

1838

John Wesley Thompson, William Faulkner's uncle, moves to Ripley, Mississippi. {JW}

Charles George Butler owns eleven lots in Oxford, valued $5,550, and seven slaves. {JW}

1840

Charles Butler administers the census. {JW}

1842

William Clark Falkner arrives in Pontotoc, Mississippi, 30 miles from Oxford, to live with his uncle John Wesley Thompson, an attorney who later becomes a district attorney and judge. {JW}

1844

In Oxford, Robert Sheegog acquires a tract of land to build a house designed by an English architect, which WF will purchase and call Rowan Oak.

1845

William Clark Falkner establishes his residence in Ripley, Mississippi.

June 8: Andrew J. McCannon murders a doctor and four members of his family. William Clark Falkner, part of the posse organized to apprehend the murderer, obtains his confession and publishes it in a profitable pamphlet. {JW}

1847

Mid-January: William Clark Falkner joins the 2nd Mississippi Volunteer Regiment at Vicksburg, in the invasion of Mexico. {JW}

April 14: Near Monterey, William Clark Falkner is found injured in one foot and hand, apparently the victim of an attack during what may have been a private errand of pleasure. {JW}

April 19: William Clark Falkner is granted a convalescent leave. {JW}

July 9: William Clark Falkner marries Holland Pearce in Knoxville, Tennessee. {JW}

October 31: William Falkner is discharged from military service. {JW}

1848

September 2: Holland Pearce gives birth to John Wesley Thompson Falkner, named after William Clark's uncle, who took William Clark under his protection after the boy had run away from his Missouri home in an altercation with his brother. {JW}

Merchant Robert Sheegog completes building his home, the future Rowan Oak, on eight city lots. {RO}

1849

February: William Clark Falkner and Holland Pearce sell their slaves "Phillis, aged 32, and her three sons, John aged 5, Joe, 3, and Peter, 1, for $1,200." {JW}

March 5: Birth of Leila Swift (Maud Falkner's mother). {JW}

May 8: In a fight, William Clark Falkner stabs and kills Robert Hindman, who had drawn a revolver, which misfires three times. {JW}

Spring: William Clark Falkner is acquitted of murder. {JW}

May 31: Holland Pearce perishes of consumption. {JW}

1850

January: William Clark Falkner purchases two slaves, "Patsey and her child Benjamin, about sixteen months old, from Holland's brother Lazarus for $256." {JW}

September: Census records that William Clark Falkner owns five black slaves. {JW}

435,000 slaves constitute 57 percent of Mississippi's population owned by 25 percent of the white families. {JW}

1851

William Clark Falkner publishes *The Siege of Monterey*, a poetic epic of the Mexican War, which is crude, melodramatic, and romantic but also energetic and brash in praise of marriage ("it makes copulation / A virtue, when under circumstances lawful") and the hazards of war. He publishes a novel, *The Spanish Heroine*, also set in Monterey. {B1}

February 28: In a dispute over a property rental, William Clark Falkner draws his pistol and shoots and kills Erasmus W. Morris, a Thomas Hindman partisan and rival of Falkner. {JW}

March 12: A jury acquits William Clark Falkner. {JW}

April 1: William Clark Falkner and Thomas Hindman make an agreement to fight a duel, but a friend intervenes to prevent violence. {JW}

October 12: William Clark Falkner marries Elizabeth (Lizzie) Vance. {JW}

1852

William Clark Falkner purchases "Emily a mulatto girl slave." {JW}

August 14: C. A. Brougham of the Sons of Temperance brings William C. Falkner to trial. "I charge Bro. W.C. Falkner for violating Article 2 of the constitution by drinking cider in my presence." Falkner moves to have the word "cider" removed from the pledge. {JW}

1853

August 1: Lizzie Vance Falkner gives birth to William Henry Falkner. {JW}

R. G. Dun, a company specializing in credit reports, notes that William Clark Falkner "is marrd has some means say 3 improved houses / lots in Town to rent out. His income from this source is some 4 $ 5c [four to five hundred dollars] per annum." {JW}

1855

A newspaper account describes William Clark Falkner as a "married man with good habits and a fair business capacity. He has about $7,000 in capital and some good property in town, including two brick stores worth about $4,000." {JW}

R. G. Dun reports that William C. Falkner is "a little wild in his hab[its]." {JW}

Caroline Barr, a slave, is born and later takes charge of WF and his brothers. {JW}

November 18: The *Ripley Advertiser* reports that William Clark Falkner has lost the election to the state legislature. {B1}

1856

July 17: Lizzie Vance gives birth to a daughter, Willie Madera, by William Clark Falkner. {JW}

William Clark Falkner casts one of 174 Democratic electoral votes for James Buchanan, who becomes the 15th president of the United States. {JW}

1857

March 21: Receipt from William Clark Falkner to John W. Thompson for payment for a slave. {MC, JW}

1858

William Clark Falkner is appointed brigadier general of the militia. {B1}

September: William Clark Falkner pays $900 for three slaves, Emeline, Delia, and Hellen, who reside in his yard. {JW}

November 24: R. G. Dun hires William Clark Falkner as a local agent. {JW}

January: William Clark Falkner sells "a negro woman named Livy" for $640 guaranteeing "the title clear & that she is a slave for life." {JW}

1859

March: William C. Falkner successfully defends James W. Whitten for illegally trading with a slave. {JW}

July 13: WF's great-great-great-uncle, John Wesley Thompson pays $100 for membership in the Book and Tract Society of the Memphis conference of the Methodist Church, South, and receives an elaborate genealogical casebook and Bible that becomes the family record of births and deaths. He specifies that this Bible should always be presented to the eldest son of its generation. {B1}

1860

Census records that William Clark Falkner, an attorney, owns six mulatto slaves.[1]

He declares $40,200 in personal property. Personal property is defined as moveable property, and included slaves. {JW}

August 31: Robert Sheegog dies.

1861

January 9: Mississippi secedes from the Union.

Late April: William Clark Falkner is elected to a captaincy in "The Magnolia Rifles" in the Confederate army. {B1}

July 21: The *Memphis Appeal* reports that at the first battle of Bull Run "The Colonel, who was ever in the van of battle, received a slight wound in the face. . . . When the second horse fell under him, he was thrown violently against a stump, and for some moments lay senseless." General Beauregard is said to have remarked to Falkner: "History shall never forget you!" {B1}

1862

April 21: William Clark Falkner loses election for colonel and is reported as disliked for "his harsh and ruthless disciplinary methods" and reckless behavior at Bull Run.[2] {B1, JW}

April 22: Brigadier General W. H. H. Whiting declares that Colonel Falkner "has been defeated by demagogues and affords another illustration of the crying evils that the election system in our army has wrought, and is producing." Whiting reads to his regiments a commendation of Falkner for his gallantry in the Mexican and Civil Wars. {B1}

December: General Grant occupies Oxford. {JW}

1863

February: General Beauregard puts William Clark Falkner in command of the 7th Mississippi Regiment organized as the "Partisan Rangers."

July 18: Grant takes Vicksburg.

End of July: William Clark Falkner recruits 600 soldiers under his command. {JW}

Early August: William Clark Falkner captures 55 horses in an engagement near Dyersburg, Tennessee but loses 31 men. {JW}

Mid-August: After burning a bridge, William Clark Falkner leads several hundred men on a cavalry attack against General Philip H. Sheridan and is routed, barely escaping without his hat. {JW}

September: William Clark Falkner engages in several skirmishes with Union troops to no great effect. {JW}

October 26: William Clark Falkner's last skirmish drives a Federal detachment toward Corinth and the Tennessee line. {JW}

October 29: All Partisan Ranger units are disbanded. {JW}

1863

January: Congressman J. W. Clapp obtains permission for William Clark Falkner to organize a regiment, and Faulkner begins an unsuccessful letter writing campaign seeking promotion. {JW}

April 8: William Clark Falkner's regiment scores a minor victory driving outnumbered Federals north toward Memphis. {JW}

April 18: William Clark Falkner's regiment sustains devastating losses near Memphis. {JW}

Late April: William Clark Falkner leads a brief, successful skirmish while still petitioning for a promotion. {JW}

Mid-May: William Clark Falkner is relieved of his command. {JW}

July: William Clark Falkner's request for a command is denied. {JW}

Late August–September: William Clark Falkner apparently abandons efforts to secure a command. {JW}

October 25: William Clark Falkner resigns from the army, citing poor health, certified by a surgeon's report specifying "indigestion and internal hemorrhoids." {B1}

1864

In Falkner family lore, Colonel William Clark Falkner becomes a blockade runner and amasses a fortune he quickly puts to use in post–Civil War Mississippi, regaining his standing as property owner, businessman, and public benefactor.

July: Emeline Falkner gives birth to a daughter, Fanny, by William C. Falkner. {JW, see entry for October 17, 1898}

August 9: General Andrew J. Smith burns the Oxford town square.

1865

April 26: William Clark Falkner makes a cash purchase of lot #137 in Pontotoc. {JW}

July 27: William Clark Faulkner purchases 20 feet of business frontage in Ripley. {JW}

August 7: William Clark Falkner purchases for $800 a block of land and erects a one-story house. {JW}

August 10: William Clark Falkner purchases several more lots in Ripley.

1866

November: Charles ("Charlie") Edward Butler enters the University of Mississippi. {JW}

1867

January 1: R. G. Dun reports that William Clark Falkner's Ripley dry goods store contains goods paid with cash valued at $6000 to $7000. "Pays punctually and is never sued on mercantile a/c [account], and very little in any way," the reporter notes. "No liens on his property, nor encumbrances of any kind." {JW}

William Clark Falkner contributes to the fund for the reopening of the Ripley Female Academy, renamed as Stonewall College, establishing a precedent his great-grandson will continue by supporting students, black and white. The colonel also writes a melodramatic play, *The Lost Diamond*, and helps with a staging a drama about orphans, false arrests, and lovers at odds. The colonel's theatrical interests will be taken up again in his great-grandson's efforts on the Ole Miss campus. {B1, JW}

April: Falkner family lore that the colonel participated in efforts to suppress the black vote will work its way into Colonel Sartoris's confrontation with carpetbaggers in *The Unvanquished*. {B1}

1868

R. G. Dun reports that William C. Falkner is a "practicing lawyer of good standing & engaged in trade with a net worth estimated at $30,000." {JW}

July 31: Leila Swift and Charlie Butler take out a marriage license. {JW}

August 2: Leila Swift and Charlie Butler marry. {JW}

1869

September: John Wesley Thompson (J. W. T.), the colonel's son by Holland Pearce, graduates from University of Mississippi law school. {JW}

September 2: J. W. T. Falkner marries Sallie McAlpine Murry, daughter of a prominent citizen, Dr. John Young Murry, and settles in Ripley, Mississippi.[3] {B1}

1870

August 17: J. W. T. and Sallie Murry's son, Murry Cuthbert (WF's father), is born. {B1}

1871

Reconstruction of the Oxford courthouse and jail begins. {B1}

May: A charter is issued to William Clark Falkner, R. J. Thurmond, and thirty-four others for a railroad from Ripley to just beyond the Tennessee line. Later in the year, Falkner is elected president of the railroad. {JW}

November 27: Maud Butler (WF's mother) is born to Lelia and Charles Butler. {B1, JW}

1872

January: The state legislature renames the railroad—Ship Island, Ripley & Kentucky Railroad Company—and expands the line to the lower tip of Illinois and an ocean port on the Gulf of Mexico. {B1}

November 21: Robert Sheegog sells his home (the future Rowan Oak) and eight lots to John M. Bailey. {RO}

December 16: J. W. T. and Sallie Murry's daughter, Mary Holland, is born. {B1}

1874

R. G. Dun estimates William C. Falkner's net worth as $100,000. {JW}

May 7: Lizzie Vance gives birth to Alabama Leroy, called "Baby Roy" by the colonel. She would become the source of stories about the colonel passed on to her great-nephew, WF, who treated her with profound respect and as an authority in the family.

1876

April 25: Charlie Butler elected Oxford's marshal and performs as tax collector as well. {JW}

1877

William Henry Falkner, the colonel's troublesome son, is killed after his affair with a married women is discovered by her husband, who is reputed to have called upon the colonel to say, "I hate to have to tell you this, but I had to kill Henry." Supposedly, the colonel replied, "That's all right. I'm afraid I would have had to do it myself anyway." {B1}

1878

July 16: Charlie Butler applies for membership in Masonic Lodge #1063 and is accepted. {JW}

1880

Census records a Lena Falkner as resident in William Falkner's Ripley home.[4] {JW}

January: Charlie Butler re-elected town marshal. {JW}

August: The first installment of William Clark Falkner's most popular novel, *The White Rose of Memphis*, appears in the *Ripley Advertiser*.[5] {B1}

1881

June: A New York publisher issues *The White Rose of Memphis*, selling out its 8,000-copy printing.

December: Sales of *The White Rose of Memphis* top 10,000 copies.

1882

July: William Clark Falkner publishes *The Little Brick Church*, set on a Hudson River excursion boat. More melodrama, the tragic story of two lovers, and one of the colonel's favorite maladies, brain fever, made this work even more hackneyed and less lively than *The White Rose of Memphis*. {CR1}

July 29: J. W. T. Falkner Jr., the colonel's grandson is born. {B1, JW}

The colonel forms a partnership in the lumber business with R. J. Thurmond. {B1}

1883

May 8: Marshal Charlie Butler shoots and kills S. M. Thompson, editor of the *Oxford Eagle*, apparently the result of a grudge between the two men. {JW}

May 9: Charlie Butler is indicted for manslaughter. {JW}

June: William Clark Falkner takes a European tour, sending travel letters home to the *Ripley Advertiser*.[6] {JW, CR1}

1884

A Philadelphia publisher, J. B. Lippincott, publishes *Rapid Ramblings in Europe*, a highly comical and self-deprecating account of William Clark Falkner's sometimes bumbling 1883 tour. {CR1}

In Ripley, William Clark Falkner builds his own version of a three-story Italianate residence, "quite palatial in style and proportions," noted an observer in the *Ripley Advertiser*. {B1, JW}

January 7: Charlie Butler re-elected as town marshal. {JW}

May: Charlie Butler acquitted of manslaughter. {JW}

1885

J. W. T. Falkner moves from Ripley to Oxford. {B1, JW}

Fall: Fannie Falkner attends Rust College in Holly Springs, Mississippi. "Family tradition asserts that Colonel Falkner paid the bills. It also says that frequently he came to see his [African American] daughter in Holly Springs, and that when he did so he brought her flowers." {JW}

1886

January: Charlie Butler, the only candidate for town marshal, is unanimously re-elected. {JW}

April 3: The *Ripley Advertiser* reports that the colonel has purchased R. J. Thurmond's shares in the Ship Island, Ripley & Kentucky Railroad, with plans to extend the line deeper into the southern part of Mississippi. {B1}

May: New track is laid on the route to Pontotoc. {B1}

October: Five more miles of track laid toward Pontotoc, using convict labor. {B1}

1887

May: William Clark Falkner visits his son J. W. T., who has moved to Oxford, and the town paper, the *Eagle*, reports that he is "as active and vigorous as his son, and this is saying a great deal." {B1}

May 1: Will Bryant marries Sallie Bailey, of the Bailey family, owners of the Sheegog property (the future Rowan Oak). {RO}

June: The *Ripley Advertiser* reports that William Clark Falkner meets Grover Cleveland in Washington, DC. {B1}

July 23: Reports of the abusive treatment of convict labor on William Clark Falkner's railroad and his coercive behavior, threatening towns would be bypassed if they do not contribute to railroad expansion. {B1}

Fall: Murry Falkner enters the University of Mississippi. {JW}

c. Christmas: Charlie Butler abruptly leaves Oxford, purportedly taking with him the town's tax collection and his octoroon mistress. {JW}

1888

Fannie Falkner graduates from Rust College. {JW, see entry for fall 1885}

January 8, 3:00 p.m.: The Oxford Board of Alderman calls a meeting to audit Charlie Butler's books after it has determined he has "absconded" with much of the town's money (approximately $5000). {JW}

May: Forty-five miles of track completed between Middleton, Tennessee, and New Albany, Mississippi. {B1}

July 4: Celebration of sixty-three miles of track completed between Middleton, Tennessee, and Pontotoc, Mississippi. "The people could call the town whatever they wanted," WF declared fifty years later, "but, by God, he would name the depots." {B1}

December 31: Murry Falkner attends a New Year's Eve costume party dressed as a cowboy, reflecting his reading of Westerns. {B1}

1889

April 4: William Clark Falkner announces his candidacy for a seat in the state legislature. {B1}

Summer: Murry Falkner stops attending the University of Mississippi. {B1}

August: The colonel travels to New York City to help secure the merger of the Ship Island, Ripley & Kentucky line with the Gulf & Ship Island. {B1}

September: Maud Butler enters Industrial Institute and College for the Education of White Girls of Mississippi in Columbus, Mississippi. {JW}

October 25: The colonel visits his friend and attorney, Captain Thomas Spight, informing him that Richard Thurmond intends to kill him. The colonel spurns the advice to carry a pistol, declaring he has killed enough men as he signs his will.[7] {JW}

The chancellor of the chancery court declares Falkner the sole owner of the railroad. {JW}

November 5: William Clark Falkner wins election to the state legislature and presumably arouses his chief rival's fears of retaliation. {B1, B3}

4:00 p.m.: At the courthouse on the Ripley Square, Richard J. Thurmond points a pistol at the colonel's head and fires right after the colonel says, "Don't shoot!" Falkner falls, dropping his pipe.[8] {B1}

November 6, 10:40 p.m.: Colonel Falkner dies with his family in attendance. {FK}

1890

Mid-February: R. J. Thurmond is indicted for manslaughter. {B1, JW}

February: William Clark Falkner's eight-foot marble monument is erected in Ripley's cemetery.[9]

March 12: Ripley *Sentinel* reports: "Mr. Murry Falkner, the handsome son of J. W. T. Falkner, Pres't of the G & C RR, came in last week and we understand is preparing himself to take charge of one of the trains as conductor." {CR1}

September: Murry Falkner goes to work for his father's railroad.

1891

February 18: R. J. Redmond is brought to trial for killing William Clark Falkner. {JW}

February 21: A jury acquits R. J. Redmond of murdering William C. Falkner. {JW}The *Grenada Sentinel* calls the trial "a mockery of justice." Rumors circulate that jury members have been bribed. {B1}

December 1: Certificate for J. W. T. Falkner's election as Mississippi state legislator signed by Governor J. M. Stone. {MC}

1892

October 13: Murry Falkner is shot in the back and mouth in retaliation for a dispute concerning his girlfriend and a seamstress, whose brother Murry had knocked down in a previous fight.

J. W. T.'s wife, Sallie Murry, probably saves Murry's life by getting him to vomit up a bullet.[10] {CR1}

1893

February 23: Phil Stone is born. {SS}

1895

November 7: J. W. T. Falkner's election as Mississippi state senator.

November 15: Governor Stone certifies J. W. T. Falkner's election as a state senator.

1896

February 19: Lida Estelle Oldham, daughter of Judge Lemuel Earl and Lida Oldham, is born. {B1}

March 25: J. W. T. Falkner's appointment as a trustee of the University of Mississippi {MC}

September 28: Murry Falkner is promoted and moves from Oxford to New Albany to work as general passenger agent for the Gulf & Chicago. {B1}

November 6: Maud Butler marries Murry Falkner, bringing with her *The Poetical Works of Robert Burns*. {B1}

November 12: *Oxford Eagle* reports: "Mr. Murry Falkner and Miss Maud Butler were married Sunday night at the parsonage by Rev. J. W. Forman. . . . The young couple took their relatives and friends somewhat by surprise, but their congratulations and good wishes were nonetheless sincere for their future happiness and prosperity." {CR1}

1897

September 25, 11:00 p.m.: William Cuthbert Falkner, the first son of Murry and Maud Falkner is born in New Albany, Mississippi. He is Willy to the family.[11]

1898

The Falkners move to Ripley, where Willy's great grandfather established his railroad and ordered the marble statue of himself that remains in Ripley's cemetery. Murry Falkner is appointed treasurer of the railroad.

May 25: The spurious date of birth is put on William Cuthbert Faulkner's Royal Air Force Certificate, born into the Church of England in Finchley in the county of Middlesex, England. {B3}

July: After a visit to Oxford, Murry and Maud Falkner return to New Albany as an outbreak of yellow fever[12] spreads resulting in a dozen deaths. Oxford's white residents evacuate.

August: Murry Falkner's father and mother, J. W. T. and Sallie Murry, evacuate from Oxford and join Murry and Maud in New Albany.

October 17: Emeline Lacy Falkner dies and is buried in Ripley cemetery not far from William C. Falkner.[13] {JW}

November 7: J. W. T., president of the Gulf & Chicago, promotes his son Murry to auditor and treasurer of the railroad at Ripley. He is also put in charge of the traffic and freight claims department. {B1}

December: Murry and Maud move from New Albany to Ripley. {B1}

1899

Early May: Lelia Butler, Maud's mother, called Damuddy by Willy, arrives in Ripley to be with her pregnant daughter. {JW}

June 14: Sallie Murry Wilkins, daughter of James P. Wilkins and Mary Holland Falkner, is born and becomes like a sister to the three Falkner brothers. {B1}

June 26: William's brother Murry (Jack) is born.

Late October: J. W. T. and Sallie Murry are called to Ripley when Willy contracts a serious but unspecified illness from which he soon recovers. {B1}

1900

Mid-March: Murry and Maud Falkner and their two young sons visit J. W. T. and Sallie Murry at their grand new home on South Street.

Murry Falkner invests in a drug company, owns a farm, and raises bird dogs.

1901

Late January: Murry Falkner travels to Grand Junction, Tennessee, for national bird dog champion contest. {B1}

March 6: Lela Butler to J. W. T. Falkner: "Little William comes to see me every few days: he is certainly a dear, most beautiful boy." {PD}

June 20: *Oxford Eagle* reports: "Mrs Lela Butler was called to Ripley Saturday by the illness of her daughter Mrs Murray Falkner."

Willy is sent to Ripley on a visit to his aunt Willie Medora and her daughters Vance and Natalie.[14] {CR1}

September 24: Brother John Wesley Thompson Falkner III (Johncy) is born.

September 28: Willy contracts scarlet fever.[15] {B1}

October 28: J. W. T. presents his recovered grandson Willy with a Shetland pony. {B1}

1902

September 22: Anticipating J. W. T's selling of the railroad, Murry and Maud leave Ripley for Oxford (population 1800), residing in the home J. W. T. occupied before his move to South Street. {JW}

September 23: En route to Oxford by way of New Albany and Holly Springs. {SO}

September 24: Arrival in Oxford. {SO}

In his memoir, Murry (Jack) Falkner, William's brother, recalls the hot, sooty trip on a coal-fired train and the speechless wonder he and Billy shared as they entered Oxford: "So many people, so many horses and carriages, and so much movement everywhere. And the lights—arc lights!" They had nothing like it in much smaller Ripley (population 600). Willy becomes Billy. {CR1}

Caroline Barr arrives to superintend the Falkner boys, telling them stories about the Civil War, Reconstruction, and the Ku Klux Klan. She sees the black and white of things and provides Billy with a powerful insight into his heritage. {CR1}

Murry Falkner establishes a hauling business and then purchases a livery stable, which becomes another hangout for Billy, who learns much from black ostlers. {CR1}

1903

April: Lemuel (Lem) Earl Oldham, a Republican, whose daughter Estelle attracts Billy's interest, is appointed clerk of the United States Circuit Court. {B1, JW}

Estelle first spots Billy riding a pony leading two smaller boys and is supposed to have said to her black nurse, Magnolia: "Nolia, see that little boy? I'm going to marry him when I grow up."[16] {B1}

Billy plays with his cousin Sallie Murry, who brings her dolls, and he brings Patrick O'Leary, a policeman figure fashioned by his grandmother (Lelia Butler). {B1, CR1}

July 1: J. W. T. sells his railroad, the Gulf & Chicago to the Mobile, Jackson & Kansas City Railroad Company, with no provision for Murry Falkner's employment.

Fall: The last of the Choctaws leave Mississippi.

1904

Sallie Murry Wilkins, Faulkner's cousin, is brought up in his home after her father's death. Murry (Jack) Faulkner in his memoirs said she became a sister to his brothers.

1905

April 20: *Oxford Eagle* reports "Mesdames Lelia Butler and MC Falkner and children spent several days of the past week with relatives in Memphis."

August 8: Another yellow fever scare. Oxford is under strict quarantine after 616 cases reported in New Orleans. Reports of malaria cases and mad dog scares abound. {B1}

September: The yellow fever scare abates. {B1}

The Falkners move to "a little White House almost directly across the street from the Big Place," owned by Murry's father, J. W. T. Falkner. {B3, SO}

September 25: On his birthday, Billy enters first grade, Oxford Graded School. Estelle enters second grade in laces, bows, and frilly dresses. Home schooled by his mother, Billy skips a grade, already exhibiting his prowess in drawing and reading. A copy of *The Clansman: An Historical Romance of the Ku Klux Klan* by Thomas Dixon Jr., signed by Billy's teacher, Annie Chandler, and apparently given to him, remains in his library. {B1, B3, CR1}

In the woods, the usually taciturn Murry feels most at ease telling his boys hunting stories. His son Jack recalled "how little I actually came to know him, and perhaps, even less to understand him. He was not an easy man to know." A father with a limited capacity for affection, his son Jack nevertheless wanted to believe "he loved us all." {CR1}

1906

September: Billy, skipped to the third grade, makes a new friend, Myrtle Ramey, giving her drawings and attending sympathetically to her delicate health. Asked what he wants to be when he grows up, he answers, "a writer like my great-granddaddy." He is on the honor roll. {B1}

J. W. T. sponsors one of several reunions of the colonel's Partisan Rangers. Billy and Jack listen to them reminisce about the war. The boys are entranced but also amused by the old timers in dingy grey uniforms with old battle flags, with Billy solemnly imitating, and then laughing at, one of them declaring: "Now what air more noble than to lie on the field of battle with your car-case filled with canyon balls." {B1, CR1}

October 6: In Oxford, Murry Falkner buys a large lot and home with plenty of space for his boys to play. {JW}

December 21: Billy's grandmother Sallie Murry Falkner dies. With his brothers, he attends funeral services. {JW}

1907

A monument to Lafayette County's Confederate heroes is erected on the Oxford town square.

April 27: Nine-year-old Billy watches a re-enactment of a Civil War battle on the Ole Miss grounds, complete with the roar of cannons and musket fire, with the winning Southern forces driving the Yankees into Bailey's woods. {B1}

June 1, 7:00 p.m.: Billy's grandmother, Lelia Dean Swift Butler (Damuddy), dies at home, as so many did then, making a vivid impression on Billy of a family clustering over a loss that will reverberate in scenes mentioning Damuddy's death in *The Sound and the Fury*. {B1}

August 15: Billy's brother, Dean Swift Falkner, is born. Murry calls him a birthday present. {B1}

August 22: Daniel's comet streaks across the sky, and Billy and Estelle decide to get married and own a chicken farm, then fall to quarreling about which chickens to purchase. {B1}

Fall: Billy enters the fourth grade. One of his classmates remembers him as small and quiet. He is an outstanding student, doing so well his teacher supposes that his mother is doing his homework. He avidly reads *The American Boy*'s stories about flying machines. His own experiments at flight end in crashes. {B1}

1908

Fall: Caroline Barr takes Billy, Jack, and Johnny bird nesting. They gather nuts, roast them, and listen to her stories about plantation life and the Klan. {B1}

Black and white photograph of WF and schoolmates. {BH1}

October 22: *Oxford Eagle* announces "one night only" production of *The Clansman*. {B1}

1909

J. W. T., the young colonel (Faulkner's grandfather) buys a Buick touring car. {B3}

June: Billy works in his father's livery stable, developing his lifelong interest in horses. {B1}

September 8: Nelse Patton, a black prison trusty, apparently drunk, accosts Mattie McMillan. As she draws her pistol, he slashes her throat with a razor. What actually happens is a confusing blend of rumor and fact. A mob breaks into the jail, after hours of pounding away at the old prison walls, and drags Patton away, castrating him and then hanging him from a tree.[17] {B1, B3, JW, CR1, FW}

September 20: Another school year begins with a quiet Billy Falkner in attendance but not doing much studying in the sixth grade. {CR1}

n.d.: Photograph of WF and his schoolmates {BH1}

October 8: *Oxford Eagle* announces the coming of *The Klansman* to the Oxford Opera House, featuring a cast of forty, "a carload of effects," a "troop of cavalry horse," and "dazzling scenery." {CR1}

October 21: At the Lafayette County Fair, Billy watches a drunken balloonist and his Negro assistant put together a flying machine powered by a sooty coal oil fire blackening the spectators as it ascends over Oxford before crashing onto the Falkners' chicken house as the astonished Maud Falkner and Caroline Barr watch a grimy Billy, Jack, and Johnny ride in on their ponies. {B1}

November: Thomas W. Dixon's dramatization of his novel, *The Clansman*, complete with cavalry horses and special effects, comes to the Oxford Opera House. {B1}

Billy Falkner makes the honor roll again, but his interest in school wanes. He prefers his father's livery stable.[18] The truant Billy, disinclined to do chores assigned by his father, visits his uncle's law office and reads law books or goes to Ripley with his grandmother's family, the Murrys, where he is made to memorize Bible verses before breakfast. He also finds refuge with the Cullens in the country, hunting and fishing.[19] Billy likes to sit with his grandfather reminiscing about the Civil War. {B1}

Winter: Billy makes the honor roll for the last time. He devises a way to avoid hauling buckets of coal to supply several fireplaces by telling stories to a classmate who does the heavy lifting during the entertainment. {B1}

1910

Sometime around 1910, William begins writing poetry as well as reading it. {DM}

March and April: Billy, Jack, and Johncy wake before daybreak and settle on a high bank to watch the fruit trains full of strawberries hum along and whistle across the countryside. {B1}

May 18: The Falkner and Oldham children gather to watch Hailey's Comet, which appears every seventy-five years. {B1}

September 12: The beginning of another school year, and Billy sits in the classroom drawing cartoons illustrating his teacher Ella Wright's tales of the Civil War. {CR1}

October 4: J. W. T. Falkner establishes the First National Bank of Oxford. {B1, JW}

Winter: Maud puts Billy into a kind of canvas harness meant to straighten his posture. He does not seem to mind this enforced sedentary appliance as he entertains Estelle with his drawing and poetry. {B1}

1911

Billy continues to bring in buckets of coal for the house's fireplaces. {B3}

James K. Vardaman is elected in a landslide to the US Senate while Theodore Bilbo is elected lieutenant governor. J. W. T. is defeated in the contest for county attorney. {JP}

September: Billy enters seventh grade but is often absent. {B1}

Murry Falkner's livery stable business declines as the automobile gains in popularity. {B1}

1912

March: Murry Falkner buys a hardware store. {B1}

Billy is often at the Oldhams', enjoying not only Estelle's company but also the lively personality of Estelle's sister Tochie. Along with Sallie Murry, his cousin, and schoolmate Myrtle Ramey, Billy has a small circle of friends who appreciate his writing and drawing. {B3, CR1}

August 16: WF's first extant letter, addresses his mother "Dear Miss Lady," while she is away from Oxford on a trip. He stays with his aunt, Holland Wilkins, called Auntee, and his grandfather, J. W. T. Falkner, aka the "Young Colonel," whom Billy refers to as "Big Dad." Hopes his mother has taken some good pictures with his camera. He mentions a trip to his grandfather's bank to get envelopes and paper to write letters his Auntee is expecting to read. "Tell Dad that we are looking after the stock all right." Reports that Ches Carothers, J. W. T. Falkner's driver, cut a leech off his foot with a butcher knife. He has seen some people who look like his Dad and brother Johnny, but none like his mother "'cause Lady, you're too pretty." Awaits her letter. {TH}

December 18: Ellen Bailey, residing at the Sheegog place, now known as Bailey place, dies leaving her sister Sallie Bryant in charge of the home. Ellen Bailey, a painter, had Maud Falkner as one of her students. Sallie and her husband, Will Bryant, settle in Coffeeville, Mississippi, and rent out the Bailey place to a succession of tenants.

1913

Cornell Franklin, Estelle Oldham's intended, is "president of the class of 1913, captain of the track team, and member of a dozen other college organizations." {B3}

Billy attends parties, sometime dances, and is, above all, the best-dressed boy. Mainly, he likes to watch Estelle dance with, it seems, all comers, until her family sends her away in the fall to study at Mary Baldwin College in Staunton, Virginia. {B1}

Eleventh-grade yearbook drawings: a speeding automobile; faculty members from different departments; cap-and-gown figure tossing away toys, with caption, "WE HAVE PUT AWAY CHILDISH THINGS"; seated figure in a basketball uniform; a bus loaded with students and driven by a teacher with a sign post "Knowledge Success"'; a seated figure with lamp and books on table with caption "BURNING THE MIDNIGHT OIL"; a bearded figure with a mug opening a barrel labeled "KNOWLEDGE"; a stern-looking teacher on a raised platform, with knife, tomahawk, and pistol hanging from ceiling aiming a cannon at a frightened student with the caption "THIS IS HOW HE LOOKS TO US"; a teacher with a funnel pouring from a large container labeled "KNOWLEDGE" into a student's head with the caption "TAKING HIS MEDICINE"; a female teacher grinding out punishment from her Demerit Mill to the hirsute culprit "A. Lincoln" while below him a large knife-wielding union soldier attacks a small figure with a Confederate flag; a stylish couple dancing. {BH5}

Camping, woodcraft, sports fill the days, all much more enjoyable than working in his father's hardware store.[20] {B1}

December: Murry Falkner purchases a new, large home for his family on North Lamar. {SO}

Mid-December: Estelle returns home, unimpressed with Woodrow Wilson, president of Mary Baldwin College, and ready to again receive the everyday attentions of Billy Falkner. {B1}

1914

Spring: Cornell Franklin receives his law degree from Ole Miss. {B3}

June: Phil Stone returns home from New Haven with a B.A., cum laude, from Yale. {B3} Drives up to the Falkner residence in an "impressive seven-passenger Studebaker." {SO} Billy shows his poetry to Phil Stone, who becomes his mentor. {B1}

August: With brother Jack tracks World War I battles on maps. {B1}

September: Enters eleventh and final grade of Oxford High School. {B1}

December: Drops out of school. {B1}

1915

March 19: *Oxford Eagle* reports William Falkner's attendance at a masked ball held at the home of Estelle's parents, Major and Mrs. Oldham. {B1}

Summer: A delighted Estelle attends classes in English, philosophy, and psychology at Ole Miss after telling her parents how much she dreaded a return to Mary Baldwin. {B1}

September: Returns to school to play football, suffering a broken nose and afterwards quits school. {B3}

November: Goes bear-hunting at "General" James Stone's camp. {DM}

December: Ends the year with no employment or discernible ambitions as far as his father and grandfather can see. {B1}

1916

Draws a man and woman dancing in black and white with pen and ink. {BH1}

January: J. W. T. aka the "Young colonel" employs his grandson as a bookkeeper in his bank. Billy hates the job but excels in making neat rows of figures.[21] {JP}

February-September: With Jack reads Memphis newspapers for accounts of the battle of Verdun. {B1}

Fall: On the University of Mississippi campus writing Swinburnian poetry when he is not imitating Housman. He is a fixture on the Ole Miss golf course.

Bill meets Ben Wasson and impresses him by quoting Housman. When Ben pays Bill a "flowery" compliment, Bill replies: "Ah, we seem to have a young Sir Galahad on a rocking horse come to our college campus." {B1}

Christmas: Bill Falkner grieves with Estelle's family over the death of her nine-year-old brother, Ned. {B3}

1917

Spring: William Falkner's drawings appear in Ole Miss yearbook.

May 24: Reads in *Oxford Eagle* about a black man accused of killing a young girl outside of Memphis. Apparently, a crowd of 5,000, including women and children, watch Eell C. Persons dragged to the scene of the crime as the murdered girl's mother urges the crowd to make Persons suffer "ten times more than her daughter suffered." The writhing man is burned at the stake in front of the cheering crowd as a man in the crowd cuts out the heart of the prostrated Persons, whose ears and then head are hacked off.[22] {JP}

Estelle Oldham wears Billy Falkner's gold ring engraved with a Gothic F. {B1}

Cornell Franklin courts Estelle. {B1}

1918

Spring: Estelle Oldham, Billy's childhood sweetheart, is engaged to Cornell Franklin, an attorney with a promising career. Nevertheless, she offers to elope with Billy, but he will not consent without their parents' approval, which is not given by Lem Oldham or Murry Falkner. Billy's mother forbids him to join the ambulance corps. Phil Stone calls on Maud, proposing that Billy join him in New Haven, where Stone is studying for a Yale law degree, so as to take Billy's mind off of Estelle. {CR2}

March 30: Billy agrees to visit Phil Stone at Yale. Deposits a $30 check into his bank account, and then cashes checks for $1, $3, and $24.05. {B3}

April: Maud and Billy's brothers drive him to Memphis, where he boards a train for New Haven. There he meets Hubert Starr, who becomes a lifelong long friend of this as yet unreconstructed southerner. {CR1}

April 4: Arrives in New Haven. {CR1}

April 5: Complains to his mother about the freezing weather in New Haven. Describes the trip there through the Blue Ridge mountains in Virginia vividly rendering the sight of "myriads of white and coral butterflies . . . And the dog wood like bits of silk upon green velvet, and wisps of clouds upon the mountains like flags." Lots of news about what he sees in New Haven and different accents of soldiers. "I'm terribly lonesome." {TH}

April 6: Writes to Dad about the big locomotives he has seen, describing them in detail, as well as the route taken to New Haven, and the cost of things. "I saw ex-President Taft yesterday." {TH}

Addresses his mother as "Darling Momsey," with a bit of news and concluding, "I love you more than all the world." {TH}

April 7, 8:00 p.m.: to "Mom and Dad," describing a walk with Phil Stone in East Haven and the harbor and a sight of Long Island "like a pale blue strip of paint on a sheet of glass." Assures them that Phil is taking care of him. "These people are always saying things to me to hear me talk, though there are lots of Southern people here." He is meeting professors, students, and soldiers. "Give Dean a kiss for brother Bill." {TH}

April 9: Mentions receiving letters from his parents and more news about the characters he meets. "I'm having a great time now." {TH}

April 10: Works as ledger clerk at the Winchester Repeating Arms Company. {B3}

April 14: "I have become a full fledged working man now, I know just what I have to do, have my badge and am getting twenty dollars a week," he reports to his mother. He describes a huge factory making Browning guns, with 18,000 workers, "probably half of them are women and girls, in the machine shops even." He is "cold all the time" but describes New Haven as a "wonderful old place." Signs off: "Give Dad my love and tell him I have seen one of the largest hardware houses in America." {TH}

April 18: Estelle Oldham marries Cornell Franklin. {B3}

Evening: WF and Phil Stone leave Phil's boarding house, run by two old maid sisters, at 120 York Street, New Haven, and cut across the Yale campus on their way to Richter's, the Taft Tap Room, in the New Haven House Hotel at the corner of College and Chapel Streets. {SS}

April 21: "I am having a good time," he reports to his mother. "All these people are awfully nice to me." He is going out to sporting events and describes the play in a La Crosse game. Sings drinking songs with a German soldier. Meets "Harvard, Yale, and Penn. Men working out here." Describes breakfasts with more pie and doughnuts than he is used to. "I tell them what hot biscuits and waffles are like. They have quite a lot of respect for Southerners up here." He concludes: "Golly, I wish I could wake up at home in the morning. Billy." {TH}

April 24: Plays bridge almost every night, he tells his parents. "I am eating more than I ever ate in my life": meat, pies but nothing that isn't machine made, so he asks them to "send grub." Describes his work and punching a time clock. "There are lots of Britishers here, in their caps and belts and plain, straight khaki trousers. No leggings or boots at all." Sends his love to "Dad" and to "Momsey": "I couldn't live here at all but for your letters. I love you darling." {TH}

April 28: Sends his mother flowers. Describes streets full of Poles, Russians, Italian Communists "all with American flags on their lapels." More sightseeing. Asks his mother to send more clothing and to have Dean write to him. "I have broken into poetry again." {TH}

May 5: Encourages his mother to let Jack enlist in the marines. Regrets he did not get to drive an ambulance "when I wanted to so much" even though his mother was against it. "Tell Mammy [Caroline Barr] that I have lunch every day with two [n----rs]. They are Hindoos, but dont tell her that." {TH}

May 19: A long letter to his mother describing his meetings with soldiers and his fun at a resort. {TH}

May 27: Tells his mother he wants to come home in July before enlisting. {TH}

May 30: Addressing his mother as "My dear Lady," describes a Liberty Bond parade, some air acrobatics of planes "dipping and daring at each other." Mentions a girl he has met "exquisite as a Dresden vase, or figure by Tanagra."[23]

Late May: WF's brother Jack enlists in the Marine Corps, "stirring the sense of rivalry always latent between these two." {JP}

June 2: Reports to his mother about more parades, football games, a boat race, and the Harvard cheer: "Hah-vud, Hah-vud. . . . I wish Dean could have seen the cheer leaders. And if Mammy could have seen the Decoration Day parade. The colored troops were there, veterans of the civil war, dolled up in blue suits and cigars and medals until they all looked like brigadiers." On swimming in the sea: I dont see how any one ever drowns in the sea. You can float like a cigar box." {TH}

June 7: To Momsey and Dad: Expecting to "join up with the British and get a commission as a second lieutenant" since "there is no thing to be had in U. S. Army now, except . . . as a private. . . . It's the chance I've been waiting for now. . . . It's rather hard to explain in a letter just now how I feel, but you both know that already, how badly I've always desired to go. At the rate I am living now I'll never be able to make anything of myself, but with this business I will be fixed up after the war is over." {TH}

June 13: Excited about his enlistment and expects to travel home afterwards, he writes to "Dearest Mother." Shows one of his mother's letters to Phil Stone, who comments "'Isn't she wonderful, God Bless her,' and I went him one better and told him that anyone who wrote letters like that and cared for me as you evidently do, didn't need God's blessing. You are an angel, Mother darling." {TH}

June 14: In New York, WF, pretending to be an Englishman, enlists in the Royal Flying Corps (later RAF) as a cadet. He returns to New Haven and then goes home. {B3}

June 15: Quits job as ledger clerk in New Haven. {B1}

June 19: Phil Stone earns a law degree from Yale University. {B3}

July 8: Writes to his mother en route to Toronto for flight training passing through Philadelphia and Baltimore. {TH}

2:30 p.m.: Telegram to mother announcing arrival in New York. {TH}

Midnight: Arrival in Albany. Describes riding along the Hudson: "The sun on the palisades is wonderful, and West Point like a grim medieval fortress glowering at us." {TH}

July 9: Reports to Recruits' Depot in Toronto, Canada. {B3}

Writes to his mother about Toronto as an "English place . . . These people are wonderful to me." Anticipates his training, including the "chair test. I have no intentions of fainting, however." {TH}

Writes to both parents about passing his examination, including whirling around in a chair in two different directions for 30 minutes. He does not faint and is about to be sick when the doctor tells him "You can dress now." Out of four, he is the only one to qualify as a pilot. {TH}

July 10: Passes another day of examinations, he reports to his mother. "I get a Cadet's uniform tomorrow, and I'll have my picture taken." Misses home cooking. {TH}

July 10–December 5: Line drawings of faun and nymph; World War I biplane and triplanes; a nude figure illustration for his handmade book *The Lilacs*.

July 11: Mentions to his mother that he is mopping floors "and such, so when I get through I'll more than likely make some one a nice wife." The food is okay. He makes his own bed and washes his own dishes. "Its a fine life—if you don't care especially what you say. I'm not grumbling, however." {TH}

July 13: Describes for "Mother darling" his new uniform: "a tiny cap with a white band, a double breasted tunic with Royal Flying Corp on each shoulder, enormous boots and spiral putties and a stick to keep our hands out of our pockets." Learns how to salute. "The British are great sticklers for this and its must be done right." Mentions "church parade—fancy my going to church. The British army is going to reform me after all." {TH}

July 15: "On parade the officer found a hook undone on my tunic. Wish I were not so careless that way, or there were not so many buttons on my tunic," he writes to his mother. Describes the day's routine. "It is a great life. I dont even have time to read. Learning the Morse code in my spare moments we are required to be able to send and receive six words a minute." {TH}

July 16: "I wish you could see some of these flight sergeants and mechanics—fierce mustaches and waists like corset models and tiny caps and swagger stick." Mentions to his mother he is quite "proficient in telegraphy now." {TH}

July 19: Forgets to shave and is given "3 extra parades." Describes Toronto: "about twice as big as Memphis." His arm is a bit stiff after his inoculation. Asks his mother to send his love to his grandfather, Sallie (his cousin), and Auntee, (Sallie's mother). {TH}

July 22: Describes his army days to his mother and a move to Long Branch: "It's another hardening process place." {TH}

July 23: Grateful for the food his mother sends: "I just cant eat the food they give us unless I am terribly hungry. . . . These Canadians are wonderful to me. So easy to get along with. They are very unselfish and good natured . . . I'm having such a hurried life that all my letters sound disjointed. However!" {TH}

July 24: Eating candy his mother sends him. More floor mopping and straightening bunks. No drill today, "for which I am deeply grateful, for they drilled me yesterday until I was limping. These army boots are ruining my feet." Expects to make a flight tomorrow.[24] {TH}

July 26: WF is posted to Cadet Wing, Long Branch, on the banks of Lake Ontario.

July 28: Better food in Long Branch, and he is going for a swim in the lake. "I passed my wireless exam," he reports to his mother. {TH}

July 31: "Did more work yesterday than any [W-p] or [N----r] living," he writes to his mother.

"Slept like a log last night . . . My tent now faces the lake and I can watch the vessels going up and down the lake, and the gulls like blown bits of dirty paper." {TH}

To his parents, he passes on the remark of a chap who sees all the letters and says "Gee, Faulkner, some one is certainly in love with you. And I told him that some one was, two for that matter." Wishes his parents were among the visitors (mothers and fathers) who are now in camp. "However, letters are the next best thing, so I am in my tent with mine, and admiring the sweater which came today. Its the softest thing I ever had on." {TH}

August 3: Imagines what it was like for the Indians on the Great Lakes. "There are lot of trees, that look like poured ink, with stiff, sharp pine trees, as though they had been cut from paper and stuck upon the sky . . . The Hurons and Iroquois fought all about here. I am acquiring the prettiest mahogany color you ever saw. I'll look like a pair of fashionable shoes soon," he writes home to his parents. {TH}

August 10: Reports a weight gain of seven pounds to his mother. "I weigh 127 now. More than I ever did. And I'll be so sunburned that I'll look like a [n----r] by Xmas." Will send a picture of himself. "This is certainly an immoral place. I have had stolen to wit: My stick, razor, mirror and brushes, knife, fork and spoon, and a pair of putties. I am going to nail every thing else I have to the floor." {TH}

August 11: Asks his parents for a bath towel and "that thin book of poems with the French grey cover." Draws what his new uniform will look like. "Just returned from Church of England services. They are about the same as our Episcopal." {TH}

August 12: "Mother darling I just got your letter and I'm home sick for the first time. . . . I've been wanting to see Dean so much . . . I almost dream about him every night." Encloses photographs and drawings. {TH}

August 15: To his mother: "I have met a very attractive girl who has a summer home in Long Branch, so now I have something to do with my holidays . . ." {TH}

August 18: To his mother: lots of attention, as usual, to clothes and a new pair of shoes. "You know how trees rustle in the wind. Thats exactly the way the lake sounds like tearing tissue paper." {TH}

August 22: To his mother: more work on Morse code and map making and reading and looking for a good pipe after losing one. "I look just like a kodak negative now. All brown my self, and my hair is burned rope color." Anticipating more food shipments from home. {TH}

August 27: The cakes and two letters have arrived. After hearing from his mother of the death of his paternal great aunt, Willie Medora Falkner Carter, oldest daughter of the old colonel, WF's great-grandfather: "I seem to have marooned myself absolutely from every thing up here." {TH}

Jack Falkner lands in France. {JW}

August 30: Describes the Canadian National Exhibition, like the Memphis fair, with horses, cattle, and peanuts. More map drawing, studying compasses, and wireless transmission. Back to Toronto soon to study aerial navigation. {TH}

September 3: Receives a package of socks, sweater, and cigarettes. At the National Exhibition: crowds, fireworks, bands, and acrobatic aerial displays. "This crowd hangs about like a crowd of vultures, waiting until some one to get a box from home. If I were not naturally rather unapproachable, they'd take it away from me." {TH}

September 5: Keenly interested in his brother Jack, who is now overseas and seeing action. "And to think of old Jack coming back with a returned man's stripes! I am looking forward to the furlough I'll get before I go overseas, so we can talk about him." {TH}

September 9: Encloses a poem, "The Ace," for his mother, encapsulating his aspirations in the last line: "He flashes through the shining gates of day." {TH}

September 12: Reports to his mother after a trip to the dentist: "I am in fairish spirits since my tooth stopped hurting." Includes a ditty: "I might be ragged and full of fleas / But my pants, thank God, dont bag at the knees." {TH}

Jack Falkner takes part in the St. Mihiel offensive. {JW}

September 15: To his mother: "I think every time I write home, it is to say—Such and such a thing arrived safely, but I believe I do get something every day, so there is nothing for me to need." {TH}

September 17: Phil Stone sends news from home, WF tells his mother. {TH}

September 19: "I've been interviewed and inoculated and vaccinated and categorized this morning." For his mother, he details all the eating and that he is still "gaining." {TH}

September 20: Posted to School of Military Aeronautics, Toronto. {B3}

Takes meticulous class notes, makes precise drawings of aircraft. {B3}

The Spanish Flu infects a quarter of the cadets, but WF escapes the illness and gains 19 pounds. {JW}

September 21: Quartered on the grounds of the University of Toronto: "This place is quite like New Haven or Yale," he writes his mother. "I mean it has an air which is quite English and quite ugly. The buildings, some of them, are individually attractive enough but they are so terribly out of taste, sort of red-face, beef-and-cheese tastelessness. It's very pretty, though, now that fall is here and the leaves are turning." {TH}

September 23: Reports to his mother that he no longer has to drill and parade and spends the day in classes about "theory of flight and airplane construction and it is very interesting." Splendid meals. {TH}

September 25: His parents send a wire on his birthday, and he tells them about learning to crank a propeller. {TH}

September 28: "Dear Mother and Dad," he writes to say the cake was "good. I have made more friends with pieces of it than you'd ever think possible." Wonders about Jack's experiences in the war. "We have all sorts of engines, maps reading wireless, artillery observation." Mentions his squadron is not allowed to leave the Toronto campus but does not mention they are under quarantine because of the Spanish influenza. {TH}

October 3: Back from a ten-mile march, he writes his parents that he is fed up with it. "The fields are full of purple and yellow flowers, and all the brick walls are covered with crimson flowers of some kind and red and yellow leaves. . . . I'd give anything in the world for a horse to ride now. . . . Dad would be crazy about this country, everything is so pretty now, almost as colorful as our falls, and it lasts so much longer." {TH}

October 6: Happy to get news from his father about Phil Stone. Mentions going to bed with "my legs so tired my neck hurts." {TH}

October 10: Another cake sent from home—much better, he tells his mother, than a Canadian dessert of "corn syrup and corn muffins." Tells his fellow cadets about Southern breakfasts of peaches, fried chicken, and biscuits. Drinks a lot of milk. {TH}

6:00 p.m.: "We have just finished our ten miles and I am very near all in—too tired to eat, all most." But then mentions recovering his appetite listing what he has eaten: roast beef and potatoes and cabbage and ice cream, purchased three apples in the canteen and ate the remainder of the crumbs of cake icing. {TH}

October 13: Still under quarantine, he writes to his mother: "My hair is so long that I am going to powder it and put a black satin ribbon in it. . . . Give mammy my love. Am going to send her a card this week." {TH}

October 14: Addresses his mother as "Dear Madam," requests a tube of Pekco tooth paste and a kiss from the kid [Dean]." Still under quarantine. Has fun pretending to be a French Canadian. {TH}

October 17: Sends "Mother Darling" line drawings of chevrons and a military medal, complete with descriptions and comments. Announces that the quarantine has been lifted. "I am still getting fat. I'll have to start reducing soon. I dont look like this yet, however. He includes a drawing of an overweight cadet. {TH}

October 21: Still under quarantine, he writes to his mother. Reminisces about his childhood, never dreaming "then that the time would come to see Jack in France and me flying in Canada."

Thinks of home for "he whose heart and soul is wrapped about his home can see beyond the utterly worthless but human emotions such as selfishness, and know that home is the thing worth having above every thing, and it is well known that what is not worth fighting for is not worth having." {TH}

October 24: Complains about not getting his pay. Eating like a horse, he tells his mother, and "plotting course on maps with instruments and compasses and learning theories of flight and 'life' and 'stagger' and more things than you ever had." {TH}

October 25: Happy to get more cake from home, he writes his mother. Tells a joke about a "Yid" who tries to get out of military service by being so gung-ho he expects to be rejected as crazy. {TH}

October 28: Tells his mother he is happy to hear from Katrina, a friend, who spent time with him making "some wild plans about Phil's office when he became a lawyer, she to be stenog. and me office boy, our job being to sit with our feet on a desk and smoke cigarettes and thus hold all customers spell bound until Phil came to fleece them. . . . I wish I could raise enough pep to write the letters I should, but I cant seem to." {TH}

October 30: Rumors about lifting the quarantine. Preparing for more exams. Hopes to complete training by Christmas so that he can be sent overseas. {TH}

October 31: Does not expect to get the flu and believes the epidemic is "about over here." Churches and theaters are reopening. Mentions various expenses and then tells "Momsey dear": "I have never been very successful at fooling you, have I?—but it made me feel rather blue to see the money I had saved ever since June go like it did. However, it's done now, and I feel allright about it. . . . Wish you could see me taking 15 words a minute at wireless. That's a letter every three seconds." {TH, B3}

November. 1: Brother Jack, a marine private, is wounded near the Argonne Forest. {B1}

November 3: Does not like the church parades, he confides to his mother. "I don't like Church of England any better than our Protestant, so I think I'll have a shot at the Roman Catholic next." His roommate, a devout Catholic, says his prayers every night. Mentions a new plane he is excited about and ends: "I can easily imagine my self freezing to death up here this winter." {TH}

November 5: Describes for his mother what his flight training is like, how he is required to plot a flight and expect incoming fire and determine his speed and petrol needed to return to home base. Tells her about a military funeral he has just attended. As in other letters inquires about family servants and asks to be remembered to them. "All the [n----rs] up here have English accents." {TH}

November 7: To "Momsey": "It looks like the whole thing is over." {TH}

November 9: Reports to his mother that even if the war is over, flight training will continue for some months. {TH}

November 10: Quarantine has been lifted, he announces to his mother. Making preparations for what he will do when he returns home and continues his interest in flying. {TH}

November 11: An armistice puts an end to the expectation of participating in aerial combat. {B3}

November 13: Finishes ground school. {B3}

Still no clear idea when he will be returning home, he writes to his mother. "Of course we are glad that the fighting is over, but I am certainly glad it lasted long enough for me to get a pilot's license which I can do quite easily now."[25] {TH}

November 15: Probably no more flying. "Glad I've gotten in what I have. Won't it be good to get home! I dream about it every night, now." {TH}

November 17: Preparing for more tests, he tells his mother, and mentions a fellow Mississippian who "knows sure enough [n----rs] and comes out . . . with sure enough [n----r] expressions." {TH}

November 18: The war is over for the RAF cadets in Toronto. All flying lessons are discontinued. WF looks disappointed in a group photograph. {TH}

November 19: Looks at train schedules and prepares to come home, he tells his parents. Looks forward to getting home and doing absolutely nothing after having to jump up when the whistle blows and getting called out at 4 a.m. to "stand shivering on an aero drome, waiting for enough light to go up and freeze by. Flying is a great game, but I much prefer walking in the winter. Still, I wouldn't take anything for my little four hours."[26] {TH}

November 22: Getting ready to be discharged, he announces to his mother. "Golly but I am glad to know that at last I am on my way home, for this country is just too cold for any use whatever. I went out last night and nearly froze to death before I could get back. It's snowing out now." He will return weighing 132 pounds. "More than I ever weighed in my life. When I joined up I weighed 113, if you remember." {TH}

Claims he has been aloft and returning "so cold he had to be helped out of the cockpit." {B3}

November 24: To Mother and Dad: "I am rather disappointed in the Royal Flying Corps, that is, in the way they have treated us, however. I have got my four hours solo to show for it, but they wont give us pilot's certificates even."[27] {TH}

November 24–25, 8:11 a.m.: Telegram to his father asking for $60 to cover rail fare. {TH}

November 28: All packed up and "marking time." No more drills. He is coming home with a cap for Dean. {TH}

November 30: Two inches of snow. Impatiently waiting to be discharged. "Just as soon as I get my papers, I'll wire you." {TH}

Claims to have soloed. {B3}

December 1: Murry C. Falkner appointed assistant secretary at the University of Mississippi. {B3}

December 4: Expects to depart Toronto in two days. Still snowing. {TH}

December 5: Physical exam, part of his demobilization, finds him fit and "pounds heavier." {B3}

December 9: Wires his mother he is on his way home and will arrive in a day or two. {TH}

Early December: Discharged from the RAF, never having flown a plane. He returns home, to parade around in a uniform that should be worn only by pilots who have seen active service. He sports a cane and claims to have been wounded in action. {CR1}

Spends part of the holiday season in the Delta, drinking and carrying on with Phil Stone in an affable manner he does not generally display at home. {CR1}

1919

Winter: Restlessly roams in Mississippi and loiters in Memphis and New Orleans. {B1}

January 2: Writes to Hubert Starr about wanting to leave Oxford but cannot while his mother is ill and not until his brother Jack returns home from military service. {CFS}

January: An official demobilization document states WF completed 70 percent of his groundwork. No flight training, no wounds. {B3}

Late January: Writes to Hubert Starr that he has had enough of his "God forsaken" home town to last him the rest of his life. But he will stay put because his mother is ill. {CR1}

February 8: Victoria Franklin ("Cho-Cho") is born to Estelle Oldman and Cornell Franklin. {B1}

March 11: A wounded Jack Falkner returns from the war, hospitalized in the navy hospital in Norfolk, Virginia. {JP, JW}

March 24: Murry Falkner writes in a journal: "The Fruit trees are in Bloom, & my Heart is blooming with thankfulness to the Ruler of all as he has brought my Boy back safely from overseas—He is today at Portsmouth Va & will be Home Soon." {B3}

March 25: Murry Falkner writes in a journal: "All the boys at home again & we are Happy & thankful." {B3}

April–June: At work on a series of pastoral poems that will eventually be collected in *The Marble Faun.*

April 6: The *New Republic* publishes "L'Apres-Midi d'un Faune."

June: Estelle arrives in Oxford with her four-month-old daughter, Victoria (Cho-Cho). WF visits them often. {B1}

August 6: WF's first poem, "L'Apres-Midi d'un Faune" appears in the *New Republic.*

September 2: A thank you note to Estelle Lake for putting up with his eccentricities.

September 19: Enrolls as "special student"[28] at the University of Mississippi, taking classes in French, Spanish, and English literature. Spends many days on the Ole Miss golf course. {B1, CR1}

September 29: Estelle and Cho-Cho depart for Honolulu. {B1}

Autumn: To escape an ice cream party at the Methodist church, WF takes Dean to Memphis, borrowing a car and arriving at Beale Street, where the "lady" who owned the house welcomes Dean "like a grownup." He sits in the parlor watching "all the pretty ladies come in." He is then sent outside to wait for his older brother and for the "long and exciting ride back to Oxford after dark." {DSF}

Mid-October: Estelle's twenty-year-old pregnant sister, Tochie, dies in the influenza epidemic. {B3}

November 12: The *Mississippian* publishes "Cathay," a neo-Shelleyan poem. {EPP}

November 13: The *Oxford Eagle* publishes "Cathay."

November 26: The *Mississippian* publishes WF's first prose fiction, "Landing in Luck," about a cadet's solo flight that seems based on his own experience but is in fact a product of observation and imagination. Swinburne could have taken credit for the poem, "Sapphics," which appears as well. {EPP}

December 10: William Falkner is initiated into Sigma Alpha Epsilon. {B1}

December 31: RAF sends WF his "Certificate of Service." {B1}

1920

January 1: Signs and dates an exquisitely hand-lettered and bound booklet, *The Lilacs,* dedicated to Phil Stone "quand il fait Sombre." {B3}

January 13: J. W. T. Falkner resigns as president of his bank, making way for upstart Joe Parks, a forerunner of Flem Snopes. {B1}

January 28: The *Mississippian* publishes "Une Ballade Des Femmes Perdues," a pastiche of François Villon's "Ballade Des dames du temps Janis." {EPP}

February 4: The *Mississippian* publishes "Naiads Song," a sort of Yeatsian mythology of the siren calls from the immortals to mortals. {EPP}

February 5: The *Oxford Eagle* publishes "Naiad's Song."

February 11: In the *Mississippian*: "Dedicated to Will Faulkner," mocks his pretentious translations, adding "If my words do not have clearness, please remember that I am modeling it after the Count's," the terms used to deride the aristocratic affect of the young poet.

February 12: The *Oxford Eagle* publishes "Dedicated to Will Faulkner."

February 25: The *Mississippian* publishes "Fantoches," a translation of Paul Verlaine. {EPP}

March 3: The *Mississippian* publishes "Clair de Lune," another Verlaine translation. "Who touches," appears in the same issue, with the explanation: "Just a parody on Count's 'Fantouches' by Count, Jr.'" {B3}

March 9: The *London Gazette* records William WF's promotion to Honorary 2nd Lieutenant on the day of his demobilization. {B1}

March 17: The *Mississippian* publishes "A Poplar," in the vein of Verlaine, with its vision of a pliant, slender, young girl" that would evanesce in his early short stories. WF's reply to his parodists can be summed up in his line, "One sees at a glance then, the utter valuelessness of an imitation of an imitation." But his undeterred detractors publish in the same issue, "Meats"—"a dainty parody on Count's 'Streets,' by Count Jr., Duke of Takerchance," attributed to "Pall Vaseline." WF's refrain in "Streets" ("Dance the Jig!") becomes in "Meats" "Hold the Pig!," with an apostrophe to "that ham what am." {B1, EPP}

March 24: The *Mississippian*: "The Mushroom Poet" attacks "a peculiar person who calls himself William Falkner," adding "wouldn't this be a fine University if all of us were to wear sailor collars, monkey hats, and brilliant pantaloons; if we would 'mose' along the street by the aid of a walking prop; and yet gods forbid, if we would while away our time singing of lascivious knees, smiling lute strings, and voluptuous toes? Wouldn't that be just too grand?" The attacker ends by quoting Byron: "He brays, the Laureate of the long eared kind." {B1, B3}

April 7: "Cane de Looney" by "Peruney Prune" intones, "Who is the beau-u-tiful man with cane?" WF, replying to a previous *Mississippian* issue, asks his critic where he has learned "English construction." Another letter in defense of WF asserts: "Poets don't sprout in every garden of learning . . . And how can they grow and bloom into a genius when they are continually surrounded by bitter weeds." {B1, B3}

April 14: In "A Clymène," WF continues his versions of Verlaine and visions of a beloved, "A nimbus that dances / In my heart and entrances."

Whatever he intends, such lines evoke the effulgent Estelle, always seeming to dance toward and then away from him, "a slender bridge, yet all dreams hover there" he writes in "To a Co-ed," published in the Ole Miss Yearbook 1919–1920. {EPP}

April 21: The *Mississippian* publishes "Study," a rhapsodic, erotic revery of nature: "Somewhere a slender voiceless breeze will go / Unlinking the shivering poplar arms . . ." {EPP}

May 5: In "Chimes," a letter to the editor in the *Mississippian*, "J." expresses surprise that WF has not been "shipped to Jackson for treatment" and urges the editor to do his duty.

May 12: The *Mississippian* publishes another parody of WF, "Alma Mater," perhaps an admission that Ole Miss had supported this wayward "special student": "Holding, and held by her embrace—At parting, her kind calmly dreaming face." {B1, B3, EPP}

June 20: WF wins $10 poetry prize offered by Professor Calvin S. Brown. {WFO}

Summer: Does odd jobs, including as painter, helps with Boy Scout troop, and plays a lot of tennis. {CR1} Spends a hot summer "in his room at his parents new home on campus, reading and writing." {JP}

September: Enrolls again as a "special student" and joins the Marionettes, a university drama club, run by Ben Wasson with the assistance of Lucy Somerville. {B1}

November 5: WF withdraws from university, having contributed to the yearbook four elegant drawings in black pen and ink, highly stylized figures, one with a caption in French, a Harlequin, the kind of decadent figure ridiculed in the *Mississippian*. It all suggests a sensibility superior to his surroundings and fortified by the enclosure of his own art. {CR1}

Spends time in Charleston, Mississippi, where Phil Stone is practicing law, and accompanies Stone to Memphis brothels. {SS}

November 10: The *Mississippian* publishes WF's review of *In April Once* by William Alexander Percy. The review reads like a self-portrait: "Mr. Percy—like alas! how many of us—suffered the misfortune of having been born out of his time. He should have lived in Victorian England and gone to Italy with Swinburne, for like Swinburne, he is a mixture of passionate adoration of beauty and as passionate a despair and disgust with its manifestations and accessories in the human race." {B1, B3, ESPL}

Mid-November: WF's commission arrives as an Honorable Second Lieutenant in the RAF. {DM}

Late December: Hand-letters six copies of *The Marionettes*, verse play reflecting the influence of Oscar Wilde and Aubrey Beardsley. {B1}

1921

Ole Miss yearbook publishes drawings and poems by WF. {BH1}

"The peculiarly intense and sometimes awkward relationship with Phil Stone continued through the winter of 1921." {JP}

January 7: *The Arrival of Kitty*, a broad farce, is staged at the Lyric Theatre in Oxford under the direction of Lucy Somerville and WF. {B3, CR1}

February 16: The *Mississippian* publishes WF's review of *Turns and Movies* by Conrad Aiken. Under the influence of T. S. Eliot's "Tradition and the Individual Talent" (1919), the review contends that "aesthetics is as much a science as chemistry, that there are certain definite scientific rules which, when properly applied, will produce great art as surely as certain chemical elements, combined in the proper proportions, will produce certain reactions." He praises Aiken's "clear impersonality." {ESPL}

March 4: The Lyric Theatre presents a play, *Green Stockings*, with WF listed as Property Manager. {B1}

May 4: The *Mississippian* publishes WF's poem, "Co-Education at Ole Miss," a slight work in which Ernest addresses Ernestine as his "little queen" who makes his heart "beat mean." If she loves him as well, he urges them off to "Gretna Green."[29]

Summer: Presents Estelle Franklin, who visits Oxford, with a gift volume of typescript poems, *Vision in Spring*. {B1}

September 21: Stark Young visits Oxford and Phil Stone tells him about an aspiring young poet, WF. {B1}

Fall: Accepts Stark Young's invitation to visit in New York. He washes dishes in a Greek restaurant and then is hired as a bookstore clerk by Elizabeth Prall. He is a soft-spoken success selling "armfuls of books." {B1}

October 6: Writes to his mother from New Haven: "Dont be downhearted about me at all, as I intend having the time of my life here." Describes the trip from Mississippi through New England, calling New Haven "a nice old place." {TH}

He rents a room in Greenwich Village and visits friends in New Haven. {B1}

October 9: Cold in New Haven he reports to his mother but finds the air "crisp and fine." {TH}

October 13: Enjoys walking in New Haven "beautiful this time of year, especially around the campus, with all the old buildings gray and white and faded ink stone absorbing sunlight, and all the trees scarlet and flame color." Still awaiting word from Stark Young about visiting New York City, he reports to his mother. {TH}

October 17: Expecting to move to New York next week after hearing from Stark Young. Describes football games with Harvard and Princeton:

"The whites and [n----rs] are always antagonistic hate each other, and yet go to the same shows and smaller restaurants, and call each other by first names. . . . You cant tell me these [n----rs] are as happy and contented as ours are all this freedom does is to make them miserable because they are not white, so that they hate the white people more than ever, and the whites are afraid of them." {TH}

October 20: Describes Indian Summer for his mother and more football. {TH}

October 25: Mentions to his mother that he has stopped traffic in a scene worthy of a Charlie Chaplin or Buster Keaton film. Includes a note to Dean about the Yale–West Point football game. {TH}

October 29: Thanks his mother for sending food: "You've got me so loaded down that I'll never be able to move at all now." {TH}

November 1: Uncertain about taking the postmaster job and asks if it has been offered to his brother Jack.

November 10: Tells his mother that his pocket has been picked and he has lost his money. Washes dishes in a Greek restaurant. "The other dishwashers, Greeks and one Irish, thought I was a [w-p], and looked down on me." Another job at a Catholic orphanage raking leaves, washing windows, and "tending the furnace." Describes New York and Greenwich Village, where he lives in a basement apartment not far from Washington Square. Beginning work soon at the Lord and Taylor book shop. "Miss Prall, the manager of the book department was very nice to me, gave me dinner last night, and smoked very gracefully while I discussed Art to her. She is a thin, slightly worn youngish woman smudges under the eyes and bobbed hair." Meets Edwin Arlington Robinson in a book shop, saying "he was too gentle to put me off abruptly." Describes first subway trip the crowding and cramming together, guards "bawling and shoving . . . It's like being shot through a long piece of garden hose. . . . It's grab your hat and get on, then get off and run a block and get on again." {TH}

November 12: Describes his garret, four flights up, close to Central Park. He prefers the Village.

He is having a "fine time" working in the bookshop, visiting the Metropolitan Museum and riding the Fifth Avenue bus. {TH}

In the Christmas rush, WF continues to charm customers, especially women, who buy "armfuls of books," enchanted by the clerk's "elegant southern accent." He has the "aura of a wounded veteran with artistic leanings" and "courtly manners." {JP}

November 15: Accepts position as postmaster. {B1}

November 16: Shows no enthusiasm for the postmaster position in a letter to his mother. {TH}

November 20: Writes to his brother Dean about missing the hunting at home. {B1}

November 23: Writes to his mother that he does not need money and is now back living in the Village. Mentions he can get a discount on books and can get books for the family as well as for himself. {TH}

December 2: Named acting postmaster of the University of Mississippi post office. {B1}

Returns home and resumes writing for the *Mississippian*. He makes use of his $1,500 salary to buy a Ford, painting it yellow. {B1}

December 10: Takes postmaster exam. {AB}

1922

Ole Miss yearbook publishes WF drawing for the French club section.

January 13: The *Mississippian* publishes WF's review of *Aria da Capo: A Play in One Act* by Edna St. Vincent Millay. He praises Millay's "strong wrist" and prefers her ideas over the way Miss Amy Lowell "festoons" her work with "broken glass, or Mr. Carl Sandburg sets it in the stock yards, to be acted, of a Saturday afternoon, by the Beef Butchers' Union." {ESPL}

February 3: The *Mississippian* publishes "American Drama: Eugene O'Neill" by WF., who calls the playwright "a contradiction to all concepts of art" because he has developed his own language of the stage not beholden to any tradition or locality. He anticipates O'Neill may derive yet more from the "strength of imaginative idiom . . . Nowhere today, saving parts of Ireland, is the English language spoken with the same earthy strength as it is in the United States." {ESPL}

February 18: Phil Stone to Al DeLacy at the Brick Row Book Shop: "Bill is getting along fine and is turning out some very good stuff." {SS}

March 7: Edwin Arlington Robinson to Phil Stone: "I am glad to infer from your note that you and your friend [WF] have found something in my work that you remember." {SS}

March 10: The *Mississippian* publishes WF's "The Hill."[30]

March 13: J. W. T. Falkner, Billy's grandfather, dies, "the loneliest man I've ever known," according to his grandson John. {CR1, FK}

March 17, 24: The *Mississippian* publishes WF's "American Drama: Inhibitions," proclaiming America's "inexhaustible fund of dramatic material," such as the "old Mississippi River days, and the romantic growth of railroads." But it is the artist's ability, not his material, that counts, as well as American idioms, which are the writer's "logical savior." {ESPL}

April 13: Murry Falkner to Ole Miss chancellor: "I am in receipt of information that my son William Falkner was one of the ones violating the

Campus Rule concerning Drinking. I wish to say so long as My Self and Family remain on the Campus we are subject to the same rules as govern the others and anything you see proper to do in reference to this matter will be satisfactory to me." {CR1}

June: *Double Dealer* publishes "Portrait," a wistful romantic poem.

September 5: A thank you note to Myrtle Stone (wife of Phil Stone's brother Jack) for her kindness while vacationing in Charleston, Mississippi. {SL}

December 15: The *Mississippian* publishes WF's review of three novels by Joseph Hergesheimer, arguing that his characters are not created from within but serve only as puppets of the author. {ESPL}

1923

Ole Miss yearbook listing: "Hardest Worker: Count Falkner." {BH1}

March 8: The Lyric Theatre burns down. WF, among the crowd watching volunteers trying to put out the fire, says to his friend Calvin Brown Jr., "This is the only good show they've ever had in that place, and there are a lot of damned fools out there trying to ruin it." {B1}

June 20: Sends a poetry collection, *Orpheus and Other Poems*, to Four Seas Company enclosing postage for the return of the manuscript if it is not accepted. {B1}

June 26: Four Seas Company replies signifying approval of the poems but also an inability to publish without payment from the author for publishing costs. {B1}

c. July: Meets W. McNeill ("Mac") Reed. {WFO}

Late summer: Replaces Reverend J. Allan Christian as scoutmaster. Christian likes the way WF undertakes nature study with the boys who "ate it up," adding that he is "good and helpful, a gentleman always and a fine influence upon the boys."

November 23: Replies to Four Seas, explaining he has no money and cannot comply with their request to subsidize publication. He withdraws the book, saying some of what he has written is not "particularly significant." {SL}

December 3: Estelle Franklin gives birth to a son, Malcolm.

Christmas: Presents Phil Stone with copies of Aldous Huxley's *Antic Hay* and James Branch Cabell's *Jurgen: A Comedy of Justice*. {SS}

1924

January: Signs a copy of James Joyce's *Ulysses*, a gift from Phil Stone. {B1}

January 11: An advertisement appears in the *Mississippian*, offering to insure students against failing courses. William Falkner is listed as one of the presidents of the Blue Bird Insurance Company. {BH1}

January 18: In the *Mississippian*, the Blue Bird Insurance company publishes its Examination Failure Rates. {BH1}

January 25: In the *Mississippian*, three advertisements of the Midnight Oil Company offer for sale a product that would obviate the need for insurance against failing courses. The second advertisement includes the endorsement of "Count Wilhelm von Faulkner, Marquis de Lafayette (County), Postmaster-General (Retired)." The last advertisement notes that because of the discovery of Midnight Oil, J. W. Bell Jr. had been able to retire and play golf with his good friend the Marquis de Lafayette. {ESPL}

May 13: Phil Stone to Four Seas Company affirming he will cover the cost of publication for a poetry manuscript by an unknown but promising poet. {SS, MC, B3}

June 30: Phil Stone obligates himself to pay Four Seas Company $400 to publish 1000 copies of *The Marble Faun* at $1.50 a copy. {B1}

July 9: Writes to Four Seas asking for publication date to be included in the contract. {SL}

July 19: Writes to Four Seas asking for a definite date for sale of book. {SL}

August 4: Returns contract, presumably with the $200 advance requested from publisher and a dedication "To My Mother." {SL}

August 18: WF takes his scouts, including his brother Dean, to Hedleston Lake for camping. {B1}

August 20: Phil Stone acknowledges Four Seas letter of August 6 and explains he is attending business for "Mr. Falkner." Stone indicates he will write a short preface, a biographical sketch, and provide a list for review copies. As to an author's photograph: "Mr. Falkner is not keen on photography and flatly refuses to put out any money on photographs." But Stone promises to supply some anyway. {B1}

September: Phil Stone sends a telegram to Four Seas Company: "Faulkner tells me to authorize you to use any facts real or imaginary that you desire to use in the book or advertising matter." {B1}

September 2: Charges against WF as postmaster: neglect of official duties, unresponsive to mail patrons, maltreatment of mail. {B3, JP}

September 9: Writes to Four Seas saying he will send two photos. In his biographical sketch mentions Colonel Falkner, *The White Rose of Memphis* and *Rapid Ramblings in Europe*. Lists experiences as undergraduate, house painter, tramp, day laborer, dishwasher in New England, bookstore clerk in New York City, bank and postal clerk, service in RAF, member of Sigma Alpha Epsilon. {SL}

September 17: Stone wires Four Seas Company that the author "TELLS ME TO AUTHORIZE YOU TO USE ANY FACTS REAL OR IMAGINATORY THAT YOU DESIRE TO USE IN THE BOOK OR ADVERTISING MATTER." {CR1}

September 29: Stone sends to Four Seas proofs he and WF have corrected. Stone suggests some design changes and relays the author's request for pale green boards and straw-colored labels for front and spine, the classic kind of presentation that Keats's publishers used. {B1}

October: Creates typescript gift booklet, *Mississippi Poems*, for a childhood friend, Myrtle Ramey. {B1}

Removed as scoutmaster after complaints about his unsavory reputation. {B1}

October 5: Stone sends a list of contacts to Four Seas for the promotion of *The Marble Faun*. {SS}

October 6: Four Seas receives WF's check for payment of publication and sends out proofs. {B1}

Jackson *Clarion-Ledger* reports a feat on the Ole Miss golf course: "William Faulkner made the rounds in 33." {CR1}

October 13: A second set of corrected proofs is due at Four Seas and Stone sends seven pages of names for book circulars. {SS}

October 15: Stone sends out more letters promoting *The Marble Faun*. {B1}

October 16: Four Seas receives second set of corrected proofs. {B1}

Works on a draft of "Mississippi Hills: My Epitaph." {B1}

October 17: Types "Mississippi Hills: My Epitaph," which ends "Though I be dead / This soil that holds me fast will find me breath." {B1}

October 31: Resigns from post office after postal inspector's investigation. {WFO, B1, B3}

Fall: Calls on Elizabeth Prall Anderson in New Orleans and meets her husband, Sherwood Anderson. {CR1}

November 5: Stone sends Four Seas a seven-page mailing list. {SS}

November 10: Four Seas declines Stone's proposal for a publication of travel letters WF would write while abroad. {SS}

November 13: *Oxford Eagle* announces WF's resignation as postmaster and reports of his plans to go abroad.

Phil Stone sends WF's "An Armistice Day Poem," to the *Atlantic Monthly*, commenting: "It is written by a man who had gone all the way through the new verse movement and learned tricks from all of them," but it is not published. {SS}

November 17: Stone to Four Seas urging immediate publication before WF leaves the country. {SS}

Early December: Estelle Franklin visits Oxford with her two children, Victoria (Cho-Cho) and Malcolm, ages five and one, and their amah. Nyt Sung. {B1}

December 2: Writes to Mrs. Homer K. Jones, wife of a Memphis physician, apologizes for an apparently drunken visit having "such a grand time then that I dont know what I wrote." He suspects it was illegible and he has sent her a correct copy of the verse. "Please forgive me and thank you for the whisky-and-soda. I don't know whether I drank it or not, but it was a beautiful tipple."[31] {BH2}

December 5: Phil Stone's secretary types a wistful poem, "To Elise," which begins "Where has flown the spring we knew together." {SS}

December 9: Another poem, "Cleopatra," speaks of fatal beauty. {B1}

December 13: "Spring," in this poem, evokes the beautiful body of the earth. {B1}

December 15: *The Marble Faun* is published. Four Seas ships twenty-five copies to Phil Stone. {B1}

December 16: New Orleans *Times-Picayune*: "William Falkner is preparing to leave the University of Mississippi campus for England and Italy, where he will spend the winter months in study."

Telegram to Four Seas: "IF YOU HAVE NOT SHIPPED MY TEN FREE COPIES MARBLE FAUN AND IF CAN BE SHIPPED FOR GODS SAKE SHIP THEM AT ONCE AS THIS IS HOLDING UP MY SAILING EVERY DAY, WILLIAM FAULKNER." {SL}

December 19: Phil Stone hosts an impromptu autograph party with WF signing books for Ella and Nina Somerville, Bess Storer, and Katrina Carter. {SS}

December 20: First known Last Will and Testament. {B1}

December 24: Signs first edition of *The Marble Faun*: "To Miss Sally McGuire/ from W Faulkner." Also signed on the title page: "William Faulkner/Oxford Mississippi/24 December 1924." {MC} Other copies signed to Joe Parks and to Myrtle Ramey, "my old friend and school mate." {BH1}

The "Hayseed" column in the *Mississippian* announces that WF had "done give up the post office. . . . It is rumored that Bill will retire to some tropical island, lay in the sweet smelling locust leaves and gourd vines and indite sonnets to the pore helpless world, which no one can diagnose." {JP}

December 25: Stays home for Christmas with his family.

December 26: Sends signed copies of his book to "Major and Mrs. L. E. Oldham, with gratitude for many kindnesses and a long and charming friendship. William Faulkner." Another to the postal inspector, who had let WF resign rather than be fired and prosecuted: "To Mr. Mark Webster, to whose friendship I owe extrication from a very unpleasant situation. William Faulkner." {BH1}

December 29: Phil Stone reports to Four Seas that he has sold 50 copies of *The Marble Faun.* {SS}

December 30: In Phil Stone's law office, WF hands his inscribed copy of his book for Myrtle Ramey and autographs 12 pages of carbon copies of his poems. {B1} Also signs a copy for Estelle. {SO}

1925

"Literature and War" reflects a familiarity with the work of several World War I novelists. {ESPL}

January 4: Leaves Oxford for a stay in New Orleans with Elizabeth and Sherwood Anderson. {B1, JW}

January 6: From New Orleans confirms to his mother plans for a trip to Europe. {TH}

c. Early January: More details about his plan to ship off to Europe and about British cruisers and crew he fraternizes with. {TH}

January 9: The *Mississippian* publishes part of Phil Stone's preface to *The Marble Faun.*

c. January 12: Lots of news about WF's fraternity brother Harry Rainold, whom he meets in the street. Enjoys walking along the New Orleans piers. "The gulf coast is certainly the place for you and pop to move to." Plays golf and says more about the British cruisers. "Mrs. Anderson has taken me to live with them. She is so nice to me—mothers me—and looks after me, and gets things to eat which I like." {TH}

January 13: Phil Stone to Four Seasons Company imploring them to send along reviews of *The Marble Faun.* {SS}

Mid-January: Eating up his mother's candy, sharing it with Sherwood Anderson's son Bob. Mentions writing a series of sketches for the *Times-Picayune.* Enjoys the French and Italian lower-class restaurants where he can eat cheaply. "Harry Rainold got me a car to a Gymnasium Club with a swimming pool and everything. Grand." {TH}

Reports to his mother that the *Times-Picayune* is publishing his pieces. He can write 500 words a day for $5.00. {TH}

January 22: "This place is FILLED with beggars, people following the races, you know. All kinds of stories." Tells his mother one of them. "Everyone is grand to me—painters and writers, etc." Mentions that John McClure, poet and literary editor of the *Times-Picayune* will be reviewing *The Marble Faun.* More golfing. Expecting to hear about a ship to Europe. {TH}

January 27: Encloses John McClure's review with no comment and asks his mother to show it to Phil Stone. More golfing. Expecting to come home in mid-February.

January 29: John McClure reviews *The Marble Faun* in the *Times-Picayune*, calling it a failure "with real honor." {WFC}

Late January: Reports to his mother about his success in publishing sketches in *Times-Picayune*. Hopes to continue the series while traveling in Europe. He is told the trip to Europe will be "the making of me." Two "more letters from strange females who saw my photo in the paper. One about 40, gushing, you know; and the other about 14–on pink paper and terrible spelling." {TH}

January–February: *Double Dealer* publishes WF's opinion of criticism in "On Criticism": "All that is necessary for admission to the ranks of criticism is a typewriter." In the same issue, "Dying Gladiator" is the grim side of love and life: "Man's life is but an April without a morrow." {ESPL}

Early February: Boasts to his mother about getting cash out of the *Double Dealer*—a rarity accorded only to Sherwood Anderson.[32] "Fame, stan' by me." {TH}

In another letter brags about his growing reputation. "People call to see me, and invite me out and I sit and look grand and make wise remarks." Spends the mornings writing, the afternoons in the parks and museums, and evenings with artists and musicians. "I'm getting along so well here that I am still putting off going abroad." {TH}

February 8: Begins to publish prose sketches in *New Orleans Times-Picayune*, showing off with "Mirrors of Chartres Street" his awareness of contemporary art in throwaway comments—"The moon had crawled up the sky like a fat spider and planes of light and shadow were despair for the Vorticist schools."

For Cho-Cho's birthday, draws a house with a cat and follows with a poem, "If Cats Could Fly."

Early February: Sends his mother his first sketch in the *Times-Picayune*. Proud of his publishing proficiency: "I am like John Rockefeller—when ever I need money I sit down and dash off ten dollars worth for them. . . . They know that someday I'll be a 'big gun' and they are glad to get it." Getting along "grand" with Elizabeth Anderson still taking care of him. {TH}

February 6: *Brooklyn Daily Eagle* in "New Books Received" mentions: "A slender volume of verse by a poet who has been both day laborer and a pilot."

February 7: *St. Louis Post Dispatch*: "A first book of poems by a young man from Mississippi and proud of it."

Happy with the RAF regimental tie Sherwood Anderson has given him. Dining at an old New Orleans establishment, Victor's. Picks up stories from a waitress and the owner. "Sky all full of fat white clouds like little girls dressed up and going to a party." {TH}

February 10: A melancholy untitled poem evokes the "aimless wind" that queries a speaker who pronounces himself dead and yet answers "O, I'm well." {B1}

February 12: Signs a copy of *The Marble Faun* for Anita Loos. {SS}

February 15: "Damon and Pythias Unlimited," in the *Times-Picayune* experiments with Jewish dialect in a race track story. {NOS}

February 16: Thinking about a novel (*Soldiers' Pay*) he tells his mother. {TH}

February 20: Worried that something is troubling his mother. Mentions the beginning of carnival, with colored lights and all traffic at a standstill for three hours. It is all "simply grand." {TH}

February 22: "Home," the *Times-Picayune*, centers on Jean-Baptiste, a Prufrockian character. {NOS}

February 26: Another poem in Eliot's style, beginning "The Raven Bleak and Philomel." {B1, SS}

c. February 28: Writes to his mother from Memphis, calling it a "fearful hole . . . I dont see how in the world you like the place." {TH}

March: Sees Estelle on a brief visit home. {JW}

March 1: "Jealousy," the *Times-Picayune*, continues an interest in Italian characters who appear in other sketches and in *Mosquitoes* and *The Sound and the Fury*. {NOS}

Drives with Phil Stone to Memphis for an appointment with Monte Cooper a literary impresario and then fails to show up. {B1}

March 3: Returns to New Orleans and decides to postpone his trip to Europe after meeting Sherwood Anderson. They begin collaboration on the Al Jackson letters. WF moves in with William Spratling and begins working on a novel, *Soldiers' Pay*. {B1}

Writes his mother that he has returned to New Orleans. {TH}

March 5: Mentions his mother's cake has arrived. "Sherwood said, after seeing the handkerchiefs and eating a piece of the cake, that he certainly would like to know my mother." Mentions that he is now living with William Spratling. {TH}

Early March: Announces he is writing a book with Sherwood Anderson.[33] Describes his apartment and his roommate, Piper. Still working on his own novel and sketches for the newspaper as well as a piece, "What Is the Matter with Marriage" in the New Orleans *Item-Tribune*.[34] {TH}

March 7: *Saturday Review of Literature* review of *The Marble Faun.* {WFC}

March 8: Describes the neighborhood around William Spratling's apartment. "Think of all that grand country to walk and ride through and yet folks will make their homes in a city!" Asks his mother to send his golf clubs. {TH}

March 11: Acknowledges another cake, clothes, a money order, and golf clubs sent from home. Describes Sherwood Anderson's outfits: "Dad should see some of the shirts and ties he has. Loud is no word. He says he likes color and he dont give a hoot who know it. He has a green corduroy shirt, and more red and orange and yellow ties! He looks like an electric sign when he is dressed up." Describes the arrival of Anita Loos "rather nice, quite small—I doubt if she is five feel tall. Looks like flapper." She earns sizable sums writing screenplays. "Gosh, I'm homesick for the hills today." {TH}

March 18: Describes the layout at Spratling's: "I can come and go when I like, sleep as long as I please, invite whom I like to come to see me—its grand." Mentions another Spratling portrait of him. "It is a good drawing but not such a good likeness. The face has more force and character than I have, I think." Mentions being "taken up by the wealthy jews lately." Wants his mother to send him two bath towels. {TH}

March 22: Reviews *Ducdame* by John Cowper Powys in the *Times-Picayune* claiming the novelist's characters are not "dramatic material." {ESPL}

Late March: Describes an outing on a yacht on Lake Ponchartrain chartered by Sherwood Anderson.[35] Tells his mother one of the Al Jackson stories he has invented with Anderson. {TH}

Phil Stone writes Four Seas Company that WF is the original of a character in Sherwood Anderson's "A Meeting South." {SS}

March 26: Driving around in a big car Anita Loos hires. {TH}

March 31: Acknowledges the cake, bacon, and cheese his mother has sent him. Mentions that Sherwood Anderson has written a story about him. "I am now giving away the secrets of our profession, so be sure not to divulge them. It would be a kind of like a Elk or a Mason or a Beaver or something giving away the pass word." {TH}

April: The *Dial* publishes Sherwood Anderson's story, "A Meeting South," with a character, David, modeled after WF.

WF works on "And Now What's to Do," and seems to have himself in mind: "Before and during puberty he learned about women from the negro hostlers and the white-night man, by listening to their talk."

The *Double Dealer* publishes "The Faun," expressing a longing and pursuit of what cannot be caught—in this case the faun's "vain pursuit / Of May's anticipated dryad." In the same issue, "Verse Old and Nascent—A

Pilgrimage," exclaims "Ah, women, with their hungry snatching little souls!" {ESPL}

April 4: WF's photograph appears in the New Orleans *Item-Tribune* with the notice that he has won $10 for answering in 250 words or less "What Is the Matter with Marriage?" He counsels preparation for the give and take of marriage. {ESPL}

April 5: "Cheest" in the *Times-Picayune* resembles a Sherwood Anderson race track story. {NOS}

Monte Cooper reviews *The Marble Faun* in the *Memphis Commercial Appeal*: "Fifty pages of monotonous, if silvery, intoning, must prove to be soporific."

Early April: Reports to his mother that his novel is "going splendidly." Recommends that his mother see a "fine movie": "He Who Gets Slapped." {TH}

April 7: To "Moms, dear heart," acknowledging her parcel of sheets, soap, and toothpaste "enough for everyone." Mentions how much his young roommate, Piper, admires him. "Makes me feel like I ought to do something quite grand for his sake." {TH}

April 10: More cake from home and a pillow case. Mentions a review in the *Memphis Commercial Appeal*: "Cheer up, things ain't so bad."[36] He has been receiving appreciative letters, one praising "true poetic lines" putting him above William Alexander Percy.[37]

c. April 10: A letter to E. Little responding to his reaction to *The Marble Faun*: "Having one's work appreciated by the people of one's native state makes the labor well worth while. If your sentiment regarding the poets of Mississippi were only more general through the state, there is no reason Mississippi should not produce verse as good as that of any state in the Union." {TH}

April 12: In "Out of Nazareth" in the *Times-Picayune*, WF introduces himself and Spratling as characters: "I remarked to Spratling how no one since Cézanne had really dipped his brush in light." {NOS}

April 13: Describes masses during Holy Week. At an evening mass mentions the candles and incense. "People in Catholic Churches sit in their pews and whenever they want to pray, they kneel whether anyone else wants to or not. When they enter they dip their fingers in the holy water basin and cross themselves, then when they pass the altar they bow." No preaching, "all music. Grand to watch, and how those little boys can sing!" Half way through his novel, he reports to his mother and has written three short stories. Mentions a thirty-year-old woman with an interest in him that he is avoiding, "an empress of stormy emotions. But then man's life is never a bed of roses. If it aint mosquitoes its something else." {TH}

April 16: Mentions a "writing slump . . . Have it all in my head but cant put it on paper for some reason. Stale, I guess." Reports to his mother that the Andersons say his half-finished novel is good. {TH}

April 18: Phil Stone writes to Four Seas reporting that WF is still in New Orleans and has postponed his departure for Europe because of his collaboration with Sherwood Anderson.

April 19: "The Kingdom of God" in the *Times-Picayune* features an idiot.[38] {NOS}

April 20: To his mother a long letter about meeting a Scotsman and learning about his war experiences and then horse racing adventures. "He has taken a shine to me, lately, comes for me in his car, a Cadillac, and we golf and swim together. He seems to be quite impressed that I am a writer." Hopes to make a story out of it all. Describes going to a masquerade dance and then to a cabaret with a "[n----r] band." {TH}

April 23: "I have got a dog-gone good novel. Elizabeth and Sherwood both say so. They have taken me in charge, wont even let me read anything until I finish it." Describes the plot and characters to his mother. Hopes to finish by June. "And Sherwood is going to try to make his publisher take it and give me an advance on it the book to appear next fall." Requests his linen suit while sending his tweeds home. {TH}

April 26: In the *Dallas Morning News*, treats Anderson as an organic outgrowth of his environment, as Anderson would regard him, saying, "All you know is that little patch up there in Mississippi where you started from. But that's all right too. It's America to; pull it out, as little and unknown as it is, and the whole thing will collapse, like when you prize a brick out of a wall." {ESPL}

May: Three WF drawings appear in a magazine, *The Scream*, depicting highly fashionable women boarding a streetcar (reflecting WF's meticulous concern with dress) as two men—one decked out in striped suit and the other in a checked two-piece ensemble with argyle socks appraise the women; a drunken figure draped over a male companion with the caption reflecting the drunk's mistaken notion that a nude statue is a real woman away from home without her clothes; a very sporty twosome, with a pipe-smoking driver in a roadster.

May 1: Another cake from home, "a grand one." Long chatty letter about meeting new people, including a man from the Palmer Institute that teaches how to write in Hollywood. Expects to be fed up with writing after he completes his novel and will seek outdoor work, perhaps farm labor. Assures his mother that he has been exercising, taking long walks. "I expect I am straighter than I was at home And I fear I am getting fat." {TH}

Early May: Cake, candy, linen suit, linen pants and lounging robe arrive, with the robe exciting admiration of "all and sundry." Novel is moving swiftly (50,000 words). {TH}

May 2: *Brooklyn Daily Eagle*: "The Marble Faun is rather melancholy, but pleasantly thoughtful and musical."

May 3: "The Rosary" (*Times-Picayune*) explores how hatred narrows the world. {NOS}

May 7: "Grand news about Jack," WF tells his mother, referring to his brother's joining the FBI. About his novel: "hate to finish it. I know I'll never have so much fun with another one. I dream about the people in it. Like folks I know." {TH}

May 10: "The Cobbler" (*Times-Picayune*) a monologue—an as-told immigrant's story of life in the old world and the new. {NOS}

May 11, 10:00 a.m.: Begins writing all day, close to 10,000 words.

Midnight: Completes *Soldiers' Pay*.

May 12: Announces to his mother he has finished his novel. His roommate, Piper, is helping to type the book. {TH}

Mid-May: Touts his new sunburn: "an elegant saddle color, like a swell colored gentleman." Describes a boat trip with mosquitoes "big as sparrows and vicious as tigers." Correcting and retyping the novel as he eats more cake from home. {TH}

May 17: "Chance" (*Times-Picayune*) pursues a down-and-out drunkard in the Sherwood Anderson mode. {NOS}

May 24: In the *Times-Picayune*, "Sunset," depicts a black character called "insane" in a newspaper account whose actions are in fact understandable as his deluded effort to find his home in Africa.

May 25: Completes *Soldiers' Pay*. {B1}

May 31: "The Kid Learns," the WF version of a gangster story in the *Times-Picayune*. {NOS}

Spring or early summer: "And Now What's to Do" an early autobiographical piece. {ESPL}

The Double Dealer publishes "The Lilacs."

June 1: More correcting and rewriting of the novel. "I am fairly satisfied with it now." Not sure about his plans, but he may go to Pascagoula before returning home. {TH}

June 6: Arrives in Pascagoula. {B1}

June 7: Swims and sails. {B1}

June 11: Arrives in New Orleans after several days in Pascagoula. Describes to his mother his activities in Pascagoula, including fishing and the kinds of fish he sees. "Sherwood Anderson is all blowed up over the novel. He has written Liveright two letters about it and Liveright has written asking me to send it on to him. Sherwood thinks it is going to be a sensation. I hope so." {TH}

June 22: Announces the possibility of getting on to boat to Spain in two days. "I am in a dreadful stew, of course, between the book and the boat, so please send my clothes which I have listed above." {TH}

June 25: From Pascagoula, where he swims and sails. "I have a grand mahogany color." Excuses not writing more often: "But when you spend most of your time writing words, as long as you are all right you want to take it out in thinking about home—writing letters is like the postman taking a long walk on his day off, or the street car motorman taking a car ride." {TH}

End of June: Returns to New Orleans from Pascagoula. {TH}

July 4: Learns that his ship to Europe is delayed somewhere near Galveston, Texas. {TH}

Early July: Writes to his mother about the delay in embarking for Europe. Asks her to send the hair brushes he forgot. {TH}

July 6: Announces to his mother that the boat is sailing tomorrow. He is taking along 500 sheets of paper and will keep a diary. He has a list of contacts to look up. "Quite a gang are coming down to see us off." Expects to land around July 30 and expects she will get his first letter by August 10. "Whatever you do, dont worry unnecessarily." He is all right for money and thanks her for the hairbrushes. {TH}

July 7, 2:00 p.m: Sails from New Orleans on a freighter, the *West Ivis*, with William Spratling bound for Europe. {TH}

July 11: The *West Ivis* docks in Savannah to pick up cargo and WF spends a few days walking the docks and the city and perhaps working on stories for the *Times-Picayune*. {B1}

July 14: The *West Ivis* sails again for Europe.

The *Times-Picayune* publishes "The Liar," a formulaic detective story. {NOS}

August 2: Arrives at Genoa and parts company with Spratling. {B1, JW}

August 3: Spratling departs for Rome while WF travels along the Italian coast. {B1}

August 5: A postcard to his nephew Jimmy announcing a walk from Rapallo to Paris. {TH}

August 6: Writes to his mother about taking the train from Genoa to Milan, which is interrupted by his curiosity about Pavia—its cathedral, bridges, and tile roofs. He eats in a wine shop with boatmen. {TH}

August 7: Arrives in Milan and likens the cathedral to "stone lace" and "frozen music." {TH}

August 8: Reunites with Spratling in Stresa. Avoiding tourists, he sets off for the mountains above Lake Maggiore. {SL}

August 9: Arrives in Sommariva, "a grand village on an Alp above Stresa." {B3}

August 10: Phil Stone to Four Seas Company inquiring about the "statement of account" due August 1. By his estimation, WF is due $81. {SS}

August 11: Writes to his mother from a village on an Alp above Stresa: "the pardoners and his wife protecting me." {TH}

August 12: Travels by train through Switzerland and spends a day in Geneva, which is quite expensive. {B1}

August 13: A postcard of Lago Maggiore to his mother: "Full of Americans—terrible." {TH} Takes the train to Paris. {B3}

c. 11:00 a.m.: Arrives in Paris on Paris-Rome Express. Finds an apartment on the left bank of the Seine not far from the Luxembourg Gardens and the Louvre. Intends to write travel articles. {B1}

August 14: Phil Stone forwards publisher's statement of account to WF. {B1}

August 16: Tours Paris—the Arc de Triomphe and walks down the Champs-Élysées to the Place de la Concorde, followed by lunch at a workingman's restaurant. He singles out Oscar Wilde's tomb and Notre Dame Cathedral, writing to his mother that it is "grand." {TH}

Works on his French and grows a beard. {B1}

Meets William Odiorne, a New Orleans figure who photographs him. {B1, CR1}

Works on articles and begins a second novel, *Mosquito* [*sic*]. {B1}

The *Times-Picayune* publishes "Episode," an account of Spratling's encounter with a woman on the street and his portrait of her that results in an expression that reminds the narrator (WF) of Mona Lisa. His exclamation ends the story: "Ah, women, who have but one eternal age! And that is no age."

An unpublished story, "Peter,'" set in New Orleans, reveals a keen interest in black people as well as a sensibility not yet fully engaged with the reality of their lives. The tradition of the tragic mulatto informs this look at Peter: "his face round and yellow as a new penny, brooded briefly. What does he see? I wondered, thinking of him as an incidental coin minted between the severed yet similar despairs of two races." {USWF}

August 17: Sherwood Anderson reports Liveright's message that two readers are enthusiastic about WF's novel and that one is "not so enthusiastic." {SS}

August 18: Writes home to his mother about how much he enjoys watching children play in the Luxembourg Gardens. Visits the Louvre. {TH}

Moves from Montparnasse to 26 rue Servandoni close to the Luxembourg Gardens. {B1}

August 23: Puts "Mosquito" aside, saying to his mother he does not know "quite enough about people," for a new novel (*Elmer*), about an artist.[39] {TH}

August 26: Calls his new novel "awfully good" and confesses to his mother "a dreadful habit of sleeping late." {TH}

Sherwood Anderson to Horace Liveright: "I am glad you are going to publish Faulkner's novel. I have a hunch this man is a comer. I'll tell you a lot about him when I see you in late October or November."[40]

August 27: Writes a whimsical poem, "What'll I do today." {B3}

c. August 30: Enjoys watching children and an old man sail their toy boats in the Luxembourg Gardens. {B1}

September 2: Working steadily on his novel and on articles but keeping no diary. {B1}

September 6, 6:30 a.m.: Bids farewell to Spratling, returning to teach another semester at Tulane. {B1}

To his mother: "I have just written such a beautiful thing that I am about to bust—2000 words about the Luxembourg gardens and death." Draws a picture of himself with a beard and comments: "Makes me look distinguished, like someone you'd care to know." {TH}

Completes 20,000 words of *Elmer*. {CR1}

September 9: Writes to his Aunt Bama about his travels and declares: "When I am old enough to no longer have to make excuses for not working, I shall have a weathered derby hat . . . And spend my days sailing a toy boat in the Luxembourg Gardens." {BH2}

September 10: 27,500 words completed on *Elmer*. {B1}

c. September 11: In Paris, writes to his aunt Vannye about an early memory. "You held a kerosene lamp, and your hair looked like honey." {BH2}

September 13: To his mother he recounts a visit from his Aunt Vannye and her daughter, noting, "Europe has made no impression on them whatever other than to give them a smug feeling of satisfaction for having 'done it.'" Puts away one novel, probably *Elmer*, and begins another one, probably *Mayday*. {TH}

September 17: Tired of cities, he tells his mother from Paris, and will soon set off for the country. {TH}

September 20: The *Times-Picayune* publishes "Country Mice," a tale of lowdown life in New Orleans. The first line sets the tone: "My friend the bootlegger's motor car is as long as a steamboat and the color of a chocolate ice cream soda." {NOS}

Attends the Moulin Rouge, confiding to his mother, "Anyone in America will tell you it is the last word in sin and iniquity." But he suggests that the "bare beef" is "only secondary," unlike America where sex is a "national disease. the way we get it into our police and religion, where it does not belong anymore than digestion belongs there." {TH}

September 21: Takes the train to Rennes. {B3}

September 22: Takes the train from Rennes to Rouen to begin a walking tour. Writes to his mother about having seen Rodin's museum and private collections of Matisse and Picasso. On Cézanne: "That man dipped his brush in light like Tobe Carothers would dip his in red lead to paint a lamppost." {TH}

September 25: Arrives in Amiens on his 28th birthday seeing the remnants of wreckage from the 1870 war with the Prussians and World War I.

September 27: The *Times-Picayune* publishes "Yo Ho and Two Bottles of Rum." Aboard the *Diana*: "There is something eternal in the East," muses the nameless narrator, "something resilient and yet rocklike, against which the Westerner's brief thunder, his passionate efficient methods, are as wind."

September 28: In Compiègne walking (averaging twenty-five miles a day) through war zone with shell cases in the hedgerows. {B1}

September 29: In Chantilly, he writes to his father about the "best looking horses you ever saw." {TH}

September 30: A postcard to his brother Dean: "You can't kill a deer like this here unless you got a red swallow-tail coat." {TH}

October 3: Feeling restless after he returns to Paris and plans to visit England soon. {TH}

Spratling writes that he has been in New York City and seen Horace Liveright, who told him the firm would publish *Soldiers' Pay*, but no official word yet. {B1}

October. 6: Leaves Paris on 6:00 p.m. train and at Dieppe boards the boat for a week in England. {B1}

October 7, Morning: Arrives in London. Finds the city dirty and expensive. Visits Buckingham Palace, Westminster, the Tower, and coffee houses frequented by Ben Jonson, Marlowe, Addison, and then on to Hounslow Heath, Piccadilly, St. Paul's, Trafalgar, and Mayfair in a fog. {TH, B3}

October 9: In Kent at Tunbridge Wells, amazed at how much the English eat (five times a day). Remarks to his mother in a letter, "Quietest most restful country under the sun. No wonder Joseph Conrad could write such fine books here." {TH}

October 15: Reports to his mother that England is too expensive for him. Mentions writing a story about reincarnation which sounds like "The Leg." {TH}

October 16: Returns to Paris and resumes work on *Elmer*. {B3}

October 17: "I have been away from our blue hills and sage fields and things long enough," he writes to his mother. Making plans for his return trip while awaiting Horace Liveright's verdict on *Soldiers' Pay*. Mentions all the walking he has done in France and England, seeing "strange people and different things . . . But after all its not like mounting that northeast hill and seeing Woodson's ridge, or the pine hills on the Pontotoc road, or slogging along those bare fields back of the campus in a drizzling rain." Expects to be home by November 1. {TH}

October 21: Enjoys dining in Paris again. "I got arrested again in Dieppe. The 6th time since I've been in France. I dont know what in the world can look suspicious about me. It must be that I have a bad face, or my trench-coat, or something. I certainly wasn't doing anything except standing on the wharf watching a fishing smack being unloaded and eating a piece of bread. But here comes the gendarme on his bicycle." He provides dialogue in French and English in his account of his interrogation. As soon as he announces he is a poet, they release him. His comment: "It takes a lot of stupidity to do anything really well, but I think it requires more down right dullness to be a cop than anything I know." {TH}

October 26: Cold and rainy in Paris, he tells his mother. "I'm writing a story now—the best one yes, as usual." Inquires about his nephew Jimmy.[41] "Good news. Just received a contract from Liveright for the novel and an option on the next two I write, and a check for $200.00." {TH}

October 30: Gives his mother the details of the Liveright contract. "I signed it: of course I'll be his bond slave for two years, but then I guess I'll have to be someone's." Mentions six stories he wants to sell: "So my future looks all right financially—only you and Pop will have to furnish the parched corn for a while longer, until the loot starts coming in." Mentions a title change for the novel.[42] He loves riding on the Paris busses in Indian summer. Expects to sail on November 19 with a stopover in New York to see Liveright. Home by December 1. {TH}

November 1: Writes as Ernest V. Simms to H. L. Mencken enclosing a WF poem, "Ode to the Louver." Simms notes "I made the corrections because my family is long a reader of your magazine [*American Mercury*] until a train reck 2 years ago." Wants Mencken to give American poets a chance: "I only made corrections in the above poem without changing its sentiments because the poet himself quit schools before learning to write because I have a typewriter." {SS}

November 3: More details to his mother about the voyage home. Angry that he has not been able to cash Liveright's check. Reports that he has a chapter finished of the "Mosquito novel, and almost half of the later one all corrected and typed."[43] Has a craving to golf. After so much rain, he compares himself to an "Indian chief: Rain in the Face." {TH}

November 6: Phil Stone writes to Four Seas Company about sending funds to WF. {SS}

November 9: Tells his mother that he still can't cash that $200 Liveright check and describes his complicated efforts to do so. {TH}

November 15: Still complaining to his mother about the weather: "Good thing the Lord gave these folks wine—they rate a recompense of some kind for this climate." {TH}

November 21: Not being able to cash the $200 check has delayed his sailing. Exasperated with Liveright for sending a personal check 2000 miles to a foreign land. Relying on his photographer-friend for help.[44] "Damn that Jew." Cold and freezing in Paris. "I've been too upset to do any more work on my novel, but I am writing another short story. . . . My beard is quite elegant: it is trimmed to a point now. Swell." {TH}

November 30: Misses the December 2 sailing because the check has still not been cashed after 24 days. He is tired of Paris and too fretted to write. "I've even read all the books I brought with me at least 5 times." {TH}

December 8: Sails from Bremen with typewriter and manuscripts and a new jacket, third class on the SS *Republic* of the United States Lines. {B1}

December 9: Aboard the boat train, stops in Cherbourg on the way to Queenstown. {B3}

December 10: Sails to New York City. {B1}

December 17: Saves the evening menu aboard the boat, with the following selections: haddock, pheasant, prime ribs, or chicken. {B1}

December 19: The *Republic* docks at the Second Street pier in Hoboken, New Jersey. {B1}

Visits Boni & Liveright to discuss *Soldiers' Pay*. {B1}

A telegram to his mother: "LANDED TODAY WIRE FIFTY DOLLARS. CARE HOTEL PENNSYLVANIA HOME WEDNESDAY." {TH}

Writes to William Odiorne, describing the voyage home among immigrants, the "goddamdest group of people," and making it through customs: "All serene—I didn't have to open the box—Inspector was a [n----r], and I kind of ran it over him." {CR1}

December 21: "Dear Moms" writing from Hotel Pennsylvania reporting that he is working on proofs of his novel. {TH}

December 25: At home for Christmas. {B1}

Late December: Back in Oxford, moves into a room in the Delta Psi house and returns to golfing and works on stories: "The Leg," "Divorce in Naples," and "Mistral," based on his European travels. Ceases work on *Elmer* and writes poetry. {B1}

1926

c. January: Addresses the Oxford rotary club about his recent European trip. {CR1}

January 25: Notation on Estelle's copy of *Vision in Spring*: "Rebound 25 January 1926. Oxford. Mississippi." {B3}

January 27: Dates *Mayday*, a hand-lettered fable composed for his beloved Helen Baird: "To thee / O wise and lovely." {WC}

February: Writes to Anita Loos expressing admiration for her creation of Dorothy in *Gentlemen Prefer Blondes*. {SL}

February 2: Boni & Liveright publishes *Soldiers' Pay*.

February 11: Acts as chairman of golf tournament committee and scores a hole in one, reported in the *Memphis Commercial Appeal*.

February 25: Liveright publishes *Soldiers' Pay* in an edition of 2500 copies.

Returns to New Orleans, after his father signals disapproval of the novel's sex scenes (not fit to read) and Oxford's censure. He "couldn't stay here," his mother admitted. {B1}

Moves in with Spratling, attends parties, but seems no longer to be as welcome. {B1}

March 3: Comptroller general of the United States writes to WF requesting overdue payment of $38.25 owed to the government because of the mishandling of money order accounts.[45]

March 17: Signs a copy of *Soldiers' Pay* "To Sherwood and Elizabeth Anderson." {B3}

Spring: Estelle returns to Oxford. {JW}

April 3: *New York Sun* review of *Soldiers' Pay*: characters "thrown together in a fashion rather reminiscent of Dostoyevsky. That is to say, haphazard." {WFC}

April 11: *Nashville Tennessean* review of *Soldiers' Pay* compares the novel to John Dos Passos's *Three Soldiers* and concludes that WF "digs deeper into human nature." {WFC}

New Orleans Times-Picayune review of *Soldiers' Pay*: a "corking first novel on this theme of the return of the hero." {WFC}

April 21: Phil Stone writes to Boni & Liveright inquiring about sales of *Soldiers' Pay* and requests that more copies be sent to Oxford. {SS}

April 29: Sherwood Anderson writes to Horace Liveright wishing the publisher success with *Soldiers' Pay* but reporting a break with WF: "He was so nasty to me personally that I don't want to write him myself." {B1}

May 19: Boni & Liveright reports sales of 2,084 copies to Phil Stone. {SS}

May 26: *Soldiers' Pay* signed and dated "For Herb Starr." {BH1}

Summer: Vacations at Pascagoula and sails with Helen Baird, which he alludes to in an undated letter about her falling into the ocean while he stayed with the boat to pick her up: "I should have gone overside . . . and you would have saved me . . ." {CCP} Hand letters presentation copy of poetry collection, *Helen: A Courtship*, for Helen Baird. {B1}

June 4: Collaborates with Phil Stone on a letter to Liveright claiming *Mosquitoes* is "much better" than *Soldiers' Pay*, citing the opinion of "several people of intelligence and taste who have read the manuscript." A request is made for a $50 advance. {SS}

June 26: *Helen: A Courtship*: "SINGLE MANUSCRIPT IMPRESSION / OXFORD—MISSISSIPPI" {B3}

July 4: *Literary Digest* review of *Soldiers' Pay*: the characters "probably had no real plans: a conventional world had crumbled, in mind and body and soul they were drifting, and to seize this tangible undertaking [returning Donald Mahon to his home] was probably the nearest approach to adjustment they could have found." {WFC}

August: Writes to Helen Baird: "Your book [*Mosquitoes*] is pretty near done." {SL}

September: Returns to Oxford, then to New Orleans.

Interviewed by a report for the *New Orleans Item* about his work as fisherman and in a lumber mill, mentions publication of *Soldiers' Pay* and *Mosquitoes*. {LG}

September 1: Completes the typescript of *Mosquitoes* in Pascagoula, Mississippi. {SS, B3}

October 29: Signs *Royal Street: New Orleans*: "To Estelle, a / Lady, with / Respectful Admiration: / This." {B3}

Autumn: Estelle returns to Shanghai. {JW}

November 10: Phil Stone writes to Liveright expressing his surprise that the August 31 and October 31 royalty checks are overdue, according to WF. {SS}

November 16: Liveright sends royalty check. {SS}

December: WF and Spratling collaborate on *Sherwood Anderson & Other Famous Creoles*. {B1, CR1}

Christmas: In Oxford, with his family. {B1}

Winter 1926–1927: Works on 17,000-word story, "Father Abraham," the genesis of the Snopes saga, and on a history of the Sartorises, who figure in several novels and stories. {B1, CR1}

1927

January: Estelle Franklin visits Oxford with her children. {B1, B3, CR1}

January 11: Writes to Horace Liveright enclosing the dedication to Helen Baird, noting that he had promised it to her and that "you can lie to women, you know, but you cant break promises you make 'em. That infringes on their own province. And besides, you don't dare." {SL}

February 5: Signs and dates a hand bound copy of his children's story, *The Wishing-Tree*: "For his dear friend / Victoria / on her eighth birthday / Bill he made / this book/." {B1, B3, CR1}

February 9: Presents a copy of *The Wishing-Tree* to Estelle's daughter Victoria (Cho-Cho). {B1}

February 18: Writes to Liveright about four passages from *Mosquitoes* deleted because of sexual content. Mentions work on a new novel (*Flags in the Dust*) and a collection of stories. Encloses Estelle Franklin's novel, *White Beeches*, "a mss. by one who has no literary yearnings whatever and who did this just to pass the time." Even so, he thinks "it is pretty fair." {SL}

February: Writes to William Stanley Braithwaite asking how he might collect his overdue royalties from the Four Seas Company: "It never occurred to me that anyone would rob a poet. It's like robbing a whore or a child." {SL}

February 25: Writes to Willian Stanley Braithwaite again concerning overdue royalties. Congratulates Braithwaite on his new anthology, "a very healthy thing in America." {SL}

March 14: Writes a sonnet about unrequited love and a broken heart like a "shattered urn in wild and bitter earth." {B3}

April 15: The Great Flood sweeps over the Mississippi Valley, leaving more than a dozen dead and 25,000 homeless.[46]

April 30: Boni and Liveright publishes *Mosquitoes*. Signs a copy of the novel "To Aunt Bama, with much love / Bill Faulkner." {BH1}

May 4: Helen Baird marries Guy Lyman.

Summer: Returns to Pascagoula. {SL}

June: Takes the train to Pascagoula and arrives with a typewriter visiting the Stones and other friends who summer there. Barefooted, he plays and swims with children, takes them on walks, and then returns to his typewriter. At dusk he tells them the story of the Headless Horseman in Washington Irving's "The Legend of Sleepy Hollow." He is also there to see his beloved, Helen Baird and present her with a sonnet sequence, with poems written in Pascagoula, Majorca, Genoa, Pavia, Lago Maggiore, and Paris. {WC}

June 2: To Hubert Starr: "Glad you liked 'Mosquitoes.' I had a grand time writing it. Worked on it 14 months. It started out as a hoax, about the middle of it I began to decide that it was literature, but when I got it done I didn't know what in hell it was and so I let it go at that." {NYPL}

June 11: *New York Evening Post* review of *Mosquitoes* praises WF's humor and satire.

June 19: Lillian Hellman reviews *Mosquitoes* in *New York Herald Tribune*: "If his first novel showed more than the usual promise then this one . . . comes in time to fulfill it. But it must stand alone; a proof of the man's versatility." {WFC}

July 3: Donald Davidson's *Nashville Tennessean* review of *Mosquitoes* praises WF's "buoyant zest," which seems to compensate for an otherwise "scornful" novelist pursuing the "principle of the grotesque," dispatching "mayhem, assault and battery upon the bodies of numerous persons with such gracious ease that you almost overlook the savagery." {WFC}

In the New Orleans *Times-Picayune*, John McClure calls *Mosquitoes* "a clever interlude." {WFC}

July 16: The *Chicago Tribune* publishes a response to the question what book would you like to have written. WF's choice is *Moby-Dick*. {ESPL}

July 22: Claims to Horace Liveright to have lost money at gambling and has drawn a draft of $200 on the publisher. {SL}

July 23: An irritated Horace Liveright writes to WF asking him to give advance warning the next time he draws a draft of $200, which the publisher can charge against the next advance against the author's royalties.[47] {B1}

Late July: Apologizes to Liveright for the abrupt draft on the publisher, but the situation was dire due to a "[n----r]" who dug up WF's whisky and sold it. Reports progress on the new novel and says he has enough verse to make a book. {SL}

September 29: Finishes draft of *Flags in the Dust*. {B3}

Late September: Reports to Aunt Bama that he has finished his novel and is now painting signs. {BH2}

October 16: To Horace Liveright: "I have written THE book, of which those other things were but foals. I believe it is the damndest best book you'll look at this year, and any other publisher." {SL}

October 20: Liveright promises to read the book quickly given WF's excitement. {B1}

November 25: Liveright rejects *Flags in the Dust* and even suggests it should not be offered for publication elsewhere. {B1, CR1}

November 30: WF replies to Liveright saying it is too bad the publisher does not like the novel, but the author still believes in the book and will submit it elsewhere. Mentions working on two other books. {SL}

1928

Mid-February: Writes Liveright about stories he has in mind and others he has sent to an agent. {SL}

February 27: Liveright gives permission to sell *Flags in the Dust* elsewhere as long as another publisher is not given an option on future work. WF replies he has begun another novel that might please Liveright. {B3}

Early March: At work on another novel he hopes to present to Liveright by May.[48]

c. Spring: To Aunt Bama: "I have something—someone, I mean—to show you, if you only would. Of course it's a woman. I would like to see you taken with her utter charm, and intrigued by her utter shallowness. Like a lovely vase. It isn't even empty, but is filled with something—well, a yeast cake in water is the nearest simile that occurs to me. She gets the days passed for me, though. thank God I've got no money, or I'd marry her."[49] {BH2}

J. R. Cofield asks Judge Falkner if he is kin to William. WF: "What, that nut! I'm sorry to say he's my nephew." Cofield begins photographing WF, commenting: "Bill should have been in Hollywood as an actor, not a writer, because I never saw him fazed by a mere camera. He was so natural that I never had to pose him for any photograph. Everything just fell into place without any sweating over getting the right angles." {WFO}

April 7: On the manuscript of "Twilight," which will transform into *The Sound and the Fury*, WF writes this day's date. Part of the novel is composed in the tower bedroom of the old geology building on the Ole Miss campus. {B1, SO}

Spring: Sends press clipping to Aunt Bama and continues to work on his new novel. {B1}

September 20: Signs a contract with Harcourt, Brace for delivery of *Sartoris* (the revised *Flags in the Dust*) by October 7. {B1}

Late September: Goes to New York for three months. {B1}

October: Announces to Aunt Bama his contract to with Harcourt, Brace: "I'm going to be published by white folks now." Of New York City, he says "I hate this place." {SL}

Lives with Ben Wasson at 146 MacDougal Street. {B1}

A bound carbon typescript of *The Sound and the Fury*: "New York, N.Y./ October 1928." {LC}

October 7: Jonathan Cape and Harrison Smith publish *The Sound and the Fury* in an edition of 1,789 copies.

November 3: Alfred Dashiell, editor of *Scribner's* magazine rejects a WF story even as the author visits with two more stories to sell. {B1}

November 13: Estelle Oldham Franklin initiates divorce proceedings in Shanghai. {PW}

November 23: Alfred Dashiell rejects the two stories WF left with him while saying he likes the atmosphere of the first and the humor of the second. He counsels straightforward narration. {B1}

c. December 8: Departs New York City for Oxford with a $200 advance from Harcourt, Brace.

c. Mid-December: Encloses two stories, "Once Aboard the Lugger" and "Miss Zilphia Gant" for editor Alfred Dashiell at *Scribner's* but admits: "I am quite sure that I have no feeling for short stories." Even so, he will persist. {SL}

December 27: Accompanies his uncle, J. W. T. Falkner Jr. on campaigning for the office of district attorney. {B1}

1929

Fannie Falkner dies. {JW, see entry for 1885}

January–May: Dates on a manila manuscript folder and bound typed carbon typescript of *Sanctuary*. {LC}

January 31: Harcourt, Brace publishes *Sartoris* in an edition of 1,998 copies with a $300 advance. Begins work on the first version of *Sanctuary*. {B1}

February 15: Alfred Harcourt writes to WF about *The Sound and the Fury*: "A couple of us have read it with mingled admiration and doubts as to whether its unusual qualities could find a profitable market." He adds, however, that Hal Smith, a Harcourt editor starting his own firm, is taking the manuscript with him to his new office at 139 East 46th Street and will write to WF. {B1}

February 17: In a *Dallas Morning News* review of *Sartoris*, Henry Nash Smith hails WF: "From such a man one might well expect the definitive utterance of the generation who went to the war and came back when it was over." {WFC}

February 18: The new firm of Jonathan Cape and Harrison Smith sends WF a contract for *The Sound and the Fury*.

Thanks Alfred Harcourt for the copy of *Sartoris*. Mentions how much he likes the book's appearance and that he is at work on another novel (*Sanctuary*). He doesn't expect Harcourt to publish *The Sound and the Fury* or that anyone else would, but Hal Smith dared him to submit it.

Mid-February: Mentions in a letter to Alfred Dashiell Estelle's story "Selvage," which he has revised. {B1}

February 20: *Outlook and Independent* review of *Sartoris*: "Although the personalities of each of the men are strong in their different ways, the reader's sympathy remains with the women in almost every situation." {NF}

c. February 20: *Scribner* editor Alfred Dashiell rejects "Selvage," calling it "too febrile." {SL}

c. April 13: Writes to Harcourt editor requesting reviews of *Sartoris*. Suggests copies of the novel could be sold at Mac Reed's drugstore. {SL}

April 14: Donald Davidson's *Nashville Tennessean* review of *Sartoris*: "Southern writers like Faulkner are "bringing back a sense of style that almost vanished in the experimentalism of the post-war period." {WFC}

April 29: Estelle divorces Cornell Franklin. {B1, JW}

May 6: Hal Smith draws up another contract for an untitled novel that will become *Sanctuary*. {B1}

May 25: Completes the first version of *Sanctuary*. {B1}

June 5: *Commonweal* review of *Sartoris*: "His faults are so much more lovable than other people's virtues." Mentions the charming space black people occupy in WF's fiction and the sensory pleasure of young frogs piping "like endless, silver, small bubbles rising." {WFC}

June 19: William Faulkner and Estelle Franklin decide to get married. {B1}

June 20: Marries Estelle in College Hill, Mississippi. {CR1}

June 21: The honeymoon couple drive to Pascagoula. {B3, CR1}

Early summer: Goes over proofs of *The Sound and the Fury* that Ben Wasson has altered. Requests that his use of breaks and italics be restored. {SL}

June 26: Estelle Oldham Franklin's divorce decree filed in Oxford courthouse. $300 a month child support but no alimony. {PW}

June 27: *Oxford Eagle* reports the marriage, adding "Mr. Faulkner is a writer of note" and "Mrs. Franklin is the daughter of former United States District Attorney Lemuel E. Oldham." {B1}

Early fall: Takes job at university power plant, working the 6:00 p.m. to 6:00 a.m. shift. {FK}

c. October: Estelle is quarantined with scarlet fever at her father's house. {B1}

October 4: Philadelphia *Public Ledger* calls *The Sound and the Fury* "arty" and a "stunt."

October 7: Alfred Dashiell at *Scribner's* magazine rejects "A Rose for Emily," calling the story "unusual" but not satisfying "our fiction needs." {B1}

Jonathan Cape and Harrison Smith publish *The Sound and the Fury* in an edition of 1,789 copies. {B1}

October 13: Lyle Saxon reviews *The Sound and the Fury* in the *New York Herald Tribune*: "I believe simply and sincerely that this is a great book." {B3, NF}

October 18: Cleveland *Plain Dealer* calls *The Sound and the Fury* "strikingly original and hauntingly effective." {WFC}

October 20: *Nation* review of *The Sound and the Fury*: "Characters are trivial, unworthy of the enormous and complex craftsmanship expended on them." {WFC}

October 25: Begins to write *As I Lay Dying*, putting the date on the manuscript. {B3, LC, MC}

Autographs manuscript with dates "25 October 1929" and "11 December 1929" Oxford, Mississippi. {MC}

Signs and dates first edition of *The Sound and the Fury*: "To Dr Brown / sincerely / William Faulkner." {BH1}

October 29: Black Tuesday.

Autumn: Henry Nash Smith in *Southwest Review* on *The Sound and the Fury*: The "spectacle of a civilization uprooted and left to die. Scope such as this is not usual in American novels." {WFC}

November 10: *New York Times* review of *The Sound and the Fury* singles out "efforts of the Negro servants, a peculiarly sane chorus to the insane tragedy." {NF}

December 11: Puts the date at the end of the *As I Lay Dying* manuscript. {LC}

1930

Signs the first edition of *As I Lay Dying*: "To Jim Devine / Baron of Hoboken / from his friend Bill Faulkner, / Earl of Beerinstein" {BH1}[50]

January: Signs a lease for house and land on Oxford and Toccopola Roads with an option to purchase.[51] {BH1}

January–May: Dates on carbon typescript of original version of *Sanctuary*, written Oxford, Mississippi. {MC}

c. January: Writes to *Scribner's* urging the publication of one of his Indian stories. Claims that *Blackwood's* in England bought the story for 125 guineas. {SL}

Writes facetious biography for *Forum* magazine emphasizing his misadventures in school, as bank clerk, pilot, and writes novels after Sherwood Anderson's encourages him so that he won't have to otherwise work. {SL}

January 10: "Rose of Lebanon" to *Woman's Home Companion*. {LC}

January 12: Completes *As I Lay Dying* typescript with date and place: "Oxford, Missippi [sic] {LC, MC}

January 23: "Fire & Clock" to *The American Mercury*. Begins keeping a list of stories sent to national magazines, circling titles accepted and crossing out those that are rejected.[52] {LC}

February 5: "Per Ardua" to *The Saturday Evening Post*. {LC}

February 6: "A Dangerous Man" to *The American Mercury*. {LC}

February 8: *The American Mercury* rejects "Drouth," later retitled "Dry September."

February 14: "Per Ardua" to *Liberty*. {LC}

February 28: From Will Bryant's diary: "William Falkner came in afternoon . . . We chimed in pretty well." {RO}

March 7: *The American Mercury* rejects "Ad Astra." {B1}

The Saturday Evening Post rejects "Point of Honor." {B1}

March 20: *The Saturday Evening Post* rejects "Hair." {B1}

March 22: To Will Bryant, owner of the Bailey Place, explains he is having trouble raising money to buy it. "I will never give up hoping to own this place until you sell to someone else, and probably not then." Wishes to pursue Bryant's offer to rent with an option to buy and suggests they have a meeting about it. {RO}

March 24: Bryant accepts the rent to buy option and outlines terms for an agreement. {RO}

March 25: *American Caravan IV* accepts "Ad Astra" for publication.

"Honor" to *Scribner's*. {LC}

Responds to Bryant's letter: "I was afraid the only proposition which I could make you was so hare-brained that you wouldn't consider it. But since you have been kind enough to do so, I dont think we shall have any trouble at all in agreeing." Estelle wants to examine the house to see what is needed in terms of wiring, piping, and other improvements. A carpenter should also look at the joists, walls, and other underpinnings. "I will be ready to act at your convenience." {RO}

March 29: Invites the Bryants to Oxford: "We will kill the fatted calf as soon as we hear from you again." He has had the Bailey property surveyed and explains how much he can afford in terms of a down payment ($6,000) and monthly payments of not more than $75. {RO}

Binds with wire between "cardboard covered with brown marbled paper with white cloth spine" original version of *Sanctuary* with note: "Oxford, Miss 25 May 1929." {MC}

Spring 1930: Refuses to provide biographical information and writes to Ben Wasson, "Dont tell the bastards anything." {SL}

Maud entertains three ladies at bridge, one of whom mentions *Sanctuary*. "Why did Bill write a book like that?' she asks Maud, who replies. "My Billy writes what he has to write." The room is silent, the ladies leave, and Maud never speaks to her inquisitor again. {DSF}

April: *The Saturday Evening Post* rejects "The Big Shot."[53] {B1, USWF}

April 16: "Selvage" to *Forum*. {LC}

April 19: Deed of trust from William Falkner [*sic*] to Mrs. Sallie B. Bryant.

April 22: *The Saturday Evening Post* rejects "Beyond the Gate." {B3}

The American Mercury accepts "Honor." {B1}

Purchases house and property and names his new home Rowan Oak. {RO}

April 30: *Forum* publishes "A Rose for Emily," the first publication of a story by WF in a national magazine.

May 1: *Scribner's* accepts "Dry September" for $200. {B1}

May 2: "Selvage" to *Liberty*. {LC}

May 12: Writes to Will Bryant about Bailey Place tenants, the Andersons. They are supposed to vacate June 1 but request a September departure. Asks for Bryant to clarify the terms of his agreement with the tenants. {RO}

May 16: Harrison Smith halts production of *Sanctuary* at galley 4 and begins production of *As I Lay Dying*. {B3}

"Miss Ziphia Gant" to *American Mercury*. {LC}

May 20: From Will Bryant's diary: "To Oxford, Miss and dinner with William Faulkner and wife once Estelle Oldham. It was nice at the old house Bailey home . . . this trip found trees had been pulled down to make road to Taylors. Falkner wanted to buy the adjacent land." {RO}

May 21: *Forum* rejects a story, "Equinox."

May 27: "Lizards" to *The Saturday Evening Post*. {LC}

May 30: Writes to Will Bryant saying that the Bailey Place tenants have told him that Bryant is willing to pay part of their rent if they vacate by July 1. "Estelle counted on the place for the first of June, and when I told her that I would not turn Mr Anderson out neck and crop and that I had given him until July 1, I might as well have told her that I had set fire to the place. But then, women seem to be like that." Wishes to know if Anderson has quoted Bryant correctly. {RO}

May 31: Bryant writes to WF telling him that he has informed the Andersons that WF has the right to evict them June 1. Tells WF he can deduct what Anderson pays him for rent from the monthly mortgage payment. "Will say that I admire your leniency in the matter." {RO}

From Will Bryant's diary: "In the afternoon came William Faulkner . . . We ate a fine water-melon." {RO}

June: The Faulkners move into Rowan Oak. {B1}

Murry C. Falkner resigns his position as assistant secretary at the University of Mississippi. {B1}

June 4: Bryant writes to thank WF for his monthly payment and asks to be notified "what arrangements made with Anderson," so that he can send a check "for liquidation of such items as assumed in my recent letter to you." {RO}

June 5: Writes to "Miss Sallie" [Bryant] asking her in Will Bryant's absence in New Orleans to send her the $45 that the Andersons owe for

June rent as agreed upon by her husband. "I wish I could make the trip with him; I lived in New Orleans at one time." {RO}

June 7: Sallie Bryant to "Dear William" about the Andersons: "I thank you for being lenient with them and hasten to send you my check for $45.00 as agreed before."

June 19: "Mistral" to *The Saturday Evening Post.* {LC}

Summer: Returns proofs of *As I Lay Dying* to the copyeditor at Jonathan Cape and Harrison Smith. {B1}

Publication of *Soldiers' Pay* in England, with an introduction by Richard Hughes.

July: Installs screens at Rowan Oak. {RO}

American Mercury publishes "Honor."

July 12: "Mistral" to *Scribner's.* {LC}

July 23: Murry Falkner signs a contract for construction of a brick home on South Lamar, where Maud Falkner lives for the rest of her life. {B1}

July 24: *The Saturday Evening Post* accepts "Red Leaves." {B1}

August: Nearly two weeks of rehearsals for *Corporal Eagen*, a comedy drama in which WF plays the part of the "funny Jewish buddy, Izzy Goldstein." {B1}

August 23: "There Was a Queen" to *The Saturday Evening Post.* {LC}

August 25: "Peasants" to *Scribner's.*[54] {LC}

August 30: "Per Ardua" to *Scribner's.* {LC}

September 6: *The Saturday Evening Post* publishes "Thrift."

September 11–12: Performances of *Corporal Eagen.* A cast member remembers "we all commented on how well Bill Faulkner played his part." Another cast member commented: "He was very sociable." {B1}

September 12: "Two on a Bench" to *The Saturday Evening Post.* {LC}

September 13: Reports to Will Bryant that he has just finished roofing his house and cleaning up the grounds. Estelle says she would like the cornices and chandeliers that Sallie Bailey took down from the house. WF says he is glad Will likes one of his Indian stories and that another one will be published soon in *The Saturday Evening Post.* "I would have sent you the manuscript to read, if I thought you could read my handwriting. . . . I believe that I have got into it something of the spirit of the times, as well as something of the Choctaw nature: a nature that is peculiar to our Mississippi, slave-holding Indians, and of which the rest of the world knows nothing at all."[55] {RO}

September 24: "Mountain Victory to *The Saturday Evening Post.* {LC}

"Two on a Bench" to *Scribner's.* {LC}

September 25: *Oxford Eagle* mentions a Sherwood Anderson essay, "They Come Bearing Gifts," in *The American Mercury* calling WF and Hemingway the "two most notable young writers who have come on in America since the war." {B1}

October 5: *New York Herald Tribune* calls *As I Lay Dying* "photographic mysticism."

October 6: Jonathan Cape and Harrison Smith publish *As I Lay Dying* in an edition of 2,522 copies dedicated to "Hal Smith."

"That Evening Sun" to *Scribner's*. {LC}

October 7: Returns to Sallie Bryant as a "present" the chandelier that they have cleaned since she had changed her mind and wants to keep it. WF mentions bed posts and other items she might want to retrieve from the house.

October 10: Signs and dates a first edition of *As I Lay Dying*: "To Phil, with love / from Bill." {BH1}

October 12: Another letter about items that Sallie Bailey might want to retrieve from Rowan Oak. {RO}

Cleveland *Plain Dealer* calls *As I Lay Dying* equal to *The Sound and the Fury* and WF "one of the two or three original geniuses of our generation." {WFC}

October 19: *New York Times* condemns "witch's brew of a family" in *As I Lay Dying*. {WFC}

To Hal Smith: "I have been pretty busy this summer, putting a roof and a bath room in the house, and making a cotton crop on the side. But now I have got the cotton on the way to the gin, and the corn is being gathered, and I have five gallons of corn whiskey, and I am to rest a while. . . . . I dont think it'll sell, either. Dont think I'll ever crash through with a book." {NYPL}

October 25: *The Saturday Evening Post* publishes "Red Leaves."

October 28: "That Evening Sun" to *American Mercury*. {LC}

October 31: The first party at Rowan Oak. WF tells the children present a Halloween story about Judith Sheegog who had lived on the property and her doomed love affair with a Yankee officer, her tragic death, and the appearance of her ghost. {B1}

John Faulkner takes Marion O'Donnell to Rowan Oak to meet WF, who signs a copy of *The Marble Faun* for him.[56] {MC}

November 3: Dated sheets (5–17) of *Sanctuary*, first version. Harrison Smith puts the book back into production. {B3}

November 5: *Nation* review of *As I Lay Dying* deplores "phosphorescent rottenness of the family." {NF}

November 7: H. L. Mencken writes, "That Evening Sun Go Down," is a "capital story," and he wants to publish it in *The American Mercury* if WF makes some revisions.

Replies to Mencken rejecting certain suggestions but also defers to Mencken's judgment on other matters.

"Rose of Lebanon" to *The Saturday Evening Post.* {LC}

November 9: A corrected version of "Rose of Lebanon" to *The Saturday Evening Post.* {LC}

November 13: Signs and dates the first edition of *As I Lay Dying* for Myrtle Ramey. {BH1}

November 14: "Dull Tale" to *The Saturday Evening Post.*

November 17: "The Hound" to *The Saturday Evening Post.* {LC}

Mid-November: Receives galleys of *Sanctuary* and decides to rewrite the novel. {B1}

November 22: *Saturday Review of Literature* calls *As I Lay Dying* "as vivid as modern caricature and as accurate as Dutch painting." {NF}

November 29: "The Hound" to *Scribner's* after *The Saturday Evening Post*'s rejection. {B1}

Another story, "Built Fence," to *The Saturday Evening Post,* which is later revised as "A Justice." {B1}

December: Dissatisfied with *Sanctuary* and begins radical revision. {CR1}

December 12: Sinclair Lewis's Nobel Prize speech mentions WF, "who has freed the South from hoopskirts." {B1}

December 14: "The Leg" to *The Saturday Evening Post.* {LC}

December 22: "Smoke" to *The Saturday Evening Post.* {LC}

Christmas Eve: In the Episcopal church with Estelle singing hymns. {B3}

Christmas: Complete with "a big tree, pine boughs in the hall, and holly and ivy from their own woods on the banister. The Oldham and Faulkner families gather to visit and for dinner. A tiring day for Estelle, six months pregnant. {B3}

December 29: General Stone's Bank of Oxford fails due in part to mismanagement and criminal activity. Shortly afterwards, Phil Stone tells WF: "You don't need me any more, and I have to make a living for my old folks." {SS}

A version of "A Fox Hunt" to *The Saturday Evening Post.* {B1}

December 30: "Per Ardua" to *Liberty.* {B1}

1931

Signs at Rowan Oak books in his personal library, including *Jude the Obscure* and *Green Mansions.*

January: *Scribner's* publishes "Dry September."

Returns corrections to H. L. Mencken for "That Evening Sun Go Down." {B1}

January 1: Makes a note on "Money Earned," with dates for sums coming in for short story sales. {B1}

Early January: Kyle Crichton writes requesting more work from WF and calling him "one of the greatest writers alive." {B1}

January 7: Discusses insurance matters with Sallie Bailey and a policy WF has taken out on Rowan Oak, although he now knows she, too, had such a policy. He understands that she has paid taxes on the house. {RO}

January 9: A version of "A Fox Hunt" to *College Humor.* {LC}

January 10: "Hair" to *Woman's Home Companion.* {LC}

Estelle, seven months pregnant, awakes her husband who calls the doctor and then takes her to the hospital. {B3}

January 11: Estelle gives birth to a daughter, Alabama, named after WF's Aunt Bama.

January 20: Alabama WF dies. {CR1}

January 27: *Scribner's* rejects "A Death-Drag." {B1}

To Will and Sallie Bryant: "The weather up here is like spring, and we are already thinking about a garden." Specifies which lots he wants to buy from the Bryants, assuring them that he is not planning a "secret subdivision and building plan . . . It is just that I would like to feel free to use this land and to improve it." He is thinking of an orchard to make the "whole place the pleasing spectacle which it once was." {RO}

January 29: "A Death-Drag," "Indians Built a Fence," "The Hound" to *The American Mercury,* and "The Brooch" to *Forum.* {LC}

"Hair" to *Scribner's.* {LC}

February 2: A revision of "The Peasants" (a version of "Spotted Horses") retitled "Aria Con Amore" to *The Saturday Evening Post.* {LC}

Memphis Commercial Appeal publishes letter from W. H. James, a black man from Starkville, Mississippi, commending an antilynching women's group. {CR1}

February 4: "Idyll in the Desert" to *The Saturday Evening Post.* {LC}

February 9: Cape and Smith publish revised *Sanctuary* in an edition of 2,219 copies.

February 10: Cleveland *Plain Dealer* review of *Sanctuary*: "I am fairly hard-boiled, but Sanctuary nauseated me." {WFC}

February 13: "Aria Con Amore" to *Scribner's* after *The Saturday Evening Post* rejects it. {B1}

New York Sun review of *Sanctuary*: "One of the most terrifying books I have ever read. And it is one of the most extraordinary." {NF}

February 15: Responds to W. H. James's letter of February 2 in *Memphis Commercial Appeal,* noting "the people of the black race who get lynched are not representative of the black race, just as the people who lynch them are not representative of the white race." Discusses the reasons for lynching from a historical perspective of a new land. "I have yet to hear, outside of a novel or a story, of a man of any color with a record beyond reproach, suffering violence at the hands of men who knew him." Concludes: "But there is one curious thing about mobs. Like our juries, they have a way of being right." {CR1}

New York Times review of *Sanctuary* refers to "that limp state which follows a frightening encounter in the dark or the sudden sickening realization that one has just escaped sudden death." {NF}

"And no one should read 'Sanctuary' who is not willing to bear the scars."—*New York Herald Tribune* {NF}

February 25: Accepts $400 for "Spotted Horses." {B1}

February 27: Explains to Sallie Bryant that he cannot make the March 1 house payment. The hard times have made it difficult to earn money from magazine publishing. He hopes to double the monthly payment in April to $150. "This is not business; I know that. By our contract, my failure renders the contract void, and, I believe, my title to the house." But he has had troubles, including the loss of his daughter and hospital bills. "But, if you wish to hold me to the letter of the contract, I will understand that you are within your rights, to which I agreed. {RO}

March: *The American Mercury* publishes "That Evening Sun Go Down," with only some of the revisions Mencken suggested.

In Oxford, signs and dates a first edition of *Sanctuary* for Myrtle Ramey. {BH1}

March 1: Sallie Bryant replies to WF's letter asking that his mortgage payment be deferred for a month. "I know what illness and hospital bills mean too, and sympathize with you very much. I hope Estelle will soon be her sweet self again." {RO}

March 1: *Atlanta Journal* review of *Sanctuary*: "This is not the novel to send your maiden aunt on her birthday." {NF}

March 2: "Idyll in the Desert" to *Scribner's*. {LC}

March 4: *Sanctuary* sells 3,519 copies in previous three weeks. {B1}

March 5: "Doctor Martino" to *The Saturday Evening Post*. {LC}

March 11: A version of "A Fox Hunt" to *Woman's Home Companion*. {LC}

March 12: *Scribner's* rejects "Idyll in the Desert." {B1}

March 15: *Daily Ilini* review of *Sanctuary*: "a potent drug for the imagination—that the book would never be finished by reading the final word but would require a tallying of events before finding out just exactly what had occurred. Sanctuary is different. I read bits of it aloud to my roommate and we were both caught in the whirlwind of its spell and swept along. I couldn't cease reading—she couldn't cease listening. My throat became dry; my eyes blurred; before I knew it, I had read so many pages aloud." {CR1}

March 16: "Doctor Martino" to *Woman's Home Companion* after *The Saturday Evening Post's* rejection. {LC}

March 20: "Hair" to *The American Mercury*. {LC}

March 23: Princeton University professor Maurice Coindreau writes to WF asking to be his translator. {B1}

March 26: *Oxford Eagle* reports: "It is said that in this novel Faulkner looses all the fury of his pen and this is one of the most stirring of the many books written by him." {B1}

March 27: *American Caravan* publishes "Ad Astra."

April: *The Bookman* praises *As I Lay Dying* for the "cinematic scene-shifting of expressionism, the almost obscure brevity and visionary sensationalism of the imagists, and the intense exploration of momentary experience characteristic of writers like Conrad, with the classic formal beauty of an intricate plot skillfully implicated, rigorously unified, and implacable in its advance to a fore-designed end." {WFC}

April 1: Cumulative sales of *Sanctuary*: 6,457. {B1}

Headline in *Brooklyn Daily Eagle*: "William Faulkner Rakes up Human Garbage to Fashion a Powerful Magnum Opus." {CR1}

April 3: "Hair" to *The Saturday Evening Post*. {LC}

April 5: "A Death-Drag" to *Collier's*. {LC}

"Divorce in Naples," "The Hound," and "Fox Hunt" to Ben Wasson, acting as WF's agent in New York City. {LC}

Writes to "Mr Will" [Bryant] to confirm "Miss Sallie" has received his check. "I thank her for her kindness in letting me double up last month." Explains that he has to go to New York in hopes of improving his finances. He believes that in person he can generate more interest in his work. In effect, he is asking that they allow him to defer further payments on the house. "My troubles appear to have descended upon me all at once, but I believe that with a—call it a breathing spell, a chance to get to where my money comes from and see to things myself, I can get into shape again." {RO}

April 11: "A Justice" to *Woman's Home Companion*. {LC}

April 12: Thanks the Bryants again for their kindness in letting him "get my head 'above water' once and for all, I believe." Confides to Will Bryant a desire to write "THE novel of Mississippi, of the action and reaction upon one another of white and red and black men, the scene to be laid in those days. That was when Mississippi WAS: integral, both its own father and its own son. Since then we have been but the apennage of the damned Yankees who set the price on cotton and force us to raise it—or starve. (You might say, and starve)." {RO}

April 15: Chatto & Windus publishes *The Sound and the Fury* with an introduction by Richard Hughes.

Thanks Bennett Cerf for sending pipes. Notes that he would like to see *The Sound and the Fury* in a Modern Library edition with Evelyn Scott's appreciation of the novel used as a preface. Asks for "what Dostoyefsky you have in the list. I have seen several reviews of my books in which a Dostoyefsky influence. I have never read Dostoyefsky and so I would like to see the animal." {RHR}

April 18: "Idyll in the Desert" to *Harper's*. {LC}

April 23: "All the Dead Pilots" to *Collier's*. {LC}

May: *American Mercury* publishes "Hair."

May 5: "A Justice" to *Harper's*. {LC}

May 14: Signs contract for publication of "A Rose for Emily and Other Stories." {B1}

May 17: Writes to "Mr Will" asking him to consider selling a lot to his brother John, who does not have much money. He would have to work out some kind of monthly payment, "equivalent to some nominal rent . . . I am only broaching the matter to you, to see if you consider the matter worth discussing further." {RO}

Signs and dates first edition of *Sartoris* for Myrtle Ramey: "William Faulkner / Oxford, Miss." {BH1}

Signs and dates in Oxford a first edition of *As I Lay Dying* for Myrtle Ramey. {BH1}

May 20: "Beyond the Talking," a review of Erich Maria Remarque's novel, *The Road Back*, revealing that defeat in war occasions the need to reflect, as it did in Germany, and, implicitly in the South. WF also makes a significant statement applicable to his own practice: "It is a writer's privilege to put into the mouths of his characters better speech that they would have been capable of, but only for the purpose of permitting and helping the character to justify him or what he believes himself to be, taking down his spiritual pants." {ESPL}

Summer: Answers a query from a reader, saying "Spotted Horses" took place around 1900. {SL}

June: "Spotted Horses" (a revision of "Aria Con Amore") appears in *Scribner's*.

Maurice Coindreau publishes an article about WF in *La Nouvelle Revue Française*. {B1}

Apologizes to Ben Wasson for not telling him where he has sent certain stories. {B1}

"To me the very title *Sanctuary* has such connotations of brooding peace that I think all those who care for sweet and sentimental books should be warned what a terrific experience awaits them within its covers"—Alexander Woollcott, *McCalls* {CR1}

June 5: To Ben Wasson in New York: "A Death-Drag," "Dr. Martino," "Idyll in the Desert." {LC}

June 8: "The Leg" to *Scribner's*. {LC}

July 7: *Scribner's* editor Kyle Crichton rejects "All the Dead Pilots," preferring to see more Yoknapatawpha stories. {B1}

July 10: *Memphis Press-Scimitar* publishes Marshall J. Smith's interview describing WF at home, his family background, and how he wrote *As I Lay Dying*. {LG}

July 17: *The Saturday Evening Post* receives and rejects "Evangeline."[57] {B1, USWF}

Phil Stone writes to E. Byrne Hackett, owner of the Brick Row Book Shop: "Bill is already one of the leading figures in American literature. He is already established and his reputation is going to grow because the achievement will be forthcoming." {CR1}

The *Brooklyn Daily Eagle* calls WF the master of "frank decadence." {CR1}

July 23: "Rose of Lebanon" to *Scribner's*. {LC}

Kyle Crichton requests more Flem Snopes stories for a series. {CR1}

July 26: The *Woman's Home Companion* receives and rejects "Evangeline." {B1}

August: *Harper's* publishes "The Hound" and pays WF $400. {B1}

c. August 10: *Scribner's* rejects "Rose of Lebanon" and again asks for more Flem Snopes stories. {B1}

August 11: "Centaur in Brass," a new Flem Snopes story, to *Scribner's*. {LC}|

August 14: Refers to an agreement made with Will Bryant the previous day. Proposes making certain changes in their contract.[58] {RO}

August 17: Begins *Light in August* titling it "Dark House." {CR1}

August 20: *Scribner's* rejects "Centaur in Brass" because it kills off Flem Snopes and the magazine wants to keep him alive for a series. {CR1}

August 23: *Harper's* rejects "Centaur in Brass." {B1}

September: *Harper's* publishes "Fox Hunt" and pays WF $400.

Professor James Southall Wilson invites WF to attend a Southern literary conference (October 23–24) at the University of Virginia that will include Ellen Glasgow, James Branch Cabell, Paul Green, Allen Tate, Sherwood Anderson, and others. {CR1}

September 19: *Time and Tide* review of *Sanctuary*: "hard to read, difficult to like, and impossible to forget." {NF}

September 21: Cape and Smith publishes *These 13* (changing the title from "A Rose for Emily and Other Stories" in an edition of 1,928 copies dedicated to "Estelle and Alabama." {B1}

September 24: WF accepts invitation to attend Southern literary conference but warns that his behavior is like a hound under a wagon, never venturing very far to meet anyone and growling when encroached upon. {SL}

Times Literary Supplement review of *Sanctuary*: "no moral or aesthetic purpose." {NF}

September 28: Alfred Dashiell at *Scribner's* asks to take another look at "A Death-Drag." {B1}

September 29: In Oxford signs and dates first edition of *These 13*: "To Aunt Bama, / with love, / William" {BH1}

October 5: "Centaur in Brass" to *The American Mercury*. {LC}

"Smoke" to *The Saturday Evening Post*. {LC}

Writes to James Southall Wilson about his arrival at the University of Virginia. {MC}

October 8: *Scribner's* rejects "Black Music" but buys "A Death-Drag" for $250. {B1}

October 16: "Smoke" to *Scribner's*. {LC}

c. October 20, noon: Boards train for Memphis. {CR1}

7:15 p.m.: Boards train for Charlottesville for a conference of Southern writers. Stops in Bristol, Virginia and sends a telegram to Elizabeth Prall Anderson. {CR1}

October 21, 5:00 p.m.: Arrives in Charlottesville for Southern Writers' Conference, and then departs for a seven-week period in New York. {CR1}

October 22: To Estelle, "I can see the Blue Ridge from both of my windows . . . The fall coloring is splendid here." Mentions he has heard nothing from Elizabeth Prall Anderson and comments "Maybe she is still mad at me." {SL} "I don't think I will need to tell you to give my love to the chillen, any more than to tell you that you already have about 1,000,000 tons of it yourself. But I do, nevertheless, tell you just darling, darling, darling." {UVA}

October 26: Arrives in New York City in playwright Paul Green's car. Several publishers avidly seek WF for their lists. He offers Bennett Cerf "Idyll in the Desert" as a special Random House publication. {CR1}

October 27: Harrison Smith, wary of other publishers bidding for WF's business and concerned about an overwhelmed author, sends him off on the *Henry R. Mallory* liner to Jacksonville, Florida. {CR1}

October 29: WF arrives in Jacksonville with an acute case of hiccups. The only cure, WF asserts, is flying in a plane upside down, which, apparently, works as a hired plane flies over Jacksonville. {CR1}

October 30: WF arrives in Chapel Hill, North Carolina. {CR1}

c. October 31: Visits the office of *Contempo* magazine, whose editor Anthony Buttitta met WF in Charlottesville during the literary conference. WF has promised to be a contributor to the magazine. {CR1}

c. November 1: Goes to a movie theater but leaves abruptly and begins talking about *Light in August.* {CR1}

November 2: Visits a college class in Chapel Hill, gives a short talk, answers questions, and is applauded. {CR1}

An interview in *College Topics*, a University of Virginia undergraduate weekly, describes WF's upbringing, early reading, views on the novel's future, his opinion of Southern literature, modern American life, Dostoevsky, and Dickens. {LG}

Phil Stone writes to WF about getting buyers for copies of *The Marble Faun* and hack work that Stone can do like writing reviews or advertisements. "I simply must add to the amount of money which I am making."[59] {BH2}

c. November 3: Boards the *Henry R. Mallory* liner in Norfolk, Virginia, bound for New York City. {CR1}

November 4: Reporter Evelyn Shelley of the *New York World-Telegram* meets WF as he docks, observing a "well-groomed shy little man with busy brows and brown eyes as bright as a squirrel." He expresses an aversion to literary life and compares himself to a hound dog under a wagon. He writes home to report the attention he has attracted, as though "I was some strange and valuable beast." {B1}

Writes to Estelle about a movie agent's claim WF could make $500 to $700 a week in Hollywood. Proposes a trip to California, although Hal Smith does not want him to do it. {SL}

On Hotel Century stationery, 111 East 46th Street, New York City, WF encloses a check made out to Will Bryant and notes that payment is for the balance of the year, until September 1, 1932. {RO}

November 5: In the *New York World-Telegram*, Harry Hansen reports that "rival publishers fought a merry battle yesterday for the favors of William Faulkner." {B1}

Meets Maurice Coindreau, translator of "A Rose for Emily" and "Dry September." {CWF}

November 7: In New York, signs and dates first edition of *These 13*: "To Jim Devine / from his friend / Bill Faulkner." {BH1}

November 7–8: Visits Hal Smith's home in Farmington, Connecticut. {CR1}

November 9: In the apartment of George Oppenheimer, a founder of Viking Press, WF inscribes a copy of *These 13*, and turns to the page where "All the Dead Pilots" begins and writes, "This is the best one." {CR1}

Autographs a copy of *As I Lay Dying*, "With gratitude to Dr Coindreau, the translator." {BH1}

c. November 11: A representative from Paramount Pictures talks WF into writing a movie for Tallulah Bankhead. "How's that for high?," he writes to Estelle, adding "I have created quite a sensation." {SL}

November 14: A *New York Herald Tribune* interview explains WF's growing reputation as the "Dostoyevsky of the South," his views of "Southern Negroes," and his reluctance to speak about his own books. {LG}

November 16: Signs a copy of *The Brothers Karamazov* for Wili Lengel. {BH1}

c. November 25: Completes an introduction to the Modern Library edition of *Sanctuary*. {B1, B3}

November 28: Interviewed for the "Talk of the Town" section of the *New Yorker*, his Southern background and work on *Light in August* is mentioned as well as stories about his flying mishaps during the war. "His mother reads every line he writes, but his father doesn't bother and suspects his son is wasting his time." {LG}

November 30: Estelle travels to Memphis to board a train to New York City. Marshall Smith interviews her for the *Commercial-Appeal* and describes an "animated, vivid person." She comments on *Sanctuary* and says she is on the way to help her husband fend off intruders. {LG}

November: *Harper's* publishers "Doctor Martino."

Professor Maurice Edgar Coindreau of Princeton University obtains permission from WF and Harrison Smith to translate into French *As I Lay Dying* and *These 13*. {B1}

December: *The Bookman* publishes a longer version of Marshall J. Smith's interview,[60] including more details about WF's work, family history, time in New Orleans and New York. {LG}

December 4: The Bankers Trust Company. To the order of William WF, $200. {RHR}

December 9: Signs and dates in New York the first edition of *Sanctuary*: "To Ben, with love." {BH1}

December 10: The Harbor Press publishes for Random House *Idyll in the Desert* in a limited signed edition of 400 copies. {MC}

Attends a Bennett Cerf party to celebrate the publication of *Idyll in the Desert*. {CR1}

The Faulkners leave for Baltimore, where Bill meets H. L. Mencken, whom Estelle dislikes. {CR1}

c. December 14: The Faulkners return to Rowan Oak. Estelle puts a photograph of Bennett Cerf on her mantle. {CR1}

December 16: Writes to Alfred Dashiell to request the return of "Smoke" if the *Scribner's* editor can't use it. Reports that the "novel is going fine." {CR1}

December 18: Agent Leland Hayward receives a telegram from Sam Marx, head of the story department at MGM: "DID YOU MENTION WILLIAM FAULKNER TO ME ON YOUR LAST TRIP HERE. IF SO IS HE AVAILABLE AND HOW MUCH." {B1}

December 20: Louis Cochran arrives in Oxford from Jackson, Mississippi for an interview with an author at work on some carpentry. New York is a place "where everybody talks about what they are going to write and no one writes anything," Cochran is told. {B1, B3}

December 23: Phil Stone produces five typewritten pages of notes on Cochran's article. Stone attributes WF's success to Stone's confidence in him. {BH2}

December 27: To Bennett Cerf: "Xmas was quiet here. Estelle and the children are with her mother in town, and so I am alone in the house. I passed Christmas with a 3 foot back log on the fire, and a bowl of eggnog and a pipe and Tom Jones. That was a special dispensation, as I have been on the wagon since reaching home, and I shall stay on the wagon until the novel is written. It is going great guns." {CR1}

1932

n.d.: Writes blurb for James Hanley's novel, *Boy*: "It's almost like a good clean cyclone or a dose of salts, since most books nowadays sound like they were written either by pansies or stallions."

Writes to Evelyn Harter at Cape and Smith declining to contribute to a book compiled by Elmer Adler about how to get published: "Tell him the best way I know to get published is to borrow the advances from the publisher, then they have to print the stuff." {BH2}

c. January: Requests $250 from Hal Smith so that he does not have to "go whoring again with short stories." Also discusses 15 percent royalty for *A Green Bough*: "I am going cold-blooded Yankee now." {SL}

January: *Scribner's* publishes "Death-Drag."

Invites Anthony Buttitta to visit in Oxford. {CR1}

Early January: Anthony Buttitta of *Contempo* visits Oxford and finds Rowan Oak still in dilapidated shape and WF in a messy workroom with recordings of Gershwin's "Rhapsody in Blue," played to "set the rhythm and jazzy tone" of *Sanctuary*." {B1}

Writes to Hal Smith and calls *A Green Bough* "2nd class poetry . . . But worse has been published." Reports making progress on his next novel. {SL}

January 13: Hal Smith writes to express his concern about publishing with journals like *Contempo* and *Salmagundi*, which may compete with Smith's plans to publish WF's poems and stories. {CR1}

Mid-January: Writes to apologize for causing Hal Smith concern about making commitments without checking with the publisher. {SL}

Writes to Ben Wasson explaining the mix-up with Hal Smith and *Contempo.* WF says his "country innocence has been taken advantage of. Which is no one's fault except mine, of course." {SL}

January 15: Hal Smith writes to reassure WF but also to caution him again about his commitments. {CR1}

To Hal Smith explains his carelessness in letting a bookshop reprint his work and that he has learned his lesson. {SL}

January 18: Ben Wasson sells "Smoke" to *Harper's* for $400. {B1}

January 26: Works on *Light in August* and thinks of trying the movies "later on." {SL}

Addresses the Oxford rotary club on the topic of aviation. {CR1}

Early winter: Completes writing *Light in August* and tells Wasson he is not ready to change publishers in spite of an offer from Harold Guinzburg of Viking Press. {B1}

February: *The American Mercury* publishes "Centaur in Brass."

February 1: *Contempo* publishes "Twilight," "Knew I Love Once," "To a Virgin," "My Epitaph," "Spring," "I Will Weep for Youth," "Visions in Spring," "April," "Winter Is Gone," and a story, "Once Aboard a Lugger," plus a review of *These 13* and *Idyll in the Desert.* In a comparison of Faulkner with Sinclair Lewis, Sherwood Anderson, Theodore Dreiser, John Dos Passos, Evelyn Scott, Ernest Hemingway, and Willa Cather, he is lauded as "the most creative of contemporary American writers."

February 10: Signs a copy of *Sanctuary*: "For Alice and Harold [Guinzberg], from Bill," and on the title page "William Faulkner / Oxford, Miss." {MC}

February 14: Henry Nash Smith in the *Dallas Morning News* sizes up WF's character and demeanor, describes his environs, his reluctance to talk about his own books, modern influences on his writing, his intimate knowledge of the characters in *As I Lay Dying*, and his war experiences. Smith notices that WF is "much interested in the new draperies which Mrs. Faulkner is planning for the living room of their fine old house, and he seemed prouder of the hand-hammered locks on the doors than of anything he has written." {LG}

February 19: Completes manuscript of *Light in August.* Autograph manuscript dated on last page with title "Dark House" crossed out. {B1}

February 27: *The Saturday Evening Post* publishes "Lizards in Jamshyd's Courtyard."

March: Corey Ford, "Popeye the Pooh," a parody of *Sanctuary*, is published in *Vanity Fair.*

Modern Library publication of *Sanctuary* with WF's introduction.

An angry Estelle throws the manuscript of *Light in August* out of a car window, and WF picks up the sheets on the road. {AB}

March 5: *The Saturday Evening Post* publishes "Turn About."

Late winter: Still making changes to *Light in August*. Tells Ben Wasson not to take less than $5000 for a serial publication. Asks Wasson to tell Corey Ford how much he and Estelle enjoyed "Popeye the Pooh." {SL}

March 16: Writes Paul Romaine of the Casanova Book Shop and publisher of *Salmagundi* of his reluctance to sign too many copies of his work since autographs are "like cotton down here: the more you make, the less it's worth, the less you get for it." Expresses his delight in Hemingway's message of good wishes via Romaine. "This is the second time he has said something about me that I wish I had thought to say first."

Early spring: Still hoping to receive $5000 for serial rights to *Light in August*; otherwise, a movie offer is still an option. {SL}

Still hoping to earn more money via Ben Wasson for short stories. {CR1}

April: *Harper's* publishes "Smoke."

April 4: Phil Stone writes on WF's behalf to the Mississippi Tax Commission inquiring into what WF can deduct on his taxes. {BH2}

April 14: Compliments Maurice Coindreau on translations of "Dry September" and "A Rose for Emily" in *La Nouvelle Revue Française* (June 1931) and *Commerce* (January 1932). He also comments on Coindreau's *La Nouvelle Revue Française* article: "I see now I have a quite decided strain of Puritanism (in its proper sense, of course, not our American one) regarding sex. I was not aware of it. But now, on casting back and rereading now and then or here and there of my own work, I can see it plainly. I have found it quite interesting." {SL, CWF}

April 15: Signs a contract with MGM for six weeks' work. {CR1}

Mid-April: Asks Wasson to inquire about royalties that Cape and Smith owe him for *Sanctuary* before committing to a Hollywood contract. {SL}

April 25: In Memphis to outfit himself for a trip to Hollywood. {B1}

April 30: Receives six copies of *Salmagundi* featuring Faulkner's poetry, printed in an edition of 525 copies under the imprint The Casanova Press. {B1}

May: In Los Angeles, signs and dates a first edition of *As I Lay Dying*: "To Herb [Starr] from Bill Faulkner." {BH1}

May 7: Arrives on a Saturday in Culver City, California, to work on film treatments for MGM and is shown to a projection room to watch a Wallace Beery film, but abruptly leaves. {CR1}

May 9: Does not show up for work. {CR1}

May 10: Does not show up for work. {CR1}

May 11: MGM contact is canceled. {CR1}

May 16: Returns to MGM, reporting he has been wandering in Death Valley. {CR1}

May 19: Sam Marx asks legal department to reinstate Faulkner. {CR1}

May 24: Signs contract with MGM. {BH1}

Completes screen treatment, *Manservant*. {MGM}

May 25: *Manservant* sent to story department. {CR1, WFH}

May 26: Completes screen treatment, *The College Widow*. {MGM, WFH}

Signs a copy of *Sanctuary*: "A heeltap to Bill Conselman / Wm Faulkner / Los Angeles, Cal" and *Idyll in the Desert* "For Bill Conselman."[61] {MC}

In Los Angeles, signs and dates a first edition of *Sartoris* "For Herb Starr." {BH1}

In Los Angeles, signs and dates a first edition of *The Sound and the Fury* "For Herb Starr." {BH1}

June 1: Completes screen treatment, *Absolution*. {MGM, WFH}

Begins working with Ralph Graves on a screen treatment, *Flying the Mail*. {MGM}

June 2: Sends $100 home out of his $450 paycheck and mentions his work on screen treatments and meeting Laurence Stallings, a friend from New York and author of *What Price Glory*, who gives good advice about "keeping my balance with these people." {SL}

June 3: Completes script for *Flying the Mail*. {MGM, WFH}

June 5: William Hawks reads "Turn About" in *The Saturday Evening Post* and tells his brother Howard Hawks: "This is the most exciting story for a picture I've read." {B1}

June 10: Signs contract with MGM assigning all rights to WF's film treatment *Flying the Mail*. {BH1}

June 16: Paramount pays $750 for a four-month option on *Sanctuary*. {CR1}

June 23: Story conferences for "Turn to the Right." {WHF}

June 26: MGM contract terminated. {WHF}

June 27: Texas Book Club publishes *Miss Ziphia Gant* in a limited edition of 300 copies, with a preface by Henry Nash Smith.

Late June: Watches equestrians preparing for the 1932 Olympics with Laurence Stallings. {B1}

July 21: Galleys for *Light in August* arrive at Rowan Oak. Rejects several proposed changes. {B1}

July 26: Put on the MGM payroll at $250 a week. {B1} Works on "Turn About" screenplay. {WFH}

August 5: Hunts on Catalina Island. {B1}

August 6: WF's father Murry dies. As eldest son and now head of the family, WF inherits the leather-bound family Bible purchased by John Wesley Thompson in 1859. {B1}

August 10: Returns home and to his new position as head of the family.

August 16: To Herb Starr and Bill Elliott: "I miss those fine cool California nights, though, even if this weather does make cotton grow. . . . Here goes a homegrown, corn whiskey mint julep to youall and California. My regards to everybody we know." {NYPL}

August 17: Dates manuscript of *Light in August* "Oxford, Mississippi" {LC}

August 24: Second draft script for "Turn About" [in pencil, "Today We Live"] "by Howard Hawks and Wm. Faulkner." {MGM, WFH}

Mid-to-late September: Finishes "Turn About" script for Hawks at home but has to return to California for final changes as soon as Hawks says so. Hopes that Paramount will purchase *Sanctuary* and asks Wasson about the prospects for short story sales. {SL}

September 26: Encloses check for $450, the balance due by September 1, 1933, to "Mr Will," requesting in an "unbusinesslike proposition" that some of it be used as a claim on the additional lots he wants to purchase. Setting off again to California and expects to return in November. {RO}

Late September: Mentions to Wasson how mad he was in California but now at home "eating watermelon on the back porch and watching it rain." {SL}

October 3: Returns to MGM for three weeks with his mother and brother Dean. {CR1}

October 6: Smith and Haas publish *Light in August.*

Signs and dates first edition of *Light in August*: "To Phil, from Bill." {BH1}

October 7: *New York Sun* review of *Light in August* suggests WF has "probably forgotten more about literary tricks than such writers as Ernest Hemingway or Sherwood Anderson will ever learn." {WFC}

October 9: *Memphis Commercial Appeal* review of *Light in August* finds the novel "more mature, broader in outlook, nearer to the final, truthful revelation of human potentialities for which the author is striving." {WFC}

October 8: *Saturday Review of Literature* review of *Light in August*: "one perfect chrysoprase." {NF}

October 17: Paramount executes its option for *Sanctuary* and Faulkner receives $6000. {B1}

October 20: *Oxford Eagle* summarizes reviews of *Light in August* calling it WF's greatest work.

October 22: Works on additional scenes for *Today We Live*. Taken off MGM payroll, having earned $6000. {B1}

October 25: Contributes to third draft of *Today We Live*. {MGM, WFH}

Late October: Writes Hal Smith: "Here I am home again, thank God." Likes the look of *Light in August*. Expects Smith to visit as soon as Rowan Oak repairs are completed. {SL}

Still awaiting the check from Paramount and planning a visit with Estelle to New York City. {SL}

November 4: To *Scribner's*, Ben Wasson sends "There Was a Queen" and "Black Music," and Alfred Dashiell accepts the first for $300 and rejects the second. {B1}

November 6: The *Memphis Commercial Appeal* publishes Louis Cochran's article on WF.

November 12: Louis Cochran sends a copy of his WF profile to Hal Smith, commenting that a "'prophet' need not necessarily be 'without honor' in his own country. . . . Knowing Bill's modesty as well as I do I doubt that you would see the article if someone other than Faulkner did not send it." {WFO}

November 17: Hal Smith responds to the WF profile Cochran has sent him: "excellent reading and I hope it will wake up the South to the extraordinary talent it possesses. I wish Bill wasn't quite so modest; I can't even get a letter out of him." {WFO}

November 28: Put on the MGM payroll at $600 a week. Works on a script eventually titled *War Birds*, based on a World War I memoir. Signs a contract assigning to MGM all rights to anything he writes while employed by the studio. {BH1, MGM, WFH}

December 3: *The Saturday Evening Post* publishes "Mountain Victory."

December 8: Bennett Cerf offers $500 for a 10-to-12-page introduction to a signed edition of *The Sound and the Fury*. {B1}

December 14: Signs a contract with MGM for "treatment of story" for "Turnabout." {BH1}

December 15: Completes work at home on *War Birds*. {B1}

Mid-December: Brings a copy of *Light in August* to Phil Stone's law office. {SS}

December 16: Rejects Cerf's offer, saying $500 for an introduction to a signed edition of *The Sound and the Fury* is not enough. {SL}

December 23: Cerf writes hoping WF will reconsider writing an introduction to *The Sound and the Fury* when he and Estelle visit New York City at Christmas. {SL}

Hal Smith writes, still worried about side deals WF makes with others to publish his work: "For Christ sake don't decide to do anything rash." {B1}

The Saturday Evening Post publishes "Mountain Victory."

December 25: Trip to New York put off because Estelle is sick. Thanks Bennett Cerf for sending a copy of *The Red Badge of Courage*, "a beautiful book." {SL}

December 26: To Hal Smith: "I have been busy as hell, writing a movie script and taking care of the sick. Estelle and the children have been sick in rotation since the middle of November, and the day after Xmas, Estelle succeeded in falling down stairs (no one would have been surprised if it had been me now . . . and she has been in bed ever since). She is getting up today, though, I think. But our trip East will be off. We have decided to save the money and put it in the house, anyway. So, I won't see you unless you can still arrange to come down here later on. . . . PS. Have four gallons of charred corn and four gallons of English tobacco Ha Ha." {CCP}

1933

Writes blurb for Clifton Cuthbert's *Thunder without Rain*: "I hated to put it down." Lauds the book's freshness . . . "As regards craftsmanship, knowing what to tell and what not to tell, it's one of the best first books I have ever read." {ESPL}

January: *Scribner's* publishes "There Was a Queen."

Early January: Answers Hal Smith's letter, explaining he has been busy writing a movie script and taking care of Estelle and sick children. {SL}

Faulkner answers a Bennett Cerf day letter: "WILL RAISE OUR OFFER TO SEVEN HUNDRED FIFTY DOLLARS AS A TRIBUTE TO THE FAULKNER PRESTIGE." The answer is still no since he does not need the money badly enough. {B1}

January 12: MGM story department produces 143-page screenplay of *War Birds*. {MGM}

January 21: Howard Hawks tells *New York Post* that Faulkner "spent four years in the British air forces and saw service both in the air and behind the lines during some of the heaviest fighting, so he knows what he is writing about. From this basis of real imagery in the author's brain we should be able to produce a result on the screen that will approximate the actual experience." {CR1}

January 27: Corrects galleys of *A Green Bough*. {B1}

In Oxford, signs and dates a portrait of himself taken in "Cofield's studio": "To Aunt Bama / from William Faulkner." {BH1}

January 28–February 7: Possibly works on revisions of screenplay for "Honor." {WFH}

February 2: First flying lesson with Vernon C. Omlie on a Waco F biplane. {B1}

February 12: Writes to Ben Wasson: "I have enough money to finish my house." {SL}

February 19: Still on MGM payroll, presumably doing revisions of *War Birds* and perhaps on *Honor.*[62]

February 20: Possibly working on film adaptation of his story "Honor." {FF}

February 21: Flying lesson with Vernon Omlie. Pilot's log: 1 hour. {UVA}

February 22: Logs one-hour flying lesson with Vernon Omlie. {UVA}

February 27: Dated proofs of *A Green Bough.* {UVA}

February 28: Logs 20 minutes flying lesson with Vernon Omlie. {UVA}

March: Paramount puts *The Story of Temple Drake* into production. {CR1}

March 3: Logs one-hour flying lesson with Vernon Omlie. {UVA}

March 5: Logs 30-minute flying lesson with Vernon Omlie. {UVA}

March 6: Accepts MGM's announcement he will have to take a 50 percent pay cut. {B3}

March 7: Logs 20-minute flying lesson with Vernon Omlie. {UVA}

March 9: Logs 30-minute flying lesson with Vernon Omlie. {UVA}

March 15: More work on *War Birds* and perhaps "Honor." {WFH}

March 16: Logs 30-minute flying lesson with Vernon Omlie. {UVA}

March 18: "Dear Mr Will," WF writes to Will Bryant comparing his plight in "these uncertain times" to a man "trying to hold to a steadfast purpose and desire . . . like a hunter in a storm in the woods, trying to hold his tent down: he no sooner has one side of it fast to earth than the other side of it blows backward over his head. I hope that the wind has ceased for a while now, though." Refers to their agreement for the purchase of four lots for $1500. WF's Hollywood contract and salary are uncertain, he notes, so he is still not "secure," although he expects to continue to earn a salary. He offers Bryant several different ways to manage payment for the lots. "Spring is here. From my window I can see three peach trees in bloom, and a strutting turkey gobbler and a hen with a brood of chickens, and across the pasture, a horse. There is no satisfaction like it anywhere under the sun, I believe." He is going to put in central heat and a room above the kitchen and an eastern portico to "match the front." His kitchen garden was the best last year and expects to do even better while also framing the inside of the stable, which he is restoring. He concludes by vowing to "own as much of this property as I can get. I dont think that even a sheriff's paper could remove me now." {RO}

MGM cuts WF's salary to $300 a week. {MGM, WFH}

March 20: Writes to Hubert Starr about his phantasmagorical hegira to Death Valley. {CR1}

March 22: Will Bryant writes WF to clarify the terms of what he is proposing in his plan to purchase lots. {RO}

Logs 45-minute flying lesson with Vernon Omlie, all "local" except the last: Oxford to Memphis. {UVA}

March 25: *Memphis Commercial Appeal* announces WF is taking flying lessons with Captain Vernon Omlie.

End of March–Early April: At work on an original screenplay, "Mythical Latin American Kingdom Story," which is not produced, although, Sam Marx, thinks highly of the Conrad-inspired work. {CR1, WFH}

c. April: Invites Will and Sallie Bryant to the premiere of *Today We Live*. {RO}

April–May: Works on 62-page screenplay variously titled "Louisiana Lou" and "Bride of the Bayou." {WFH}

April 8: Full script of *Today We Live* credits the story to WF and the screenplay to Edith Fitzgerald and Dwight Taylor. {CR1}

April 11: Discusses financial arrangements with Will Bryant and adds: "My credit is good now, and I want to keep it so. Also, I want to use it, judiciously of course as I believe a certain amount of debt is good for a young man. But I also know that credit, in the hands of one young in business as I am, can also be dynamite." {RO}

April 12: In Oxford, national premiere of *Today We Live* (based on "Turn About"). WF gives a short talk at the Lyric Theater. The *Commercial Appeal* reports: "Faulkner brought his immediate family to the theatre, together with his 'hired-help,' whom he wanted to show, he said, 'that he worked sometimes.'" {B1, B3, CR1}

The *New Republic* publishes "Night Piece," "Over the World's Rim," "The Ship of Night," "The Race's Splendor."

April 17: Logs flight with Omlie. {UVA}

April 18: Logs flight with Omlie. {UVA}

April 19: Logs flight with Omlie. {UVA}

April 20: Logs 45-minute solo flight. {B3, CR1, UVA}

Smith and Haas publishes *A Green Bough*, a poetry collection.

April 21: *New York Sun* calls *A Green Bough* accomplished but derivative. {WFC}

April 25: *Cincinnati Times-Star* deems *A Green Bough* well-read but "callow." {WFC}

April 26: In New Orleans for a few weeks to work on a script about river life for director Tod Browning. {CR1}

April 28: Hal Smith writes to congratulate WF on good review of *A Green Bough* and that he does not agree with the poet's critics. {CR1}

May 3: The *New Republic* publishes "Man Comes, Man Goes."

May 5: Sam Marx at MGM writes director Tod Browning for a progress report on WF's work on "Louisiana Lou" in New Orleans. Off to a slow start, the director reports, and difficulties with dialogue. WF is fired after he refuses to finish the script in Hollywood because he is awaiting the birth of a child. {B1}

c. May 9: Returns to Oxford. Solo flight: Pilot's Log. {UVA}

May 12: Paramount releases *The Story of Temple Drake*, based on *Sanctuary*.

May 13: Taken off MGM payroll. Sam Marx wires asking WF to send his work to director Tod Browning in New Orleans. {MGM, WFH}

May 14: Sends Tod Browning several pages of script and says he can send more in a week, but "dont say anything more to the studio about keeping me on. Just let it go." {MGM}

Buys a Waco-210 monoplane.

May 22: Jackson *Clarion-Ledger* review of *The Story of Temple Drake* praises Miriam Hopkins as Temple Drake, portraying the "complexities of literature's most spirited character . . . a strange composite of good and evil forces, a curious mixture of conventional attributes and uncontrollable desires."

May 27: Logs solo flight. {UVA}

June 24: Estelle gives birth to a daughter, named Jill.

June 26: Addressed to First National Bank with a note explaining a check for $1800 for US Bonds. {RO}

June 27: Announces the birth of a "gal baby" to Ben Wasson. Accepts the idea of a Random House edition of *The Sound and the Fury* in different colored inks and is willing to write an introduction for $750 now that it is virtually certain that a bankrupt Smith will not be able to send royalties for *Sanctuary*. {SL}

Summer: Commenting on "Beyond" in a letter to Ben Wasson, Faulkner hesitates to make the story plainer, calling it "a tour de force in esoteria." {SL}

In another letter to Wasson, mentions that he is "hot with a novel now" and that Rowan Oak now has heat and two rooms papered and painted. {SL}

Writes to Morton Goldman, who takes over as WF's agent, that he is thinking of writing an article about Mississippi for *Vanity Fair*. {SL}

July 17: Logs solo flight. {UVA}

July 19: Mentions in letter to Sam Marx that he has looked over but not changed the script of his story, "Honor," written by another screenwriter. Asks about Tod Browning, director of *Louisiana Lou*, who worked with WF on the script. "I was getting pretty steamed up over it when I got the air." {SL, MGM}

July 20: Hal Smith receives WF's letter acknowledging a check without specifying for what and asking that the option clause be removed from his contract. Mentions completing three stories since the end of his employment in Hollywood. {SL}

August 3: *Story* publishes "Artist at Home."

August 11: *Memphis Press-Scimitar* reports that WF "finds peace in the sky." Says he made about $35,000 in Hollywood, but "it's a rotten way to make a living."

August 15: Logs two-hour solo flight in the Waco for a total of 33 hours flying time. {UVA}

August 15: Logs solo flight. {UVA}

August 19: Finishes draft of introduction to *The Sound and the Fury.* {ESPL}

Mid-August: Sends introduction to *The Sound and the Fury* to Random House, calling it "a poem almost." {B1}

August 24: Sam Marx reports that Tod Browning has also been fired from "Louisiana Lou." {CR1}

Ben Wasson sends introduction to *The Sound and the Fury* to Bennett Cerf. {B3, CR1}

Faulkner writes to Bennett Cerf saying he will send a color-coded copy of the novel and asks for its return since it is his only copy. {SL}

August 26: Files with MGM story department script for *Mythical Latin American Kingdom Story.* {MGM, WFH}

August 29: Cerf acknowledges receipt of WF's three-color marking up of the Benjy section of *The Sound and the Fury* and sends $500 to Ben Wasson, WF's agent. Another $250 is due when Faulkner signs the sheets of the new, limited edition. {B1}

September 5: Logs a two-hour cross-country flight. {UVA}

September 8: Logs another two-hour solo flight. {UVA}

Memphis Press-Scimitar announces plans to take Jill flying.

September 13: *Memphis Press-Scimitar* photographs of WF before a two-hour flight. {UVA}

September 15: Logs a 400-mile round trip flight from Memphis to Jackson, Mississippi. {UVA}

September 16: Logs a five-hour 400-mile flight from Memphis to Vicksburg and back. {UVA}

Late September: With Vernon Omlie flies to Little Rock, Arkansas, and Abilene, Texas. {UVA}

Autumn: Writes to Ben Wasson about Rowan Oak: "The house not elaborate but heat in and two new rooms and paper and paint which it has not had in 25 years, and lights, which it has never had." {CCP}

Early October: WF's plane crashes and turns over. He emerges without injuries, but the plane requires repairs, including a new propeller. {B1}

October 26: *Memphis Press-Scimitar* reports a flight with Dean Falkner and Vernon Omlie to New York.

October: In an undated letter, announces work on a Snopes book and another novel, *Requiem for a Nun.* "It will be about a [n----r] woman. It will be a little on the esoteric side, like AS I LAY DYING." Will consider putting together a collection of stories for book publication. {SL}

Virginia Quarterly Review calls *A Green Bough* "jangled but sometimes moving music." {CR1}

Autumn: Asks Morton Goldman to send "Black Music" to *Minotaure, Paris.* "I dont believe anyone in America will want it." {SL}

Mails a story, "Bear Hunt," to *The Saturday Evening Post.* Tells Morton Goldman to ask for $1,000. {SL}

November 1: Takes off with brother Dean and Vernon Omlie, stopping in Murfreesboro, Tennessee. {UVA}

November 2: Stopover in Washington, DC. {UVA}

Harper's buys "Wash" for $350.

November 3–10: Arrives in New York City, checking in at the Algonquin Hotel. {CR1}

Morton Goldman officially takes over from Ben Wasson as WF's agent. {CR1}

Makes friends with Hal Smith's new partner, Robert Haas. {B1}

Consults with Bennett Cerf about the limited edition of *The Sound and the Fury.* {CR1}

Cerf hosts a party, inviting Dorothy Parker, publisher Harold Guinzburg and his wife, Alice, and WF's other New York friends. {CR1}

November 11: Vernon Omlie flies the Faulkner brothers out of New York, stopping in Washington, DC, before returning to Memphis. {UVA}

November 27: Morton Goldman submits "Pennsylvania Station" to *Scribner's.* {SL}

December: Accepts $900 from *The Saturday Evening Post* for "A Bear Hunt" and $200 from *The American Mercury* for "Pennsylvania Station." {B1}

December 14: A 90-minute flight with Department of Commerce inspector on a flight test that WF passes and is issued a pilot's license. {UVA}

December 17: Begins a new manuscript with the title "Requiem for a Nun." {CR1}

December 30: First flight as a licensed pilot. {UVA}

December 31: Alfred Dashiell at *Scribner's* rejects "Pennsylvania Station." {B1}

Writes Morton Goldman about a Christmas tree story (eventually titled "Two Dollar Wife") that he willing to revise. {SL}

1934

January: Four flights in the Waco with Vernon Omlie, Dean, Cho-Cho. {UVA}

January 4: *Oxford Eagle* publishes a profile "Prominent Citizens of Oxford": "EMINENT NOVELIST, POET AND SCENARIO WRITER, LICENSED AIRPLANE PILOT." {B1}

January 29: WF lands in Memphis after a flight to Batesville, Mississippi. {B1}

January 31: Rejects Hal Smith's suggestion to review Malraux's *Man's Fate*. Reports that he estimates the Snopes book will take two years. {SL}

February: *Harper's* publishes "Wash."

The American Mercury publishes "Pennsylvania Station."

Story magazine publishes "Elly."

February 10: *The Saturday Evening Post* publishes "A Bear Hunt."

February 11: Begins another novel titled "A Dark House," the preliminary stage of writing what would become *Absalom, Absalom!* {AB}

February 15: Flies with Vernon Omlie to New Orleans for dedication of Shushan Airport and to see an air show which becomes the basis of *Pylon*. {CR1}

March: Mails to agent Morton Goldman a two-page account of the genesis and editing of *Flags in the Dust*, retitled *Sartoris*. {B1}

In Oxford, signs and dates first edition of *Light in August*: "For Myrtle Ramey." {BH1}

Early March: Plans a series, *A Child's Garden of Motion Picture Scripts*, "burlesques of the sure-fire movies and plays, or say a burlesque of how movies would treat standard plays and classic plays and novels, written in a modified form of a movie script." {SL}

March 31: WF, his brother Dean, and Vernon Omlie organize an air circus, sponsored by Oxford's merchants. {CR1}

c. April: Undated clipping in *Oxford Eagle* reports barnstorming with "a Negro pilot they call Black Eagle." {B1}

George McEwen, the brother of Narcissus McEwen, Jill's nurse, does odd jobs around Rowan Oak and accompanies WF in several flights, in charge of turning the propeller after WF warms up the engine. {B1}

April 1: In the air over Oxford. {UVA}

Phil Stone publishes, "William Faulkner: the Man and His Work," in *The Oxford Magazine*.

April 10: Phil Stone writes to Hal Smith for permission to quote from WF's books. {B1}

April 16: Hal Smith approves Phil Stone's request for permission to quote from WF's work: "Extraordinarily little has been written about him . . . I think the mystery with which he surrounded himself has been especially valuable. He had been the sort of writer about whom legends of all kinds collects. Perhaps it is now time to bring him out in the limelight, although I am sure he will always remain a strange figure in our literary history." {B1}

Smith and Haas publish *Doctor Martino and Other Stories.*

April 21: Practices aerobatics in Vernon Omlie's Waco F. {UVA}

April 22: *New York Times Book Review* calls *Doctor Martino and Other Stories* magazine fiction that will harm WF's reputation. {WFC}

April 26: Morton Goldman sends "This Kind of Courage" to *Scribner's*, which Alfred Dashiell rejects a week later.

April 28: Brother John and Maud Falkner accompany WF on a flight from Memphis to Ripley. {B1}

Late spring: Writes to Morton Goldman trying to work out a deal with *The Saturday Evening Post*: $10,000 for six Civil War stories that will eventually become *The Unvanquished.* {SL}

May 6: *Brooklyn Daily Eagle* review of *Doctor Martino and Other Stories*: "Murder figures in six stories; death in ten," with three cases of comic relief. {CR1}

May 10: Morton Goldman sends "Lo!" to *Scribner's*. Alfred Dashiell suggests revisions, but Faulkner works instead on *post*–Civil War and Reconstruction stories. {SL}

June: Draft of will prepared by Phil Stone. {BH5}

June 1: *The Oxford Magazine* publishes the second part of Phil Stone's Faulkner profile.

June 26: Executes a three-page will in Phil Stone's law office, leaving his property and income to Estelle during her lifetime or until she remarries. Jill then would inherit the estate. Maud Falkner would receive income and manuscripts of *Soldiers' Pay* and *Sanctuary.* {B1}

Accepts Howard Hawks's contract offer of $1000 a week to work at Universal Studios when the *Post* does not agree to Faulkner's request for $10,000 for six Civil War and Reconstruction stories. {B1}

July 1: Leaves for three-week assignment to write *Sutter's Gold* in collaboration with Howard Hawks. Reports to Universal Studios. {WFH}

July 7: Writes to Estelle that he is making good progress and living with his friend Hubert Starr. {SL}

Completes a synopsis of *Sutter's Gold.* {B3}

July 12: Reports to Estelle about finishing another screenplay synopsis and the possibility of work on another about Mary of Scotland. Writes about her two letters, the nicest ones he has received. He says she sounds happy with a good grip on herself, as if she is at peace. {UVA}

July 20: Writes to Estelle, explaining work on *Sutter's Gold*, the possibility of other projects, and his frustration with awaiting word on the fate of his scripts and his desire to get home. "Done a little on the novel [*Absalom, Absalom!*] from time to time."

July 21: Writes to Estelle: "I'm hoping to wangle via the studio, the camera I have wanted, the little one with the German lens that takes pictures indoors and out both. The good ones cost $200, but I hope to be able to get one for about $75. If I can do so, I may buy it. Then we can keep a regular diary of the children and Rowanoak [*sic*]." {CR1}

July 23: In Santa Monica, signs and dates on half-title page of *Mosquitoes*: "To Herb Starr, from his friend, Bill Faulkner." Also signs and dates first edition of *Sanctuary*: "To Herb, from Bill Faulkner," and a first edition of *Doctor Martino and Other Stories*. {BH1}

July 24: Arrives in Memphis with Richard Halliburton, a fellow southerner and travel writer, who comments to reporters: "I've wanted to meet Bill Faulkner most, not only because I liked his books, but because to me he's a home boy. . . . I liked him immensely." {B1}

July 29: Tells Goldman he is still hoping to do more *Post* stories if the magazine can wait until he finishes up work in Hollywood. {SL}

August: *Scribner's* publishes "Mule in the Yard."

Tells Hal Smith he is not sure when *Absalom, Absalom!* will be ready for publication. Making money on other projects has interrupted the novel, and he is even thinking of writing another novel before he can bring *Absalom, Absalom!* to full term. {SL}

Writes to Goldman that the main point is to get as much money as he can for his stories no matter where they are published. {SL}

August weekends: WF, Estelle, Jill, and her nurse, Narcissa, head to the Memphis airport. In the hot weather, they sit on chairs in the shade of the hanger with Louise, Dean's wife, while Dean and Vernon Omlie fly customers. Narcissa nurses and fans, Louise and Estelle converse, and WF supervises. {DSF}

August 11: To Hubert Starr: "And I have missed California: sleeping cool at night, and the ocean beginning about where my mailbox is. Remember me to Decker and the Gables." Phil [Stone] sends his best. {NYPL}

September: *The Saturday Evening Post* agrees to publish a series of stories set in the Civil War and Reconstruction. WF completes and sends to the *Post* "The Unvanquished" (later revised as "Riposte in Tertio") and "Vendée." {B1}

September: *Harper's* publishes "Beyond."

September 3: Finishes the script for *Sutter's Gold*. {CR1}

September 4: Writes a long letter to Will Bryant saying his correspondence has suffered because he has been working on the script for *Sutter's Gold*. He provides Bryant with a detailed account of the "very interesting" story, framing it as part of his own "expedition to California." He concludes:

"It is a good story, I think and I have just finished it (yesterday). I have worked at it pretty steadily." {RO, CR1}

September 9: Flies a Command-Aire, owned by E. O. Champion, an Oxford automobile dealer and airplane mechanic. {B1}

September 15–16: Participates in another air circus with Vernon Omlie as the chief pilot. {B1}

Meets George Grider, the son of Mac Grider, whose story WF used for *War Birds*. {B1}

September 29: *The Saturday Evening Post* publishes "Ambuscade."

September 30: Dean Falkner marries Louise Hale after a barnstorming weekend. {FK}

October 4: "Drusilla" to *The Saturday Evening Post*. {LC}

October 13: *The Saturday Evening Post* publishes "Retreat."

October 18: Revises "Vendée" according to the *Post*'s specifications. {B1}

Writes to Morton Goldman, asking him to withdraw "This Kind of Courage" because it has turned into a novel. {SL}

October 27: Hosts a dinner dance for a young friend of Estelle and several Memphis debutantes and their escorts. {B1}

October 30: Flies Champion's Command-Aire again. It loses a pin in one of the overhead valves, but he manages to get the plane home and later repairs it with the help of the Black Eagle. {B1}

November: *Story* publishes "Lo!"

November 1: *The Oxford Magazine* publishes the third installment of Phil Stone's Falkner family history.

November 3: *The Saturday Evening Post* publishes "Raid."

November 6: A mishap in the Waco, damage to the undercarriage on landing. {B1}

Logs 90 minutes in the Command-Aire. {B1}

November 11: Hal Smith receives the first chapter of *Pylon*. {B1, B3}

November 20: Invites Hal Smith to come deer hunting, adding, "I will be sober (I have not had a drink since you left) and I want to show you the South." {SL}

November 23: Hal Smith receives "An Evening in New Valois," a chapter of *Pylon*. {B1, B3}

November 25: Completes the manuscript of *Pylon* in Oxford. {B1, B3}

November 30: Third chapter of *Pylon* to Hal Smith. {B1}

December 5: Fourth chapter of *Pylon* to Hal Smith. {B1, B3}

December 12: Fifth chapter of *Pylon* to Hal Smith. {B1}

December 15: The last two chapters of *Pylon* arrive in New York. {B1, B3}

Writes to Morton Goldman that *Pylon* is finished and mentions sending the novel to Howard Hawks.

Christmas: At home, with his family, including brother Dean and his wife, Louise. {DSF}

Late December: Tells Hal Smith that "New Valois" in *Pylon* is a "thinly disguised . . . New Orleans." But the characters and story are fictional, although "someone may read it and see into it what I didn't. Someone may or may not see a chance for a suit." {SL}

Writes Goldman: "I can use money right now to beat hell." {SL}

December 28: Hal Smith writes to assure Faulkner that no one is likely to sue over the representation of characters in *Pylon*. {CR2}

1935

January 2: Excuses himself to "Mr Will" for not attending to business (paying taxes), mentioning a busy year taken up with his father's death, supporting his mother and brothers, publishing stories in *The Saturday Evening Post*, and in December finishing a novel (*Pylon*), and getting sick after deer hunting season. He will send a check to cover what he owes Bryant. {RO}

January 6: Signs and dates *A Green Bough* "To Byron Sage," including on the title page "William Faulkner / Fox-20th Cent Studio. / California."[63] {MC}

January 7: Will Bryant: "'Raid' kept my thoughts on Robert Peel, manager of Polk plantation, whose farmhands in 1866 took up a march of religious fervor to 'cross the Jordan & go over into Canaan.' They got as far as Yocona River & some crossed tho Peel retrieved most of them." {UVA}

January 9: Hal Smith brings 84 pages of *Pylon* galley proof with him to Oxford. {B1}

January 23: Suggests Goldman try to place "Golden Land" with *Cosmopolitan*, but *The American Mercury* buys it in late February or early March. {SL}

Assures "Mr Will" he is taking care of the taxes. Although it has snowed, he ends by saying he hopes Bryant's health has improved. "We have spring to look forward to now; I think that the smell of plowed earth and the sign of greening willow buds and the sound of birds is always the best tonic which a man can have." Mentions that his baby is thriving. {RO}

January 30: WF and friends incorporate Okatoba Fishing and Hunting Club. {B1, B3}

Early February: Writes Hal Smith about boiling the pot to get time for two months of work on *Absalom, Absalom!* {SL}

February 2: Looks ahead to purchasing more lots from Will Bryant, although he still has to pay off what he owes for the last two purchases. {RO}

February 5: Receives $2000 advance from Smith and Haas for *Absalom, Absalom!*

February 12: Will Bryant offers to sell Bailey's Woods after receiving two offers from others, saying WF has first pick. {UVA}

February 15: "I am watching your literary growth," Will Bryant writes to WF. Suggests he is willing to sell WF "Bailey Woods." {RO}

WF writes the same day that he is working on straightening out the taxes on Rowan Oak property and the assessments of lots he has acquired from Bryant. {RO}

February 18: Rejects proposals to publish *The Marionettes*, to write a book about the Mississippi River, and an offer to write about a lynching, saying he has never seen one. {SL}

March 9: Asks Goldman if the agent is due a commission on "This Kind of Courage," which became the basis for *Pylon*. {SL}

March 23: *Macon Telegraph* review of *Pylon*: "a breathless experience in reading." {WFC}

March 24: Cleveland *Plain Dealer*: "He adds the power of loving the people who he scorns and of sparing us no brutality or vulgarity concerning the people whom he loves." {WFC}

New York Herald Tribune review of *Pylon*: "Mr. Faulkner has never written a better story than this, or a more painful one." {WFC}

Nashville Banner review of *Pylon:* a bad book that "seems to mark the end of William Faulkner." {WFC}

March 25: Smith and Haas publish *Pylon*.

Brooklyn Daily Eagle review of *Pylon*: "reeking with the hot smell of engine oil" and with "alcoholic nausea." {WFC}

March 27: In Oxford, signs and dates first edition of *Pylon* "For Myrtle Ramey." WF sends the book from Mac Reed's drugstore with a note from Mac Reed: "His autograph for you bears the date of yesterday 26th, but he made the entry just a few moments ago, forgetting the true date." {BH1}

March 30: Begins a new manuscript with the title "Absalom, Absalom!" {B1, B3, JW}

April: Needs $10,000 to pay debts and insurance. Writing two stories a week in hopes of paying the bills. Sends first chapter of *Absalom, Absalom!* to Smith and Haas. {B1, SL}

Scribner's publishes "Skirmish at Sartoris."

April 2: In Oxford, signs and dates first edition of *Pylon*: "For my daughter, Victoria." {BH1}

April 27–28: A Faulkner "air circus" in Oxford. {CR2}

May: *The American Mercury* publishes "Golden Land."

May 18–19: Flies to Lexington, Tennessee, to another air circus with brother Dean and Vernon Omlie. {B1}

May 26: *Miami News* review of *Pylon*: "a genius astray." {CR1}

June 29: Second chapter of *Absalom, Absalom!* to Smith & Haas. {B1, B3}

July: *The American Mercury* publishes "That Will Be Fine."

July 1: Becomes a "Quiet Birdman," with wings and engraved metal plate worn by experienced pilots. {B1}

July 20: Flies with E. O. Champion on the Command-Aire. {B1}

July 22: Third chapter of *Absalom, Absalom!* to Smith and Haas. {B1, B3}

July 29: Sends a check to Will Bryant and adds: "It is hot here, and I am working steadily on a new novel (*Absalom, Absalom!*) which I hope and believe that you will like better than some, many, of the others." {RO}

Late July: Writes to Goldman about the possibility of selling manuscripts since he needs at least $2,000 by September. Asks whether there is a market for these titles: *The Sound and the Fury, As I Lay Dying, Sanctuary, Light in August, Pylon.* {SL}

August 19: Fourth chapter of *Absalom, Absalom!* to Smith and Haas.

August 21: Flying. {UVA}

September 23: Boards the train from Memphis to New York City, relying on a loan from Hal Smith and hoping to get assignments in New York and later in Hollywood.

September 25: Checks into Murry Hill Hotel on Park Avenue between 40th and 41st streets.

September 27: *The American Mercury* rejects a chapter of *Absalom, Absalom!* {B1}

Visits with Hal Smith, Dorothy Parker, Bennett Cerf, and others. {B1}

October: *The American Mercury* publishes "Uncle Willy."

October 2: On Smith & Haas stationery, itemizes more than $3000 in debts. {SL}

October 5: Writes to Estelle that he will be going to California for eight weeks. Reports news about their New York friends: the Connellys have divorced, and Madeleine Connelly is now "Mrs. Playwright Sherwood." The Guinzbergs send their regards. "I have seen 2 shows, dined out once, and I have a typewriter in my room and I am working on a story for Scribners." {SL}

October 10: Meets with Graeme Lorimer, publisher of *The Saturday Evening Post.* {B1}

October 13: Arrives in Memphis. {B1}

October 14: At Rowan Oak. {B1}

October 15: Dates chapter 5 of *Absalom, Absalom!* {CR2}

November: *American Mercury* publishes review of *Test Pilot* by Jimmy Collins and "this whole new business of speed." {ESPL}

November 2–3: WF and his brother Dean perform as "The Flying Faulkners" in an air show. {B1}

Continues work on *Absalom, Absalom!* {B1}

November 9: Dean, William, and Hal Smith fly over Oxford leafleting announcement of "Mammoth Armistice Day Pageant." {CR2}

November 10: Brother Dean is killed in plane crash.

November 11, c. 10:00 a.m.: Goes into Dean's room to see his wife, Louise. He sits by her on the bed and says: "Dean's body is here. But I know you want to remember him the way he was." The casket remains closed and placed in the living room. The afternoon funeral is private. {DSF}

December: *Harper's* publishes "Lion."

December 4: Tells Goldman he expects to have completed *Absalom, Absalom!* In another month. Agrees to Cerf publishing a limited edition of "the Elmer story," although the publisher did not follow through. {SL}

December 10: Departs for five-week assignment at Twentieth Century-Fox at $1000 a week. {B1}

December 16: Employee Number 27545 begins his contract at $1,000 a week for four weeks. Reports to the Fox lot and is assigned to *The Road to Glory*. {TCF}

Mid-December: Reports to producer Nunnally Johnson at Twentieth Century-Fox and works with script supervisor Meta Carpenter, who becomes his lover. He continues to work on *Absalom, Absalom!* {AB}

December 16–21: Works on "Zero Hour"/ "Wooden Crosses"/ "Road to Glory" screenplay with Joel Sayre. {WFH}

December 23: To Hubert Starr: "I have been busy all last week. I went down to the beach yesterday and found you had moved." {NYPL}

Christmas: Signs "Afternoon of a Cow" to Joel Sayre. {B3}

December 31: With collaborator Joel Sayre finishes rough first draft of script for *The Road to Glory*. {TCF} They celebrate at the Brown Derby and board a chartered bus to the Rose Bowl game in Pasadena. Loses his shoes. {B1}

1936

January: *College Life* publishes "Two Dollar Wife."

Scribner's publishes "The Brooch."

Early January: Finishes final draft of *Absalom, Absalom!* and presents it to screenwriter David Hempstead, commenting: "I think it's the best novel yet written by an American." {B2}

January 7: Payroll suspends him for temporary illness. He is taken off *The Road to Glory*. {TCF, WFH}

January 12: In Los Angeles, signs and dates first edition of *Pylon*: "To Hubert Starr, god damn him." {BH1}

January 16: "Not to return here on same deal" (Fox file). {TCF}

Mid-January: Writes to Helen Baird about the time she fell off a sailboat and he tried to steady the boat rather than diving in to save her. When he picked her up out of the water, she bawled him out for not jumping in right away to save her. If he had acted more quickly, he would not now have to go to Hollywood to get rich so that he can write his Snopes novel. {CCP}

January 17: Departs Hollywood for Mississippi. {B1}

January 24: Screenplay for *The Road to Glory*, marked "final" by William Faulkner and Joel Sayre. {TCF}

January 27: "Zero Hour" script, a revision of *Wooden Crosses*, retitled *The Road to Glory* [in pencil], with the names "Faulkner & Sayre" [also in pencil]. {BH1}[64]

January 31: Random House absorbs Smith & Haas, becoming WF's publisher. Dates the completion of *Absalom, Absalom!* {B1, B3}

February 20: WF, Stone, and their wives dine together. Stone is proofreading *Absalom, Absalom!* and seeking without success to get WF to "abandon some writing peculiarities . . . I think the book will make a grand movie," Stone tells WF's agent. {SS}

February 26: Returns to Fox at salary of $1000 a week, checking into the Beverly Hills Hotel. Works on treatment, *Banjo on My Knee*. {TCF, WFH}

February 26–March 3: Works on treatment for *Banjo on my Knee*. {WFH}

March: Possible revisions on set for *Zero Hour/Wooden Crosses/Road to Glory*. {WFH}

March 2, 5:30 p.m.: Reports to Estelle that he is getting along fine but wishes "I was at home, still in the kitchen with my family around me and my hand full of Old Maid cards." {SL}

March 3: Story conference for *Banjo on my Knee*. {WFH}

March 5: Zanuck instructs WF to make the female characters free from sexual innuendo. {TCF}

March 9: Sends home $250 from his first paycheck. Likes Estelle's plans for them to meet in New Orleans. He can see things are going right with her. {UVA}

March 10: Revised treatment of *Banjo on My Knee*. {TCF, WFH}

March 22: Louise, Dean's wife, gives birth to a daughter and names her Dean. WF sends a telegram: "YOU TAKE CARE OF THE GIRL TILL I GET THERE TO DO IT FOR YOU."

Late March: Accepts new contract beginning August 1, with a guarantee of twenty weeks' work, starting at $750 a week with a six-month option specifying a $250 rise if renewed. {B1}

Works on a new version of first chapter of *Absalom, Absalom!* {B1}

Appears frequently at the Musso & Frank Grill on Hollywood Boulevard next to the Stanley Rose Book Shop, where he meets Nathanael West. {B1}

Accompanies Nathanael West on a boar hunt. {B1}

c. Spring: Writes to Will Bryant that he is "broke at present." Work on the novel has delayed writing short stories, although his agent now has five to sell. "I will send you whatever I can, $100.00 or $500.00 and, I hope, the thousand. Please accept my regrets for being unable to do so now." He is sorry to hear about the Bryants' bad health. {RO}

April 9: On loan to RKO for $1000 a week to work on *Gunga Din* treatment and dialogue revision. {FF, WFH}

April 10–13: Working on story outline and sequences for *Gunga Din.* {WFH}

April 26: To Estelle: "Getting along. All right and working hard." {CR2}

May 14–16: Working on story line and sequences for *Gunga Din.* {WFH}

May 16: To Estelle: "Damn this being an orphan." {CR2}

May 15: Works on chronology for *Absalom, Absalom!* Signs two pages of it to Meta Doherty (Carpenter's married name).

End of May: Returns to Oxford. Works on typescript revisions of *Absalom, Absalom!* {B1}

c. June: To Morton Goldman: "Since last summer I seem to have got out of the habit of writing trash but I will still try to cook up something for Cosmopolitan. . . . That's probably hard work too and requires skill, but I seem to be so out of touch with the Kotex Age here." {SL}

June 3: Hal Smith wires to ask if he can change the italics of chapter 5 of *Absalom, Absalom!* to roman type. WF wires back: "NO." {B3}

June 22: *Memphis Commercial Appeal* classified advertisement: "I will not be responsible for any debt incurred or bills made, or notes or checks signed by Mrs. William Faulkner or Mrs. Estelle Oldham Faulkner." {ESPL}

June 23: Responds to reporters: "It's just a matter of protecting my credit until I can pay up my back debts." {B2}

June 24: Celebrates Jill's third birthday. {CR2}

July 6: *Time* reports on WF's ad [see entry for June 22].

July 11: To Will Bryant: "I believe I can promise to send you five hundred dollars in August." Returning to his California job in a week. He can't afford to acquire more property right now and has not given up hope that it won't be sold to someone else. {RO}

July 15: Departs for work at Fox accompanied by Jill and Estelle, Jack Oliver (driver), and Narcissus McEwen (nurse). {B1, B3, CR2}

Late July: Arrives in Los Angeles and stays at an expensive hotel before renting a house at 620 El Cerco, Huntington Palisades, north of Santa Monica and about six miles from Twentieth Century-Fox. {B1}

July 27: Estelle writes to her children, Malcolm and Victoria, about finding a place near the ocean. She has trouble figuring out where the suburbs stop and start: "All look alike to me." They have a "lovely view of the mountains," and Jill likes playing in the sand. {B1} WF includes a line drawing of the house. {BH1, BH5}

August: *Scribner's* publishes "Fool about a Horse."

The American Mercury publishes a version of the first chapter of *Absalom, Absalom!*

August 1: Reports for work at Fox at $750 a week. {DM, WFH}

August 7–September 1: Works with Nunnally Johnson on *The Last Slaver*, later released as *Slave Ship*. {TCF, WFH}

August 11: Twelve-week contract with Fox at $750 per week.

August 13: On Twentieth Century-Fox Corporation stationery includes note to Will Bryant and check for $500. {RO}

August 28: To Phil Stone, written on Twentieth Century-Fox stationery: "I am going to miss the shooting at home this fall, though I still hope to come home for a while at Christmas and get out once or twice at least. I am going to buy an English setter puppy out here." {UM}

September 1: Completes work on galleys of *Absalom, Absalom!* and script of *The Last Slaver*. {TCF}

September 2–3: Assigned to "Four Men and a Prayer." {WFH}

September 4: Writes to Morton Goldman: "I am in California again up to my neck in moving pictures, where I shall be for about a year." Vows to sell *Absalom, Absalom!* to the pictures for $100,000, but there are no takers. {SL}

Writes to Hal Smith that he is gradually getting out of debt and expects to pay Smith and Robert Haas the money he owes them. {SL}

September 4–November 30: Working on *Splinter Fleet*. {TCF, WFH}

September 12: Attends Daryl Zanuck's story conference about *Splinter Fleet*. Zanuck instructs WF to "block out new treatment" and to "fight way from FORMULA." {TCF}

September 19: Logs thirty minutes on a Fairchild 22. {UVA}

September 24: Completes temporary film script for *The Last Slaver*. {TCF}

October 8: Wires Hal Smith: "HAVE FLU STOP WILL SIGN PAGES QUICKLY AS POSSIBLE."[65] {SL}

October 10: Revised temporary draft of *The Last Slaver*. {TCF}

October 23: Second printing of 2500 copies of *Absalom, Absalom!*

Estelle's attorney sends a letter to WF's attorney, Hubert Starr, initiating divorce proceedings. {CR2}

October 25: *Macon Telegraph* calls *Absalom, Absalom!* "chaotic," and "abnormal."

October 26: Random House publishes 6,000 copies of *Absalom, Absalom!* and a limited edition of 300 signed copies. Copy 1 inscribed "for Meta Carpenter, wherever she may be." {CR2}

Starr writes to Estelle's attorney that his client wants to modify "certain statements which he thinks might be construed by some busybody as uncomplimentary to Mrs. Faulkner."[66] {CR2}

October 30: *New York Sun* review of *Absalom, Absalom!* refers to its map and WF's naming himself the "sole owner and proprietor": "A queer sort of county" that apparently deforms its owner's sensibility, making him think he could make it a "'symbol of the world.'" {NF}

October 31: *The Saturday Review of Literature* dismisses *Absalom, Absalom!*, citing the "familiar hypochondria of Mr. Faulkner's prose. . . . In book after book now he has dropped tears like the famed Arabian tree, in a rapture of sensibility amounting to continuous orgasm." {NF}

New York Herald Tribune review of *Absalom, Absalom!*: "I suspect that Mr. Faulkner is not really talking about the South at all but about a region of his own and kindred minds; and that if any war oppresses and burdens his imagination it is not the Civil War but the World War." {NF}

November: *The Saturday Evening Post* publishes "The Unvanquished."

November 1: The *Charlotte News* reviewer of *Absalom, Absalom!* admits to being "lost and terrified in the shadows and thunders" of Faulkner's "involved prose" and yet calls the novel his "master work." {WFC}

November 5: Writes to Louise Bonino expressing his pleasure at the limited edition of *Absalom, Absalom!* {SL}

San Diego Union calls *Absalom, Absalom!* "macabre and sadistic."

November 7: *Fort Wayne News* calls *Absalom, Absalom!* "morbid."

November 9: Logs two hours on the Fairchild 22. {UVA}

November 14: *The Saturday Evening Post* publishes "Riposte in Tertio."

November 15: *Hartford Courant* dismisses *Absalom, Absalom!* as a "wearying welter of degeneracy and extravagant sordidness."

November 19: Third printing of 1400 copies of *Absalom, Absalom!*

Signs and dates #224 of limited edition of *Absalom, Absalom!* "To Bill Conselman /Bill Faulkner / Studio."[67] {MC}

November 29: Wallace Stegner's *Salt Lake City Tribune* review of *Absalom, Absalom!*: "a significant contribution to the theory and art of fiction . . . more searching, more profound and (in the progressive spell of inescapable doom which it lays upon the reader no less surely than upon the hapless characters that people its pages) more dramatic than anything Faulkner had hitherto given us." {JB}

November 30: Taken off work on *Splinter Fleet*, released as *Submarine Patrol.* {B1}

December 4: Studio layoff. {B1}

December 5: *The Saturday Evening Post* publishes "Vendée"

December 7: With Kathryn Scola produces first draft of *Splinter Fleet.* {TCF}

December 10: On Twentieth Century-Fox stationery sends holiday greetings to the Bryants and encloses a $500 check. {RO}

December 22: "First Draft Continuity" of *Splinter Fleet* by William Faulkner and Kathryn Scola. {TCF}

December 25: Christmas with family in Pacific Palisades.

December 28: Assures Morton Goldman that he will write more stories and that he has another novel "in my bean." {SL}

Writes to Bennett Cerf about six stories centered on "a white boy and a negro boy during the civil war," and proposes them as a book. {SL}

December 29: Robert Haas writes that Hal Smith has resigned from Random House but that the firm will continue its enthusiastic publication of WF. {B1}

1937

Early January: Very pleased to hear from his stepdaughter, Victoria, and to learn that Jill likes the Robert Louis Stevenson poems he has sent to her as a Christmas present. {SL}

January 21: *Scribner's* accepts "Monk" for publication.

Writes to Morton Goldman about writing more short stories and a novel. {SL}

February 26: Returns from Fox layoff. {WFH}

Welcomes Maurice Coindreau's request to translate *The Sound and the Fury*. Offers to "draw up a chronology and genealogy and explanation, etc, if you need it, or anything else." {SL, CWF}

Early spring: On RKO Studios Inc. stationery writes note to Will Bryant saying he is sorry to hear that Bryant is still ill. Looks forward to seeing him when he returns home from California. {RO}

March 9–11: Works on *The Giant Swing*, later released under the title *Dance Hall*. {FF, WFH}

Writes to Will Bryant expressing his relief that Bryant feels better. He is prepared to acquire more property and to pay off some of his debts to Bryant. Hopes Sallie is feeling better. Reports that Jill is attending a private kindergarten and likes it. She is learning French, and he has already taught her to ride. {RO}

March 12: Assignment on *The Giant Swing* ends, and he begins work on *Drums along the Mohawk*. {TCF}

March 14: Bryant replies to WF's letter of March 9, expressing his appreciation for his sentiments. He sends a "statement of credit" as requested, explaining the taxes on Bailey Woods, adding: "They are a bargain at 1500.00 and the interest at 4% is below the price of any banking or utility bond notes except Gov't issues. . . . All my household join in kindest regards and best wishes to you and wife and bushels of love to Jill." {RO}

March 15: Completes and has typed a 26-page treatment of *Drums along the Mohawk*. {TCF}

March 18: Fox weekly wages increase from $750 to $1000. {TCF}

April 1: Writes to Will Bryant: "You and I have dealt together for so long without any suggestion of haggling or trading, that I dont know just how to express my answer, which after all is not an answer so much as a request." Asks for more time to consider Bryant's terms and explains how he expects to pay for the property. {RO}

April 5: Meta Carpenter marries Wolfgang Rebner and accompanies him to Europe. {CR2}

April 14: Interoffice memo: "One week off for illness." {B2}

April 29: Returns to work. {B2}

May: *Scribner's* publishes "Monk."

May 13: Logs more flying time. {UVA}

May 25: Writes on Twentieth Century-Fox stationery and encloses a check that he hopes Will Bryant will accept as an option on the rest of the Bailey property. He wants to get a survey done and settle the price later. {RO}

Late May: Estelle and Jill return to Oxford driven by a chauffeur. {CR2}

June 4: Responds to Maurice Coindreau's letter, explaining he will be in California until August 15 and available to "explain any confusions" about *The Sound and the Fury*, which Coindreau is translating. {CWF}

June 14: Signs his name on Thomas Mann's *Stories of Three Decades*.

June 16: Last day of work on *Drums along the Mohawk*. {TCF}

June 20: Maurice Coindreau visits to go over questions about translating *The Sound and the Fury*, some of which, WF confesses, he cannot answer. The translator notices that WF is constantly drinking. {CWF}

June 25: At a dinner party reads "Afternoon of a Cow" to Coindreau and Wasson. {B3

June 26: Signs a copy of *Absalom, Absalom!* as a souvenir of Coindreau's visit. {CWF}

June 28: Writes to Estelle saying that nice letters from Rowan Oak have cheered him. Asks to hear about Jill's birthday party. {SL}

June 30: Fox distributes Faulkner's 238-page dialogued treatment of *Drums Along the Mohawk*. {TCF}

c. July: Works with Dudley Murphy on treatment of *Absalom, Absalom!* titled *Revolt in the Earth*. {WFH, CR2}

July 21: Expects to be home soon since his contract has not been renewed. {SL}

July 24: Writing "An Odor of Verbena" for publication in *The Unvanquished.* {B3}

July 3: Completes "dialogued treatment" of *Drums along the Mohawk.* {TCF, WFH}

July 21: To Estelle: "Contract not taken up and renewed. Mammy and I will be home sometime between Aug 22–Sept 1, if we live and nothing happens." {B3}

July 28: Writes to Estelle announcing he expects to be home in mid-August. "It's hot here and I dont feel very good, but I think it's mostly being tired of movies, worn out with them." {SL}

August 8: Writes Estelle he expects a termination notice from studio. {SL}

August 15: Contract with Fox ends. {WFH}

August 16: Officially notified his option will not be exercised. {B2}

August 18: Flies from Mines Field. {B2}

Late August: Returns to Oxford. {B2}

September 1: Drives to Memphis for 45-minute flight on Waco C. {B2}

September 2: To Will Bryant: "returning to my house and oaks and cedars with the same pleasure, the same lift of the heart which, God willing, the sight of it will always give me and which I shall very likely take into the earth with me when my time comes." The survey of the property is underway. "I will come down to see you—not of course just to discuss business, but to renew the friendship which is a part of my home too." {RO}

September 3: The *New York Sun* publishes Laurence Stallings's account of his friendship with WF in Hollywood. {CWF}

September 15: Dates first page of *The Wild Palms* manuscript. {B3}

September 22: Victoria (Cho-Cho) gives birth to a daughter, Victoria. Abandoned by her husband, WF takes care of her, reciting from *A Shropshire Lad.*[68] {B3, JW}

September 25: Celebrates birthday with Estelle and Jill at Rowan Oak.[69] {B2}

Decides to purchase Bailey's Woods. {DM}

c. **October 17 or 18:** Checks into the Algonquin Hotel and works on *The Unvanquished* at Random House and attends several parties with old friends Hal Smith and Jim Devine. {CR2}

During nearly a month in New York, WF drinks heavily, passes out, and falls on a radiator, badly burning his back. {CR2}

November 10: Arrives home in the company of Jim Devine, who reports to Robert Haas at Random House about an uneventful trip free of sedatives and liquor. {CR2}

November 16: To Memphis to fly the Waco C. {B2}

November 17: Harold Burson, a university student, interviews WF, who calls Hollywood "a very wealthy, over-grown country town." He has not read *Gone with the Wind*, which he calls "too long." {B2, B3}

November 18: *Memphis Commercial Appeal* reports that WF "believes his best novel has yet to be written." Gives his impressions of Hollywood and says he does not like "scenario writing." He does not know enough about it to do it justice. Describes writing his novels in longhand and then revising and rewriting on the typewriter. {LG}

November 19: Reports to Robert Haas about his painful back, cursing his own "folly." Wants to establish a balance with Random House by returning a check credited to an account he can draw on. {SL}

November 23: Resumes work on "The Wild Palms," which had begun as a short story. {B3}

November 29: Signs contract for *If I Forget Thee, O Jerusalem*, later retitled *The Wild Palms*. {B3}

Writes to Robert Haas about beginning slowly on the novel but expects to complete it by May 1938. {SL}

December 9: *Oxford Eagle* publishes photograph of WF and two fellow bird hunters.

December 21: Writes to Robert Haas that the novel is "coming pretty well. I found less trouble than I anticipated in getting back into the habit of writing, though I find that at forty I dont write quite as fast as I used to." {SL}

Christmas: With his family. He discusses Darwin with Malcolm, now studying anthropology, and plays with Jill. Cho-Cho spends the holiday in Shanghai, invited by her father and with WF's encouragement. {B3}

December 28: To Jim Devine: "Novel going pretty well. I have about a third of it done, should come in under the wire May first with my tail up and my eyes flashing; under blankets even." A painful back has resulted in writing at night, but he puts off grafting until after quail shooting season, when he will have to remain quiet with no lifting or stooping. {SL}

Exasperated with the surveyor, WF tells Will Bryant. Discusses business details about acquiring Bryant's property. Asks Bryant to execute a new deed specifying one dollar for the four lots, "My reasons for this being that when I record these deeds, I would like to keep the sum I paid for the property a private matter which I think it is. I do not like the idea of the idle and curious being familiar with my private affairs." {RO}

1938

January 12: In the *New Republic*, Stark Young recalls his first meeting with WF in 1914 and contradicts the claim that Sherwood Anderson discovered Faulkner, insisting that it is Phil Stone who deserves the credit.

January 20: At Rowan Oak signs first edition of *The Unvanquished*: "Estelle, Jill, William Faulkner." {BH1}

January 31: Faulkner flies. {UVA}

February 2: Pilot's license is renewed. {UVA}

February 8: Writes a $200 check as first payment for purchase of Bailey's Woods. {RO}

February 10: Deeds for four lots, with no signatures or amounts specified. {RO}

February 15: Random House publishes *The Unvanquished.* MGM acquires screen rights for $25,000, 20 percent of which goes to Random House. {SL}

February 16: Signs contract with Loew's Incorporated for motion picture rights. {BH1}

February 19: Goes over complicated business details with Morton Goldman about stories sold and commissions and what happens when material is resold and bought for film adaptations. Expects to pay Goldman 10 percent ($357.14) out of the sale of *The Unvanquished.* {SL}

St. Louis Globe-Democrat review of *The Unvanquished*: "This is not the hard-boiled Faulkner of old. This is a southerner and sentimentalist and, for all his pretense, he is a sentimentalist, writing sincerely and effectively about his home country." {WFC}

February 20: Cleveland *Plain Dealer* review of *The Unvanquished:* "Toned-down and brushed up Faulkner." {WFC}

February 25: Will Bryant writes a thank you note for *The Unvanquished*, which he is enjoying. {RO}

Late February: Purchases land he calls Greenfield Farm. {B2}

February 28: Grateful to Goldman for compromising and accepting 5 percent for sale of *The Unvanquished* for film adaptation, on top of 20 percent that Random House receives. {SL}

Mid-March: Suffers from infection from failed skin graft for his burned back. {CR2}

March 22: *Harper's* purchases "Barn Burning."

April 1: The burned back slows up work on the novel, so that it cannot be delivered until June. The grafts did not work, the back got infected, and the wound had to be scraped. Three months of constant pain. {CR2}

April 7: Writes to "Mr Stone" acknowledging the deeds for the lots he has just purchased. {RO}

May: Joins 418 prominent Americans responding to Spanish Civil War: "I most sincerely wish to go on record as being unalterably opposed to Franco and fascism, to all violations of the legal government and outrages against the people of Republican Spain."[70] {CR2}

May 7: Records servicing of mare in studbook. {UVA}

May 8: Hosts an elaborate hunt breakfast in full hunt costume at Rowan Oak. Phones photographer J. R. Cofield to memorialize the happy event. On the back of the photograph, Estelle lists the names of the guests. {BH1}

May 21: *Saturday Review of Literature* publishes Anthony Buttitita's profile and tour of the sites Faulkner said he used for his fiction. {CWF}

June 15: Dates the final page of "Old Man": "Rowan Oak /Oxford, Mississippi." {B3}

June 17: Wires Random House: "NOVEL FINISHED SOME REWRITING DUE TO BACK COMPLICATIONS. SENDING IT ON IN A FEW DAYS." {SL}

June 24: Jill's birthday party. {B2}

c. June 25: Sends novel to Random House. {B2}

July: Reads Emily Stone's novel and offers to write a foreword, but she cannot find a publisher. {SS}

July 4: A barbecue at Greenfield Farm. {B3}

July 8: Writes Robert Haas about objectionable words in *The Wild Palms* and suggests taking them all out for consistency. For the ending of Old Man, he suggests replacing "Women, shit," with "Women,. . . ." He adds "It is only what people see that shocks them, not what they think or hear, and they will recognize these words or not and no harm done in either case." Nevertheless, he defends the original words as true to his characters. Still prefers *If I Forget Thee, O Jerusalem* for the novel's title. Reports that his back is improving. {SL}

July 9: From Faulkner's farm account book: "On or after Nov 15, 1938 I promise to pay to Falkner Bros the sum of ten dollars ($10.00) at 8% interest the above amount is secured by 1 hog which is owned sole by me." {CR2}

Late August: Takes Estelle and Jill to Gulf Coast. {CR2}

Gives the Stones the address of Howard Hawks's production company with a letter from Faulkner endorsing Emily Stone's novel, but the work gets no attention. WF tells Emily that 300 rejections are "required just to get up to zero." {SS}

September 15: Writes to Will Bryant about the exact location of his lots and the matter of deeds overlapping with a neighbor. He asks Bryant to have his lawyer (Phil Stone) draw up a new deed with the description WF specifies.[71] {RO}

September 23: Writes to Will Bryant again about the surveyed lots and how they are to be described. {RO}

Late September: Reads proof of *The Unvanquished* at Random House. {B2}

October 2: Writes to Jill about a plaid dress he is getting for her. {SL}

October 4: Drives to Teterboro Airport in New Jersey to fly a Monocoupe for an hour. {B2}

October 6: Tells Estelle the book title is changed from *If I Forget Thee, O Jerusalem* to *The Wild Palms*. {B2, B3}

October 9: In New York, signs and dates first edition of *A Green Bough* for Jim Devine. {BH1}

October 10: Asks Estelle to convey to Malcolm WF's account of the Army vs. Columbia football game. {SL}

October 11: Finishes galley proofs of *The Wild Palms*. {B2}

October 13: Returns home. {B2}

October 20: Writes his name in books by Homer, Ben Jonson, Walt Whitman, Cervantes, Synge, and Ford Maddox Ford, acquired in New York. {B2}

October 24: Contributes to purchase of a Travel-Aire, a three-seat open cockpit biplane, which he flies for 90 minutes. {B2}

November 7: Rewrites "Barn Burning." {B2}

Autograph manuscript of *The Hamlet*. {MC}

November 20: "Barn Burning" to a new agent, Harold Ober. {SL}

December 3: Jimmy (WF's nephew) and stepson Malcolm attend the Mississippi-Tennessee football game and then pick up journalist Robert Cantwell for his visit to Rowan Oak as part of his *Time* profile. {CWF, CR2}

December 4: Cantwell is unable to get Uncle Ned Barnett to talk about the old colonel. {CR2}

WF gets in some flying time. {CWF}

December 15: Robert Haas receives detailed letter outlining the plan and plot for a Snopes trilogy. WF is half way through the first volume. {SL}

December 19: Flies the Travel-Aire. {B2}

1939

January 18: Elected to National Institute of Arts and Letters.

January 19: Random House publishes *The Wild Palms*.

Reports to Bennett Cerf that he expects to finish volume 1 of the Snopes trilogy in April. Asks Cerf to send a copy of *The Wild Palms* to Mrs. Wolfgang Rebner (Meta Carpenter). {SL}

January 23: *Time* publishes Robert Cantwell's cover story feature on Faulkner. {DM}

January 25: Malcolm Cowley's *New Republic* review of *The Wild Palms*: Harry and Charlotte "fall in love, instantly and fatally, like two characters in a late-Elizabethan tragedy, forsaking security for passion even as the convict forsakes passion for security." {WFC}

January 27: *Brooklyn Citizen* review of *The Wild Palms*: "something overwhelming and terrible . . . An evil spell so unutterably fascinating that one cannot escape its black magical power." {WFC}

January 28: *El Paso Herald-Post* review of *The Wild Palms*: "the agonizing struggle of living organisms in the grip of mighty forces." {CR1}

February 7: Reports to Robert Haas that he is putting together the final stories to be incorporated in the first Snopes novel. {SL}

February 10: Begins a new section of *The Hamlet*, the flashback of Ike and the cow. {B3}

February 22: Writes to Sallie Bryant a long letter of tribute to her husband, who has just died, praising his lively mind which never failed him, his adaptability to the present, and to the inevitability of change, and the outlook for the future. "To me he bridged a time which far exceeded seventy-five years. He took the history of this north Mississippi country which we both loved because to him too that history was not dead, and because he believed it was not dead he brought the shadowy figures and the names which moved through it into the present, not as ghostly visitors but as men and women with warm and living flesh and blood. When I talked and listened in his company I talked and listened not only to his and my forbears but to all the men whose passions shaped and tamed the land where we were born and lived." {RO}

March: Receives $1200 advance for *The Hamlet* and uses it to pay off debts to Phil Stone. {B2}

March 1: Fifty-five minutes on the Travel-Aire. {UVA}

March 6: Writes to Robert Haas asking him to give Meta Carpenter $150 to cover her costs for a trip to New Orleans where she meets WF. {B3, SL}

March 12: Another flight on the Travel-Aire. {UVA}

March 17: Tells Robert Haas he is "not a movie writer" but hopes Hollywood will buy his novels. Has found it impossible to write pot-boiler stories. Asks for advice on whether he should borrow to pay insurance premiums or drop the insurance. {SL}

March 22: Asks Random House to lend him money to help a friend (Phil Stone) in debt. Cashes in an insurance policy. {CR2}

March 25: Thanks Robert Haas for sending a check and discusses the contract details for the Snopes trilogy. {SL}

March 29: More discussion with Haas about how he can use Random House royalties, or the expectation of royalties, to help pay his insurance policy and mortgage. {SL}

March 31: Donald Klopfer: "We want to publish every single thing that you write." {UVA}

End of March: *The Wild Palms* is selling more than 1000 copies a week, surpassing the success of *Sanctuary*.

April 5: In a New Orleans *Item* interview, WF mentions working on the trilogy, interrupted for "boiling the pot." {B2, LG}

Robert Haas writes to report his satisfaction with *The Hamlet*, still a work in progress. {SL}

April 19: Another flight on the Travel-Aire. {UVA}

April 24: Writes to Robert Haas about revisions of the first Snopes novel. Hopes to come to New York in the fall to go over the whole manuscript. Adds: "I am the best in America, by God." {SL}

May: Interrupts work on *The Hamlet* to write "Hand upon the Waters," a detective story. {B2}

May 3: Reports to Haas that he has cashed in an insurance policy to pay premiums on two their policies and income tax. "Maybe what I need is a bankruptcy, like a soldier needs delousing." {SL}

June: *Harper's* publishes "Barn Burning."

Summer: *Virginia Quarterly Review* of *The Wild Palms*: a "love story, full of stripped and quivering passion that never relaxes, is almost too harrowing to be read through consecutively. Mr. Faulkner's power of evocation is so great, his voltage so high, that the love story, in spite of its pitiful beauty, would exhaust a reader. The convict story, though intense itself, furnishes relief because the tensity in this second tale is pure muscularity, pure determination, without the emotional strain of the other." {CR2}

July 4: Celebration at Greenfield Farm, with Negro singers in red bandanas. {B2}

Works on revisions of "The Peasants" to be renamed *The Hamlet*. {B2}

August 17: MGM file indicates WF asks for $1250, but no contract is offered. {B2}

Mid-August: Rewrites stories to be included in *The Hamlet*. Tells Haas that he expects to be in New York by October 10. Looking for a room to rent for $50 a month. "I could then buy liquor, and cadge grub from you all." {SL}

August 22: Donald Klopfer writes to assure Faulkner that Random House could help him find a cheap place for a month's stay in New York to work on polishing his novel. {UVA}

September 2: Asks Miss Sallie for a delay in certain payments because of the assessment of additional taxes for 1937. {RO}

c. September: Writes to Maggie Lea, daughter of Sallie Bailey, about *The Plantation Overseer*, a book he borrowed from her father, Will Bryant. He is returning the book to her, but he cannot find another book she evidently thinks he borrowed from her father. He will keep looking for it. "Being a book man myself, I try to be very careful with all books, and with borrowed ones particularly . . ." {RO}

October: Confirms the titles of the Snopes trilogy: *The Hamlet*, *The Town*, *The Mansion*. Concerned about discrepancies in dates for certain parts of the novel. Sends editor Saxe Commins the last chapter of *The Hamlet*. {SL}

October 2: In the air. {UVA}

October 3: In the air. {UVA}

Harold Ober receives "The Old People."

October 6: In the air. {UVA}

October 9: In the air. {UVA}

October 10: In Washington, DC to testify in a plagiarism trial concerning *The Road to Glory*. {B3}

October 14: With Joel Sayre watches Temple defeat Texas Christian. {B2}

October 17: Lunch at the Plaza Hotel in New York City interviewed by Michael Mok for the *New York Post*, reporting on a "jolly little man who likes nothing better than telling droll yarns [especially about the Snopeses] between puffs of a well-seasoned pipe." {B2, LG}

October 24: From Oxford, responds to the League of American Writers, affirming his antifascism and opposition to Franco and the revolt against Republican Spain. Sends manuscript of *Absalom, Absalom!* to Vincent Sheean as his contribution to the antifascist cause. {B3}

November 4: *The Saturday Evening Post* publishes "Hand upon the Waters."

November 29: Reports to Haas that he has done well selling stories this year, although still $300 in the red. Will need $2000 by January 1. {SL}

December 7: Writes to Robert Haas about obtaining $500 from Random House, which along with $300 O'Henry Memorial award for "Barn Burning," and perhaps a sale to *The Saturday Evening Post* should keep him going for about six months. {SL}

1940

January 4: Harold Ober receives "A Point of Law."

January 27: Caroline (Callie) Barr suffers stroke.

January 21: Reads the galleys of *The Hamlet*. {CR2}

January 31: Caroline Barr dies.

February 3: In the *Memphis Commercial Appeal*, comments on his relationship with Caroline Barr: "As oldest of my father's family, I might be called her master. That situation never existed between 'Mammy' and me." {CR2}

February 4: Delivers funeral sermon for Caroline Barr. {ESPL}

February 5: Returns the galley of *The Hamlet* to Random House. Excuses his lateness due to the death of the "hundred-year-old matriarch who raised me . . . So I have had little of heart or time either for work." {SL}

Reports sale of "A Point of Law" to *Collier's* for $1000 and so "am in fair condition." {SL}

Memphis Commercial Appeal publishes the funeral sermon for Caroline Barr. {ESPL}

February 7: Writes to May Bell Barr, Caroline's daughter, describing Caroline's comfortable last years with a young couple who took good care of her. "I'll be glad to show you her grave if you ever come to Oxford." {SL}

Thanks Robert Haas for sending a news clipping about WF's remarks at Caroline Barr's memorial service. WF writes that from her "I learned to tell the truth, to refrain from waste, to be considerate of the weak and respectful of age. I saw fidelity to a family which was not hers, devotion and love for people she had not borne." {SL}

Writes to Harold Ober grateful for the sale of "A Point of Law" for $1000. {SL}

March 14: Harold Ober reports that *Collier's* has rejected "Gold Is Not Always" and "The Fire and the Hearth." {B3}

March 18: "Pantaloon in Black" arrives at Harold Ober's office. {B3}

March 19: Ober sends "Pantaloon in Black" to *Collier's*. "This is a good story . . . Hope someone takes it quick," WF comments. {SL}

March 27: *Collier's* rejects "Pantaloon in Black," specifying its need for comic stories. {B3}

Last will and testament with changes in pencil by WF and Phil Stone. {BH5}

April 1: Random House publishes *The Hamlet*.

April 14: Cleveland *Plain Dealer* reviewer of *The Hamlet* deplores the reverie of Ike Snopes in love with a cow: "Why, but for the gratification of the author's perverted judgment, should any reader endeavor to interest himself for 60 pages in a minute description of a gruesome creature who grovels habitually in filth?" {WFC}

April 16: *New Masses* reviewer of *The Hamlet* praises the reverie of Ike Snopes in love with a cow: "sheer primitive myth—apocalyptic poetry, too." {WFC}

April 18: Tells Robert Haas and Bennett Cerf about problems paying income tax. He has written four stories, but he has not been able to sell them, remarking, "Maybe a man worrying about money can't write anything worth buying." {SL}

April 28: Informs Haas he now needs $1000 to "pay debts and current bills." Only one of six stories has sold, and he has mortgaged his mares and colts to "pay food and electricity and washing and such, and watching each mail train in hopes of a check." Mentions a "blood-and-thunder mystery novel which should sell,"[72] but he does not dare devote six months to writing, "haven't got six months to devote to it." Instead, he proposes another book of linked stories (*Go Down, Moses)* using a "method similar to THE UNVANQUISHED." Proposes a contract that would give him $300 a month in addition to a $1000 advance. {SL}

May 3: A long letter to Robert Haas about "this really quite alarming paradox which my life reveals"; how he has taken on the responsibility of financially supporting numerous family members with help from no one, even though he is a first-class artist who ought to be "free even of his own economic responsibilities and with no moral conscience at all." Outlines a projected novel about a boy of thirteen or fourteen, a "big warmhearted, courageous honest, utterly unreliable white man with the mentality of a child," and "an old negro family servant, opinionated, querulous, selfish, fairly unscrupulous, and in his second childhood, and a prostitute not very young anymore and with a great deal of character and generosity and common sense, and a stolen race horse which one of them actually intended to steal."[73] Ends the letter with a request: "May I have $1,000.00 at once?" {SL}

May 6: *Santa Barbara News Press* reviews *The Hamlet*, acknowledging WF's "sheer genius to ignite images that cut open new worlds upon our sensibilities." {WFC}

May 22: Writes to Robert Haas that he is still considering a collection of stories he could get together in about six months. Another novel would take at least a year and would need at least a steady $200 a month. Offers this suggestion on approaching his agent, Harold Ober, who has several stories to sell: "If somebody dont buy something of Faulkner soon, I dont know what Random House will do." {SL}

May 27: Asks Ober about stories that might be sent to *Esquire* or *The Saturday Evening Post.* Tells his agent: "I'm so busy borrowing money from Random House I dont even have time to write." {SL}

A letter to Ober discusses the war in Europe. "I got my uniform out the other day. I can button it, even after twenty-two years; the wings look as brave as they ever did. I swore then when I took it off in '19, that I would never wear another, nohow, nowhere, for no one. But now I don't know." He has had trouble writing but also knows he can still write. Asks for $500, so he can pay his back income tax. {SL}

June 1: Tells Haas he has signed a contract for a novel, which may turn out to be one of connected short stories. Still asking for $200 a month for the next 12 months. "If you think this is a bad risk, say so. I have learned damned well what a goddamn nuisance anyone becomes who, each time you see or hear him, you think, 'How much does he want now?' You and Don [Klopfer] and Bennett have been my good friends for a long time, and I would hate to spoil it like this." Has tried to get a Hollywood job but "that's out for me. No good for them." {SL}

June 4: Robert Haas sends a check for $500 in response to Faulkner's financial distress. {B3}

June 7: Needs $9,000, which would give the economic freedom to write for two years, or $5,000 for one year. The other option is to sell off his property, but he won't do that unless there is no other option. Itemizes his debts to the bank, income tax, insurance policies, his mother's household, his home and farm. Assets: 35 acres of wooded parkland, which could be sold as a subdivision, farm stock, a new novel, and five short stories. To remain solvent, he would have to sell six commercial stories a year. Suggests perhaps selling his novel elsewhere so he can pay back Random House. He knows of one publisher (Harold Guinzberg of Viking Press) who told him "I could almost write my own ticket with him." {SL}

June 10: Haas writes that Random House cannot continue to provide advances and indicates WF might have to look to another publisher. {SL}

June 12: Tells Haas he will contact another publisher, but if there is no interest, then the $1000 Haas has offered is acceptable, and he will try to sell some short stories. {SL}

June 18: Telegram notifying Random House that Viking Press has offered to become his new publisher. {B3}

June 19: Bennett Cerf writes to WF expressing everyone's regret over his leaving Random House. Offers $2000 plus a $1000 advance already owed to him. {SL}

June 20: To Bennett Cerf, WF explains his financial situation and how he and Haas have dealt with it. At this point, he has accepted the Viking offer and does not want to "blackjack another into advancing me money, which that second publisher had otherwise declined to advance." {SL}

June 22: *Collier's* publishes "A Point of Law."

June 24: Cerf reiterates his offer and notes Viking Press would have to pay for the plates of *The Hamlet*. {SL}

June 25: In New York, WF meets with Harold Guinzberg of Viking Press, and the publisher notes he will talk with Cerf about buying the plates to *The Hamlet*. {B3}

June 27: Meets with Harold Ober to discuss several short stories, including "The Old People," rejected by *The Saturday Evening Post*, *The American*

Magazine, Collier's, Country Gentleman, Red Book, Cosmopolitan, and *This Week.* {B3}

June 28: *Harper's* purchases "The Old People" for $400.

June 30: Arrives in Memphis and flies the Travel-Aire. {UVA}

July 1: *The Saturday Evening Post* rejects "Almost." {B2}

July 3: Viking Press withdraws its offer to publish WF because of the $1500 cost of plates and stock of *The Hamlet.* But Harold Guinzberg writes to WF of his continued interest in publishing him. {B3}

Ober writes to say *The Saturday Evening Post* has rejected "Almost" (a version of "Was"). {B2}

July 8: Cerf writes to explain his meeting with Guinzberg and to say the June 19 offer still stands. {SL}

July 12: Writes to Ober requesting the return of the "Almost" typescript. {SL}

July 18: Revises "Almost" as Ober suggested.[74]

July 19: Signs two pages of the "Almost" typescript for Dan Brennan, a visitor to Rowan Oak.[75] {B3, CR2}

July 20: Sends Ober the revised "Almost." {B2}

July 24: Writes to Bennett Cerf about his disappointment in *The Ox-Bow Incident* and contemporary writing in general. {SL}

Mails "Go Down, Moses" to *The Saturday Evening Post.* {B2}

July 25: Flies his brother Jack's plane, the Aeronca. {B2}

July 28: Goes over his dealings with Harold Guinzberg and Viking Press in a letter to Bennett Cerf and concludes: "I have not approached any other publisher, and at present I do not intend to." He is close to finishing *Go Down, Moses.* Still thinking about his "Huck Finn novel."[76] Mentions that his brother John has written a novel, *Men Working,* and asks, "Do you want to look at it."[77] {SL}

Late July: Cho-Cho (Victoria) marries William Fielden in Shanghai. {B3}

August: At Rowan Oak signs and dates a copy of Dorothy Cameron Disney's *The Balcony* and gives it to Malcolm Franklin. {BH1}

August 5: "Tomorrow" to *The Saturday Evening Post.* {LC}

August 9: *Harper's* purchases "Pantaloon in Black" for $400. Ober sends a check. {B3}

August 13: *The Saturday Evening Post* purchases "Tomorrow" for $1000, Ober reports. {B3}

August 16: A grateful letter to Ober who does not take his customary commission for selling a story to *The Saturday Evening Post.* Mentions that Robert Haas has declined to publish John Faulkner's novel and asks Ober to look at it. {SL}

August 17: Sends Maggie Lea a $100 check and again regrets he cannot find the book she says he borrowed from her father, Will Bryant. "I have thought about it often, tried to remember the book, but I still cant recall having had it. I am distressed over the possibility that I might have had it and lost it. I never lost a book before." {RO}

August 30: Writes to Maggie Lea about the details of property WF bought from her father and mother. {RO}

September: *Harper's* publishes "The Old People."

September 11: *The Atlantic Monthly* purchases "Gold Is Not Always" for $300. {B2}

September 15: *Collier's* purchases "Go Down, Moses" for $1,000. {B2}

October: *Harper's* publishes "Pantaloon in Black."

Makes eleven flights, piloting four different aircraft as he works on figure-eights, spot-landings, and instrument flying. He also gives himself a refresher course in Morse code. {B3}

October 31: Writes to Maggie Lea with more details about his transactions with her father and says he can bring to her all his papers. "I should have kept the record clearer. But throughout the whole transaction between Mr Will and myself while I was buying this property, the relationship was not that of two men doing business with one another, but rather that of a young man with an older man for whom he had a considerable respect and admiration and who, the young man believed, held for him a warmer feeling than mere acquaintanceship." {RO}

November: *Atlantic Monthly* publishes "Gold Is Not Always."

With friends drives 150 miles into the wilderness to hunt. {B3}

November 12: "An Error in Chemistry" arrives in Harold Ober's office, but several magazines reject it. {B2}

November 23: *The Saturday Evening Post* publishes "Tomorrow."

November 30: In Oxford, signs and dates first edition of *Doctor Martino and Other Stories* owned by Polly Jordan. {BH1}

December 7: In the air. {UVA}

December 9: Thanks Ober for selling his brother John's novel. Includes a poem, "The Husbandman" published as 31 in *A Green Bough* and "brought up to date . . . It is timely now." {SL}

December 15: Writes to wish the staff at Random House a merry Christmas and happy new year. Says hunting takes his mind off of war. "But I'm only 43, I'm afraid I'm going to the damn thing yet." {SL}

December 16: "Delta Autumn" arrives in Harold Ober's office. {B3}

Christmas: A gift: Earnest Albert Hooton's *Twilight of Man* to "Malcolm A. Franklin / from Mama and Billy." {BH1}

1941

January 16: Telegram to Harold Ober: "WIRE ME COLLECT WHAT POSSIBILITY OF ANY SUM WHATEVER AND WHEN FROM ANY MSS OF MINE YOU HAVE. URGENTLY NEEDED ONE HUNDRED BY SATURDAY."[78] {SL}

January 18: Grateful to Ober for sending money. "When I write you I did not have $15.00 to pay electricity bill with, keep my lights burning." {SL, B3}

January 25: *Collier's* publishes "Go Down, Moses."

January 31: Encloses a $10 check and a note to the owner of Oxford's Neilson's department store: "If this don't suit you, the only alternative I can think of is, in the old Miltonic phrase, sue and be damned. If you decide on that step, be assured that I shall do my best to see that the people who have fed me and my family will be protected, and after Uncle Sam gets through his meat-cutting, J. E. Neilson can have what is left. You may even get an autographed book. That will be worth a damn sight more than my autograph on a check dated ten months from now." {CR2}

February 15: In the air. {UVA}

February 19: Sends Estelle a happy birthday telegram from New Orleans. {B3}

March: Works on stories. {B3}

March 19: "The Tall Men" arrives in Harold Ober's office. {B2}

March 21: Reports to Robert Haas that he is still writing stories. "I am flying fairly steadily still very restless. Civilian Pilot Training is not enough." Even thinks of trying to get to England and serve "under my own commission," but he has a family and other dependents to care for. Hopes to teach navigation for the US Air Corps. Has a new book in mind. {SL}

March 30: In Oxford, signs and dates first edition of *The Wild Palms* "Vance C Broach, / from his kinsman."[79] {BH1}

Spring: Joins the barbecues and songfests at Sardis Reservoir, singing "Water Boy." {B2}

April 11: Rejects the idea of a profile advanced by a *Life* editor to Harold Ober. {SL}

May: William Herndon works on getting WF a Hollywood contract. {B3}

May 1: Explains to Robert Haas the plan and contents of *Go Down, Moses,* composed of stories that he will rewrite "to an extent." But he wants to make sure Haas wants to publish such a book. {SL}

May 13: Investigating where he is employable in Hollywood. Asks Haas to send $500. {SL}

May 22: William Herndon, acting as Faulkner's agent, asks MGM for $500 a week for 12 weeks. {B2}

May 31: *The Saturday Evening Post* publishes "The Tall Men."

June 5: Asks Robert Haas to send his books to William Herndon, a Hollywood agent hoping to sell some of WF's work to the movies. {SL}

Robert Haas receives "The Fire and the Hearth," a reworking of "A Point of Law."

June 18: Ben Wasson visits Rowan Oak, bringing along with him a young Greenville, Mississippi, writer, Shelby Foote. {B2}

June 30: Asks Robert Haas for $500. {SL}

Organizing Aircraft Warning Service. Distributes booklet "Meet Your Air Warden" with guides to air raid procedures. Occupies an office on the Oxford Square. {SS}

July: Works on *Go Down, Moses*, revising stories to be reshaped as a novel. {B3}

July 6: Thanks Warren Beck for sending three articles about him: "I agree with them. You found implications which I had missed. I wish that I had consciously intended them; I will certainly believe I did it subconsciously and not by accident." Presents a view of his fiction that is in line with his later Nobel Prize address, saying there are some who read him and say, "Yes. It's all right. I'd rather be Ratliff than Flem Snopes. And I'd still rather be Ratliff without any Snopes to measure by even." Claims he has "written too fast, too much, but "I discovered then that I had rather read Shakespeare, bad puns, bad history, taste and all, than Pater, and that I had a damn sight rather fail at trying to write Shakespeare than to write all of Pater over again so he couldn't have told it himself if you fired it point blank at him through an amplifier." {SL}

July 12: In a letter to the *Memphis Commercial Appeal* protests the punishment of an army unit for "crying 'yoo-hoo' at golfers and ladies in shorts." {ESPL}

July 25: The first section of "The Bear" arrives at Harold Ober's office. {B3}

August 21: Explains to Ober that he has no contract with William Herndon, but if an "authentic offer" materialized in Hollywood he would be "committed to Herndon." {SL}

August 25: Explains to Robert Haas he is running late with the "one more chapter to rewrite" on *Go Down, Moses* because of defense work. Asks for $500. {SL}

To William Herndon: "I am not very successful in making a synopsis (outline) for the reason that, in my own writing, the additional characters and even the course of the story invent themselves as I write it." {UM}

Cashes $25 check made payable to him by "Mrs. Phil Stone."[80] {BH1}

September 9: Robert Haas receives second chapter of "The Bear." {B3}

October 27: Tells Ober he is rewriting "An Error in Chemistry" to simplify it. {SL}

November 5: Complies with *The Saturday Evening Post* request to clarify the ending of "The Bear." {SL}

November 6: Informs Haas that he expects to be finished with *Go Down, Moses* by December 1. {SL}

November 9: Robert Haas receives chapter 3 of "The Bear." {B2}

November 10: Working on revisions of "The Bear" for *The Saturday Evening Post* and tells Ober: "I am in a situation where I will take almost anything for it or almost anything else I have or can write." {SL}

November 14: Ober reports that *The Saturday Evening Post* has purchased a much-revised version of "The Bear" for $1000. {B3}

November 18: Makes suggestions to Warner Bros. on the adaptation of a novel, *The Damned Don't Cry*. {BH2, B3}

November 29: Mentions planting oats while Ole Miss loses a football game to Mississippi State. {B2}

December 2: Harold Ober reports *Story* has purchased "Delta Autumn" for $25. {B1}

Writes to Robert Haas about delay in delivering *Go Down, Moses*: "There is more meat in it than I thought, a section now that I am going to be proud of and which required careful writing and rewriting to get it exactly right." Now hoping to deliver by December 15. {SL}

c. December 7: Tells Saxe Commins that "Delta Autumn" needs to be rewritten. Asks for books for Jill, now 8 and can read books meant for 10- or 12-year-olds. {SL}

Mid-December: Turns in *Go Down, Moses* to Saxe Commins. {SL}

December 20: WF's ledger records transactions with his farm tenants: Nathalie Avent, James Avent, Uncle Ned Barnett, and Renzi McJunkin. {UVA}

1942

January 19: "Knight's Gambit" to Harold Ober, adding "As always, I am broke." Would like quick payment. {SL}

January 21: Sends Robert Haas the dedication to "Mammy," Caroline Barr, for *Go Down, Moses*: "Who was born in slavery and who gave to my family a fidelity without stint or calculation of recompense and to my childhood an immeasurable devotion and love." Complains about congressmen who "refused to make military appropriations . . . I'd send them to the

Philippines." In charge of air and communications in case of air raids and has organized observation posts. {SL}

January 29: "Two Soldiers" to Harold Ober. {SL}

February 5: *The Saturday Evening Post* purchases "Two Soldiers" for $1000.

February 17: Ober receives "Snow." {B3}

February 18: *Harper's* rejects "Knight's Gambit" as too obscure and complex. {B2}

February 21: Works on revisions of "Snow" and "Knight's Gambit."[81]

March 24: In Oxford, signs and dates first edition of *Go Down, Moses, and Other Stories*: "Phil Stone, from Bill." {BH1}

March 27: Tells Robert Haas he is still hoping to get a commission in the navy, Bureau of Aeronautics. "I am to get full Lieut. and 3200.00 per year, and I hope a pilot's rating to wear the wings." Does not want an office job but thinks it unlikely he can get "nearer the gunfire." Asks for $100. "I think a change of environment will freshen me." Concerned that he may not pass the medical exam. {SL}

March 28: *The Saturday Evening Post* publishes "Two Soldiers."

March 30: "My Grandmother Millard and General Bedford Forrest and the Battle of Harrykin Creek" arrives in Harold Ober's office. Calls the story a "message for the day . . . of a willingness to pull up the pants and carry on, no matter with whom, let alone what." Asks Ober for $100. "I'm the only writer I ever heard of who got advances from his agent; I wish to keep this distinction constant." {SL}

Late March: Receives copies of *Go Down, Moses, and Other Stories* and points out that the book is a novel. {SL}

April 6: Phil Stone writes to Robert Daniel, who is putting together the first major exhibition of WF's work, explaining that many of his WF manuscripts perished in a fire that destroyed his 100-year-old home. "With reference to Horace Benbow, I really suspect that I am the original of Horace Benbow. It is so much trouble getting details out of Faulkner in oral conversation that I long ago gave up trying to find out. . . . Bill has a way of telling people anything they want to know and this has been the origin for a lot of fairy tales about Faulkner." Stone goes on to correct the record on WF's war service, pointing out he was not wounded in France "or anywhere else." {BH2}

May–June: *Story* publishes "Delta Autumn."

May 1: The *Post* rejects "Shall Not Perish," objecting that a 12-year-old boy uses language too sophisticated for the son of a tenant farmer. {B2}

May 2: Reviewer's reaction to *Go Down, Moses* in *Saturday Review of Literature*: "Reading the stories with Hitler's war going on tends to make you give certain names to certain of their motifs. You seem to recognize the stern and bloody surviving which the Nazis preach, the pure democracies Walt Whitman sang, and the fatal heredity and environment which made the late Clarence Darrow pity all men for their crimes." {CR1}

May 6: Asks *Post* if he should rewrite "Shall Not Perish." {SL}

Boston Globe review of *Go Down, Moses*: "our most distinguished unread talent." {WFC}

May 9: *The Saturday Evening Post* publishes "The Bear."

May 11: Random House publishes *Go Down, Moses, and Other Stories.*

May 12: Phil Stone writes to Robert Daniel: "Faulkner used to write out his stuff in longhand first in ink with a very minute handwriting and then type it. He still does this a little but, like most modern writers, he has gotten lazy and types most of it directly now."[82] {BH2}

May 14: Ober receives Faulkner's instruction to hold "Snow" for a rewrite while he tries to write something for the *Post* "to get enough money to go on military service and leave something for dependents." {SL}

May 25: Revised version of "Shall Not Perish" to the *Post.* Tells Ober: "I think it's all right now. I should have written it this way at first; it never had tasted quite right to me. Goddamn it that's what having to write not because you want to write but because you are harassed to hell for money does." {SL}

May 29: *Post* rejects "Shall Not Perish" for a second time. {B2}

June 3: Bennett Cerf sends congratulations on the good reviews of *Go Down, Moses* but adds: "There simply isn't very much that can be done with a collection of short stories in times like these." Suggests writing a World War II book that would be a money maker. Mentions Faulkner's introduction to *Sanctuary* and his confession that he wrote it to sell. "Maybe you would like to take another whack at the old jackpot!"[83] {RHR}

June 4: Ober receives the third revision of "Shall Not Perish," along with "A Courtship." {B2}

c. June 6: Informs Bennett Cerf that air force rejected him for a war job "didn't say why, may have been age, 44." Says he has a definite offer from the navy but still prefers air force and wonders what "influence I might wangle." Or: "do you know of anyone who wants to send a missionary to California for a few weeks?" {SL}

Mid-June: Writes to Whit Burnett, editor of *This Is My Best,* to include any story "you want to and that is convenient," concluding, "I have been so worried lately with trying to write potboilers and haunting the back door of the post-office for checks that dont come to keep a creditor with a bill from catching me on the street, that I dont remember anything anymore." {SL}

June 22: Writes Ober his writing has gone stale. Suggests military service or a stint in Hollywood would help. Supporting his family and other dependents is beginning to hurt his work. "I believe I have discovered the reason inherent in human nature why warfare will never be abolished: it's the only condition under which a man who is not a scoundrel can escape for a while from his female kin. But now the formation of these WAACs and such gives a man to blink." {SL}

June 23: Writes to Bell Wiley about the war and his efforts to enlist and comments on the genealogy of the McCaslins in *Go Down, Moses.* {WC}

c. June 23: Writes Bennett Cerf he is broke, with only 60 cents in his pocket. {SL}

June 25: Writes Ober he is still hoping to get a California assignment. Owes the grocer $600 and cannot pay telephone bill or fuel for the winter. {SL}

June 28: Informs Ober he will take anything about $100 for film work in Hollywood. Has been borrowing small amounts of money from his mother. Will send a story soon although only one has sold in six months. "If a man with my experience and reputation has reached that point, there is something wrong and something had better be done. I think a change of scene is the answer." {SL}

June 29: Malcolm Cowley's *New Republic* review of *Go Down, Moses*: "There is no other American writer who has been consistently misrepresented by critics, including myself." {JB}

June 30: Cerf sends $200 and writes about possible work in Hollywood and again presses Faulkner to write a book about World War II. {CR2}

Early July: *New York Times* critic Brooks Atkinson visits Oxford and meets a subdued WF. {CR2}

July 11: Ober wires to confirm a job possibility in Hollywood. {B3}

July 15: Ober wires that Warner's is ready to offer a contract but does not know who to deal with because earlier WF had casually allowed another agent, William Herndon, to represent him. {SL}

Robert Daniel writes to WF's Aunt Bama about his WF exhibition. "To me one of the most interesting things is the corrected galley-sheets of *Sanctuary*. You know he tells in the Introduction how he tore it down and rewrote it, and these sheets certainly prove it." {BH2}

July 16: Ober encloses $100 check. {B2}

July 17: "Shingles for the Lord" arrives in Harold Ober's office. {B3}

William Herndon wires claiming his right to represent WF, who denies underhanded dealing and promises that Ober will work out an equitable arrangement. {B3}

To Ober a letter written to producer James Geller expressing enthusiasm about a new assignment. {SL}

July 18: To Ober about Herndon's accusation that WF has not behaved honorably, and WF acknowledges he should have clearly cut ties with Herndon before allowing Ober to seek employment for him in Hollywood. {SL}

To Herndon denies underhanded dealing, noting he had not heard from Herndon for six months and did not realize the agent was still working on his behalf. Explains he has asked Ober to make an "equitable adjustment" with Herndon, adding: "If this is not satisfactory to you, then make your threat and cause whatever trouble you wish." {SL}

July 19: To Ober, WF admits that Herndon's charge that he has not behaved honorably bothers him, "even if it is not true." Worry over money led to WF forgetting about Herndon's claim for a commission. Hopes that Ober will agree that Herndon should make the Hollywood deal. {SL}

July 20: Ober receives WF's letter saying that although Herndon's claim is weak, he did bring WF to the attention of producer Robert Buckner at Warner Bros. "So my feeling is that, whether he actually deserves anything or not, I would rather pay his commission than have him on my mind as thinking I owed him anything." {SL}

c. July 22: Ober forgoes his commission and advises WF to deal directly with Warner Bros. {B3}

Sends telegram to James J. Geller at Warner Bros. accepting deal made by Herndon. {SL}

Ober receives a rewritten version of "Snow." {B2}

July 23: In Oxford, signs and dates for James W. Silver the first edition of *Go Down, Moses, and Other Stories.* {BH1}

To Bell Wiley: "The ledger excerpts in *Go Down, Moses* were a little to set a tone and atmosphere, but they also told a story of how the negros became McCaslins too. Old McCaslin bought a handsome octoroon and got a daughter on her and then got a son on that daughter; that son was his mother's child and her brother at the same time; he was both McCaslin's son and his grandson." {CCP}

July 27: Reports to Warner Bros. lot as part of a seven-year contract, beginning at $300 a week. He stays at the Highland Hotel, close to Hollywood Boulevard. {B3}

July 28: Ober sells "Shingles for the Lord" for $1000 to *The Saturday Evening Post.* {B3}

WF wires Ober that he has arrived in Hollywood and should send *Post* check to him at the studio. {SL}

Types 9 pages of a story outline, "Journey toward Dawn." {BH3}

July 29: Confers with producer Robert Buckner about *The De Gaulle Story* and takes eight pages of notes and completes a story outline. {BH3}

July 30: Two pages of suggestions for Buckner. {BH3}

July 31: More suggestions for Buckner. {BH3}

August 1: Dismayed that he is committed to a long-term contract with Warner Bros. on unfavorable terms but is assured by Geller and Buckner that if he does "all right," the contract will be "torn up and a new arrangement made." Apologizes to Ober "for getting things bitched up like this." {SL}

Writes to Estelle about her handling of finances: "You are doing all right. I am not worrying at all." {CR2}

Early August: Mentions Thomas Mann's exile from Hitler's Germany: "What an immortality that brute has got himself: an immigrant, he has expelled from his native land the foremost literary artist of his time." {SL}

August 3: Writes an expanded treatment off *The De Gaulle Story*, including a 45-page section titled "Free France." {BH3}

August 10: Buckner writes a memo to WF with suggestions for *The De Gaulle Story*. {BH3}

August 13: Completes 39-page treatment of *The De Gaulle Story*. {BH3}

August 15: Writes to Maggie Lea from Hollywood enclosing payment on a note due to her. {RO]

August 17: Writes to Estelle: "Would like some more preserves if you can spare it. I have a coffee pot in my office and will eat some preserves and bread too. Gave all other jam to Mrs. Buckner." Reminds her to take care of the furnace. {CR2}

August 19: Completes 44 pages of *The De Gaulle Story* per Buckner's instructions. {BH3}

August 31: To Jill: "If there is one thing I always did like, it's a Jill." {UVA}

c. September: Adrien Tixier, a De Gaulle representative, issues 5-page "Observations on Inexact Details" in *The De Gaulle Story*. {BH3}

September 1: Buckner writes a memo directing WF to complete a "full treatment of the De Gaulle story" by September 4 or 5. {BH3}

September 4: Completes 79-page treatment of *The De Gaulle Story* per Buckner's schedule. {BH3}

September 14–October 5: Howard Hawks borrows WF to rewrite a death scene for *Air Force*. {CR2}

September 19: In *The Saturday Review of Literature*, Phil Stone publishes "William Faulkner and His Neighbors." The same issue contains a favorable review of John Faulkner's novel, *Dollar Cotton*. {CR2}

Writes to his stepdaughter, Victoria, that he is sober and "writing to the satisfaction of the studio." {SL}

September 22: Writes Maggie Lea that he is home again but has to return to California. Provides more details about his business dealings with her parents. "I will send a payment of some amount this fall, and I hope that after I get back on salary again, I can discharge the whole business. But with regret, as I will never again find such nice creditors as you and your mother and father have been." {RO}

September 30: Warner Brothers research department memo to WF about *The De Gaulle Story*. {BH3}

c. October: French Research Foundation supplies six pages of information for *The De Gaulle Story*. {BH3}

October: Meets Ruth Ford in Hollywood. {CR2}

October 2: Warner Bros. renews WF's option at $300 a week, commencing October 26 for thirteen weeks with seven more options escalating from $350 to $1,250 if all options are renewed. {CR2}

October 5: Revises 58-page screenplay and adds 17 pages to *The De Gaulle Story*. {BH3}

October 12: Expands treatment of *The De Gaulle Story* to 66 pages. {BH3}

October 13: Warner Brothers research department responds to WF's request for a list of typical first and last names of Breton men and women. {BH3}

October 20: Twenty-eight-page treatment of "De Gaulle Story" filed in Warner Brothers Story Department. {BH3}

October 30: Completes 153-page typescript of *The De Gaulle Story*. {BH3}

c. Early November: Henri Diamant-Berger provides critique of *The De Gaulle Story*. {BH3}

November 9: Buckner sends memo to Faulkner relaying the critique submitted by De Gaulle's representatives. {BH3}

November 13: To Ober a three-page poem, "The Old Ace," about Eddie Rickenbacker's survival of a plane crash. Then wires to advise waiting for a revision. {SL}

Visits Consolidated Aircraft in San Diego as part of work on *Life and Death of a Bomber*. {CR2}

Rewrites several pages of *The De Gaulle Story*. {BH3}

November 14: Airmails the revision of "The Old Ace" to Ober. {SL}

Files 8-page report on his visit to the Consolidated Aircraft Factory for "The Life and Death of a Bomber. {BH5, WFH}

November 15: Writes to his mother about coming home for Christmas if he gets the studio's permission. He is counting on a raise "since I have done pretty good for them this time." {SL}

November 16: Completes 153 pages of *The De Gaulle Story*. {BH3}

November 17: Rewrites several pages of *The De Gaulle Story*. {BH3}

November 18: Completes rewriting of 69 pages of 153-page typescript of *The De Gaulle Story*. {BH3}

November 19: Makes the last revisions of *The De Gaulle Story*. Sends a 2-page memo to Buckner: "Let's dispense with General De Gaulle as a living character in the story." It is the only way to free the story from French supervision. Otherwise, "we must either please them and nobody else, or probably please nobody at all." {BH3}

November 23–December 7: Works with Daniel Fuchs on revised, final screenplay for "Background to Danger." {WFH}

November 26: Airmails another revision of "The Old Ace" to Ober and asks for a copy of "Tomorrow," which he hopes to sell as a treatment to the studio. {SL}

December: In Oxford, on furlough from Warner Brothers. {CR2}

Types up instructions for "CURING HAMS SHOULDERS BACON." {BH5}

December 5: Writes to his stepson, Malcolm Franklin, thanking him for news about home. Describes wartime Hollywood: blackout, rationing, and public attitudes. Approves of Malcolm's wish to "get into the service," even though "the same old stink is rising from this one as has raised from every war yet: vide Churchill's speech about having no part in dismembering the Br. Empire. But it is the biggest thing that will happen in your lifetime. All your contemporaries will be in it before it is over, and if you are not one of them, you will always regret it." He hopes there will be a place for older men like himself "old enough and have been vocal long enough to be listened to, yet are not so old that we too have become another batch of decrepit old men looking stubbornly backward at a point 25 or 50 years in the past." {SL}

December 14: Jack Warner gives permission to return to Mississippi. {CR2}

December 16: Lands at Memphis airport. {B2}

Christmas: An elaborate family gathering at Rowan Oak. {B3, CR2}

New Year's Eve: Estelle plays the piano. WF sings "Water Boy." Fireworks. {CR2}

1943

January 1: At Rowan Oak, a dinner of hog jowls, black-eyed peas, and cornbread. The company ends the day with a fishing expedition. {CR2}

January 7: Jack Warner picks up Faulkner's option at $350 a week for another 26 weeks. {CR2}

January 13: *Story* purchases "My Grandmother Millard" for $50. {B2}

January 16: Resumes work at Warner Brothers and residence at the Highland Hotel. {B2}

January 21–22: Working on *Life and Death of a Bomber.* {WFH}

January 23: Completes work on *Life and Death of a Bomber.* {B3, CR2}

January 25: Studio picks up his option. Tells Ober he may try for the Ferry Command but has resigned himself to at least part-time script work since nothing else pays as well. Hopes to accumulate more funds before attempting to volunteer for service. {SL}

February 13: *The Saturday Evening Post* publishes "Shingles for the Lord."

February 17–25: Working on an Errol Flynn film, *Northern Pursuit.* Reports to Robert Haas that he is "surrounded by snow, dogs, Indians, Red Coats, and Nazi spies." {SL, B3, CR2, WFH}

February 26: Completes work on *Northern Pursuit* with screenwriters Alvah Bessie, Frank Gruber, Thomas Job, A. I. Bezzerides, and Robert Rosen. {WFH}

March 5–9: Works on *Deep Valley* screenplay. {WFH}

March 27–April 16: Works on *Country Lawyer,* incorporating new characters in an original story about Yoknapatawpha, although it is ostensibly an adaptation of a novel by Bellamy Partridge. {CR2, WFH}

March-April: *Story* publishes "My Grandmother Millard and General Bedford Forrest and the Battle of Harrykin Creek."

March 8: Writes to a reader objecting to a technical error (the use of a frow) and explains he is well aware of the error but took a "minor liberty in order to tell the story. . . . But I regret sincerely having offended anyone's sense of fitness, and I will be doubly careful from now on to be explicit in facts." {SL}

March 15: Asks Ober for permission to adapt an F. Scott Fitzgerald story, "The Curious Case of Benjamin Button." Finds life dull but enjoys riding "a tremendous big roan Tennessee walking gelding, and feel better for it." {SL}

April 3: Writes to his stepdaughter, Victoria, and her husband, William Fielden, about having the "damned worst bloody rotten bad cold in human captivity . . . I am a rachitic old man in the last stages of loco-motor ataxia," but he can still "invent a little something now and then that is photogenic, and I can still certainly sign my name to my salary check each Saturday." {SL}

A long letter to his nephew Jimmy with a wild story about his exploits in World War I, including his claim that the Gestapo has his dogtag. Cautions against "foolhardiness. A lot of pilots don't get past that. Uncle Dean didn't." Talks about beating fear: "The brave man is not he who does not know fear: the brave man is he who says to himself, 'I am afraid. I will decide quickly what to do, and then I will do it.'" Parting advice: "Learn all you can about the aero plane: how to check it over on the ground. Aero planes very seldom let you down; the trouble is inside cockpits." {SL}

April 5: To Victoria (Cho-Cho): "I feel pretty well, sober, am working to the satisfaction of the studio. Mentions De Gaulle script: "Don't tell publicly what I am even writing." {CFS}

April 7: Assigned to *Battle Cry* directed by Howard Hawks. They work on the screenplay in June Lake, California. {CR2}

April 21: Completes a 140-page script for *Battle Cry* but after script conferences starts over. {BH4}

April 26: Mentions to Ober he is still thinking of adapting a Fitzgerald story—this time as a play. Relays to Ober his statement to Herndon that he is involved only in the Warner Bros. contract. "I think I am no good at movies, and will be fired as soon as the studio legally can. I will have to try something else then." Still considering wartime service, although "I really am too old for anyone to want, even if I still dont believe it." {SL}

April 27: To his son-in-law, William Fielden, expressing a yearning to return to "my town, my land, my people, my life." Admits Estelle has done fine without him. Gives his regards to "Vickie-pic," his step granddaughter. "See Air Force [a Hawks film]. I wrote Quincannon's death scene, and the scene where the men in the aero plane heard Roosevelt's speech after Pearl Harbor." {SL}

Mid-May: Malcolm Franklin departs for service in the army. {B2}

May 16: Writes to Jill saying he has heard from Mama and Granny about Jill's nice haircut. "Pappy misses that yellow hair that had never had an inch cut off of it since you were born, but since Pappy knows and can remember and can see in his mind whenever he wants to every single day you ever lived, whether he was there to look at you or not, why any time he wants to he can imagine into his mind and his sight too every single one of those days, and how you looked then." Describes his daily routine for her and how he gets to work, picked up on the corner by Mr. Bezzerides and Mr. Job. "I am writing a big picture [*Battle Cry*] now, for Mr Howard Hawks, an old friend, a director . . . It will last about 3 hours, and the studio has allowed Mr Hawks 3 and 1/2 million dollars to make it, with 3 or 4 directors and about all the big stars." Mentions he has purchased two Victory Bonds for her. {SL}

May 19: *Story* purchases "Shall Not Perish" for $25.

May 24: To Malcolm Franklin: "War is bad, of course, unnecessary among civilised peoples. We are fighting, as always, the long battalioned ghosts of old wrongs and shames that each generation of us both inherits and creates. We will win this one, then we must, we must, clean the world's house so that man can live in peace in it. I believe we will. I envy you being young enough to have a part in it." {UVA}

June 2: Completes a 231-page script for *Battle Cry* that requires revision and the services of another writer, Steve Fisher. {BH4}

June 15: Producer William Bacher approves of WF's script but suggests revisions. {BH4}

June 18: Bacher makes some cuts and other revisions of WF's script. {BH4}

June 21: Completes third version of *Battle Cry*. {BH4}

Writes to Harold Ober that he expects his Warner Bros. option to be renewed. {SL}

June 24: Turns in revisions of French scenes in *Battle Cry* script. {BH4}

Late June: Estelle and Jill join WF in California. {CR2}

July 1: Writes a consolatory letter to Robert Haas about the loss of his son in the war: "My nephew, 18, is about to be posted to carrier training. He will get it too. Then who knows? The blood of your fathers and the blood of mine side by side at the same long table in Valhalla, talking of glory and heroes, draining the cup and banging the empty pewter on the long board to fill again, holding two places for us maybe, not because we were heroes or not heroes, but because we loved them." {SL}

July 4: Writes to Malcolm Franklin about a "squadron of negro pilots," the Tuskegee Airmen, making it a parable about what he expects will happen when these African Americans return to a racist America. "A change will come out of this war. If it doesn't, if the politicians and the people who run the country are not forced to make good the shibboleth they glibly talk about freedom, liberty, human rights, then you men who live through it will have wasted your precious time, and those who dont live through it will have died in vain." {SL}

July 5: A completely revised 117-page *Battle Cry* script is typed up, including WF's revisions of American and Greek scenes. {BH4}

July 11: To Jill: "Tell Granny I am going to the mountains tomorrow with Mr. Hawks to go fishing. Will be back next Sunday and write about it. I sho do love you. Pappy." {UVA}

July 12: Option picked for 52 weeks at $400. {USC}

July 15: Earl Robinson,[84] collaborating on *Battle Cry* script, believes WF's rewrite promises to be "an honest-to-God great picture" with "scenes that will really be new and startling but at the same time simple and true and embodying real people and believable characters and situations." But he also calls attention to parts that are "spotty and confusing." {BH4}

July 26: Completes revision of Russian segment of *Battle Cry*. {BH4}

July–August: *Story* publishes "Shall Not Perish."

August 1: Writes to Estelle that he expects to continue working on *Battle Cry* so long as Hawks needs him. A successful job may yield a new, better contract. Hawks is setting up an independent production unit with WF as his writer. "He says he and I together as a team will always be worth two million dollars at least. . . . When I come home, I intend to have Hawks completely satisfied with this job, as well as the studio. If I can do that, I wont have to worry again about going broke temporarily. . . . I am so impatient to get home, I am about to bust. . . . If I were just sitting here, waiting for a contract to expire, I reckon I would blow up." {SL}

August 3: Submits to Warner Bros. story department revision of Russian and Chinese segments of *Battle Cry*. {BH4}

August 4: Estelle writes of her suspicion that her husband remains with Hawks so that he can continue an affair with Meta Carpenter. {CR2}

August 5: "Second temporary Draft" of *Battle Cry*. {BH4}

August 9: Jill writes to her dear Pappy saying she supposes he had a good time in June Lake (a resort) working with Hawks. {UVA}

August 12: Estelle sends her son, Malcolm, news from home, adding: "My letter seems to be made up of exclamations, which Billy thinks a serious fault, but I do love to emphasise." {MFP}

August 13: Last day on the payroll for *Battle Cry* after the decision not to produce the film. {CR2}

Mid-August: Jack Warner approves leave of absence without pay until November 15. {CR2}

August 16: Turns into Warner Bros. story department 9-page revision of Chinese segment. Signs contract assigning ownership of *Battle Cry* to Warner Brothers. {BH4}

In Oxford, WF works on a film treatment with a $1000 advance from producer William Bacher. {CR2}

August 22: "I called Nannie [Maud Falkner] tonite and she told me Pappy arrived today. I know how happy the house is now," Malcolm Franklin writes to his mother. {CR2}

August 25: W. G. Wallace, Trust Dept, Warner Bros.: "You have requested, and we have agreed, that you may absent yourself from our studio for a period of approximately three (3) months commencing August 14, 1943, with the understanding and agreement, however, that the present term of your said contract with us shall be deemed suspended, both as to services and compensation, during such period of absence, and that we shall have the right or option to extend said contract and the present term thereof, including the terms and conditions thereof . . ."[85] {USC}

September–November: Works on screenplay for William Bacher, "Who?," an early version of *A Fable*. {WFH}

September 30: From Oxford, reports to Ober that he is writing a new work, "a fable, an indictment of war perhaps, and for that reason may not be acceptable now." {SL}

October 30: Reports to Ober that he expects to remain in Oxford until February 15, by which time he will run out of money and "go back into slavery for another 6 plus months."

November 17: Sends Ober 51 pages of his fable. Explains how Bacher and director Henry Hathaway pitched the idea to him and said, "I was the only man to write it . . . in any form I liked: picture, script, play, or novel, any revenue from a play or novel to be mine exclusively." Does not expect to do anything with the property until after his "status with Warner is cleared up." Considers rewriting the piece as a magazine story but also advises Ober to show it to Robert Haas or Bennett Cerf. {SL}

December 2: "I can hardly wait to hear about Pappy killing the deer. Write me all about it & ask him to," Malcolm Franklin writes to his mother. {CR2}

December 21: In New York, Malcolm Franklin misses Christmas at Rowan Oak and comforts himself hearing a "negro basso-baritone who was very good and sang some of Pappy's favorites—Water Boy—among them." {CR2}

1944

January: Fred Woodress, an aspiring writer, visits Rowan Oak and is advised to travel "as much as you can and by getting as much out of life as you can." {CWF}

January 8: Reports to Ober that he has finished the first draft of his fable. {SL}

January 15: Writes to Robert Haas at Random House inquiring about an advance for *A Fable*, which is not forthcoming. In this retelling of the Christ story, in which Christ returns to give humanity "one more chance, will we crucify him again, perhaps for the last time." {SL}

c. February: Malcolm Cowley writes expressing his interest in meeting WF and writing "a long essay" about his "life and aims." {FC}

Works on *God Is My Co-Pilot.* {FF}

February 14: Resumes work at Warner Bros. {WFH}

Meets screenwriter Stephen Longstreet who would later publish an article about their friendship. {CWF}

February 17–24: Works on "God Is My Co-Pilot," notes on Steve Fisher script. {WFH}

February 21–22: A rewrite is due on *To Have and Have Not.* Faulkner is working from Jules Furthman's draft. {B3, CR2, WFH}

March 1: Shooting begins on *To Have and Have Not.* {CR2}

March 19: Signs and dates *Light in August* "For Robert Weil/William Faulkner/Studio."[86] {BH5}

April 2-May 6: Works on revising Jules Furthman's script of *To Have and Have Not.* {WFH}

April 17: Addressed to "Dear Ladies" [Estelle and Jill]: "There have been fierce domestic upheavals in the studio. Warner seems to be in some state of almost female vapors. He fired his main producer, Mr. Wallis, and all Wallis' writers. Two other producers are about to quit. I think Warner has forgotten me. But someday he will look out his window and happen to see me pass, so I may be fired too. None of us know what's going to happen. Half the writers are gone now, and the whole shebang might blow up at anytime." {SL}

April 22: Suspends work on his fable to work on *To Have and Have Not,* in production with script changes every day. "I have been trying to keep ahead of him [Hawks] with a day's script." Expresses mixed feelings about war: "Still too young to be unmoved by the old insidious succubae of trumpets, too old either to make one among them or to be impervious . . . I have a considerable talent, perhaps as good as any coeval. But I am 46 now. So what I will mean soon by 'have' is 'had.'" Hopes to return to writing his fable after he is done with "the frantic striving of motion pictures to justify their existence in a time of strife and terror . . ." {SL}

April 30: Writes to his stepdaughter, Victoria Fielden, about finding an apartment that Jill and Estelle can occupy, "a little cubbyhole but in a quiet convenient *not Hollywood* neighborhood, with no yard, etc. But after several years of Rowan Oak and trees and grounds, maybe Big and Little Miss will enjoy living in a city apartment, with nothing to break the silence but the shriek of brakes and the crash of colliding automobiles, and police car and fire wagon sirens, and the sound of other tenants in the building who are not quite ready to lay down and hush at 1 or 2 a.m." {B3}

May 1: Completes a 118-page script for *To Have and Have Not.* {B3}

May 7: Replies to Malcolm Cowley's letter about writing a WF profile. "I would like the piece, except the biography part." Mentions working the Hollywood "salt mines." {SL, FC}

Completes revisions on script for *To Have and Have Not.* {B3}

May 15: Assigned to *The Damned Don't Cry.* {B3}

May 18: Writes to Ober about producer Jerry Wald, who wants some "Faulkner" in a picture. Hoping to see his fable as a story if he can get clear of any studio claim on it. {SL}

May 22: Malcolm Franklin writes to his mother: "Now that I am becoming mature in my thoughts I realize that he has shaped my character & mode of thinking greatly. He is truly a great man, not because of his writings but because of his knowledge, his kindness and his understanding." {CR2}

May 26: Ober writes that Whit Burnett wants to recommend "Two Soldiers" for a radio series and wants WF to provide a brief explanation of why he liked the story. {SL}

May 29: In response to Ober's May 26 letter, WF writes, "Handle the story as you see fit," and then he adds: "I like it because it portrays a type which I admired—not only a little boy, and I think little boys are all right, but a true American: an independent creature with courage and bottom and heart—a creature which is not vanishing, even though every articulate medium we have—radio, moving pictures, magazines—is busy day and night telling us that it has vanished, has become a sentimental and bragging liar." {SL}

Early June: Completes 79-page treatment of *The Damned Don't Cry*, which the studio does not use. {FF}

June–July: Revises second draft of *The Adventures of Don Juan*, the work of other writers. {WFH}

June 17: Warner Bros. producer Jerry Wald writes a memo to Jack L. Warner enclosing the first draft of the *Don Juan* script. "Last Wednesday I had Bill Faulkner put on to cut and polish the present script. he should complete his work within the next two weeks." {BH2}

June 24: On Jill's 11th birthday, she moves with her mother into an apartment house just off Sunset Boulevard. {B3}

Early July: Works on *The Amazing Dr. Clitterhouse*. {B3}

Estelle writes to her son, Malcolm, about a pleasant meal at Musso & Frank. {MFP}

Estelle writes to Malcolm that WF is happy about having found an apartment in which she can cook his favorite meals. {MFP}

July 3–15: Works on outline of "Fog Over London." {WFH}

July 11: Jerry Wald to Warner Bros. executive Steve Trilling: "Attached is the revised draft on DON JUAN as written by William Faulkner. I don't think it's quite right yet, but nevertheless it's a good script for budgeting." {BH2}

Estelle writes to Malcolm: "Your letters are the very breath of life to me. . . . Billy, Jill, and I read them avidly before I send them home. Bless your heart!" {CR2}

July 12–August 19: Reassigned with A. I. Bezzerides to *Strangers in Our Midst* aka *Escape in the Desert*, a remake of *The Petrified Forest*. {WFH}

July 22: Malcolm Cowley writes to WF giving a "market report" on his "standing as a literary figure." Inquires about WF's use of symbolism. {SL, FC}

August 7–19: Works on *God Is My Co-Pilot* and second treatment of *Fog over London.* {FF, WFH}

August 28: Begins work on *The Big Sleep.* {CR2}

September 7: Estelle and Jill depart on the Southern Pacific for home. {CR2}

September 11: *The Big Sleep*, first draft of script, WF and Leigh Bracket. {HHP}

c. Mid to late September: Estelle, breaking into tears, tells Buzz Bezzerides: "Something went wrong," about her marriage to WF. "I don't know what went wrong. We used to go fishing together. We loved each other." Bezzerides answers, "Nothing is wrong. You know I love you, always have, always will, you know I miss you, stay awake at night, dreaming of you. The only reason I have not written is because the things I want to say to you must be breathed, whispered, how I wish I were there. I would look at you mooneyed, hold your hand, besides I am lazy, negligent, careless, and slightly busy. Forgive me for not writing sooner." {CR2}

September 22: Candace House to Jill: "Your pappy was out and rode Lady Bug the Sunday after you left but hasn't been out since . . ." {MFP}

September 26: *The Big Sleep, Part I* by WF and Leigh Brackett. {HHP}

September 30: Buzz Bezzerides writes to Estelle about WF: "I like the guy, even with his faults, I don't think I'd ever let him down, he gets pretty dependent and helpless. But he is fine now, the picture he is writing is to be shot very soon, and he is feeling tiptop." {CR2}

October 9: Sends Maggie Lea a check for $500 and wants to know what the balance is on the note. He is close to "cleaning up the whole thing." Mentions he is anxious to get home. {RO}

October 10: Candace House to Estelle Faulkner: "Mr. Faulkner was out again Sunday and rode Lady. He said he wished he could hear of race horses shipping East and he'd ship her down to Jill. It's a long way but perhaps something will turn up so he can." {MFP}

October 11: *To Have and Have Not* is released. {AB}

October 29: In consultation with WF, Malcolm Cowley publishes "William Faulkner's Human Comedy" in the *New York Times Book Review*, recounting WF's sensational success with *Sanctuary* and the decline in public interest in his work, most of which is out of print. {CR2}

November: Lee Barker of Doubleday, Doran calls Harold Ober to propose a $5,000 advance for a WF book about the Mississippi River, so that WF could be rescued from Hollywood. {B2}

Howard Hawks purchases the rights to Irina Karlova's novel, *Dreadful Hollow*, and turns the project over to Faulkner. {CR2}

Early November: A long letter to Malcolm Cowley about his piece in the *New York Times Book Review* saying it was "all right . . . I am telling the same story over and over, which is myself and the world." He attributes his long, complex sentences to trying to "say it all in one sentence, between one Cap and one period. . . . I don't know how to do it. All I know to do is keep on trying in a new way. I'm inclined to think that my material, the South, is not very important to me. I just happen to know it, and dont have time in one life to learn another one and write at the same time . . . Though the one I know is probably as good as another, life is a phenomenon but not a novelty, the same frantic steeplechase toward nothing everywhere and man stinks the same stink no matter where in time." Discusses his creation of Quentin Compson and Thomas Sutpen. Compares himself to an old mare that has "only 3 or 4 more in her, and cant afford to spend one on something from outside." Refers obliquely to his fable and says "it's not Yoknapatawpha." {SL, FC}

Assigned to work on an adaptation of an Eric Ambler novel, *Uncommon Danger*, retitled *Background to Danger* and is praised for his magnificent two-week job. {CR2}

November 13–December 12: Assigned to *Mildred Pierce*. {WFH}

November 18: Reworks the original script of *Mildred Pierce*. Does not respond to director Michael Curtiz's detailed comments. {B3}

December?: Writes complete screenplay of *Dreadful Hollow*. {WFH}

December 2: Rewrites parts of *The Big Sleep*. {B3}

December 7: Producer James Geller informs WF his request for a three-month suspension beginning December 13 is granted.

December 12: Visits the stables where Jill rode her horse to say goodbye to Jack House who takes care of Jill's horse.

December 12–15: On the way to Oxford by train, during a stop in New Mexico, makes a few more revisions of *The Big Sleep*. {WFH}

December 15: Final revisions of *The Big Sleep* dated in Oxford with a note to James Geller: "Done by the author in respectful joy and happy admiration after he had gone off salary and while on his way back to Mississippi." {B3, CR2}

December 20: Writes to Ober that he is considering the book on the Mississippi River that is meant to save him from Hollywood. "I am grateful to the blokes who thought of it, very pleased and comforted that such men exist, not just on my account but for the sake of writing, art, and artists, in America and the world." He doubts, however, whether he can do it since it is not his idea and is not the kind of book he set out to write. He is not sure; therefore, he should expend his energy on this outside project unless "I will take fire myself over the idea of such a book . . . I would not insult the men who made the offer possible by taking the money for anything less than my best, if I did that, the whole purpose of the offer would be exploded, as I would still be morally and spiritually in Hollywood. Please express to them my gratitude, and more, my sincerest congratulations and the comfort it gives me, and through me, all writing sincere people, that good writing is not dead and will never be." {SL}

1945

January 10: Writes to Bennett Cerf and Robert Haas about his fable: "I'm doing something different now, so different that I am writing and rewriting, weighing every word, which I never did before; I used to bang on like an apprentice paper hanger and never look back." Expects to need two or three thousand dollars by March and will have to "pot boil or go back to the salt mine" (Hollywood). {SL}

January 11: Malcolm Franklin to his mother: "And then Billy's letter of day before yesterday. That letter made me feel very good. I have received few letters that I have appreciated anymore." {MFP}

January 20: Premiere of *To Have and Have Not* with a writing credit for WF.

January 24: Writes to Ober that he is still considering the Mississippi book but is reluctant to interrupt work on his fable. Completes 64 pages of the novel. {CR2}

January 25: Writes to Joe C. Brown, an African American school teacher, mentioning their talk three years earlier in front of Neilson's store on the Oxford Square and his disappointment that Brown has not sent him his poetry. {SL}

January 29: Writes to Joe C. Brown after his visit to Rowan Oak, enclosing WF's editing of a poem and counseling that his passion has to be kept under control and not spoiled by rhetoric. {SL}

February 2: Malcolm Franklin to his mother: "In your letter of the 24th, the part telling of the beautiful spring-like weather and of your long walks with Billy made me homesick and brought back the beautiful memories of the past." {MFP}

March 8: Writes to producer James Geller at Warner Bros.: "It's been a wet winter here. I've got little done except cleaning ditches, fixing fences, repairing houses, etc. hope to start breaking ground this month to get some early corn planted. Dammit, I wish I could have a different system: be at the studio working Jan.–Feb.–March, be here farming April-May-June, at the studio July-Aug.–Sept., then back here for rest of the year to gather and sell crop." {USC}

March 16: *The Big Sleep*, cutter's script by WF and Leigh Brackett. {HHP}

March 19: Tells Ober he expects to return to Warner Bros. in early June. Hopes to renegotiate his long-term contract into a one-year agreement. "If they had any judgment of people, they would have realized before now that they would get a damn sight more out of me by throwing away any damned written belly-clutching contract and let us work together on simple good faith and decency, like with you and Random House." More work on his fable, paring down 100,000 words to about 15,000. {SL}

Malcolm Franklin to his mother: "I did receive your delightful letter of March 4th and one from Jill of the same date. I was so happy to hear about Jill singing in the choir and you and Billy going to church (I am sure just to see her)." {MFP}

April: *A Rose for Emily and Other Stories* is published in an Armed Services pocket edition with a foreword by Saxe Commins. {LC}

April 14: *The Saturday Review of Literature* publishes "William Faulkner Revisited" by Malcolm Cowley. {CR2}

April 20: Meets with Major Bernard A. Bergman about a tour of combat theaters for a book on air force operations. {B3}

April 21: Wires Ober about meeting with Major Bergman: "INCONCLUSIVE BECAUSE I WAS TIGHT WRITING DETAILS CAN ANYTHING BE DONE AS I WANT THE JOB."[87] {B2}

April 26: Editor Whit Burnett at *Story* offers $25 for "Two Soldiers," provided that that the words "hell" and "[n----r]" are removed from the story.

April 30: Phil Stone writes to Malcolm Cowley saying it is the best article he has read about WF. But Cowley is "all wet about a number of things" and Stone writes a detailed letter of correction. {BH2}

May 6: Lem Oldham, WF's father-in-law, dies of kidney failure.

May 7: *Oxford Eagle* announces the end of war in Europe.

May 16: Finlay McDermid, head of Warner Bros. Story Department, writes to Ed Williamson, manager of the Warner Bros. Exchange in Memphis, asking for help, saying WF has not been able to arrange transportation from Oxford to Los Angeles. {BH2}

McDermid writes to WF to say he is trying to arrange transportation. {BH2}

May 18: Ed Williamson reports to Finlay McDermid that he has assisted WF in confirming his travel plans. {BH2}

May 21: Counters Whit Burnett's offer of $25 for "Two Soldiers," asking for $50 and requesting an asterisk and footnote explaining the deletions of "hell" and "[n----r]," telling Ober: "This may be good for the children in fact. it will be teaching them at an early and tender age to be ever on guard to protect and shield their elders and teachers from certain of the simple facts of life."

May 25: Still on old Hollywood contract, now getting paid $400 a week with six-month raises to $450 and $500. Tells Ober he is rewriting his fable as a novel. {SL}

June 7: Resumes work at Warner Bros. {B3, WFH}

June 8: Warner Bros. Inter-Office memo from Finlay McDermid to Roy J. Obringer: "Please return WILLIAM FAULKNER to payroll as of Thursday June 7th." {BH2}

June 12–16: Completes 17-page story outline of *Stallion Road*. {CR2, WFH}

June 16: Warner Bros. salary raised to $500. {USC}

June 25–July 28: Works on screenplay of *Stallion Road*. {WFH}

June 28: Writes to Estelle's mother, Lida Oldham, comparing the flowers in California and Mississippi. "Everybody has a garden, but they look pretty amateurish: corn too thick, etc., though tomatoes do better. Gardening people miss the Japanese, who used to do all that around private homes. They made a bad mistake not watching their Japanese gardeners and learning something while they had the chance." Mentions missing home and his family in the evenings. {CR2}

June 29: Signs contract assigning ownership of *The De Gaulle Story* to Warner Brothers. {BH3}

Summer: Works off the books for Jean Renoir on *The Southerner* and on spec with Buzz Bezzerides on an adaptation of "Barn Barning," which is shown to Howard Hawks. But no sale. {FF, WFH}

July 5: In a Warner Bros. envelope sends Maggie Lea a check and writes he is well "but wish to hell I was back home." {RO}

July 17: Herndon threatens to sue WF. {CR2}

July 25: Terminates his business relationship with William Herndon as of August 18, 1945. {SL]

July 26: Writes to Ober about his expectation that Herndon will continue to claim commissions on WF's Hollywood work. {SL}

Reports to Estelle that since June 7 he has completed a screenplay, fixed up a picture for Ginger Rogers. Still trying to get rid of Herndon, and spends three hours a day on busses because Bezzerides is not working and driving him to the studio. Recounts his work on *Stallion Road* and two weekends "writing a 50 page story with Bezzerides which we hope to sell to Howard Hawks."[88] He is trying to make "enough money to get the hell out of this place and come back home and fix Missy's room and paint the house and do the other things we need." He is also trying to keep up (by correspondence) with what the farm needs. Expects to write home at least once a week. {SL}

July 28: Completes 134-page script of *Stallion Road*. {WFH}

July 30: Tells Ober that Mr. Obringer at the studio advises WF to wait for Herndon's next move. Goes over the sequence of events that resulted in Herndon's claiming a commission. He is considering leaving Hollywood, although the studio will probably suspend him. {SL}

July 31: Finlay McDermid to Steve Trilling about WF's trouble with William Herndon. Roy Obringer, the studio's attorney, prefers that WF "let things ride until Herndon actually does something and then get his own lawyer. Faulkner may be, I believe, contemplating the idea of taking another walk rather than face the general unpleasantness. Will have to be a little careful in handling him, I imagine, during the next few weeks." {BH2}

August 6: Talks to William Herndon about releasing him from their contract. Herndon claims the contract is worth $21,320 and could be sold to another agent, or WF could pay Herndon $10,000 at the rate of $100 a week. {B3}

August 8: Writes to Ober about Herndon. Working on *Stallion Road,* he concludes "Apart from this Herndon matter, I think I have had about all of Hollywood I can stand. I feel bad, depressed, dreadful sense of wasting time, I imagine most of the symptoms of some kind of blow-up or collapse. I may be able to come back later, but I think I will finish this present job and return home." Regrets that his books have never sold and he does not have "enough sure judgment about trash to be able to write it with 50% success." Realizes that leaving may make it impossible for him to return. {B3}

August 9: Malcolm Cowley reports Viking Press has accepted his proposal to do a *Portable Faulkner.* Wants to consult about what to include in the book. {SL, FC}

August 10: Premiere of *The Southerner* with no credit for WF because of his contractual obligations to Warner Brothers.

August 16: WF responds to Cowley: "By all means let us make a Golden Book of my apocryphal county." Discusses which works to include in the anthology. Includes a map of Yoknapatawpha County. {SL, FC}

Writes to an Oxford friend, Professor A. P. Hudson now teaching in Chapel Hill about a manuscript by Thomas Reed concerning the Confederate State Naval Academy and a love story. Believes the story merits book publication, not a movie treatment. "I don't like this damn place any better than I ever did." {SL}

August 17–September 1: Works on revised screenplay of *Stallion Road.* {WFH}

August 20: To Ober: "I think I have had about all of Hollywood I can stand." {SL}

August 23: Ober promises to work on releasing WF from his Warner Brothers contract. {CR2}

August 24: *Ellery Queen's Mystery Magazine* purchases "An Error in Chemistry" for $300 and enters the story in its contest. {CR2}

August 25: Writes to Estelle about homesickness and how kind the Bezerides family has been to him. Hopes to start for home soon. {SL}

August 31: Finlay McDermid to Steve Trilling: "As you know Faulkner has been a quietly unhappy man during his stay in Hollywood." Points out the relationship with WF has been pleasant, and he has been turning in scripts without complaint, even though "any Hollywood writer" could have done the work. McDermid wants the studio to rewrite WF's contract, giving him more artistic freedom. "I feel if Faulkner could really cut loose on a story in which he was terrifically interested that we might get something pretty spectacular, but it seems a shame to waste one of the country's top novelists on routine melodramas . . ." Trilling writes in pencil on the memo: "Suspend & extend when returns." {BH2}

September 1: Completes a 151-page revised draft of *Stallion Road.* {WFH}

September 8: Clears out his desk at the studio. {B3}

Finlay McDermid writes to Steve Trilling that WF "in a very mild and friendly manner" says he will not sign the "usual extension and suspension papers." He wants to write more fiction. Roy Obringer suggests drawing up a new contract. "It is my feeling that Bill will retire to his native haunts, come what may, unless we can hold out a more tempting bid to him than his present deal offers." {BH2}

September 9: Cowley writes with questions for *The Portable Faulkner.* {SL}

c. September 11: Recommends to Richard Wright the work of Joe Brown, a fellow townsman.

Praises both *Black Boy* and *Native Son*, although the latter as fiction is more powerful than the memoir. {SL}

September 17: Mentions Tom Reed, a screenwriter, to Ober: "He is a good man, an amateur sailor. I've found that any man with an active hobby like sailing or hunting or horses or whiskey is pretty liable to be all right, whether he can write or not." He is going to ask Reed to send a manuscript to Ober. Although the Doubleday offer for a book about the Mississippi River is tempting, he decides that "perhaps the job is not for me. I'll sell myself here to do what I am not sure I can do, but I have too much respect for my ancient and honorable trade (books) to take someone's money without knowing neither of us will be ashamed of the result. I will keep it in mind though." Instructs Ober not to "refuse or accept it either until you have heard from me later." {SL}

Cowley writes from Hemingway's Cuban home with questions about which versions of WF's stories to include in *The Portable Faulkner*. Reports what Hemingway has said about WF. {FC}

September 18: Finlay McDermid informs Roy Obringer of a deal that allows WF to work on his novel [*A Fable*] while on suspension with rights to what he produces belonging to the studio, if the studio exercises its option to purchase the material. {BH2}

McDermid writes to Steve Trilling that the studio has "first refusal on Faulkner's literary material during the remainder of his contract term, which will expire in July, 1950. One advantage of writing a new contract would be the procurement of two additional years of WF's exclusive motion picture services—if any—and an increased feeling of good will." {BH2}

September 19: WF goes off the Warner Bros. payroll. {BH5}

September 20: Goes over with Malcolm Cowley choices for *The Portable Faulkner*. Calls Percy Grimm "the Fascist Galahad who saves the white race by murdering Christmas. I invented him in 1931. I didn't realize until after Hitler got into the newspapers that I had created a Nazi before he did." Comments wryly on Hemingway's marriages and concludes: "Apparently man can be cured of drugs, drink, gambling, biting his nails and picking his nose, but not of marrying." {SL, FC}

September 21: Drives off for home with a horse, "Lady," for Jill and without permission from the studio. {B3}

September 25: Midnight: arrives home for his 48th birthday. {B3}

September 26: Signs copies of Kenneth Roberts's *Rabble in Arms: A Chronicle of Arundel and the Burgoyne Invasion* and *The Lively Lady: A Chronicle of Arundel, of Privateering and of the Circular Prison on Dartmoor.*[89]

Compiles a list of his stories for Harold Ober. Mentions reading "An Error in Chemistry": "Until I had read through the first page, I didn't even recognise it, thought for sure I had finally caught my impersonator." {SL}

September 30: Works with Leigh Bracket on revised temporary screenplay of *The Big Sleep*. {WFH}

October 5: Likes Cowley's suggestion of producing a book of stories with sections on Indians, town life, and so on. Acknowledges his awareness of his European reputation. Mentions a party in which writers, including Christopher Isherwood, were on their heels and knees "in a kind of circle in front of me. I'll have to admit though that I felt more like a decrepit gaffer telling stories than like an old master producing jewels for three junior co-laborers." {SL, FC}

Mid-October: Completes an appendix on the Compson family for Cowley's *Portable Faulkner*. {B3}

October 15: Writes to "Colonel Warner" that he does not want to commit himself to more studio work: "I feel that I have made a bust at moving picture writing and therefore have mis-spent and will continued to mis-spend time which at my age I cannot afford." He notes that everyone at the studio "could not have been pleasanter," and he is relying on Warner's sense of fairness. {SL}

October 18: From Oxford, sends Compson appendix to Cowley, noting, "I should have done this when I wrote the book. Then the whole thing would have fallen into pattern like a jigsaw puzzle when the magician's wand touched it . . . It took me about a week to get Hollywood out of my lungs, but I am still writing all right, I believe . . . Let me know what you think of this. I think it is really pretty good to stand as it is, as a piece without implications. Maybe I am just happy that that damned west coast place has not cheapened my soul as much as I probably believed it was going to do." {SL, FC}

October 22: Jack Warner denies WF's request to end his contract. {CR2}

October 26: With Leigh Brackett completes final screenplay of *The Big Sleep*. {WFH}

October 27: Goes over for Cowley various details in the stories included in *The Portable Faulkner*. Says the Compson appendix is written from "a sort of bloodless bibliophile's point of view. I was a sort of Garter King-at-Arms,[90] heatless, not very moved cleaning up 'Compson' before going on to the next 'C-o' or 'C-r.')" Mentions having underlined a copy of *The Sound and the Fury* in "different color crayons" that Bennett Cerf never sent back. "Maybe they can dig it up." {SL, FC}

October 29: Robert Haas sends WF a watch his daughter Betty has purchased for him. {B2}

October 31: Children gather at Rowan Oak to hear ghost stories. {CR2}

November: Hog killing time. {CR2}

November 2: Writes to Haas from Oxford, declaring, "If Warner really intends to try to starve me into fulfilling the contract, I may be able to make enough stink through publicity over it to free myself." He is concerned that Warner will make a claim on everything he writes. {SL}

Cowley writes about tearing apart WF's books to cut and paste together *The Portable Faulkner* while proposing a few changes to avoid inconsistencies in the presentation of characters from one story to another as well a few cuts. {FC}

November 3: Eugenion Vaquer writes asking permission to publish a translation of "Turn About" in an Italian literary magazine. {B2}

c. November 6: Asks Haas for $125 and thanks him for sending the watch. {SL}

November 7: Cowley receives WF's admission that he never "made a genealogical or chronological chart, perhaps because I knew I would take liberties with both—which I have." Explains the chronology of the Indian stories, noting that "Red Leaves" precedes "A Justice." Endorses Cowley's sequence of stories and promises to resolve some discrepancies. {SL, FC}

November 10: Cowley discusses more changes and corrections, which WF endorses. He tells WF he has suggested to an enthusiastic Robert Linscott at Random House an edition of WF's collected stories. Asks WF to include a map of Yoknapatawpha County in *The Portable Faulkner*. {FC}

November 22: Thanksgiving dinner: roast duck on a silver platter, with a platter of squirrel and dumplings, and then collard greens, cornbread, and butter. Cognac served in the library, in the delicate little glasses. {CR2}

November 23: Beginning of two-week deer hunt. {CR2}

November 26: Robert Haas tells WF to accept the watch he has sent with "best wishes and genuine affection." {B2}

Early December: Returns to writing *A Fable*. {B2}

December 4: To Robert Haas: Mentions returning home from a "two weeks' deer hunt," accepts the gift of the watch with "gratification and pleasure, not just the gift but its commemoration of a long and happy relationship which is to continue for three or four times these fifteen years since we are all still young men yet." Reports he saw seven does and did not shoot them. They "ran every day, fine sport, hell-for-leather on a strong horse through the woods after the dogs, ran one old buck almost fifty miles, from 7 a.m. until the dogs gave out about 3 p.m., came back to camp after dark, leading the horse and striking matches to read the compass. The buck got away, I was glad to know, was shot at three times but he still ran." Announces that Cowley's *Portable Faulkner* is "going to be a good book." {SL}

December 8: Writes to Cowley: "It's not a new work by Faulkner. It's a new work by Cowley, all right though." Provides more detail about Falkner family history, education, but would prefer no biography. Explains adding the u to his name. {SL, FC}

December 12: Sends Robert Haas 65 pages of his fable. "I think it's pretty good and I'd like for Ober to see it. . . . Maybe good enough for me to quit writing books on, though I probably won't quit." {SL}

December 24: Approves of Cowley's introduction to *The Portable Faulkner*. Suggests the following lead: "WHEN the war was over—the other war—William Faulkner, at home again in Oxford, Mississippi, yet at the same time was not at home, or at least not able to accept the postwar world." Prefers "no mention of war experience at all." {SL, FC}

December 25: Signs several Christmas presents: *The Complete Writings of Ralph Waldo Emerson* and Kenneth Roberts's *Captain Caution*. {LC}

Signs a carbon typescript of *The Hamlet* for his godson Philip Alston Stone: "May he be faithful / fortunate and brave /William Faulkner / Xmas 1945/ Oxford, Miss." {LC,. BH1}

Colonel William C. Falkner: Civil War veteran, railroad tycoon, best-selling novelist. Young William said he wanted to be a writer like his great-granddaddy. Illustrations by Evelyn J. Mayton.

William Faulkner's birthplace in New Albany, Mississippi.

Baby William, the oldest of four sons.

The home of Caroline Barr, the family servant and second mother to William and his brothers.

Not yet the great novelist.

Under some duress, he decides to marry his childhood sweetheart, Estelle Oldham, a divorcee.

With Estelle's approval, purchases a run-down antebellum establishment that he works hard to restore and calls Rowan Oak.

Attains his first popular success with *Sanctuary* but does not seem to enjoy the attention or the prospect of becoming a public man.

The enticing Estelle Oldham who returns from life abroad with her first husband to add panache to the Faulkner household.

Caroline Barr took care of Jill in her early years just as she had taken care of Jill's father.

Faulkner liked to get away to Sardis Lake and sail, often with daughter and friends, but sometimes with distinguished visitors such as Eudora Welty.

The adult Jill admitted it had been difficult to live with two parents who drank too much and acted roles that made it difficult to know what they really felt for one another and their daughter.

Andrew Price with Faulkner's horse, Tempy. Faulkner grew up in a livery stable with African American hostlers and enjoyed their company all of his life.

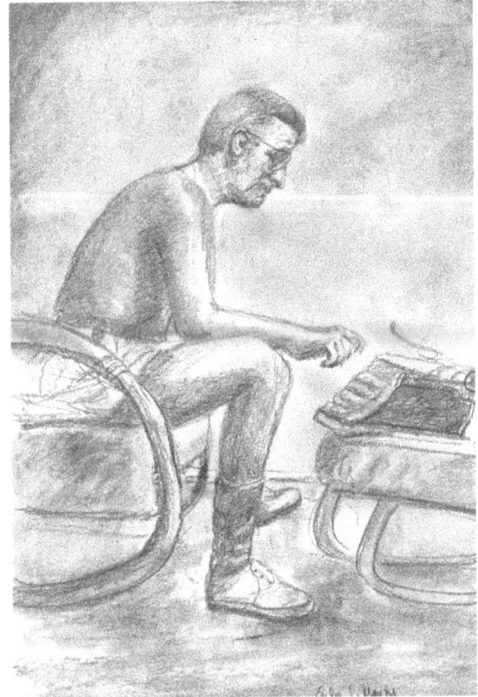

Faulkner spent more than twenty years of his career writing scripts, sometimes in the baking sun, for Hollywood productions that financed the purchase of an airplane, a farm, and all the accoutrements of a landed gentleman.

With the publication of *The Portable Faulkner* in 1946, edited by Malcolm Cowley, Faulkner's career began to revive. Most of his work had been out of print. Faulkner visited Cowley's home in Sherman, Connecticut, while recovering from a drinking episode, and the critic took the novelist on a restorative drive. Photograph courtesy of Susan Locke.

Faulkner hated to answer the telephone, even when the call came to Rowan Oak announcing that he had won the Nobel Prize.

Faulkner, the owner of Greenfield Farm, often liked to think of himself as a farmer, not a writer, as many reporters learned when they tried to talk to him about his writing.

An older Faulkner, as many people saw him in and around Oxford, in the square talking to the townspeople.

Evelyn
21,18

1946

Writes 36-page treatment, *One Way to Catch a Horse*. {FF}

Early January: Reiterates to Cowley his "hope for no biography. . . . I'm old-fashioned and probably a little mad too; I dont like having my private life and affairs available to just any and everyone who has the price of the vehicle it's printed in . . . I'll be glad to give you all the dope when we talk together. Some of it's very funny. I just dont like it in print except when I use it myself . . . I don't see much Southern legend in it." Attributes his rhetoric to "Oratory out of Solitude." Comments on the role of writing and oratory in Southern history, why the South and not the North produced literature about the war. Speculates about the future of Southern literature. {SL, FC}

January 5: Goes over contractual commitments with Ober. Comments on his check for winning a magazine contest prize: "What a commentary. In France, I am the father of a literary movement. In Europe I am considered the best modern American and among the first of all writers. In America, I eke out a hack's motion picture wages by winning second prize in a manufactured mystery story contest." Recommends *The Portable Faulkner*: "Malcolm Cowley has done a fine job in Spoonrivering my apocryphal county." {SL}

January 16: Mentions to Robert Haas his "satisfaction of owning and using" the chronometer, a "first rate instrument, even though at present its main purpose is to notify me when to drive in to the village and fetch my daughter from school. I am also using it to clock a new mare, a pretty fast quarter horse. I brought her from California last fall." Mentions a Walter Winchell report that he is having a nervous breakdown "in expensive privacy. It's nice to be rich, even if only on the air waves." {SL}

January 18: Warner Brothers memo from Don Moore to Finlay McDermid noting WF's illness is exaggerated. His publisher is said to marvel "at how well he feels in view of this reported New York nervous breakdown." {BH2}

January 21: Still fretting with Cowley over the description of WF's war service. Wants only this statement: "Was a member of the RAF in 1918." Expresses his skepticism about a friend of Cowley's decision to farm. "I hope he's rich; he'll need to be. . . . If he really wants a farm, I'll sell him mine, including 4 span of mules and 11 head of [n----rs]." {SL, FC}

January 24: Finlay McDermid writes to WF that he has tried to relieve the writer of his agent, Herndon, "but am sorry to report that I got nowhere." {BH2}

January 29: Writes to McDermid thanking him for trying to deal with Herndon: "It's a curious situation to me. It's like having a woman fasten onto you for alimony for the rest of your life: not like a man." {USC}

February 1: Reiterates to Cowley that he does not want his war service to make him out to be a hero but continues the fiction that he had a cockpit malfunction in a crash. {SL, FC}

February 4: Informs Robert Linscott at Random House that the appendix on the Compsons should be included in the Modern Library edition of *The Sound and the Fury* and *As I Lay Dying*. He does not want to write an introduction. {SL}

Signs a first edition of *The Hamlet* "To Phil Stone / from Bill."[91] {BH1}

Roy Obringer of Warner Bros. writes to WF denying his request to be released from his contract. {USC}

February 5: Asks Cowley to forward a copy of the Compson appendix to Robert Linscott at Random House. "Damn to hell, I have never yet been able to afford a secretary; I never missed one much until these last few years. Now I dont know where about half of what I have is, nor even (at times) whether I ever wrote it or not." {SL, FC}

February 18: Reports to Robert Haas that Jack Warner claims he owns everything WF writes. Out of money again and considering a return to Hollywood. {SL}

To Harold Ober about "Afternoon of a Cow" translated by Maurice Coindreau: "If he says I authorized this through him, I will accept his statement." {SL}

To Cowley: "You cant stand a fact up, you've got to prop it up, and when you move to one side a little and look at it from that angle, it's not thick enough to cast a shadow in that direction." Declines to write an introduction to *The Portable Faulkner*. He does not mind the remaining inconsistencies and won't read *The Sound and the Fury* again to square it with the appendix. {FC}

February 23: Tells Ober he is broke and has to go back on Warner's salary in March. Trouble finding a place near the studio unless the studio can help. "They probably wont; they have never yet done anything for me." {SL}

Writes to Finlay McDermid at Warner for help in locating a place to live. {USC}

c. February 24: Complains the studio never made good on its promise to offer him a better contract. "My only hope is to get fired." {SL}

February 28: Tells Ober he acquiesces in publication of "Turn About" in an Italian literary magazine. Mentions working with screenwriter Tom Reed on a treatment for a light comedy, "Continuous Performance." {SL, WFH}

March 2: Swedish writer Thorsten Jonsson, WF's Swedish translator, arrives at Rowan Oak and predicts he will win a Nobel Prize. {CR2}

March 4: Finlay McDermid writes that to his surprise he has been able to arrange accommodations close to the studio." {BH2}

March 13: Tells Linscott the appendix is the key to *The Sound and the Fury*. Dislikes the pairing of *The Sound and the Fury* and *As I Lay Dying*: "It's as though we were saying 'This is a versatile guy; he can write the same stream of consciousness style about princes and then peasants,' our 'This is a universal river; he has written about all the kinds of people in Miss. in the same style.'" {SL}

March 16: Signs and dates in Oxford Mississippi the third printing of the first edition of *The Sound and the Fury*: "To Malcolm Cowley / Who beat me to what / was to have been the / leisurely pleasures of my / old age." {BH1}

March 20: Asks for Haas's help in repairing his chronometer. Considers returning to Hollywood, staying away from Warner, and earning "some money under the nose." {SL}

Signs and dates in Oxford first French edition of Sartoris: "To Malcolm Franklin" and first British edition of *The Hamlet*: "To my son, / Malcolm Franklin: and first British edition of *As I Lay Dying*: "For my son, Malcolm Franklin." {BH1}

March 22: Writes to Robert Linscott opposing the idea of Hemingway writing a preface to the Modern Library pairing of *The Sound and the Fury* and *As I Lay Dying*: "It's like asking one race horse in the middle of a race to broadcast a blurb on another horse in the same running field . . . This sort of mutual back-scratching reduces novelists and poets to the status of a kind of eunuch-capon pampered creatures in some spiritual Vanderbilt stables, mindless, possessing nothing save the ability and willingness to run their hearts out at the drop of Vanderbilt's hat." {SL}

Writes to Ober contemplating a return to Hollywood, perhaps to work out something with William Bacher who has the film rights to the fable. {SL}

March 24: Tells Haas the fable cannot be completed in the next three months, which is why he has to return to Hollywood. {SL}

March 26: Ober sends part of *A Fable* to Warner Brothers asking permission for WF to stay home and complete the novel. {SL}

March 28: Ober is told Jack Warner grants WF's request to stay home and complete his novel and makes no claim to the film rights of "Who?" (An early script draft of the fable). {SL}

March 30: Reports to Robert Haas that he has resumed work on his fable while trying to sell some pot-boiling fiction. Asks for $1000 now and $500 on May 1 and June 1. Prefers to have the Compson appendix serve as an introduction to the Modern Library edition of *The Sound and the Fury* and *As I Lay Dying*. {SL}

April 2: R. J. Obringer of Warner Brothers writes to confirm the studio has no claim on WF's novel and that he will need to return to the studio as soon as the novel is completed. He requests WF's signature on this agreement. {SL}

April 3: Finlay McDermid writes to Harold Ober about WF's tangled business relationship with agent William Herndon. Explains the terms of the Warner Brothers contract, his uncertainty about WF's intentions, and his hope that Ober can clarify WF's "writing plans. You may rest assured that I have Bill's welfare in mind and will do whatever I can to make his Warner contract as small a burden as possible. If he'll only co-operate!" {BH2}

April 13: McDermid writes to Jacob Wilk in the legal department at Warner Bros., about a letter of agreement granting WF time to complete a novel and waiving the studio's claim to the work. "I have periodically tried to get approval for a complete rewriting—or even abandoning—the Faulkner contract. So far, however, I have had no success . . ." {BH2}

April 15: McDermid communicates to Wilk that Ober "feel positive that everything will be worked out satisfactorily." {BH2}

April 18: Harold Ober receives WF's letter with Obringer's request for signature on an agreement to return after a fable is finished. But WF estimates he won't be able to finish his work for two years, "as this is going to be a lot of book something new for me, really not a novel." {SL}

April 19: Ilya Ehrenburg and other Russian writers arrive and try to arrange a meeting with WF. {CR2}

April 23: Congratulates Cowley on *The Portable Faulkner*: "The job is splendid. Damn you to hell anyway. But even if I had beat you to the idea, mine wouldn't have been this good. By God, I didn't know myself what I had tried to do, and how much I have succeeded." Mentions that Random House and Ober have succeeded in getting Warner to let him stay home to work on "what seems to me to be my magnum o." {SL, FC}

April 29: Viking Press publishes *The Portable Faulkner*. Signed copy for Malcolm Cowley: "To Malcolm Cowley, Who beat me to what was to have been the leisurely pleasure of my old age." {CR2}

May 5: Caroline Gordon reviews *The Portable Faulkner* on the front page of the *New York Times Book Review*. {WFC}

Includes a "batch" of his fable in letter to Robert Haas, calling it "a big book." Still planning to return to the studio before he can complete the book. "It's not a novel at all. I think it's more than just a fable." Still trying to write a preface to the paired edition of *The Sound and the Fury* and *As I Lay Dying* to please Linscott, but "I'm not a preface man." {SL}

c. May: Sends Robert Linscott a brief introduction note to Compson appendix. Compares his earlier accounts of the family to the "first moving picture projector—warped lens, poor lighting, undependable mechanism and even a bad screen—which had to wait until 1946 for the lens to clear, the light to steady, the gears to run smooth." {ESPL}

Early May: Completes more work on *A Fable*. {CR2}

May 5: Sends Robert Haas a "batch" of new pages of his work in progress: "The central idea has not changed, it just has more in it that I knew at first." {SL}

May 12: *Nashville Tennessean* reviews *The Portable Faulkner*: "an original approach." {CR2}

May 17: Asked again about an Ehrenburg visit, WF agrees to an hour meeting, but that is rejected by Ehrenburg, who wants to spend two days in Oxford. {CR2}

In a letter to Cowley, complains about visitors who take up his time. "I swear to Christ being in Hollywood was better than this where nobody knew me or cared a damn." {FC, SL}

May 22: Robert Linscott reports to WF that they have found his original introduction to *The Sound and the Fury* written in August 1933. {B2}

Late May: Calls the August 1933 introduction to *The Sound and the Fury* "smug false sentimental windy shit" in a letter to Linscott. "I will return the money for it, I would be willing to return double the amount for the chance of getting it out of danger and destroyed." Mentions he is "hot" with his new book now and will try to take a day off to write an introduction to the Modern Library edition of *The Sound and the Fury* and *As I Lay Dying* "if you can wait that long." {SL}

In another letter to Linscott about the efforts to get *The Sound and the Fury* published, concluding "To me, the book is its own prologue epilogue introduction preface argument and all. I doubt if any writing bloke can take seriously this or any other manifestation of the literary criticism trade." {SL}

Late May or early June: To Malcolm Cowley: "I am for no introduction at all." {FC, SL}

June: *Ellery Queen's Mystery Magazine* publishes "An Error in Chemistry."

June 3: Linscott finally agrees to no introduction. {SL}

Writes to Robert Haas that he believes the fable is "not just my best but perhaps the best of my time. . . . I see a rosy future for this book, meaning it may sell, it will be a War and Peace close enough to home, our times, language, for Americans to really buy it." {SL}

Haas replies agreeing to Faulkner's proposal that he receive $500 per month. {SL}

June 7, 7:00 p.m.: Madeleine Simons shows up at Rowan Oak's front door. She is invited in, and WF discusses his work, including *Absalom, Absalom!* and *The Hamlet*. {CR2, CCP}

June 23: The *Chicago Sun* publishes Sidney Landfield's encounter with WF in Oxford, who prefers to talk about farming, not writing, although he mentions he can write "most everywhere." {CWF}

June 24: Recommends to Harold Ober a book by Emily Whitehurst Stone (Phil Stone's wife), adding, "I haven't seen it. I have known her husband many years, have confidence in his judgement about books, I mean literary." Reports significant progress on his fable. {SL}

July: Ober sells screen right to "Death Drag" and "Honor" for a total of $6600.

July 3: Ober receives some pages of the fable that might interest a literary quarterly, WF suggests. {SL}

July 25: Thanks editor Lambert Davis at Harcourt, Brace for sending a copy of Robert Penn Warren's novel *All the King's Men*. "The Cass Mastern story is a beautiful and moving piece. That was his novel. The rest of it I would throw away. The Stark thing is good solid sound writing but for my money Stark and the rest of them are second rate. the others couldn't be bigger than he, the hero, and he to me is second rate . . . He was neither big enough or bad enough. . . . He should have taken the Cass story and made a novel. Though maybe no man 75 years from that time could have sustained that for novel length." {SL}

July 27: Edmund Wilson reviews *The Portable Faulkner* in the *New Yorker*: "a new kind of Faulkner book . . . a real contribution to the study of Faulkner's work." {CR2}

End of July: Ober receives 178 pages of *A Fable*. {SL}

RKO buys rights to "Two Soldiers" for $3,750. {B2}

Early August: Ober now has close to 200 pages of *A Fable*. {SL}

August 2: Explains to Ober that powerful Hollywood agent Charles Feldman, is attempting to extract Faulkner from his Warner Bros. contract and from William Herndon. Assures Ober that he has final say on all other contracts dealing with Faulkner's writing. {SL}

August 6: Ober writes cautioning Faulkner not to sign Herndon's Famous Artist's Agency contract. Ober says he will contact Feldman. {SL}

August 8: Tells Ober that Feldman is expecting to hear from him. Projects he will finish his fable by January 1. Includes more of his fable for Ober. {SL}

c. Mid-August: Thanks Robert Haas for sending the monthly $500 check. Disappointed that no movie rights have been purchased for his stories. Mentions he will be harvesting crops until November but will continue work on his fable. Hasn't been to New York: "I've been buried six years now." {SL}

August 15: Publishes letter, "His Name Was Pete," in *Oxford Eagle* describing Jill's dog run over by a motorcar. {ESPL}

August 21: Maggie Lea receives another check for $100. "I have hopes of sending in a more substantial one soon. We are all well, and send our best to your family. Your friend, William Faulkner." {RO}

August 26: Robert Penn Warren's review of *The Portable Faulkner* in the *New Republic*, cautioning: "no writer is more deeply committed to a locality than Faulkner, [but] the emphasis on the southern elements may blind us to other elements, or at least other applications of deep significance" WF's fiction constituted a "legend of our general plight and problem. The modern world is in moral confusion. It does suffer from a lack of discipline, of sanctions, of community, of values, of a sense of a mission." {CR2}

August 31: Premiere of *The Big Sleep*, with a writing credit for WF.

October: *The American Mercury* publishes "Honor."

Early October: Nearly 250 pages of *A Fable* completed. Tells Ober he is surprised to get an army sergeant's request for a copy of *Sanctuary* and wants the agent to send him one. "Though god knows what he wants with a book. Should think a 10 cent address book for girls' telephone numbers would be his meat." {SL}

November 2: LSU Tigers play Ole Miss in Baton Rouge. WF shows up at the Sigma Alpha Epsilon Fraternity "in his cups" and sleeps in a room used by women guests at fraternity dances. The next morning, he reports that "when he arrived the seat on the toilet was up and that this would cause a scandal on the campus if it got out."[92] {CCP}

November 10: Mentions to Robert Haas that he is working on an unnamed movie script off the books that Warner Bro. does not know about.[93] {SL}

November 18: Tells Ober about the unnamed movie script he is still working on. He has put aside work on his novel (fable) but will return to it as soon as the script is finished. {SL}

November 26: In hunting camp. {B2}

November 28: In Oxford, signs and dates first edition of *The Portable Faulkner* to "Vance Carter Broach / from his cousin." {BH1}

December: Malcolm Cowley asks WF to contribute to the Chinese Writers' Association.

WF replies: "Will see about it." Recounts how a beautiful stag eluded him. "It's a dull life here. I need some new people, above all probably a new young woman." Anticipating a return to Hollywood. "At 30 you become aware suddenly that you have become a slave of vast and growing mass of inanimate junk, possessions; you dont dare look at any of it too closely because you'll have to admit there is not one piece of it you really want. But you bear it for the next eighteen years because you still believe you will escape from it someday. Then one day you are almost 50 and you know you never will." {SL, FC}

December 5: Informs Ober he has finished his screenplay job and is back at work on his novel (fable). {SL}

December 8: Tells Haas he is still working on his novel (fable) and thinks he might have to return to Hollywood in January. Describes the "beautiful sight" of a stag "running too fast. . . . I'm glad now got away from me though I would have liked his head." {SL}

December 13: Ober writes to reiterate that Warner Bros. has said he can stay home until he finishes his novel. The agent confirms the film rights for "Death Drag" and "Honor" have been sold. {BH1}

December 20: Publication of Modern Library edition of *The Sound and the Fury* and *As I Lay Dying*, with the Compson appendix as an introduction.

December 30: Encloses Ober's commission, saying "I got 35 hundred . . . Here is yours."[94] {SL}

1947

Late January: Ober now has 275 pages of *A Fable.* {SL}

January 25: Settles up with Maggie Lea with his final payment. "This concludes the matter. In a way, I am a little sorry to sever at last even this slight thread with the memory of one for whom I could have felt no more warmth and admiration if I had been kin in blood." Expresses his wish to call on her again "for the pleasure of seeing you again." {RO}

January 27: Ober receives a letter from WF approving the publication of "Afternoon of a Cow" in *Furioso.* {SL}

February 13: *Oxford Eagle* publishes Faulkner's inscription on the monument to Lafayette County's World War II dead: "THEY HELD NOT THEIRS, BUT ALL MEN'S LIBERTY." {ESPL}

February 25: Mentions to Ober "Afternoon of a Cow" as funny. "I suppose I tried it out on the wrong people." {SL}

March 13: Letter to the *Oxford Eagle*: "Bravo your piece about the preservation of the courthouse." {ESPL}

March 24: Sends Ober revised pages of his novel (fable). "I dont write as fast as I used to. It will take another year, probably two. . . . do you have any trouble keeping Warner off me?" {SL}

c. March 24: Reports to Robert Haas that he now has "300 correct pages" of his novel. Expecting to come to New York in a month or so to go over the new work. "If the book can be accepted as a fable, which it is to me, the locale and contents wont matter." {SL}

March 25: Tells Ober he is rewriting his novel because the "course of my present story pays off too fast." {SL}

c. March 31: Reports to Haas that Ober expects no trouble from Warner Bros. while WF works on his novel. {SL}

April 14–17: Speaks to six classes at the University of Mississippi. A student, Gene Roper Jr. describes WF's appearance, his opinions of his contemporaries and other writers as well as comments on his own work. {CWF}

Later, Lavon Rascoe publishes in *Western Review* a transcript of the question-and-answer session on April 16, and A. Wigfall Green and Rich M. Allen provide their account of Faulkner's Ole Miss visit. {B3, LG, CWF, CR2}

April 24: To Ober: "I have just found another serious bug in the ms. No wonder nobody seems to have any definite idea about it. Seems to have taken me longer than I imagined to get movie scripting out of my reflexes." {SL}

Spring: "I am a little stale; I would like to come up East for a week or so. If mss goes all right through summer, I will come up then."

May 11: *New York Herald Tribune* reports on WF's appearances in Ole Miss classes, quoting him as saying Hemingway had no courage. {CR2}

May 12: Writes to Ole Miss English Department chairman W. Alton Bryant objecting to the press release issued by the Director of Public Relations: "I just hate like hell to be jumbled head over heels in to the high-pressure ballyhoo which even universities now believe they must employ: the damned eternal American BUY! BUY!! BUY!!! 'Try us first, our campus covers ONE WHOLE SQUARE MILE, you can see our water tank from twelve miles away, our football team almost beat A & M., we have WM FAULKNER at 6 (count them: 6 English classes.' That sort of thing I will resist with my last breath." {SL}

May 24: Obringer writes to McDermid noting the date, June 14: "exercise option" for 52 weeks, with 12 vacation weeks, with a raise from $500 to $600 a week. {BH2}

June 2: McDermid to Steve Trilling about Warner's contract option: "My personal inclination would be to let the option lapse, since I would be extremely surprised if FAULKNER showed up on the scene again." {BH2}[95]

June 9: Asks Ober if he wants to look at the work of writers who sent pleas to WF about getting published. On the novel: "It's getting right now. It was a tragedy of ideas, morals, before; now it's getting to be a tragedy of people." {SL}

June 24: Warner Bros. option picked up for 52 weeks at $600. {USC}

June 28: Responds to General C. T. Lanham's letter on behalf of Ernest Hemingway in response to WF's claim that Hemingway lacked courage. WF points out he made no "reference whatever to Hemingway as a man: only to his craftsmanship as a writer. I know of his record in two wars and in Spain, too." Explains the background of his remarks at the University of Mississippi. "A copy of this goes to Hemingway, with a covering note. Whatever other chances I have to correct it, I shall certainly take."

WF's covering note to Hemingway: "I'm sorry of this damn stupid thing. I was just making $250.00, I thought informally, not for publication, or I would have insisted on looking at the stuff before it was released. I have believed for years that the human voice has caused all human ills and I thought I had broken myself of talking. Maybe this will be my valedictory lesson." He hopes it "won't matter to a man like you," but concludes "please accept another squirm from yours truly." {SL}

July: Buzz Bezzerides visits WF at Rowan Oak. {CR2}

July 13: "The book is going all right, but slow," WF writes Ober. Still concerned about going back to Warner Bros. in view of what he owes on his taxes. With 400 pages completed, he estimates his novel will run to at least a 1000. {SL}

July 18: Tells Ober he has turned over the matter of his taxes to a specialist in movie writers' taxes on the advice of Buzz Bezzerides. Suggests that perhaps Warner could be diverted from his claims on WF's time by suggesting WF is in demand elsewhere in Hollywood. {SL}

Summer: *Furioso* publishes "Afternoon of a Cow."

August: More work on *A Fable*. {B2}

August 24: Tells Haas he is slowly progressing on his ms. Mentions a new chapter about "a white man and an old Negro preacher and the preacher's 14-year-old grandson who stole a crippled racehorse and healed its broken leg and spent a year dodging from one back country track to the next racing the horse before the police ever caught them, then the white men shot the horse . . . They did it not to win money . . . The thieves knew that what the horse wanted to do was to run races: a champion: a giant among horses."

September 4: Tells Robert Haas about the complications of trying to order a pipe and getting sent the wrong one: "That's a symptom of what's wrong with this country. People have to make too many pipes to sell to too many people to pay too much tax to support too much government which we really can no longer afford: to pay for which people have to make too many pipes to sell to too many people, etc." Regarding *A Fable*, "perhaps the last book I'll write." {SL}

September 21: Finally gets the right pipe via Robert Haas. Considering again "another Hollywood hitch" since the novel is not finished and perhaps at 500 pages could even be published as an incomplete work. {SL}

October: Works on screenplay of "The Shadow." {WFH}

October 3: Proposes to Haas that *A Fable* could be published in incomplete form the same way the "old Dial I think printed some of *Ulysses*."[96] Still uncertain about how much longer it will take the complete the work.

"I seem to write so slowly now that it alarms me sometimes: now and then I think the stuff is no good, which is the reason it takes so long. Yet I wont stop it; when I stand off a moment and bring to mind the whole pattern, I have no trouble in believing in it." Household chores and lack of servants because of GI money have slowed him down. He is also concerned about estimated taxes.

October 5: Tells Ober he no longer wants to try to change the Warner Bros. contract or seek a new one. He will just serve his time and get out when he can. {SL}

October 14: Replies to Haas who says forget worrying about Hollywood and that Random House will continues its financial support, including $900 for 1944 income tax and another $1500 when needed. They can talk it over in New York. WF feels uncomfortable about taking money from Random House for a book he has not finished. "Then I think of Hollywood; that after all, I can go back there and get out of arrears again. Maybe I need to know that is out; i.e. instead of a bale of hay in the safe distance ahead of him maybe what the mule needs is a stick behind him. I dont know why I keep on freezing and stewing this way. You wrote me years ago not to worry about the money but to write the book; I dont know why I cant remember it." {SL}

October 18: Confides in Robert Haas his concerns about *A Fable*: "I believe it is a tremendous idea; some of the trouble I seem to have getting it written to suit me is because of its size and (myself) being so close to it all the time. It's like standing close to an elephant; after a while you cant see the elephant anymore at all." {SL}

October 30: Explains to Ober a key passage in the horse thief section of *A Fable*: "The lawyer begins a political speech, the sort of thing which has held American crowds for a hundred years, full of rhetoric and meaning nothing. But as soon as the crowd realizes what it is, they rise up and . . . just push him out of the way and overtake the turnkey and the Negro and set the Negro free . . ." Still worried about money: "My trouble is simply, I dont want to be broke in my old age when I cant earn anything more, as so many artists do at the end of their lives. I dont save anything much in Hollywood but at least I dont spend now what Random House will advance me."

November 14: Still expressing to Ober the hope that a magazine will publish an excerpt from *A Fable*. {SL}

November 26: *Partisan Review* requests significant cuts to "Notes on a Horsethief." {B3}

November 28: Wires Ober that *Partisan Review* can edit but not rewrite "Notes on a Horsethief." {SL} Writes to Ober suggesting where to cut the story for *Partisan Review*. {SL}

In Oxford, signs and dates a first edition of *Sanctuary* to "Aunt Bama / with love" a first edition of *Go Down, Moses, and Other Stories* "For Aunt Bama / with love." Also signs and dates a first edition of *A Green Bough*: "For Aunt Bama / with love / William / not through mistake but affection, / besides she owns us both anyway / to Cousin Vance Carter Broach / From Cousin William Faulkner." Signs and dates Modern Library edition of *The Sound and the Fury*: "For Vance Carter Broach / from his cousin." {BH1}

December 5: Asks Ober if *Partisan Review* found his story dull. Asks Ober's opinion: "Dull? Too prolix? Diffuse?" Suggests that perhaps the magazine does not exist that will print such a work any more than Joyce's *Ulysses* could now appear in a journal. Describes himself as a man "crouching in a Mississippi hole trying to shape into some form of art his summation and conception of the human heart and spirit in terms of the cerebral, the simple imagination, is as out of place and in the way as a man trying to make an Egyptian water wheel in the middle of the Bessemer foundry would be. . . . There is nothing wrong with the book as it will be, only it may be 50 years before the world can stop to read it. It's too long, too deliberate." {SL}

December 23: Works on programs for Jill's tea dance. {B2}

Ober now has 500 pages of *A Fable*. {SL}

1948

Untitled science fiction scenario (2 pages). {FF}

January: Working on a houseboat with his friends. {B3}

January 15: Puts *A Fable* aside to begin work on *Intruder in the Dust*. {B3}

February 1: Describes work on *Intruder in the Dust* to Ober: "a Negro in jail accused of murder and waiting for the white folks to drag him out and pour gasoline over him and set him on fire, is the detective, solves the crimes because he goddam has to to keep from being lynched, by asking people to go somewhere and look at something and then come back and tell him what they found." The theme of this "mystery-murder" is the "relationship between Negro and white, specifically or rather the premise being that the white people in the south, before the North or the govt. or anyone else, owe and must pay a responsibility to the Negro." {SL}

February 22: Reports to Robert Haas about rewriting *Intruder in the Dust*. Involved in a dispute with the government about his income tax. {SL}

c. February 22: Responds to H. L. Mencken who asks for copies of WF's novels for a German professor preparing a seminar at the University of Berlin. He has forwarded Mencken's request to Random House. "I am looking forward to the new *American Language Supplement*. It's good reading, like

Swift or Sterne. You and they seem to have the same problem: there are just too goddam many of the human race and they talk too much." {SL}

March 1: A legal expert is working on his tax problems, WF tells Haas, adding that he is going to let Hodding Carter at Levee Press publish the horse thief section from *A Fable.* Faulkner will receive 25 percent of the $2.50 per copy sale. {SL}

March 15: To Robert Haas: *Intruder in the Dust* will "certainly be ready" for fall publication. Expects a June 1 delivery, but observes: "I seem to write so much slower, have to do so much more rewriting before sentences come exactly right than I used to, that I am a little afraid to commit myself." Not sure about the title, what word should go with the phrase "in the dust": "shenanigan, skullduggery, jugglers"? {SL}

March 16: Haas suggests Imposture in the Dust, or Masquerade, Stratagem, Pattern, Cabal. {SL}

c. March 21: WF suggests more possibilities: Imposter in the Dust, Sleeper in the Dust, Malfeasance in the Dust, Substitution in the Dust, Malaprop in the Dust, Malpractice in the Dust, Trouble in the Dust but rejects them all as either too long or too esoteric and notes he still likes Intruder in the Dust. {SL}

April 7: Signals his approval of proposed short story collection and will go over Haas's list of stories. Almost done with *Intruder in the Dust,* which has proven longer than the novella he originally planned. {SL}

April 20: Finishes *Intruder in the Dust.* Still not absolutely certain about the title, he tells Haas. "Please think again, ask Saxe, Don, Bennett, anyone." The novel began as a "150 page whodunit but jumped the traces, strikes me as being a pretty good study of a 16 year old boy who overnight became a man." {SL}

c. April 27: Describes *Intruder in the Dust* to Harold Ober as "a mystery story plus a little sociology and psychology." Provides instructions on how to excerpt the novel for magazine publication. "This paring, editing, as you see, will leave it a simple story of movement." {SL}

April 28: Hoping *Intruder in the Dust* has a magazine sale, WF tells Haas, noting he will not get back *A Fable* until he is done with planting and farming "about July 4th, though I shall work at it from time to time." {SL}

May: *The Magazine of the Year* publishes Roark Bradford's profile reporting WF's political views, aversion to publicity, an account of his home and family, the nature of Oxford and Ole Miss, legends of Faulkner's drinking, his time in Hollywood, and the writer's work in progress. {CWF}

May 2: Tells Ober to make sure *The Sewanee Review* changes the name of Calicoat to Hogganbeck in "A Courtship." "I wrote that story before I had my Yoknapatawpha genealogy straightened out. The steamboat pilot, David Hogganbeck, was the grandfather of the hunter, Boon Hogganbeck, in GO DOWN MOSES." {SL}

c. May 5: Explains to Bennett Cerf why "BEAT FOUR" cannot work as a replacement title for *Intruder in the Dust*. Returns to *Intruder* as the best word in the title. {SL}

c. May 8: More income tax troubles. Asks Bennett Cerf for $375. "I would like to come up this fall, haven't seen anybody to talk to in 8 years now. I will have to borrow money to come on though, unless a studio buys the book." {SL}

May 12: Ober receives a 26-page story titled "Lucas Beauchamp." {B3}

May 18: Discusses letting Warner Bros. bid first on film rights to *Intruder in the Dust* first because the studio was "amicable" about his leaves of absence. If they refuse, then show it to James Cagney's independent production company. {SL}

Late spring: Puts in brasswork and mahogany paneling for houseboat. {B2}

June: Completes two pages of screenplay outline, "Morningstar." {WFH}

June 1: Albert Erskine joins Random House as Saxe Commins's assistant and supervises the typesetting of *Intruder in the Dust*. {B2}

June 8: Warner Bros. option picked up for 52 weeks at $750. {USC}

June 18: *Intruder in the Dust* finishes printing.

June 29: One page of an untitled treatment for a science fiction film with a letter to Howard Hawks. {LC}

July 11: MGM acquires screen rights to *Intruder in the Dust* for $50,000, 20 percent of which goes to Random House. {CR2}

c. July 13: Suggests to Bennett Cerf a few changes in *Intruder in the Dust*. Pleased with the film sale to MGM. {SL}

July 16: "Will see you this fall I think," WF writes to Ober. "I want to come up and consult you and Bob both about what to do with this money so my friends and kinfolks dont or cant borrow and spend it." {SL}

Tells Malcolm Cowley he will turn down an invitation to talk at Yale: "I don't think I know anything worth 200 dollars worth talking about but I hope to be up East this fall though I still dont believe I will know anything to talk about worth 200 dollars so I would probably settle for a bottle of good whisky." {SL, FC}

August: Tells Robert Haas about sailing a houseboat on Sardis Resevoir with his friends. "I supervised the launching and since have been busy helping them learn to sail a biggish craft, set out two cans to moor between, marked channels, etc., getting her shaken down. {SL}

August 15: Dedicates the houseboat he has made with his friends: "Out of Confusion by Boundless Hope: Conceived in a Canadian Club bottle She was born a.d. 15th August 1947 by uproarious Caesarian Section in prone position with her bottom upward in [Colonel Hugh]'s back yard eleven miles from the nearest water deeper than a half inch kitchen tap and waxed and grew daily there beneath the whole town's enrapt cynosure." {CR2}

August 16: Signs movie contract for *Intruder in the Dust.* Hopes to settle matters with the IRS now that his novel has been sold to the movies. Asks Haas if he can "count on you for the money, in case MGM check not yet in?" {SL}

Writes to Emmanuel Harper at Random House: "I think we all did mighty well on this book. I have not read the contract, since your legal staff has checked it and I couldn't make head nor tail of it anyway; too much verbiage for me." {SL}

c. September 12: Reports to Robert Haas that he is going on September 15 to New Orleans with a lawyer to "argue with the income tax people about 1944 additional assessment." He may need more money, as much as $2000. Had to purchase a Ford station wagon because his 1936 Ford is "about used up." Hopes to get to New York in the fall. Likes the look of *Intruder in the Dust* and wants six more copies. {SL}

September 15: In New Orleans to settle income tax claim reduced to $1000.

Hamilton Basso, who befriended WF in 1925 in New Orleans, writes to say the *New Yorker* has asked him to do a profile of WF, if he consents.

September 18: Needs only $1000 after income tax settlement and tells Haas he needs another list of the proposed stories for the collection Random House wants to publish. "The big mss. is coming but slow at present. I will probably not get seriously at it until winter and the bad weather." Wants to finish it by next year. Trouble with an ulcer but getting better. {SL}

September 23: To Hamilton Basso's request for an interview, WF replies: "Oh hell no. Come down and visit whenever you can, but no piece in any paper about me as I am working tooth and nail at my lifetime ambition to be the last private individual on earth & expect every success since apparently there is no competition for the place."

September 26: *Dallas Morning News* review of *Intruder in the Dust*: "It should not seem particularly strange that Faulkner, having dealt with the displacement of people from war and poverty, should finally come to deal explicitly with the most dispossessed and displaced of all, the Negro." {WFC}

New York Herald Tribune review of *Intruder in the Dust*: "One of the marks of Faulkner's genius is that he can write of the Negro without false pity, without the usual haze of shallow sentiment in which so many 'men of good will' scatter patronage, and the sweet, slightly rotted fruits of 'good intentions.'" {WFC}

September 27: Random House publishes *Intruder in the Dust*. Copies go on sale in Oxford.

In Oxford, signs and dates first edition of *Intruder in the Dust*: "To Phil / from Bill." {BH1}

Elected to the American Academy of Arts and Letters.

September 28: Thanks Bennett Cerf for the invitation to stay with his family, but "one purpose of my expedition is vacation from the nest-and-hearth business." Prefers a hotel like the Algonquin if it has not "changed too much." Expects to come between October 15 and 20 and stay for about a week. {SL}

Tells Robert Haas he will come to New York after squirrel and dove shooting season ends. Will show some of his "big mss." Malcolm Cowley has invited WF to stay at the Harvard Club, "but being an old Yale man (vide the two days I spent at the Yale club on your cuff in 1935) this might be lese majesty unless it may be considered post graduate work." {SL}

At Rowan Oak, signs and dates the first edition of *Intruder in the Dust*: "Buddy,[97] from Pappy." {BH1}

Autumn: *The Sewanee Review* publishes "A Courtship."

Sends annotated list of stories to Robert Haas, discussing which stories are strongest, which weakest, which are parts of novels, and proposing other stories Haas has not included in his list.

In *Partisan Review*, Elizabeth Hardwick, reviewing *Intruder in the Dust*, observes that WF having "created this myth of the 'possessed, legendary writer,'" has written a polemic, "even in its odd way a 'novel of ideas,'" as if he "ran down from the hills to make a speech in the public square." {CR2}

October 2: Phil Stone writes to WF after reading *Intruder in the Dust*: "A skillful job, Bill, but it seems too trickey [*sic*] in places and there is too much damned talk in it." {SS}

October 23: In the *New Yorker*, Edmund Wilson complains of WF's "snarled-up" and tract-like prose in *Intruder in the Dust*.

October 18, 5:15 p.m.: Bennett Cerf meets WF at La Guardia airport. {B2, B3}

Checks into the Algonquin Hotel. {B3}

Dines with Ruth Ford. {B3}

October 19: Sees Ruth Ford. Visits new Random House offices. {B3}

Attends a party at the home of Robert Haas. {FK}

October 20: Visits Random House offices. {B3}

Lunch at 21 with Donald Klopfer. {B3}

Attends dinner party in his honor at Robert Haas's New York apartment. {B3}

October 21: Declines Ruth Ford's invitation to a party. {B2}

October 22: Declines another Ruth Ford invitation to go out. Malcolm Cowley arrives at the Algonquin, observes the whiskey and beer bottles on the dresser, and the writer on his back "naked and uncovered except for a silk pajama top." {CR2}

October 23: Malcolm Cowley calls to confirm a luncheon engagement, and WF's friend Jim Devine answers and asks Cowley to call back the next day. {CR2} In his notebook, Cowley describes WF's neat figure and melancholy demeanor reminiscent of Poe. {AB}

October 24: Ford calls again but there is no answer. {B3}

Noon: Cowley shows up at the Algonquin, knocks on the door to WF's room, and hears a faint "Come In." Cowley gives WF a drink and departs. {CR2}

4:00 p.m.: Ruth Ford and Harvey Breit (who had interviewed WF) find him semiconscious after three days of drink. {CR2}

Cowley returns to the Algonquin and meets *New York Sun* theater critic and Robert Haas. Calls are made to put WF in the Fieldstone Sanitarium on 250th Street. {CR2}

After several hours, during which WF objects to the sanitarium, Cowley drives him late at night to his home in Sherman, Connecticut. {CR2}

October 25: Slowly recovers, nursed by Cowley's wife, Muriel. Cowley describes WF's condition, comments on his work, his time in Hollywood, and a proposed profile *Life* asks Cowley to write. {FC}

In Sherman, Connecticut, signs and dates a first edition of *Light in August*: "For Malcolm Cowley," and a first edition of *The Portable Faulkner*. Also signs and dates first editions of *Pylon*: "For Malcolm Cowley," and *Absalom, Absalom!*, and *The Unvanquished*. Signs and dates first edition of *Go Down, Moses, and Other Stories*: "For Muriel Cowley / a charming and delightful lady / with gratitude." {BH1}

October 26: Suffers withdrawal pains but improves, telling Cowley about *A Fable* and then about Sherwood Anderson and New Orleans. {FC}

October 27: Cowley takes WF for a drive in the fall color. {CR2}

October 28: Cowley drives WF, with a copy of *The Lost Weekend* in hand, to the Brewster station headed back to New York City. {CR2}

Harvey Breit meets WF at Grand Central station and takes him to a planetarium. {CR2}

7:00 p.m.: Attends Ruth Ford's dinner party and drinks the cocktails and cognac but manages to control his intake. {CR2}

October 29: Lunch with editor Saxe Commins and Cowley. Signs and dates first edition of *Intruder in the Dust*: "For Saxe Commins / from Bill Faulkner." {BH1}

October 30: Purchases a coat for riding at Abercrombie & Fitch. Sends a dozen long-stemmed roses to Muriel Cowley. {CR2}

Signs and dates the first edition of *Intruder in the Dust*: "for Jim Devine." {BH1}

Works at Random House on a collection of his stories. {CR2}

Flies home. {CR2}

Midnight: Arrives home and goes to bed. {CR2}

October 31: For editor Saxe Commins lists the table of contents for the story collection, noting how "each noun [is] in character and tone and tune with every other." Anticipates working on a foreword to the collection. {SL}

In the *New York Herald Tribune*, John K. Hutchens records WF's comments on *Intruder in the Dust* and politics, especially the Dixiecrats. {LG}

November 1: Writes Cowley about the projected collection of stories. Lists the contents page and explains his conviction that "even to a collection of short stories, form, integration, is as important as to a novel—an entity of its own, single, set for one pitch, contrapuntal in integration, toward one end, one finale." Wants a coat like Cowley's: "white or near white corduroy, bellows pockets and a loose belt and a vent in back so I can ride a horse in it. Brooks said they had not had them in two years The next time you are in there, will you see if they can get the corduroy and make me one like yours." {SL, FC}

Returns to work on *A Fable*. {SL}

November 3: Cowley sends comments about the structure of WF's collected stories. {FC}

November 7: To Ralph Thompson of the *New York Times*, WF describes his reputation in Oxford and how in New Orleans, Sherwood Anderson encouraged him to write a novel. {LG}

November 11: Thanks Haas for sending his sonnets and photograph. "You ought to write more verse. I mean for the sake of the verse itself." Reflecting on Haas's loss of his son in the war, WF adds: "The only difference between you and the sonless grief less natural poet is, the poet is capable in his imagination alone of all grief and degradation and valor and sacrifice." Mentions writing more of the "big mss" interrupted by deer hunting. With the death of two senior camp members, it has been WF's responsibility to gets dogs and horses set up to the camp, along with arranging the cooking, tents, feed, and so on. {SL}

November 20: In response to Hubert Starr's query about WF's genealogical line, WF supplies a capsule history, beginning with his great-grandfather's trek from Tennessee to Mississippi and ending with his murder on a Ripley Street. {NYPL}

November 23: Elected to American Academy of Arts and Letters.

c. November 24: Proposes the idea of a Gavin Stevens volume, a collection of stories in which he "solves or prevents crime to protect the weak, right injustice, or punish evil. It would include a new, unpublished novella, "Knight's Gambit," which he is the "hottest to write now." The volume could be ready for fall publication. {SL}

Late November: MGM location manager visits Oxford to consult with local officials. {CR2}

December 10; In Oxford signs and dates the first edition of *Intruder in the Dust*: "For Mrs Calvin Brown." {BH1}

Christmas: Types and binds a new copy of *The Wishing-Tree* dedicated to Phil Stone's son, "Philip Stone II." {SS, BH1}

December 30: Random House sends $4,000 of MGM money for film rights to *Intruder in the Dust.* {B3}

December 31: Explains his delay (he was in hunting camp) in acknowledging the honor of his election to the American Academy of Arts and Letters to the president of the Academy. {SL}

1949

n.d.: Writes short note to Saxe Commins that he cannot "go to hear the music Friday p. m. Please thank Dorothy, and excuse me."[98] {BH2}

January 5: Rejects the idea of Malcolm Cowley's *Life* profile of him, adding "the only plan I can accept is one giving me the privilege of editing the result. Which means I will want to blue pencil everything which even intimates that something breathing and moving sat behind the typewriter which produced the books." He does not think *Life* will stand for such an approach but is amenable to thinking up some way for Cowley to collect on the assignment. {SL, FC}

January 10: Robert Haas writes that Random House's intention is to reprint *Go Down, Moses*, *The Hamlet*, and *The Wild Palms* and asks if WF wishes to make minor changes. {SL}

January 11: Cowley accepts WF's prohibition of writing about his private life and suggests concentrating on the creation of Yoknapatawpha. {FC}

January 19: Working on the Gavin Stevens volume, he informs Saxe Commins. Lists the stories, and mentions he is rewriting the novella, "Knight's Gambit." {SL, BH2}

January 21: Explains to Ober his permission for a ballet to be based on *As I Lay Dying*. {SL}

January 26: Requests a change of title from *Go Down, Moses, and other Stories* to *Go Down, Moses*. Does not want to make changes in the other reissued novels but would like to add something to *Intruder in the Dust* if that is reprinted. {SL}

February 2: Director Clarence Brown arrives in Oxford to survey film locations for *Intruder in the Dust*, confers with WF, who agrees to read the script and to help with revisions. {CR2}

c. February: Writes to Bennett Cerf saying that director Clarence Brown is "the best to work with I ever knew. Revised dialogue in jail cell scenes and coached Hernandez, although the actor quickly picked up the right inflections." WF's horse, trained to flinch at quicksand, is used in the film. {RHR}

February 7: To Robert Haas: includes an insertion for *Intruder in the Dust*.[99] {BH2}

February 11: Mentions seeing Cowley's Hemingway profile in *Life*, but without reading it tells Cowley he is sure "it's all right" and has Hemingway's approval and will "profit him—if there is any profit or increase or increment that a brave man and an artist can lack or need or want." But WF demurs: "I will protest to the last: no photographs, no recorded documents. It is my ambition to be, as a private individual, abolished and voided from history, leaving it mark less, no refuse save the printed books." He even claims he wishes that, like the Elizabethans, he had not signed his work. "It is my aim, and every effort bent, that the sum and history of my life, which in the same sentence is my obit and epitaph tool, shall be them both: He made the books and he died." Alluding to his drinking during his last time with Cowley, he promises he will "furnish someone to do the actual drinking; not myself this time." {SL, FC}

February 17: Cowley mentions discussing the *Life* profile with editor Robert Coughlan. Predicts that sooner or later such a profile will appear regardless of WF's wishes. {FC}

February 19: Tells Ober he is rewriting "Knight's Gambit" as a novella, which perhaps will help sales of the Gavin Stevens story volume. {SL}

February 23: To Eric J. Devine, WF describes the contents of his navigator's kit aboard the home-made steamboat his friends have fashioned, and a party of 42 people and one sheep with two cases of whiskey, and a barbecue, poker and crap game, and one fight. He considers himself and his friend Evans "probably the best flat-bottom boat sailors in the world." Mentions the excitement about filming *Intruder in the Dust* in Oxford: "It's too bad I'm no longer young enough to cope with all the local girls who are ready and eager to glide into camera focus on their backs." {SL}

c. March: Informs Robert Haas about the costly draining of his farmland and that he will need to draw the balance of his $10,000 movie money. {SL}

March 5: Goes over for Saxe Commins the details of stories in *Knight's Gambit*. {SL, BH2}

March 8: Letter from Saxe Commins discusses the knight's gambit move in chess, "an unorthodox opening." {BH2, CR2}

March 9: Clarence Brown and an advance crew return to Oxford. {B3}

April 23: Instructs Ober not to charge a commission for the ballet adaptation of *As I Lay Dying*. Even if it makes a few dollars, he considers the production noncommercial and advises to let it go "unhampered." {SL}

April 24: Mollie Darr, a Northwestern University student encloses a permission form for WF to sign, approving a dramatic adaptation of *As I Lay Dying*. {SL}

April 25: Assures Valerie Bettis that she has his permission to produce her ballet of *As I Lay Dying*. He does not expect his 5 percent unless she actually makes a profit and notes that Harold Ober, a "good friend," is simply protecting his author's interests. {SL}

May 1: Goes over the order of the stories in *Knight's Gambit* in a letter to Saxe Commins. {SL, BH2}

May 2: Writes to Ober enclosing his signed permission form for a dramatic production of *As I Lay Dying*, specifying that his approval is for a noncommercial production and that should there be a profit, they would make a new agreement. {SL}

May 4: Ober rejects WF's permission letter for the Mollie Darr production of *As I Lay Dying*. Ober also disapproves of WF's agreement with Valerie Bettis for a ballet production of the novel, noting that she is a professional doing sell-out performances. {SL}

May 6: "The harm is done now," WF writes to Ober, referring to his agreement with Bettis. He proposes writing to her again and asking her to send Ober a weekly accounting for all performances. {SL}

c. May 18: Announces to Saxe Commins the completion of the novella, "Knight's Gambit," although he is still doing some rewriting to be completed by June 1 in time to meet the publishing schedule. {SL}

May 20: Malcolm Cowley writes to confirm that Robert Coughlan of *Life* is doing a profile of WF. {FC}

June: Artist Stuart Purser describes his encounter with WF at the Courthouse Square discussing art while the artist watches WF interacting with "country folks, talking to both black and white, not groups but to individuals." WF comments to the artist: "You get your ideas and inspiration from observing these people while I get mine through talking with them." He describes WF's interest in African American artist M. B. Mayfield. {CWF}

June 2: Typescript of "Knight's Gambit" sent to Saxe Commins. {SL}

Commins writes to WF about "Knight's Gambit, with a query about term in it referring to a young girl's "ephemeride." The word is changed in the published book to ephemeris at WF's suggestion. [See entry for July 5] {SL}

June 23: Vicky to her parents: "Pappy, Jill, Grandmama, and I have been painting everything, so it really looks nice. Pappy built Jill and I a ping-pong table. (I am just a whiz at it.) The tennis court in the pasture is nearly fixed, and we have croquet, and badminton too." {CFS}

July 5: Reports to Robert Haas that he is going to run out of money "as usual." Wants $5,000. Describes work on his sloop, *The Ring Dove*, going out in all sorts of weather. "She sails in dry little wind, and can sail in and out of any hole she can turn around in. Two neighbor boys and my 16 year old daughter are my crew." Suggests *ephemeris* is the right form of the word for "Knight's Gambit." {SL}

Mid-July: Galleys of *Knight's Gambit* arrive in Oxford. {B2}

July 27: Writes to Manuel Komroff, an editor at Liveright when *Soldiers' Pay* was published. Remembers only one letter that Sherwood Anderson gave him to deliver to Komroff, who thought there was a second one about *Mosquitoes*. Mentions the estrangement from Anderson: "I never did know why . . . Though I ran into him in New York several years later and everything seemed to be all right again. Spent an afternoon with him, and never saw him again." {SL}

August: Joan Williams meets WF at Rowan Oak. He rebuffs her, but her letter to him leads to a correspondence and further meetings. {WFJW}

Malcolm Franklin conversation with Carvel Collins: WF, drunk while sailing, breaks the mast of his sailboat. {CC}

August 31: WF writes to Joan Williams saying he is charmed by her letter and apologizes for not attending to it earlier. {WFJW}

Early September: A sneak preview of *Intruder in the Dust* appears to please WF. {CR2}

September 2: "William Faulkner took us sailing on his sailboat on a big inland lake they've cut out of the woods there—waves and everything, big."—Eudora Welty {CR2}

Autumn: Joan Williams writes: "many times I have heard people remark that you are the only person writing to day worth reading." {WFJW}

c. October 5: Congratulates Saxe Commins on publication of *Knight's Gambit*: "Beautiful job." {SL}

October 6: *Oxford Eagle* stories about the film of *Intruder in the Dust*: "World Premier Excitement Ready to Break." {BH1}

October 9: MGM sets up searchlight in preparation for premier of *Intruder in the Dust*. {B3}

October 10, 4:30 p.m.: A mile-long parade with university and high school marching bands and floats celebrate the opening of *Intruder in the Dust*. {B3}

October 11: With his family, WF attends the premier of *Intruder in the Dust.* WF acknowledges the audience's applause but declines to make a speech. {B3, CR2}

October 12: Recalls in a letter to Sam Marx, head of MGM story department, "our mild fiasco of twenty years ago."[100] Reports seeing Clarence Brown's production of *Intruder in the Dust* the previous evening and concludes: "I may still be on MGM's cuff, but at least I am not quite so far up the sleeve." {SL}

October 14: Replies to composer Virgil Thompson's plan to make an opera out of *The Wild Palms*: "I am pleased and flattered by the idea." Notes he is sending on Thomson's letter to Harold Ober. {SL}

Writes to Ober calling *Intruder in the Dust* "a good picture, I think." Offers to pay a commission to Ober, even though he was not able to sell "Knight's Gambit." {SL}

October 15: Writes to Joan Williams that her questions are best asked of a man in bed, but he promises to answer her queries. {WFJW}

Williams asks what she should read and tells WF she is reading a Memphis newspaper about the film adaptation of *Intruder in the Dust.* {WFJW}

November 5: Tells Robert Haas that he has been so fortunate with agents and publishers that he does not even read the contracts he signs. He realizes that he has "imposed on" Harold Ober" by not taking into account Random House's handling of certain rights to adaptations of his books. From now on, he will inform both publisher and agent when a request is made to adapt his work. Hopes to come to New York after hunting season. Ends by saying "Anything you do in Faulkner book affairs has already received my ok." {SL}

c. November 16: Explains to Saxe Commins that he cannot find the sheets he is supposed to sign for a limited edition of *Knight's Gambit.* {SL}

November 16: *Milwaukee Journal* review of *Knight's Gambit* compares Stevens to Sherlock Holmes and Chick to Watson while noting the other characters are "substandard folks" and "animalistic bayou billies, naive and ferocious by turns." {WFC}

November 27: Random House publishes *Knight's Gambit.*

In Stockholm, 15 members of the Swedish Academy vote to award WF a Nobel Prize, but the vote of 18 members has to be unanimous.

November 28: Vicky writes to her parents: "About a week ago, Pappy went deer hunting and will probably be back tomorrow. Pappy has fixed the sailboat for the winter and there won't be any more sailing." {CFS}

November 29: Tells Robert Haas about a stag he missed shooting three times on a recent hunt. Needs $1000 by end of year. He is pleased Haas likes the film of *Intruder in the Dust.* "Last night, lying in bed, I suddenly realized that I was bored, which means I will probably go to work on something soon." Does not expect to visit New York until the following year because he cannot afford it. {SL}

December: Fred Woodress visits WF and is invited to observe a hog dressing. He finds Estelle "gracious to such a brash young man. She invites him into the living room and is "as much a conversationalist as her husband is not, asking me a lot of questions about myself and my family." WF's advice to aspiring writer Woodress: "Don't write by associating with other writers . . . I don't believe in it . . . Get to know people but not particularly writers." He offers advice on other topics, including style, reading, and education" before lapsing into silence. CWF}

December 3: Signs and dates first edition of *Knight's Gambit*: "Buddy,[101] on his birthday. 1949 / Pappy." {BH1}

December 4: Newark, New Jersey *Sunday Star-Ledger*: "If this is not Faulkner's best work, it still is Faulkner and even not-so-good Faulkner is so very much better than the best of many another."

December 17: In Oxford, signs and dates first printing of *Knight's Gambit*: "Phil and Emily Stone." {BH1}

December 26: Joan Williams writes: "I want to work hard because of you." She tells him about going to see *Intruder in the Dust* and wanting to say to the "usher, the ticket seller, the woman in front of me—I know him in some ways, and he is a great man—but of course I couldn't." {WFJW}

December 29: Wants to meet Joan Williams but not in Oxford, which might have repercussions. {WFJW}

December 30: Phil Stone writes to WF scholar Glenn O. Carey: "Faulkner does not mind what is said about his work but does not want anything written about him personally." {BH2}

December 31: Writes to Joan Williams suggesting an outing on a friend's houseboat on Sardis Lake. {WFJW}

1950

January 1: Phil Stone writes to WF about *Knight's Gambit*: "A damned good job." {SS}

January 3: Joan Williams visits Rowan Oak, and Estelle fixes a picnic. {AB}

January 7: Joan Williams returns to Bard College. {WFJW}

January 10: Thanks Dayton Kohler for his article about WF in *College English*, saying Kohler has understood WF's aim and joins Malcolm Cowley, Warren Beck, and "one twenty-one-year old Tennessee school girl [Joan Williams]," who understand his work. {SL}

January 13: Mentions to Joan Williams that he has read her story, "Rain Later," in *Mademoiselle* and calls it "all right. It is, moving and true, made me want to cry a little for the sad frustration of solitude, isolation, aloneness in which every human being lives, who for all the blood kinship and everything, cant really communicate touch." She has to keep working at her writing and be ready to "sacrifice everything for it—happiness, peace, money, duty too if you are so unlucky. Only, quite often, if you are really willing to sacrifice any and everything for it, everything will not be required, demanded by the gods." {SL}

January 21: Phil Stone writes to WF scholar Glenn O. Carey with details about WF's time in New Haven, his service in the RAF, his time in New Orleans, and his education. {BH2}

January 25: Saxe Commins announces that Random House is ready to publish a collection of WF's stories in August if he is ready to do so. {SL}

February 2: Arrives at the Algonquin Hotel and then visits Random House. Discusses publication plans for *A Fable* and a collection of stories. {SL}

Arranges with Joan Williams to visit her at Bard. {FK}

February 7: Joan Williams accompanies WF to a party at Robert Haas's apartment, with several friends, including Ruth Ford, in attendance. {CR2}

February 9: Phil Stone writes to WF scholar Glenn O. Carey: "As far as his actual writing is concerned I helped him very little except with the humor, but I actually made his humor for him. At the beginning he was a very humorless person." {BH2}

February 11: Declares to Joan Williams that her first letter to him made him fall in love with her. {WFJW}

February 12: Boards the train in New York for Memphis. {B3}

February 13: Notes to Joan Williams at Bard concerning his play, *Requiem for a Nun*. {SL}

Williams replies critiquing the play and calling for more development of Nancy's character. She is also hopeful, if somewhat doubtful, about their collaborating on the play. She concludes: "To have found someone, embodying so many things I've looked for, in so strange a way, under strange circumstances . . . it was all so wonderful and means so much to me . . . Bill, I do love you." {WFJW}

February 14: Instructs Joan Williams to send her letter in plain envelopes with no return address so that the mail cannot be identified when it reaches him at home. {WFJW}

Mid-February: Sends Joan Williams a few pages of the play, pointing out that much will be changed after the first draft is completed. {WFJW}

February 17: Encourages Joan Williams to rewrite the first scene of *Requiem for a Nun*. {SL}

February 20: Writes to Merle Haas, wife of Robert Haas, thanking her for his stay at the Haas home and for helping him select watercolors and brushes. {SL}

February 21: Williams writes to say that *Requiem* is really WF's play, and she does not want credit for it. But she is torn between working on the play and finishing her degree at Bard. "A wide vista has opened through you and I hope that I am capable enough to enter." {WFJW}

February 22: Mentions to Joan Williams hearing about his prospects as a Nobel Prize winner. "Been hearing rumors for about three years, have been a little fearful. It's not the sort of thing to decline; a gratuitous insult to do so but I dont want it. I'd rather be in the same pigeon hole with Dreiser and Sherwood Anderson, than with Sinclair Lewis and Mrs. Chinahand Buck." He has the first act of *Requiem for a Nun* "laid out, rough draft of about twelve pages." {SL}

Williams writes to WF about a "great man offering love and friendship to me." She worries about what WF will tell Estelle about their collaboration. {WFJW}

February 23: Writes to Joan Williams saying how much he misses her while he is in New York. {WFJW}

Early March: Joan Williams writes to WF: "Talking to you things come that are good enough to write down." {WFJW}

In another letter, she dreams about his coming to Bard to speak as a literary lion. {WFJW}

March 2: Still expects Joan Williams to work on the play and says, "I tell you again, the play is yours too." Tells her just to get "*everything* down on paper." {SL}

March 3: Writes to Joan Williams claiming something she said at the Biltmore Hotel gave him the idea for *Requiem for a Nun.* {WFJW}

March 12: Joan Williams sends a poem to WF to "remind me, help me to / remember, be happier." {WFJW}

March 22: Reports to Joan Williams that he is working on the second act of *Requiem for a Nun* "going slow but it moves. Maybe you can write the 3rd one while you are at home." He insists the play is also hers but encourages her to finish her schooling. He hopes they will be able to meet over her spring break. Advises her on how to treat Estelle when they meet. {SL}

March 26: Letter to the *Memphis Commercial Appeal* commenting on the conviction of three white man for killing three black children in Attila County, Mississippi. {ESPL}

March 28: Responds to Marjorie Lyons, who wonders why the reporter in *Pylon* is not given a name: "He was not anonymous: he was every man." In this case, the reporter is the man who is capable of one great love even if it is not reciprocated. He quotes Harry Wilbourne in *The Wild Palms*: "Between grief and nothing, I will take grief." {SL}

April 1: Explains to Mark Van Doren why he cannot accept in person the Howells Medal for Fiction. He is a farmer and has to take care of his crops: "No Mississippi farmer has the time or money either to travel anywhere . . . I doubt I know anything worth talking two minutes about." But he takes "great pride" in the honor and grateful for the letter. {SL}

April 5: Phil Stone writes to WF scholar Glenn O. Carey about WF's knowledge of the Civil War and his World War I service. Calls the stories about WF's fighting in France "laughable." Mentions that WF's brother John and his mother laughed when Carvel Collins questioned them about WF's combat experience. {BH2}

April 6: Attends Jill's junior class performance as Cornelia Otis Skinner in *Our Hearts Were Young and Gay*. {B2}

April 9: Comments on a response to his letter of March 26 about the murder of black children. {ESPL}

c. April 9: Meets Joan Williams in Memphis. {WFJW}

April 18: Asks Ben Wasson to excuse the delay in sending his excerpt from *A Fable* for publication by the Levee Press. He has been writing a play and forgot about it. He welcomes a visit from Wasson. {SL}

April 20: Phil Stone to Carvel Collins: "I saw Bill at the post office a few minutes ago and he says he is not feeling well again. He has not been feeling well for almost a year, off and on, and I am gently needling him now, to get him to go to the Clinic but he probably won't do it. As I told you before, the Faulkners think they can even defy the laws of Nature." {BH2}

April 30: Writes to condemn the recent murder of a black man and the ignorance and bigotry that disgrace a country founded on freedom from oppression. {ESPL}

Early May: Writes to Joan Williams expressing his doubts that he can write a play but still thinking "it will be beautiful." They will have to rewrite all of it. Reflects on their unhappy meeting in Memphis with too many people that precluded intimacy. {WFJW}

May 5: Joan Williams writes that she was not "particularly nice in Memphis." She had a terrible time during her week at home. "I think of you often and regret the day in Memphis as time lost in which we could have come to a closer understanding." {WFJW}

May 6: Sends Joan Williams several pages of *Requiem for a Nun*. He mentions an awards ceremony in New York on May 25 and wonders if Joan can join him. He loves her and misses her. {WFJW}

May 7: Visits Phil Stone at home to reiterate his opposition to a Carvel Collins *Life* profile. {SS}

May 8: Phil Stone tells Carvel Collins about a conversation with WF the previous day: "He was very positive that he did not want any such article about him to appear in Life Magazine. He was quite disturbed about it and came out to my house later in the morning to be sure to see if he could prevent it being done." Stone relays WF's reasons. {BH2}

May 9: Writes to Joan Williams cautioning her about middle-class morality. She will have to fight her family to save her art. {WFJW}

May 15: Robert Haas receives a letter from WF saying he won't be at the Howells Medal ceremony because of farming. Two acts of the play completed, although he doubts his ability to write a play. He may turn it into a novel. {SL}

c. May 15: Repeats his reasons to Bennett Cerf for not attending the Howells Medal ceremony and adds: "Too many people for one thing if no other reason." {SL}

c. Mid-May: Admits to Saxe Commins he was right about a collection of stories: "The stuff stands up amazingly well after a few years, 10 or 20. I had forgotten a lot of it; I spent a whole evening laughing to myself about mules and the shingles." {SL, BH2}

Reports to Robert Haas that he has finished the play, *Requiem for a Nun*, and now is writing three introductory chapters that hold the three acts together. Projects a fall publication at the earliest. Needs to draw $5000 from his Random House account to buy a new tractor to replace his old one, worn out after fifteen years. Hopes to come to New York City sometime in the winter. {SL}

May 19: Forwards a letter to Joan Williams about a possible job. Tells her that he has finished the third act and now realizes *Requiem for a Nun* is a novel and will have to be rewritten as a play. He still expects her to work on it with him. {SL}

May 22: Rewriting first draft of play, which will now reside inside of a novel, with the help of Joan Williams. Long speeches need condensing for a "workable play script." Anticipates calling on a playwright for help. Relates his adventures on his sailboat during a storm. {SL}

May 25: Awarded American Academy's Howells Medal for Fiction.

June 12: Accepts the Gold Medal for fiction and reflects on his attitude toward his achievement. {ESPL, FC}

June 17: Writes to Joan Williams about Estelle's discovery of one of Joan's letters to him. The couple argue in front of Jill. Complains of Estelle's drinking and lack of respect for his work. He warns Joan that Estelle might write to her parents. {WFJW}

July 1: Sends Ober "A Name for the City" (the first prologue of *Requiem for a Nun*) hoping to get a sale to *The Saturday Evening Post* or to *Harper's*.

July 4: At an Independence Day celebration in the Oxford Square, WF takes care of a lost little boy, treating him to an ice cream soda in Mac Reed's drugstore until the boy's parents arrive. {B2}

July 9: Writes to Joan Williams about Estelle, who is jealous and unbalanced. {WFJW}

July 13: Suggests Joan Williams write to him using the name A. E. Holston, general delivery. He cautions Joan to beware of Estelle's "insanity" but proposes more meetings. {WFJW}

July 15: Suggests to Joan Williams they have worked too long on the play to stop now. {WFJW}

Joan Williams writes that Estelle has called and invited her to a lunch meeting at the Peabody Hotel in Memphis. Confused about Estelle's motivations, Williams mentions her mother is worried Estelle might name Joan in a divorce suit. Joan is worried about the safety of continuing their correspondence. But she hopes, as WF does, that "things will be better soon." {WFJW}

Mid-July: For Joan Williams, draws a picture of a man smoking a pipe behind a plow and mule. He asks Joan to think over what is wrong with Temple Drake. He mentions an invitation to Rowan Oak and that Estelle wants to see her and put an end to gossip.[102] {WFJW}

July 19: Proposes a visit with Estelle to Joan Williams's home so that Estelle's character can be assessed.[103] {WFJW}

Summer: At the Peabody Hotel, Estelle tells Joan that WF is suffering from male menopause. Estelle appears frail and dignified and to Joan not at all the mad woman WF describes. {WFJW}

August: Visits the Williams home and appears quiet and old fashioned. He concludes her family has no interest in her writing. {WFJW}

August 2: Random House publishes *Collected Stories*. Joan Williams sends some rewritten pages of *Requiem for a Nun*. {SL}

August 3: Discusses a scene from *Requiem for a Nun* with Joan Williams and asks her advice. {SL}

August 4: Explains Temple's motivations in a letter to Joan Williams. {WFJW}

August 5: Shelby Foote signs his book *Follow Me Down*. WF replies: "I read your book and liked it. Do better next time." {CFS}

August 14: Tells Joan Williams it was only after five or six times that he realized her face is pretty and only after their attending a New York party that it is beautiful and unbearable to contemplate. {WFJW}

August 20: Emphasizes to Joan Williams that they are working on the play for the fun of it, and she does not have to continue if she does not want to finish it. He regrets he has not seen more of her during the summer. {WFJW}

In Oxford, signs and dates first edition of *Collected Stories*: "To Phil Stone. From Bill Faulkner." {BH1}

New York Times Book Review: "For the reader not yet lost from the world of literature, Faulkner can be a deep and continuous source of wisdom. For this kind of reader Faulkner reveals the laws of existence and the conditions of survival—and how people behave under them." {CR2}

New York Herald Tribune review of *Collected Stories* lauds the "Elizabethan richness . . . [i]ts humors, its ironies, its ancient tempers, its latest fashions, its masks of horror, its violence, its comedy, its pathos." {WFC}

August 21: Random House publishes *Collected Stories.*

August 28: *Time* review of *Collected Stories* conveys "the excitement that comes from never knowing when, amidst pages of failure, there will come a masterpiece." {WFC}

August 29: Joan Williams goes sailing with Estelle and WF. {B2}

August 30: Williams writes to WF calling their sail "strange all right." She wishes they could go off by themselves. {B2}

September 1: WF has a circular printed advocating the sale of beer in Oxford. {ESPL}

September 3: Writes to Joan Williams about her youthful attractiveness and wishes she could accompany him on a trip to Jackson, Mississippi. {WFJW}

Hartford Courant review of *Collected Stories*: "There are no extrinsic trappings, no introduction, only intelligent grouping which ends the book wisely with the voluptuous death dream 'Carcassone.'" {WFC}

September 5: Modern Library edition of *Light in August* is published.

September 8: A letter about his beer broadside. {ESPL}

September 26: Sends Joan Williams a happy birthday telegram. {WFJW}

September 29: Presents a story idea to Joan Williams about a famous fifty-year-old man and a young woman, with whom he shares "everything, anything, whatever you like." The young woman is curious but also troubled by what the famous man wants from her. Then she receives a telegram announcing his death, and she realizes she sensed it all along and that "what he wanted was to walk in April again for a day, an hour." {SL, WFJW}

Autumn: Contributes to a fund to send African American artist M. B. Mayfield to Chicago to see the Van Gogh show at the Art Institute. {Stuart Purser, CWF}

October: *Harper's* publishes "A Name for the City."

October 2: Addresses UNESCO meeting in Denver about the conflicting systems of communism and capitalism and concludes: "The last sound on the worthless earth will be two human beings trying to launch a homemade space ship and already quarreling about where they are going next." {ESPL}

October 11: Signs and dates a copy of *Go Down, Moses, and Other Stories* "for Else [Jonsson]." https://www.christies.com/lotfinder/Lot/faulkner-william-go-down-moses-and-other-5331760-details.aspx.

October 16: Comments to Saxe Commins about Budd Schulberg's novel *The Disenchanted.* Assesses the novel in terms of the values expressed in his Nobel Prize speech and pays tribute to "the real ones before us who have not yet got the recog. they deserve: Anderson, and the clumsy giant Dreiser for instance, and Cather." {BH2}

October 18: Williams writes that WF is the only one who understands her. She cherishes his faith in her. {WFJW}

October 23: In a letter to Joan Williams affirms his faith that they will write something together. {WFJW}

October 25: Joan Williams, unhappy at home, leaves for Bard and then New York City rather than staying home to see WF. {WFJW}

Late October: An unhappy WF laments the 1500-mile distance from Joan when even 70 miles (from Oxford to Memphis) also separated them. {WFJW}

November: Newspaper stories include WF in lists of possible Nobel Prize winners.

November 1: Joan Williams writes to "dearest Bill . . . Hell hell hell—I want to see you too. I want to somehow reach you, lose my restraint, timidity—all the things that keep us from being close I would give anything to be somewhere alone, to do, think as we pleased." She mentions her struggle to write about them. {WFJW}

November 3: Cautions Joan Willams about the claims of her family: "People need trouble, fret, a little of frustration, to sharpen the spirit on, toughen it. Artists do; I dont mean you need to live in a rathole or gutter, but they have to learn fortitude, endurance, only vegetables are happy." {SL, WFJW}

November 9: Joan Williams writes to tell WF how proud she is of him. "I have missed you terribly." {WFJW}

November 10, early morning: WF is out liming a field when a Swedish journalist calls Rowan Oak to say WF has won the Nobel Prize. {SO}

WF says he will not be able to attend the ceremony. {B3}

2:15 p.m.: Learns officially he has won 1949 Nobel Prize for Literature.

November 11: *New York Times* on the Nobel Prize award: "Incest and rape are perhaps widespread distractions in the Jefferson, Mississippi of Faulkner, but not elsewhere in the United States." The *New York Herald Tribune:* "Nothing would justify an open quarrel with regard to the Prize, even though one would have preferred the choice of a laureate more smiling in a world which is gradually getting darker."

November 13: Writes a letter to *Time* defending Hemingway after the negative reviews of *Across the River and into the Trees*. {ESPL}

"I have been confronted with you at every turn with your picture all over every front page," Joan Williams writes to WF. {WFJW}

November 16: Informs the Swedish Academy that he will not be able to attend the award ceremony, adding, "I hold that the award was made not to me, but to my works—crown to thirty years of the agony and sweat of the human spirit, to make something which was not here before me, to lift up or maybe comfort or anyway at least entertain, in its turn, man's heart. That took thirty years. I am past fifty now; there is probably not much more in the tank. I feel that what remains after the thirty years of work is not worth carrying from Mississippi to Sweden, just as I feel that what remains does not deserve to expend the prize on himself, so that it is my hope to find an aim for the money high enough to be commensurate with the purpose and significance of its origin."

Mid-November: In hunting camp, a coon collard supper to celebrate the Nobel Prize. "We was proud that William won that. He was just old William Faulkner."—John Cullen {FWP}

November 27: Returns home from hunting camp after much drinking and with close to a case of pneumonia but sends a telegram to the Swedish Academy stating he will attend the award ceremony. {B3}

December 5: Writes to Joan Williams about missing her: "I don't know when I will see you, but you are the one I never stop thinking about. You are the girl's body I lie in bed beside before I go to sleep. I know every sweet red hair and sweet curve on it. Dont forget me. I love you." {WFJW}

December 6: With Jill departs for the Nobel Award ceremony in Stockholm and arrives in New York with a high fever. {CR2}

December 7: In New York treated with penicillin for the flu. {CR2}

December 8, 11: 30 a.m.: Departs from New York for Stockholm with stopover in Newfoundland. {B2}

December 9, 5:00 a.m.: Arrives in Prestwick, Scotland, near Glasgow, arriving later in the day in Stockholm, after a brief layover in Oslo. {B2}

A press conference in the afternoon, followed by a dinner party, where WF meets Else Jonsson. {B2, CR2}

December 10: At the American Embassy in Stockholm, a scared WF works on his speech—his first, he tells the staff. {CR2}

He delivers his speech too far from the microphone, so it is inaudible to most listeners. Speaks of writing about the "problems of the human heart in conflict with itself . . . I believe that man will not merely endure: he will prevail." {ESPL}

December 11: Signs and dates the Chatto & Windus editions of *Sanctuary*, *Sartoris*, *The Sound and the Fury*, *These Thirteen*, and *The Unvanquished*: "William Faulkner/For Else." {Patrik Andersson catalogue, http://patrikandersson.net/en/} Signs and dates the Chatto & Windus edition of *Soldiers' Pay*: "William Faulkner for Else." {https://www.peterharrington.co.uk/catalogsearch/result/?q=soldiers+pay}

December 12: WF and Jill arrive at Le Bourget airport in Paris. {B2}

December 15: Departure for London. {B2}

December 16: Writes to Joan Williams that he discovered in Stockholm that he wasn't quite as old as he thought.[104] {WFJW}

December 18: Arrives home with Jill, greeted by the local high school band. {FK}

December 20: Joan Williams writes a poem lamenting the loss of anonymity now that WF is world famous. She speaks of a desire "to create something together." {WFJW}

December 21: Answering Joan Williams's letter, WF longs for anonymity and worries about the risk to Joan if she is discovered with him. {WFJW}

December 27: Writes to Swedish ambassador, Erik Boheman thanking him for his kindness during the pleasant trip to Sweden: "I hope that it was within my power, and that mine and my daughter's conduct was such to leave as high an opinion of Americans in Sweden as the regard and respect for Sweden which we brought away." {SL}

Writes to Merle Haas about his return home to "lots of family, plenty of Xmas" as Jill sorts out all her impressions of the Swedish trip. "I dont at all regret going to Stockholm now; I realise it was the only thing to do; you can commit mistakes and only feel regret, but when you commit bad taste, what you feel is shame. Anyway, I went, and did the best I knew how to behave like a Swedish gentleman, and leave the best taste possible on the Swedish palate for Americans and Random House." {SL}

Sends a telegram to Joan Williams about his arrival in Memphis the next day. {WFJW}

December 30: A love letter to Joan Williams with a fantasy about them going away together. {WFJW}|

c. Late December: Aunt Bama writing to her nephew Vance Broach: "At air port so many recognized him & came up to say 'Isn't this Mr Wm Faulkner? & he would smile graciously & say 'Yes.'" {BH2}

From Jill to Aunt Bama: "We had a wonderful time in Stockholm and then went on to Paris and London. Pappy looked so very nice at the presentation ceremony and I was so proud of him and all the ambassadors said what a fine stroke he made for America in Sweden." {BH2}

December 31, Midnight: WF raises a toast: "Here's to the young people—they are our hope." {B2}

1951

January 1: Comments to Robert Haas about his Nobel Prize speech: "The piece was what I believe and wanted to say, though I might have said it better with more time to compose it. But then, maybe not; I might have lost its thread in trying to make literature out of it." Postponing work on his fable to finish with *Requiem for a Nun*, which he hopes Random House will publish in the fall. Would like Haas to ask Robert Sherwood to look at the play portion of the novel and assess "whether I can write a play or not."[105] Farming and considering how to use his Nobel Prize money is also taking up his time. In good health except for a lingering cold. {SL}

c. January: To Phil Mullen, associate editor of the *Oxford Eagle*: "I fear that some of my fellow Mississippians will never forgive that 30,000$ that durn foreign country gave me for just sitting on my ass and writing stuff that makes my own state ashamed to own me." {SL}

January 2: Telegram to Joan Williams saying he will arrive in Memphis at 10:00 a.m. {WFJW}

January 7: Two letters to Joan Williams proposing a love affair and continuing with his thoughts about writing. {WFJW}

January 9: A note to Joan Williams about one of her stories. He likes it but suggests she rewrite it. {WFJW}

January 14: Proposes a February meeting with Joan Williams and compliments her on a *Mademoiselle* story and says she has to be willing to sacrifice everything for her art, although she may not have to. {WFJW}

January 16: Maud Falkner to Sallie Burns: "Billy has gotten so touchy we don't dare mention his fame, and believe me, we edge off. He is so very proud and happy over winning the prize, but is his own shy self about publicity." {CCP}

January 17: Joan Williams writes to WF discussing her reading and mentions writing down WF's advice. She wonders what kind of love WF means but signs her letter "with love." {WFJW}

January 20: In Greenville, Mississippi, signs and dates first edition of *Notes of a Horsethief*: "For Ben, much love much/ long time. / Bill" "For Mrs. Wasson, with love, / A lady who has remained / completed unspoiled by my / success" {BH1}

January 21: Writes to Joan about a screenwriting assignment for Howard Hawks in Hollywood. {WFJW}

January 23: Writes to Joan Williams presenting himself as a sort of Cyrano figure. {WFJW}

January 25: Darryl Zanuck declines to produce *Dreadful Hollow* {CR2}

January 28: To Joan Williams: "Writing is important only when you want to do it, and nothing nothing nothing else but writing will suffice, give you peace." Mentions he is setting off for Hollywood.

January 29: Writes to Meta Carpenter that he will soon arrive in Hollywood. {AB}

Late January: Consults with Phil Stone about reworking his will canceling all of Stone's debts to him. Other provisions are for gifts to friends and family members, an insurance policy to fund his niece Dean's education. {SS}

c. January 31: Sends Saxe Commins the "first section of new mss. (*Requiem for a Nun*)." Mentions going to "the coast tomorrow to do a movie job [*The Left Hand of God*] for Howard Hawks." {BH2}

February 1: In Hollywood for work on *The Left Hand of God* in collaboration with Howard Hawks at $2000 a week. {CR2}

Last will and testament with codicil about Nobel Prize trust fund. {B2, BH5}

February 1–March 4: Works on screenplay of *The Left Hand of God.* {WFH}

February 2: In left-hand corner of black and white photograph of WF: "For Saxe commins / old friend, long time, Bill Faulkner." {BH1}

February 7: *The Left Hand of God,* first draft script and synopsis by WF. {HHP}

February 10: The Levee Press publishes *Notes on a Horsethief.*

February 11: Writes Joan Williams about his stay at the Chateau Marmont and collaboration with Howard Hawks; "Fantastic place, fantastic work, almost worth the 2000 a week they pay me." {CR2}

February 12: Phil Stone writes to WF about his will and trust and tax implications. {BH2}

Mid-February: Asks for Saxe Commins's help in getting to Europe while his family thinks he is working on his "play-novel." {BH2}

February 24: To Malcolm Franklin about his sailboat, *The Ring Dove.* Draws a recently purchased Irish pipe.[106] {UVA}

Late February: Discusses European travel arrangements with Saxe Commins and the "official reason to go" provided by Robert Haas. {BH2}

February 28: Perrin H. Lowrey Jr. to Phil Stone asking him to convey to WF that his "books are things that strengthen us for what we are writing and for what we hope to write." {BH2}

March: National Book Award for *Collected Stories.*

Script revisions first draft of *The Left Hand of God.* {HHP}

March 3: Stone replies to Lowrey, saying he appreciates his letter and will read it to WF when he returns from California. {BH2}

March 4: Receives a bonus for finishing his script for *The Left Hand of God* early. {B3}

Describes Hollywood to Joan Williams: "This is a nice town full of very rich middle class people who have not yet discovered the cerebrum, or at best the soul. Beautiful damned monotonous weather, and I am getting quite tired of it, will be glad to farm again." {SL, WFJW}

Meta Carpenter drives WF to the airport. {SO}

March 8: Robert Haas approves the "plan that you take Random House's blessing and go and look at these places [in France] yourself, and get whatever information and atmosphere you will need at first hand."[107] {BH2}

March 13: Phil Stone writes to WF collector William Wisdom: "If and when I see you I shall tell you about the trouble we had about getting Faulkner off to Sweden but I would not want to write it. It is quite a saga, sounds like one of his Snopes tales, and I think it will amuse you." {BH2}

March 27: A letter to the *Memphis Commercial Appeal* opposing the execution of Willie McGee. {ESPL}

Late March: Mentions to Saxe Commins his desire to include an epigraph from "Mr. Eliot's Sunday Morning Service" at the beginning of Act 2 of *Requiem for a Nun.* {SL, BH2}

Enumerates his travel itinerary for Commins, including visits to 1918 battle fields in France and consultations with his French publisher, Gallimard. {BH2}

March 29: Telegram to Commins: "PLEASE TAKE UP TICKETS BEFORE DEADLINE NOTIFY ME BY LETTER." {BH2}

April 2: Saxe Commins receives the second section of *Requiem for a Nun.* {BH2}

Signs and dates a copy of *Notes on a Horsethief* "For Else {Jonsson}/Bill." {Patrik Andersson catalogue, http://patrikandersson.net/en/}

Early April: Asks Commins to do more booking at hotels in Paris and London and arranging flight connections. {BH2}

In another letter from Oxford apologizes to Commins: "Am sorry to put this all on you, but cant do much myself from here, since I hope to keep down fanfare about the trip." {BH2}

April 12: Flies to New York at beginning of trip to France and England. {B3}

April 13: Conveys to Robert Haas his desire that Random House remain his publisher after his death, with Saxe Commins making editorial decisions if Saxe agrees. He asks that they sign his letter, which they do. {SL}

Confirms with Ben Wasson and Hodding Carter that *Notes on a Horsethief* is to be an exclusive edition with no reprint without WF's permission. {BH2}

April 15: Flies to London. {B2}

April 17: Shops for handmade footwear in London. {B2}

Visits Gallimard publishers in Paris. {B2}

April 23: Phil Stone to William Wisdom, who has complained about not receiving a reply to his letter to WF. "I am not going to tell Bill anything. Sometimes he makes me so damn tired I would like to kick the seat of his pants clean off. Back in 1924 when we were trying so hard to get started and met with nothing but defeat, I got my friend, Stark Young, to put Bill up in New York at his own apartment and to get him a job there in New York. Mr. Stark has written Bill a letter and Bill, the last I heard, had not even answered that letter." This has nothing to do with genius, Stone insists: "If you had known four generations of them [Faulkners] as I have you would understand." {BH2}

April 26: Scraps a plan to return to London and decides to fly directly home. {B2}

April 30: Arrives in New York City. {B2}

May 1: Signs the first French edition of *Le Bruit et la Fureur*: "For Joan, with love Bill / William Faulkner / Bard / Mayday." {BH1}

May 2: Visits Bard College for a talk and is introduced by Joan Williams. Afterwards, Williams and a friend drive him to New York City, and he is irritated because he cannot be alone with her. {WFJW}

May 5: Arrives in Lexington for the Kentucky Derby. {B2}

May 11: Printer receives Act Two of *Requiem for a Nun*. {B2}

May 15: Joan Williams publishes a sketch of WF in the *Bardian*, Bard College's school newspaper. {WFJW}

May 18: Jill hosts a Rowan Oak garden party for high school seniors and their teachers. {B2}

May 20: Malcolm Cowley writes to say that Robert Coughlan of *Life* is preparing to write a profile of WF. {SL}

May 21: Joan Williams sends her *Bardian* sketch [see May 15]. She is anxious to hear from him and get his reactions. {WFJW}[108]

May 23: Reports to Else Jonsson about resuming work on *A Fable* and his expectation that he is close to completing it, so that he can "break the pencil and cast it all away, that I have spent 30 years anguishing and sweating over never to trouble me again." {SL}

May 25: Awarded Legion of Honor by French president Vincent Auriol. {B2}

May 28: Delivers commencement address in Fulton Chapel expressing his concern over the attacks on individuality coming from systems, foreign and domestic. {B2}

c. Early June: Instructs Saxe Commins on the layout of Acts 2 and 3 of *Requiem for a Nun*. "This is a good piece. If I were only older, and had the big book behind me, I would be almost tempted to break the pencil here and throw it away." {SL}

June 7: Writes to Joan Williams about wanting to dedicate *Requiem for a Nun* to her but dreads the consequences at home. {WFJW}

June 11: Joan Williams suggests it might be better if they did not write so often since WF is concerned about Estelle intercepting their letters. {WFJW}

June 14: Thanks French publisher Gaston Gallimard in French for his kind treatment during WF's visit to France. "Avec mes hommages sincerements, William Faulkner." {SL}

Mid-June: Ruth Ford telephones from New York City to say *Requiem for a Nun* now has a producer. {B2}

June 18: Still regards *Requiem for a Nun* as their play, WF writes Joan Williams, "even though you have repudiated it." He believes he has a producer interested after reading the galleys. {SL, WFJW}

c. June 18: Reports to Ruth Ford, who wishes to star in *Requiem for a Nun*, that Random House has received inquiries about the play. Realizes the second act has to be rewritten and expects to consult with her when he finishes farming in a week. "It will be pretty fine if we can make a good vehicle for you. I would like to see that title in lights, myself. It's one of my best, I think: Requiem for a Nun." {SL}

June 22: Supplies Else Jonsson with details about his play, which he hopes will be produced in Europe. "I may be able to wangle a workable reason to go to Europe, maybe before next year." {SL}

Early July: Departs for work in New York on stage version of *Requiem for a Nun*. {B2}

Writes to Else Jonsson that he is returning home from New York on July 11 after doing as much as he can with the play but will have to return whenever rehearsals are scheduled. {SL}

July 19: Confesses to Else Jonsson: "I know so little about theatre myself." Spending his time in the hot weather farming. {SL}

August 3: Reiterates to Robert Haas an objection to Robert Coughlan's proposed *Life* profile of him. "I have deliberately buried myself in this little lost almost illiterate town, to keep out of the way so that news people wont notice and remember me." He will do everything he can to prevent publication. Still farming, still hot, still working on the play. Getting ready to take Jill to college, traveling by car on September 9 with a stay in New York City by the 14th. {SL}

August 8: Writes to Meta Carpenter saying he wants to see her again. {CR2}

August 13: Telegram to Hal Smith opposing Robert Coughlan's visit to Oxford to research a profile: "PLEASE ASK HIM NOT TO COME. WILL DO ALL I CAN TO PREVENT THIS. BILL." {SL}

August 16: Hal Smith writes WF about Robert Coughlan's proposed article for *Life*, which WF still opposes. {B2}

Coughlan arrives unaware of WF's attitude but manages to gain entrance to Rowan Oak after expressing his admiration for WF's work. {B2}

August 20?: Announces to Robert Haas that he is thinking of writing his memoirs, "a book in the shape of a biography but actually about half fiction." Material would include "essays about dogs and horses and family [n----rs] and kin"—but more like short stories, including, perhaps, photographs and drawings. Asks for Haas's opinion.[109]

August 27: A long, detailed letter to Else Jonsson about farming. {SL}

September 4: Asks Joan Williams to report on her impressions of California, suggesting she will like some of it but should not take it seriously. {WFJW}

Writes to Jill with advice "important for a young woman to learn." {UVA}

In Oxford, signs and dates first edition of *Requiem for a Nun*: "Phil, with love. Bill." {BH1}

September 6: Writes to Saxe Commins about travel plans to Boston and Princeton: "The book [*Requiem for a Nun*] is very fine, handsome." {BH2}

September 9: To Joan Williams: "I am too old to have to miss a girl twenty-three years old . . . By now I should have earned the right to be free of that." {WFJW}

September 12: With Estelle, drives Jill to Wellesley, Massachusetts, to enter Pine Manor Junior College. {B3}

Joan Williams sends her mixed impressions of California and vows not to give up writing. {WFJW}

September 19: Jill enrolls at Pine Manor Junior College. {B3}

September 20: In New York, signs and dates first edition of *Requiem for a Nun*: "For Saxe." {BH1}

September 22: *New Yorker* review of the play, *Requiem for a Nun*: preposterous. {WFC}

September 23: *New York Post* review of the play, *Requiem for a Nun*: "absolutely worthless." {WFC}

September 24: *Richmond News-Leader* review of *Requiem for a Nun*: one of WF's "strongest novels." {WFC}

September 25: Home for his birthday, looking in on his farm, preparing for a trip to Cambridge, Massachusetts, where he will confer with Ruth Ford and producer Lemuel Ayers on the staging of *Requiem for a Nun*. {SL, B3}

Informs Random House that he authorizes Harold Ober to be the agent of record for "all matters pertaining to my play REQUIEM FOR A NUN." Acknowledges the publisher's right to earnings from "dramatic, moving pictures, and other rights as stipulated in the contract between Random House and myself." {SL}

September 26: A happy birthday telegram to Joan Williams. {WFJW}

September 27: Random House publishes *Requiem for a Nun.*

September 29: *Nation* review of *Requiem for a Nun*: an "ambitious failure." {WFC}

September 30: Reports to Else Jonsson that he has returned to farming after delivering Jill to college. Gives Jonsson his itinerary for trips play rehearsals and acceptance of the Legion of Honor from the French Consul General in New Orleans. {SL}

Delta Democrat-Times review of *Requiem for a Nun*: the "major change from the earlier Faulkner being that he now chooses to write about the struggle for affirmation of belief rather than about the outrage felt by the potential believer." {CR2}

October 2: In Oxford, signs and dates first edition of *Requiem for a Nun* "For Aunt Bama." {BH1}

Departs for Cambridge, Massachusetts. Stays at the Hotel Continental, one block from Harvard Square. {B3}

October 2–17: In Cambridge, Massachusetts, to work on stage version of *Requiem for a Nun.*

n.d.: Types draft of telegram to Estelle: "Decided to do rewrite [of *Requiem for a Nun*] here. May remain week more. Will telephone this week-end. Pappy." {BH2}

October 5: Asks Jill to tell him about her visit to West Point. {UVA}

October 7: Estelle writes to Dorothy and Saxe Commins, thanking them for their hospitality to "Jill, Billy and me." She mentions that she is worn out—so much to do "in the house and grounds." She is hoping they will visit. "Dorothy and I could scout the country-side for pretties for our houses, while Saxe and Billy work. . . . With a heart *full* of love." {BH2}

Brooklyn Daily Eagle calls the play *Requiem for a Nun*: "Greek tragedy, in three acts, with the public and the history of the county taking the part of the chorus." {CR2}

October 15: To daughter Jill: "Pappy loves [her] more than even his soul." {CR2}

October 25: *Oxford Eagle* announces the premier of *Requiem for a Nun* in Cambridge on November 10 "for a trial run of two weeks before the first opening in New York at the beginning of January."

October 26: Receives Legion of Honor in New Orleans and reads a very brief statement in French. {ESPL}

October 29: *New Orleans Item* publishes an interview with a relaxed WF, who chats in a "hill-country" accent about not really being a writer, preferring silence and horses, with occasional stays in Hollywood to earn money. Some interplay with Estelle as well and memories of childhood and New Orleans. {LG}

Writes to Joan Williams praising one of her stories. He is happy to hear from her. {WFJW}

November 5: Returns to Cambridge to do more work on stage version of *Requiem for a Nun*. {B3}

November 17–23: The annual hunt. {B3}

November 27: Returns home from New Orleans. {B3}

November 28: Continues to encourage Joan Williams to write a novel based on a plot line he has suggested to her. {SL}

November 30: Reports to Else Jonsson he has been deer hunting but has seen no deer, went to New Orleans but has returned to resume farming and expecting to return to Boston to "rewrite the damned play again, of which I am quite sick now, except that as soon as it works, the producer has agreed to take it to Europe which is to be in the spring." {SL}

c. December 4 or 11: Informs Saxe Commins he does not need to meet Jill at La Guardia since her plane will fly direct from Boston to Memphis. Asks for $2500. "I will try to finish the year on this." {BH2}

December 20: More suggestions to Joan Williams for the story she is working on. Proposes talking out the story, beginning with one sentence. "Any good story can be told in one sentence, I mean the line, the why of it . . . Rewrite that first letter you sent me, a young woman girl, writing to a famous poet say, whom she called on against his will probably, and wrote to apologize: 'I didn't intend to bother you, interfere, I just wanted, hoped, you would tell me why life is, because you are wise and you know the answers' . . . This story will be a series of letters." {SL}

Christmas: A quiet holiday, complete with tree, Yule log, and holly decorations. {B3}

December 29: Writes to Lemuel Ayers, producer of *Requiem for a Nun* emphasizing the play is for Ruth Ford, and her role in it has to be protected. He will have Ober go over their agreement. {SL}

Late December: Asks Commins to make reservations for Jill at the Baltimore Hotel in New York and to send $15,000 after January 1. "All well here, a good Xmas. I am getting bored, and shall get to work at something soon now." {BH2}

1952

Aspiring writer Pinckney Keel arrives at Rowan Oak seeking advice: "Then go plow a while until a thought comes. Then sit under a tree and write it down," WF responds, but above all "keep writing." He shows her his typewriter and stresses "You don't have to look for people to write about . . . They're everywhere." {CWF}

Loïc Bouvard interviews WF who uncharacteristically discuss his Bergsonian idea of time. {LG}

c. January: Tells Saxe Commins the play was scheduled to open May 30 in Paris, but the producer (Ayers) could not raise enough money and then book publication of *Requiem for a Nun* "has taken the original 'shine' off the thing." More talk of opening in November, but without Ayers, with the director Albert Marre taking over the production. But in order to proceed WF will have to risk about $15,000 of his own money, which he is inclined to do for a production during a French literary festival. Concerned about the impact of his investment on his taxes, WF proposes a telephone talk with Commins. {SL, BH2}

January 4: Requests that Ober make sure that Ruth Ford's part in *Requiem for a Nun* is protected in the contract. {SL}

January 15: Tells Joan Williams her story has improved, if not enough to suit his own judgment. {SL}

January 22: Recalls a pleasant two days with Harold Raymond, senior partner of Chatto & Windus, and the honor of meeting Mrs. Raymond. Still hopes he can accept their invitation to visit the Kentish countryside. Sends his regards to Mrs. Smallwood, a Chatto & Windus partner, whom he met at a party in Chelsea given Mr. and Mrs. J. A. Cochran. Mentions reading Graham Greene's novel *The End of the Affair*, "for me one of the best, most true and moving novels of my time, in anybody's language." {ESPL}

January 24: Completes "First Draft Continuity" of *The Left Hand of God.* {TCF, HHP}

January 26: Suggests to Joan Williams that she visit him at Rowan Oak while Estelle is away visiting Jill at college. {WFJW}[110]

January 28: Telegram to Saxe Commins: "FORGOT ON TELEPHONE PLEASE GET AT LEAST THREE TICKETS FOR THE KING AND I. EITHER FRIDAY OR SATURDAY February FIRST OR SECOND" {BH2}

January 29: In Oxford, signs and dates the first edition of *Intruder in the Dust* for Myrtle Ramey. {BH1}

January 30: Telegram to Saxe Commins: IF JILL AND ESTELLE ARRIVAL CONFLICT PLEASE MEET JILL GRAND CENTRAL I THINK 5PM. ESTELLE AND MISS SOMERVILLE WILL BE ALL

RIGHT UNASSISTED. WOULD YOU CARE TO ASK LINSCOTT FOR DINNER TOO.[111] {BH2}

February 13: Hopes he can meet Joan Williams, if only at the Memphis airport. {WFJW}

February 29: Writes to Joan Williams that he wishes he could ride into the dynamite saloon and rescue her.[112] {WFJW}|

March 2: Writes to Else Jonsson about work on his "big book" and farming. Describes his misadventure with two horses. "No harm though; I learned years ago how to fall off horses." Says the play will open in Paris May 1 and that next week the director will visit him to make plans. {SL}

March 4: Writes to Jill about his horse Tempy. {UVA}

March 14: Another love letter to Joan Williams hoping she will not recoil at his advances. {WFJW}

Additional work on *The Left Hand of God.* {TCF}

March 15: Additional work on *The Left Hand of God.* {TCF}

Mid-March: Invited to attend a festival, "Oeuvres du XXe Siècle," sponsored by the French Liberty of Culture. {SL}

March 21: Additional work on *The Left Hand of God.* {WFH}

March 25: President Rufus C. Harris of Tulane University offers to confer a Doctor of Letters degree and invites WF to attend the commencement exercises on May 27. {SL}

March 28: Reports to Harold Ober about the director Albert Marre's visit. WF decides not to invest $15,000 but offers to put in $2,000 after Marre raises $7,500. Asks Ober to look into the situation, adding, "I will follow your instructions." {SL}

c. April: Likes the idea of a Ford Foundation documentary film about his work. Busy farming but wants to visit France in May. He is pleased with the horses he is training. {SL}

Asks Saxe Commins to return part of a speech mistakenly included in a letter to him. {BH2}

Tells Saxe Commins he will attend a literary festival in Paris but does not want to be an official delegate. The festival "will be a fine excuse to leave here with, since mine is the sort of family which, if I refused to take it to Europe with me, on my return I would find had bought itself a new fur coat, just to keep the books balanced, you might say." {BH2}

April 1: The *New York Times* reports that WF is at home working on *The Left Hand of God.* {TCF}

April 6: Accompanies Shelby Foote to Corinth, Mississippi to visit Civil War battlefields. {B2}

April 9: "The play in Paris has failed," Faulkner writes to Else Jonsson. Lack of funding. {SL}

April 11: Declines honorary doctorate from Tulane acknowledging the honor but stating such a degree should not be bestowed on someone who had not even graduated from grammar school. {SL}

April 13: Describes for Jill the new paddock he has had built at Rowan Oak. {UVA}

April 19: Writes to Else Jonsson about his proposed trip to Paris, where he will have no commitments and act as a "free agent." {SL}

c. Spring: Compliments Joan Williams on her progress as a writer and wants to know about how she is feeling. Offers some criticisms of her story which remains prolix. "A child's loneliness is not enough for a subject. The loneliness should be a catalyst, which does something to the rage of the universal passions of the human heart, the adult world, of which it—the child—is only an observer yet. You dont want to write just 'charming' things. Or at least I dont seem to intend to let you." {SL}

c. May: Draws map of Brown's hotel area of London. {BH5}

Early May: Asks Saxe Commins to book a room for him at the New Weston and cautions him not to send Estelle any money. "In ten minutes, she can have you believing that black is white. Of course, in eleven minutes you know better, but sometimes it is too late by then." {BH2}

May 1: Joan Williams writes from New Orleans addressing a "great man whom I do still love in the depths that no one else has touched." {WFJW}

May 7: To Joan Williams: "I'm leading a dull, busy, purely physical life these days, farming and training a colt and working every day with a jumping horse over hurdles, a long time now since I have anguished over putting words together, as though I had forgotten that form of anguishment." But this just means he is storing up energy to do more writing, he adds. {SL, WFJW}

May 15: Addresses Delta Council in Cleveland, Mississippi. Speaks as much as a fellow farmer as a writer, emphasizing individualism and opposition to centralized government policies. {ESPL}

n.d.: Discusses travel arrangements with Saxe Commins. {BH2}

May 16: Departs for France, England, and Norway. {B2}

May 17: Writes to Joan Williams that he carries her last two letters with him and will come at her call. {WFJW}

May 19: Arrives in Paris, visits Gallimard, meets Else Jonsson, attends a writers' congress, and meets André Malraux. {B3}

May 27: Suffers acute back pain that he treats with liquor. X-rays reveal a broken back and arthritis. {B3}

May 30: Delivers a few words at the Salle Gaveau in Paris and receives an ovation. "I believe that in the intelligence of the French members here, and the muscle of Americans may rest the salvation of Europe." {ESPL}

May 31: Arrives in London as the guest of publisher Harold Raymond. {B2}

June: Harvey Breit of the *New York Times Book Review* asks WF to review *The Old Man and the Sea.* {B2}

June 2: Visits Chatto & Windus to discuss an English edition of *Requiem for a Nun.* {B2}

June 4: Arrives in Oslo for back therapy arranged by Else Jonsson. {B2, CR2}

June 6: Harold Ober sends a memo about *Requiem for a Nun* to Saxe Commins, explaining that the producer, Lemuel Ayers, and WF believe the play does not have enough action. Ayers has ideas about introducing scenes from *Sanctuary* working with Whitfield Cook, an Alfred Hitchcock collaborator, if WF agrees. "Ayers is still enthusiastic about the play and wants to do it and make it a great success." {BH2}

June 8: Writes from Oslo to Saxe Commins about making hotel arrangements in New York City. {SL, BH2}

June 14: Departs Oslo for New York. {B2}

June 15–16: Meets with Saxe Commins, who arranges more medical treatment for WF, who also manages a visit to Random House and sees New York friends. Over dinner enjoys a long conversation with Robert Penn Warren, followed by ferry ride. {SL}

June 16: Writes to Monique Salomon, novelist and editor devoted to WF's work, and her husband, Jean-Jacques Salomon, about the masseur in Oslo who relieved him of back pain for the "first time in years." Explains that he suffered a "collapse" in London. Asks them to redeem a ticket he had lost and found and which has to be presented in Paris and use the money to buy a gift for his god-daughter, the child Monique just gave birth to. {SL}

June 17, 6:30 p.m.: Arrives in Memphis. Dines with Joan Williams. They make love in her car. {WFJW}

2:30 a.m.: Arrives at Rowan Oak. {B3}

June 19: Writes to Joan Williams about both his frustration and fulfillment in his love for her. {WFJW}

June 20: Writes a letter to Harvey Breit saying Hemingway's great work needs no defender while noting that if what Hemingway has recently published "had not been as honest and true as he could make it, then he himself would have burned the manuscript before the publisher ever saw it." {SL}

Writes Billy Winn of the Delta Council that he can do as he likes with his Council speech, which was part of a pleasant experience that included a case of whiskey. {SL}

June 22: In the hot weather watches Jill train her horse while "I sit on the rail and supervise," he tells Saxe Commins. {SL, BH2}

June 28: Writes to Harold Raymond at Chatto & Windus thanking him for the "pleasant dinner and evening" and asking him to convey his compliments to Mrs. Raymond and others in attendance. The back gives him no trouble, thanks to the Swedish masseur, but he is staying away from horses for a while. Includes a blank check for the doctor's fee incurred during treatment in England. {SL}

July: Writes to Joan Williams that he is still concerned about the implications of their making love. {WFJW}

July 2: Fears that Estelle is intercepting the correspondence with Joan Williams even though he has a private post office box. {WFJW}

July 8: Provides a brief biography for editor Anthony Brett-James at Chatto & Windus for the English edition of *Requiem for a Nun*. Minimizes his World War I experience and emphasizes his occupation as farmer. {SL}

July 11: Proposes to Joan Williams that they work together on a television script ["The Graduation Dress"] for James Geller, WF's former boss at Warner Brothers. {SL}

July 14: Comments on Joan Williams's story, "The Morning and the Evening," saying she can use whatever she likes from his contribution. "I am only trying to help you become an artist. You owe me nothing in return for what I try to do or succeed in doing for you." {SL}

Writes to *Harper's* recommending Williams's story: "I hope you will look at this twice, if necessary." {SL}

July 23: Writes to Joan Williams's father thanking him for advice about cutting down a cedar tree, sending his respects to Joan's mother and apologizing for keeping Joan out late. {SL}

July 29: Mentions to Joan Williams a check for $500 for "The Graduation Dress" and asks about her story for *The Saturday Evening Post*. {SL}

July 30: To Saxe Commins, confesses he is not feeling well, his back hurts, has trouble sleeping, and he is bored and fed up, "my days being wasted." Expects to do something "drastic." Talks of getting away for as long as a year, "almost vanish. Then maybe I will get to work again, and get well again." He wants to be free and has always believed that someday he would be. "I have waited, hoped too long, done nothing about it, and so now I must, or—in spirit—die." Anticipates "scorn and opprobrium . . . but perhaps I have already sacrificed too much already to try to be a good artist, to boggle at a little more in order to still try to be one." {BH2}

July 31: Confesses that he does not understand his wife and suspects he knows very little about women. {WFJW}

c. August: To Saxe Commins: "I have never been able to write fiction even on demand or to a pattern; I could never write propaganda on demand when I cant even do it by volition." {BH2}

Telegram to Joan Williams assuring her that he is not antagonistic toward her or her work. {WFJW}

Estelle is hospitalized for treatment of alcoholism. {JW}

August 7: Tells Joan Williams that he continues to be frustrated with their lovemaking and her reluctance to resume an affair. He continues to express his willingness to help with her writing. {WFJW}

August 8: Complains to Joan Williams about injuring his back in a boating accident. Decides to go back to work on the "big book," realizing that like *The Wild Palms*, this new work is the treatment for a broken heart. Mentions rereading her story "The Morning and the Evening," which has been rejected by *Harper's*. "Where I beat you was, I set out to learn all I could sooner in my life than you did. I mean the reading." He apologizes for an earlier, mean-spirited letter. {SL, WFJW}

August 10: Writes that he will reschedule his deer camp outing if Joan Williams can arrange to meet. {WFJW}

August 12: Reports that Ober wishes to see Joan's story. He advises opening herself up "because the heart and the body are big enough to accept all the world, all human agony and passion." Continues to work well on the "big book." {SL}

c. Mid-August: A critique of Joan Williams's story "The Morning and the Evening": "It's all right, this time. I think you can stop worrying, and just write. The next one may not be this good, but dont let that trouble you either." {BH2}

August 19: Continuing back problems, he tells Else Jonsson, made worse by his inability to "be still, inactive, and the farm work," although he has not worked with horses. "Though probably the great trouble is unhappiness here have lost heart for everything, farming and all, have not worked in a year now, stupid existence seeing what remains of life going to support parasites who do not even have the grace to be sycophants. Am tired I suppose. Should either command myself to feel better, or change life itself, which I may do." {SL}

August 20: Encloses Joan Williams's story in a letter to Harold Ober. Believes in the story but also acknowledges he may be wrong about it and wants Ober to give him an honest opinion. Does not want to go to Hollywood except when he can work with Hawks and may have to do some other kind of "hack work" for the *Post*. "I seem to have lost heart for working." {SL, WFJW}}

August 21: Encourages Joan Williams to do more television work for producer James Geller using WF's name if Geller wants it. Laments losing intimacy with Williams. {SL, WFJW}

August 26: Writes Joan Williams implying he misses their physical intimacy. {WFJW}

Early September: Reports that he is working on the "big book" [*A Fable*] again." Expects he may actually finish it this time. Asks for $5000. Mentions that Joan Williams will be coming to New York with parts of his novel.[113] {BH2}

September 18, 5:45: Suffers a convulsive seizure. Taken to the Gartley-Ramsay Hospital in Memphis. Seconal prescribed to allow sleep and recovery from back pain. {CR2}

September 20: Writes to Jill: "I love you. I believed that I would never hurt you. I wish I could recall it, which I cannot of course, but believe Pappy when he says he loves you and regrets having ever hurt at all his child, his only child, that he has always been and will always be so proud of." {UVA}

September 24: Begins to feel better and recover. {CR2}

September 25: Continues convalescence. {CR2}

c. September 25: Joan Williams writes from New York: "There will not be anybody to fill your place in my heart . . . [P]robably I will go through life looking for another you." {WFJW}

September 26: Fidgety but refuses spinal fluid test and leaves hospital. {CR2}

Robert Coughlan of *Life* magazine writes to Phil Stone asking for advice on the WF profile he has written. {BH2}

A happy birthday telegram to Joan Williams. Also writes to her wishing they could spend every day together, an impossibility now that she is in New York. {WFJW}

September 27: Writes to Joan Williams that he expects to be in New York City in October, hoping to hold and touch her then. Tells her about the forthcoming Ford Foundation documentary on the history of Yoknapatawpha and work on a TV adaptation of a story, "The Brooch." {WFJW}

2:00 p.m.: Tells Joan Williams, who has met Hal Smith at WF's suggestion: "Smith is a good man for you to have seen. He will do a great deal for me that doesn't cost actual cash money. Don't hesitate to demand of him nor of anyone at Random House in my name." {WFJW}

September 28: Explains to Saxe Commins that he did not write earlier because of bad back and his lapse into alcohol to treat it. Hospitalized and in a back brace. Asks Commins to help Joan Williams, who has sold a television script agented by Harold Ober. WF wants her to write a novel for Random House. "She is shy and independent and will probably ask nothing of you." {BH2}

September 29: Phil Stone writes to Fred Wieck of the Newberry Library, Chicago, noting WF does not write letters "unless he has to do it." {BH2}

Acknowledges receiving from Harold Ober a letter from the *Atlantic Monthly* accepting Joan Williams's story "The Morning and the Evening." Explains that she has been "my pupil 3 years now, when nobody else, her people, believed in her. I am happy to know my judgment was right." Notes that she is "shy and independent, will ask for no help" but wants Ober to do what he can for her. Says he is interested in doing a piece about Mississippi and has done more work on the "big book," even though he has been hospitalized. "I still feel pretty bad, but should improve from now on." {SL}

Responds to Thomas H. Carter's request for a review of *The Old Man and the Sea* to be published in *Shenandoah*. Although he has written a few paragraphs for Harvey Breit of the *New York Times Book Review*, he is willing to write fresh review if Carter wants one. {SL}

Writes to Joan Williams about his aching back and aching heart. {WFJW}

September 30: Phil Stone sends Robert Coughlan a detailed critique of his WF profile, calling it "extremely good." {BH2}

Joan Williams writes that she hopes he is happy in spite of his unhappiness about her. Describes her mixed feelings about WF's agent, Harold Ober. "Whatever I have achieved, Bill, its been you that made it possible. I want to see you and anytime . . . I would demand nothing in your name from anyone." {WFJW}

Autumn: *Shenandoah* publishes WF's review of *The Old Man and the Sea.*

October 7: Saxe Commins arrives in Oxford to deal with WF's medical care after a fall at Rowan Oak. {CR2}

October 8: Commins writes to his wife, Dorothy, describing a WF in extremis. {BH2}

Commins writes to Robert Haas and Bennett Cerf with a detailed report about WF's deterioration. {BH2}

October 10: Arrives at the Campbell Clinic in Memphis for fitting of a steel back brace. {CR2}

Estelle Faulkner wires Saxe Commins: "PLEASE, IF YOU WILL, KEEP BILLS WHEREABOUTS CONFIDENTIAL. THANK YOU." {BH2}

Estelle writes to Saxe and Dorothy Commins that WF is cooperative and improving. "We can never thank you enough, Saxe, for, in your gentle way, taking charge of the situation and getting our 'Pappy' back to the hospital . . . [*Y*]*ou* turned the tide." {BH2}

Phil Stone sends a letter to Robert Coughlan with more corrections of his WF profile. {BH2}

c. **October 15:** Estelle reports to Saxe Commins about WF's continued improvement. "I was a little startled when I saw your letter addressed to Mrs. *Estelle* Faulkner—Aren't you a bit premature—or has something happened that I'm in the dark about."[114] {BH2}

October 18: Writes to Joan Williams declaring his love for her is greater than any other he has known. {WFJW}

October 21: Estelle wires Saxe Commins: "BILL HOME TODAY. GREATLY IMPROVED. WILL WRITE LATER LOVE ESTELLE." {BH2}

October 24: Lets Else Jonsson know that he has been sick and depressed and hospitalized. Expects to feel strong in a week and will write "a better letter then." {SL}

Reports to Joan Williams that Estelle has read her letters while he was in the hospital. {WFJW}

October 25: Reports to Saxe Commins that Estelle has read one of Joan Williams's letters and is now drunk, and he is trying to nurse her. "I cant really blame her, certainly I cant criticize her, I am even sorry for her, even if people who will open and read another's private and personal letters, did deserve exactly what they get." Describes his own unhappiness and claims Estelle "has never had any regard or respect for my work, has always looked on it as a hobby, like collecting stamps." Worries about the impact of all this on Jill. "I used to be the cat who walked by himself and wanted, needed nothing from anyone. But not any more. Let me have your advice, if you have any. I probably wont take it, but it should comfort me." {BH2}

October 27: Tells Joan Williams that he will stay with Saxe and Dorothy Commins in Princeton but hopes to see her in New York City on the weekends. {WFJW}

October 29: Estelle to Saxe Commins about a stronger "Billy" catching up on correspondence and "farm duties": "Truly, he has too much to do here—It is bad, I know, for an artist to undertake all Bill does—but how to circumvent it? I am at loss—" Expresses gratitude to Commins and resolves to keep "an even keel mostly!" {BH2}

c. November: Expresses the hope to Joan Williams that her soul and spirit match the beauty of her body. {WFJW}

Draws a map for Joan Williams with directions from the Princeton railroad station to Saxe Commins's residence. {BH5}

November 1, 10:00 p.m.: Responds to Joan Williams's reservations about Harold Ober, telling her, "He is a fine agent and good person," although they have nothing to talk about except in correspondence. "Let that be your attitude toward him. He is all right, just horribly shy, and I mean horribly." He is delighted to learn that Williams is working on her first novel. {SL, WFJW}

Confesses to Saxe Commins that he wants to work quietly in Princeton. A crop failure has him worrying about money again. Still working on his novel. "I seem to have reached a point I never believed I ever would: where

I need to have someone read it and tell me, Yes, it's all right. You must go ahead with it." {BH2}

Writes a note to Dorothy Commins about the peace and pleasure of his anticipated trip to Princeton. {BH2}

November 2: In a letter to Joan Williams, WF takes some credit for her early success. {WFJW}

c. November 3: Joan Williams describes a call from Saxe Commins, who offers to publish her book and then inquires about WF's health. She is hesitant, but Commins assures her that WF confides in him. "I could tell how much he loved you . . . Write me what you are *doing*."

November 4: Votes for Adlai Stevenson for president. {JW}

Saxe Commins writes that *A Fable* is "as near perfection as we can make it." {SO}

November 6: To: Joan Williams: "You must expect scorn and horror and misunderstanding from the rest of the world who are not cursed with the necessity to make things new and passionate, no artist escapes it." The passion in her work has come from their intimacy. {SL, WFJW}

November 9: Carvel Collins writes to Phil Stone mentioning that with his wife, Mary, he hosted a visit from Jill, Malcolm, and his wife, Gloria, at Martha's Vineyard last spring. {BH2}

November 10: Telegram to Saxe Commins: "PLEASE RESERVE ROOM ALGONQUIN FOR FRIDAY. SHOULD REACH TOWN IN TIME TO SEE YOU. OTHERWISE MONDAY" {BH2}

November 13: Phil Stone reports to Carvel Collins about the Ford Foundation film: "They took shots of me and Bill all day long one day in the office. Bill was just as gracious and patient about this as possible, and I am quite alarmed about him. I want to get him to a doctor soon to be sure that he is not developing a split personality." {BH2}

Mid-November: Works on *A Fable* in Princeton and New York. {CR2}

November 26: To Jill: "All the boys here wear dirty white shoes too, I suppose until the weather turns warm in May, then they will go back to brown leather ones." {UVA}

Late November: Writes an affectionate goodbye note to Dorothy Commins {BH2}

Admitted to Westhill Sanitarium in the Bronx. Undergoes, according to Dr. Eric P. Mosse, a series of electroshock treatments. {B2}

November 29: Faulkner scholar Ward L. Miner describes WF's appearance at a Paris literary conference last spring: "The hall was packed and it was quite evident they were there for one person—Faulkner—even though people such as Malraux, Auden, etc, were also on the platform. When Faulkner stood up, there was a tremendous ovation for several minutes.

Unfortunately, his talk was rather feeble, and so the applause was not nearly as great at the conclusion. But it was apparent to anybody that Faulkner the novelist was looked up to with awe even though Faulkner the speaker was not." {BH2}

Early December: At the New Weston Hotel in New York City and working on *A Fable* at Random House. {B2}

December 2, 1:30 a.m.: Recounts for Joan Williams the record of agonizing partings and wonders if he can write without her. This is what has come from her first visit to Rowan Oak to meet him. {WFJW}

7:00 a.m.: Apologizes for sending Joan a depressing letter. {WFJW}

December 4: Reports to Else Jonsson that he is in Princeton getting work done on his novel. Decides to ignore his back and to get back up on a horse when he returns home. {SL}

Anna Louise Davis of the Ober agency writes to Richard L. Field of *Holiday* magazine: "William Faulkner came in to see Mr. Ober today and he told him that he still wants to try the piece on Mississippi for Holiday, but he has not yet thought of a peg on which to hang it. Will you be willing to give him a little more time to ponder this issue?" {UVA}

December 9: Writes to Saxe Commins that Joan Williams's right to the manuscript of *The Sound and the Fury* is "not to be challenged."[115] {BH2}

December 10: Writes a kind of fable to Joan Williams about what his love for her has meant to him. {WFJW}

Mid-December: Resists producer Lemuel Ayers's suggestion that Ruth Ford should be replaced in *Requiem for a Nun.* {SL}

December 17: Responds to a moving letter from Joan Williams, claiming that someday they will read it together when they have become one. {WFJW}

December 18: Harold Ober writes that producer Lemuel Ayers says he cannot raise the money for the play version of *Requiem for a Nun* so long as Ruth Ford is given the lead. The play needs a "really great actress." Ober goes over Faulkner's options and asks for his response. {BH2}

December 19: Asks Harold Ober to work on Ruth Ford's behalf since producer Lemuel Ayers has dropped his option on the play. {SL}

December 23: Permits *The Freeman* to publish his speech to the Delta Council. {SL}

December 24: Explains to Saxe Commins that he does not believe television adaptations of his work will hurt the books Random House prints. All is calm now with Jill in the house, but he expects that after Estelle has a "few drinks in her, the lightning flicks a little. Hope to God I can keep J out of it, but I dont know of course." {BH2}

December 25: A traditional Christmas morning with Jill, Dean, and Vicki (Cho-Cho's daughter) and the toast to the younger generation. {CR2}

December 27: Phil Stone writes to Howard Magwood asking for a print of the Ford Foundation film he appeared in with WF and hunting companion, Ike Roberts. "Bill and I were talking about it the other day and we are anxious to get one and to let Ike Roberts see it at a private showing while Ike is still here. He is very frail and he might go out almost any time." {BH2}

December 28: Speculates that Joan Williams may not do what is necessary to nurture her talent, telling her about the courage required to become an artist. {WFJW}

December 30: A note to Joan Williams: "I love you."

December 31: Reports to Joan Williams that he has "run dry" on his novel. He can no longer write in Oxford and has to "get away." He suggests a letter from Joan might stimulate his writing. {SL, WFJW}

1953

January 2: To Joan Williams: "I was wrong. The work, the mss. is going again. Not as it should, in a fine ecstatic rush like the orgasm we spoke of at Hal's [Smith's] that night. This is done by simple will power; I doubt if I can keep it up too long. But it's nice to know that I still can do that: can write anything I want to, whenever I want to, by simply will, concentration . . ." {SL}

January 5: Requests that Saxe Commins send him $5000 to pay off small pending debts. Working deliberately on the novel. Asks for help locating an apartment in Princeton for February. {SL, BH2}

Malcolm Franklin date book: With Pappy drives Jill to the airport to return to college. {UVA}

January 7: Joan Williams responds to WF's dream about shopping in New York with Joan for a new dress for a party and then traveling back to Princeton, where she is to receive a Nobel prize: "Sometimes, you are very funny . . . a wonderful dream." {WFJW}

January 8: Encourages Joan Williams to keep writing short stories. His own work is going "damned well. Very hard to do here, and slow. Am doing new stuff now: it is all right. I still have power and fire when I need it, thank God." He hopes their separation will have increased her desire for him. {SL, WFJW}

Malcolm Franklin datebook: dinner at Rowan Oak. {UVA}

Phil Stone writes to E. Melville Price, an old New Haven friend, about the Ford Foundation documentary, which took up his time from 8:30 a.m.

to 6:20 p.m. "I told Bill I would be glad when he got through being famous." {BH2}

Estelle writes Dorothy Commins thanking her and Saxe for taking care of WF, who returned to Oxford "a new man." Mentions that her eyes are growing "steadily worse." {CFS}

January 10: Writes to Saxe Commins about leaving Oxford. Expects to tell Estelle the next day and the "subsequent explosion will determine just when and under what conditions." He also expects her to ask to come with him. {SL}

Proposes to Joan Williams that they spend five days together in Hal Smith's New York apartment. {WFJW}

January 14: Estelle's cataract surgery. {B3}

January 15: Malcolm Franklin datebook: Estelle returns to Rowan Oak. {UVA}

January 16: Urges Jill to keep up with her school work. {UVA}

January 18: Malcolm Franklin datebook: "Faulkners over for dinner." {UVA}

January 19: Malcolm Franklin datebook: "went to F for dinner." {UVA}

January 20: Malcolm Franklin datebook: "M has other cataract removed. Called Jill." {UVA}

January 22: Malcolm Franklin datebook: "Faulkners for dinner."

January 24: Malcolm Franklin datebook: "Faulkners over for duck." {UVA}

January 26: *The Freeman* reprints the Delta Council speech.

Malcolm Franklin drives WF to the bus station on the way to New York City. {CR2}

January 29: Malcolm Franklin datebook: "Faulkners for dinner." {UVA}

January 31: Returns to New York and stays in Hal Smith's apartment at 9 East 63rd Street, suffering more back pain and drinking bouts. {B3, CR2}

c. February: Spends time with Robert Linscott, visiting the Whitney Museum, talking about writing, which he finds difficult now to do in Oxford, his unreliable response to interviewers, window shopping on Fifth Avenue, and his talk with a butcher about his writing, lunching in New York. "He was wholly without the loose change of small talk." {CWF}

February 5: Malcolm Franklin datebook: "supper at Faulkners."

February 7: Accompanies Hal Smith and Saxe Commins to the National Book Awards at the Commodore Hotel and lapses into another drinking bout. {B3, CR2}

February 8: Taken to Charles B. Townes private hospital on Central Park South, where he recovers quickly. {CR2}

February 9: Malcolm Franklin datebook: "Faulkners for drinks."

February 11: Malcolm Franklin datebook: "supper at Faulkners."

February 13: In New York, signs the Modern Library edition of *Sanctuary* "For Joan Williams" {CFS}

February 16: Apologizes for worrying his stepson, Malcolm. "I know that I have not been quite myself since last spring." He has been suffering blackouts, perhaps from taking a bad fall while riding his horse, Tempy. Saxe Commins is taking care of him, so Malcolm should not worry his mother, Estelle. Malcolm can rely on Saxe for an honest report. {SL}

Saxe Commins reports to Malcolm and Gloria Franklin that WF is in the Random House office every day and has recovered and feels he should remain in New York to finish his work. {UVA}

February 19: The *New Yorker* rejects "Weekend Revisited" based on WF's hospital experience and a response to Charles Jackson's *The Lost Weekend.* {CR2}

Malcolm Franklin datebook: "Faulkners for supper. Mama's birthday." {UVA}

February 22: Writes to Else Jonsson saying he is in New York and not much happier, but he is busy writing, finishing a piece about Sherwood Anderson, working on a television adaptation of one of his stories ("Old Man"), and a piece about his state for *Holiday* magazine, plus continued labor on *A Fable*. Back troubles continue with medical consultations. "Because something is wrong with me; as you saw last spring, my nature has changed. I think now that when I fell off the horse last March, I may have struck my head too. I will know this week." {SL}

Malcolm Franklin datebook: "supper at Faulkners." {UVA}

February 24: Ober sells a memoir about Sherwood Anderson to the *Atlantic Monthly* for $300.

February 25: Undergoes a medical exam and is pronounced normal. {B3}

February 27: The Omnibus documentary about WF in which he appears is shown at the Civic Auditorium in Oxford. {CR2}

February 28: A detailed description of WF working in Saxe Commins's office at Random House in a *New Yorker* interview. {LG}

March: Works on television script of "Shall Not Perish." {WFH}

March 2: Another medical exam with other tests and x-rays recommended. {B3}

March 5: Writes to Jill that he loves her "always, always, always." {UVA}

March 10: Malcolm Franklin datebook: "Lunch at Faulkners."

March 11: Admitted to Doctors Hospital under supervision of Dr. S. Bernard Wortis. Skull x-rays show no abnormalities, liver function normal, some hypersensitivity brain waves, but no sign of illness. {B2}

March 17: Malcolm Franklin datebook: "Lunch at Faulkners." {UVA}

March 31: WF visits a psychiatrist, refuses Dr. S. Bernard Wortis's probing of his childhood and relationship with his mother. Like Dr. Mosse at the Westhill sanitarium, Dr. Wortis observes a man with an intense need for affection. {B3, CR2}

Tells Else Jonsson he continues working on television scripts. He has had two more "spells." A doctor has told him about a brain lobe that is "hypersensitive to intoxication"—not just alcohol but "worry, unhappiness, any form of mental unease, which produces less resistance to alcohol." But the doctor has not advised quitting drinking completely. Brain function is normal but "near the borderline of abnormality. which I knew myself; this behavior is not like me." Yet he can still work and continues with plans to farm, drive Jill to school, and deliver an address at her graduation. He has recorded his Nobel speech for broadcasting Europe by Voice of America. {SL}

Turns over to Ober the manuscript of "Mississippi," 3,000 words longer than *Holiday* requested. {B3}

Completes television script of "The Brooch." {WFH}

April: Works on television script of "Old Man."[116] {WFH}

April 3: Writes to Joan Williams that in spite of their recent intimacy she has still not given herself to him completely. {WFJW}

"The Brooch" is broadcast. {WFH}

April 6: Malcolm Franklin datebook: "Martinis and dinner at Faulkners." {UVA}

April 10: Stone writes to WF about memories of Yale friends and discussions of Swinburne. {BH2}

Malcolm Franklin writes in his datebook: "Mama had gastric hemorrhage." She is taken to the hospital. {CR2}

April 11: Estelle's condition is fair and blood donors are lined up. {CR2}

April 12: Estelle returns home in fair condition. {CR2}

April 16: Dated carbon typescript of Faulkner's adaptation of "Old Man" for television. {LC}

April 18: Returns to Rowan Oak after Estelle suffers another hemorrhage. {CR2}

April 19: Jill and her father arrive at Rowan Oak and Estelle is taken to Oxford Hospital.

April 20: "I just saw Bill a while ago and he tells me that he made a lot money out of the TV," Phil Stone writes to Carvel Collins. Mentions Estelle's hemorrhages: "We knew she was sick but we didn't pay any attention to it because we just took it for granted that she was probably getting off of a drunk." {BH2}

Malcolm Franklin datebook: "M better." {UVA}

April 21: Malcolm Franklin datebook: "M seems better." {UVA}

April 22: Reports to Saxe Commins about Estelle's sickness, blood transfusions, and forthcoming tests. "She was almost gone Saturday, but rallied and has improved." Still hoping to spend May in New York. Mentions costly medical bills and that "another TV job will help." {BH2}

c. April 23: Writes to Joan Williams that Estelle is better and thinks his own ability to work is due to Joan's encouragement. {WFJW}

April 24: Estelle is convalescing, WF tells Commins. Asks him if he can find a mislaid pipe. Hoping to visit Commins in June. {BH2} Draws a pipe that he has mislaid at Commins's house. {BH5}

April 25: Admits to Joan Williams that he needs her and is no longer a proud man on his own. {WFJW}

April 26: Malcolm Franklin datebook: "Pappy home supper at F's." {UVA}

April 29: "Working at the big book," WF reports to Joan Williams. "I know now—believe now—that this may be the last major, ambitious work; there will be short things, of course. I know now that I am getting toward the end, the bottom of the barrel. The stuff is still good, but I know now that there is not very much more of it, a little trash comes up constantly now, which, must be sifted out." Believes he now has a perspective on his body of work. "I realize for the first time what an amazing gift I had: uneducated in every formal sense, without even very literate, let alone literary, companions, yet to have made the things I made. I dont know where it came from. . . . I wonder if you even had that thought about the work and the country man whom you know as Bill Faulkner—what little connection there seems to be between them." He suggests all these years of creativity have led to the night of love making with Joan. {WFJW}

April 30: Admits to Joan Williams that he is worried that Hal Smith will make a pass at her. {WFJW}

Malcolm Franklin datebook: "supper at Faulkners." {UVA}

c. May: Draft of a telegram to Ernest Hemingway on winning the Nobel Prize: "Splendid news. stop not that quote the old man unquote needs more accolade than it already has from us who know the anguish it took and have tried to do it too." {SL}

May 1: Robert Coughlan to Phil Stone: "Bill went on one of his big, economy size toots here in New York not long ago and had to be hauled off to the hospital. But they fixed him up and he was out soon and is behaving himself now, so far as I know." {BH2}

May 3: Estelle travels to Memphis for hospital tests.

May 4: A convalescing Estelle accompanies WF and Malcolm Franklin to see *High Noon*. "Supper at Faulkners." {CR2, UVA}

May 6: Writes to Meta Carpenter about Estelle's illness. {CCP}

May 7–8: Writes three letters to Joan Williams, continuing to express his need for her and asking her to wire him and say when he can call her. Promises to control himself. {WFJW}

May 9: Departs for New York.

Mid-May: Meets and gets on well with e. e. cummings.

Attends a Dylan Thomas reading and speaks briefly to him afterwards. {B3}

Signs a copy of *Soldiers' Pay* for Brandon Grove in Joan Williams's apartment. Williams tells WF that Grove, a young man she has been dating, has taken advantage of her relationship with WF. He replies, "That's what people do." {WFJW}

May 15: Reports to Else Jonsson that Estelle is recovering, and he has returned to New York City to work until his visit to Jill's school, after which he will return home. He is wearing a polo player's belt to help with his back. {SL}

Writes to Meta Carpenter: "Devine and I liked each other well in the old age. Change in people: the saddest thing of all, division, separation, all left is the rememberings, the dream, until you almost believe that anything beautiful is nothing else but dream." {CCP}

May 17: Malcolm Franklin datebook: in New York "met by chance Pappy—he came on to the hotel where we had a drink & chat." {UVA}

May 24: Attends the YM-YWHA Poetry Center to see Dylan Thomas perform. Meets and drinks with Thomas afterwards. {B2}

June: *Atlantic Monthly* publishes "Sherwood Anderson: An Appreciation."

June 1: Writes a short note to ask where Joan Williams is. Then in a longer letter counsels against traveling by bus to see the country, which is as foolish as attending a writers' conference. {WFJW}

Early June: William and Estelle depart for Jill's Pine Manor graduation. {CR2}

June 8: *Atlantic Monthly* publishes "A Note on Sherwood Anderson."

Delivers address to Jill's Pine Manor Junior College graduating class.

June 14: Returns to Rowan Oak. Corrects proofs on Pine Manor graduation speech, which Ober sells to the *Atlantic Monthly* for $250. {B2}

June 16: Salvages his sailboat sunk in Sardis Lake and throws a party. Dances the soft shoe with an Ole Miss student. {B2}

c. June 16: Counsels Joan Williams never to be "afraid about money. That is death to an artist." Discusses his plans for a writers' colony, delayed because of work on the big book. "I could not do justice to a group which trusted me, and do my own work too." {SL}

June 18: Advises Joan Williams about one of her stories. Praises her hard work but believes it is not the best she can do. He does not want her to copy his style but adds: "I learned to write from other writers. Why should you refuse to?" Suggests she show the story to Ober to see if it is salable. {SL}

Estelle extols her three-day visit with Saxe and Dorothy Commins and is looking forward to their visit to Oxford in the fall. She describes WF's address to Jill's graduation class as "perfect—He looked very handsome and distinguished in his cap and gown—and evidently remembered Saxes' instruction—for every word was clearly and carefully spoken." {BH2}

June 22: Telegram to Saxe Commins: "PLEASE SEND 5000 ALL WELL HERE. TRYING TO WORK." {BH2}

June 25: Jill sends a thank you note to Dorothy Commins, adding: "My brother Malcolm found the enclosed [thank you note] this morning, rather the worse for wear . . . My mistake was relying on Pappy, with so very many things on his mind, to mail it for me.[117] {BH2}

June–July: Works steadily on *A Fable*. {B2}

c. July 2: Joan Williams is rewriting a story to submit to Harold Ober and waiting to get WF's comments, worried that this is the best she can do but that he won't be satisfied. She would like to spend the summer in Memphis and see him but does not want to sneak around with him. {WFJW}

July 3: Working at the big book, but it has run dry. He will try again tomorrow. Still believes Williams's story needs more work after reading it twice. Nothing wrong with the story itself but rather with the way it is told. Goes into detail about how the first sentence should be handled, what the second paragraph should look like, and how the tension should increase. {SL}

July 4: Replies to Joan Williams, agreeing that Memphis is not a good place for them to meet. Runs dry on *A Fable* but has not resumed with the expectation that he will run dry again. {WFJW}

c. July 6: Reports to Joan Williams, saying he had a good day writing *A Fable*. {WFJW}

July 10: Howard Hawks calls from Paris about a film starring Gary Cooper, which is delayed due to Cooper's operation. {B2}

July 13: Mentions to Saxe Commins he is awaiting word from Howard Hawks. "Big book [*A Fable*] is going well now. Slow, very hard to work here, will have to get away regardless soon, whether the Paris thing comes through or not." {BH2}

July 16: Invites Joan Williams to accompany him to Europe.[118] He advises her to keep writing and not wait for inspiration. {WFJW}

Malcolm Franklin datebook: "Lunch at Faulkners. Hot and clear." {UVA}

July 25: Malcolm Franklin datebook: "hot and clear, supper at Faulkners." {UVA}

July 27: Telegram to Saxe Commins: "HAVE 500 PLUS PAGES. END OF BOOK POSSIBLE IN TWO MONTHS. WILL ADVISE PLANS SOON. PLEASE SEND 25 HUNDRED."

July 29: Estelle to Dorothy and Saxe Commins: "Bill has done a prodigious amount of work on his book, despite interruptions of all sorts that I've been unable to prevent." But he is "frightfully unhappy here, and Jill and I will be relieved and glad when he decides to 'take off' again." Mentions Joan Williams has arrived, and so Estelle may leave "*first* after all." She mentions reports of WF that are the result of "envy" and "malice . . . Luckily I have managed a stiff upper lip—and retained my dignity." {BH2}

In a letter to Joan Williams, WF speculates that editor Seymour Lawrence's rejection of her story might have something to do with the editor's knowing WF and Joan. {WFJW}

July 30: Writes to Joan Williams suggesting a fall rendezvous at Robert Linscott's farm and perhaps a trip to Mexico. {WFJW}

July 31: Writes to Joan Williams declaring she should tell her father that WF will take care of her and her future. {WFJW}

Malcolm Franklin datebook: "Lunch at Faulkners—Faulkners for gimlets on terrace—supper at Faulkners." {UVA}

August: *Atlantic Monthly* publishes "Faith or Fear," the graduation speech to Jill's graduation class, emphasizing, "We must break ourselves of thinking in the terms foisted on us by the split-offs of that old dark spirit's ambition and ruthlessness: the empty clinging terms of 'nation' and 'fatherland' or 'race' or 'color' or 'creed.'" {ESPL}

August 3: Saxe Commins writes about two New American Library editions of *Sanctuary* and *Requiem for a Nun* together and another that would print "Wild Palms" and "Old Man" separately instead of by alternating chapters of the two novellas. {BH2}

On Commins's letter Faulkner writes: "Dismembering THE WILD PALMS will in my opinion destroy the over-all impact which I intended." Nearing the completion of the "big one . . . I am frightened, that lightning might strike me before I can finish it. It is either nothing and I am blind in my dotage, or it is the best of my time. Damn it, I did have genius, Saxe. It just took 55 years to find out. I suppose I was too busy working to notice it before." Expects the book to be about 700 typed pages and that they will need two weeks to go through it. {SL, BH2}

In another undated letter to Commins, Faulkner reports the manuscript will be finished after one more chapter. He needs to draw $2500 to invest in an unspecified business. "Please send $10,000.00 now." {SL}

August 4: Finishes what he calls the "Three Temptations scene" in *A Fable*. {B3}

Malcolm Franklin datebook: "Faulkners on terrace for gimlets & frankfurters." {UVA}

August 5: Writes to Joan Williams exhilarated about writing the "Three Temptations scene" and crediting her as his inspiration. {WFJW}

Malcolm Franklin datebook: "Faulkners for steaks on our terrace—gimlets." {UVA}

August 6: Malcolm Franklin datebook: "rained all day. Supper with F uptown. Watermelon at Oldhams." {UVA}

August 8: Predicts to Joan Williams that he will have a draft of *A Fable* by the end of the month. {WFJW}

August 13: Telegram to Saxe Commins: "YES TO FAULKNER READER." Inquires about a deadline for a foreword. {BH2}

Writes to Joan Williams predicting a successful season of work and love. {WFJW}

August 14: Telegram from Saxe Commins stating foreword can be written at Faulkner's convenience after his return to New York. {BH2}

Mid-August: Writes Saxe Commins asking him to let Estelle "have what money she asks for, to my acct." {BH2}

August 20: Writes to Joan Williams after meetings in Memphis and Holly Springs, expressing his disappointment that she is traveling to Florida since he hoped to have her to himself while Estelle and Jill were in Mexico. {WFJW}

August 25: Estelle and Jill depart for a holiday in Mexico. {B3}

August 29: A telegram responding to Commins's heart attack: "GLAD TO HEAR IT. BEGGED YOU LAST SPRING TO REST AND LET JOINT EXPLODE. MAYBE YOU WILL NOW. LOVE TO DOROTHY. BILL" {SL}

September: A draft of *A Fable* finished, WF falls into a depression and accepts an invitation to spend a few days in Greenville, Mississippi, but at a party refers to *A Fable* as "possibly the greatest of our time." {B2}

Writes to Joan Williams crediting her own determination to write as a reason why he finished *A Fable*. {WFJW}

Before leaving for Greenville, accepts Howard Hawks's invitation to work on *Land of the Pharaohs*, to be filmed in Egypt. {CR2}

In Oxford, organizes a party at Rowan Oak, preparing dinner and supervising the chilling of the wine. {B3}

Writes Saxe Commins that he has not yet read the proof of *The Faulkner Reader*. {BH2}

September 1: Phil Stone writes to Carvel Collins: "Bill stopped me on the street the other day and told me that he had just finished the best thing that he had ever written [*A Fable*] and probably . . . the best thing anybody had ever written, and yet there are still people who believe in Faulkner modesty." {CR2}

September 4: Decides not to send flowers to Joan Williams after she discourages his gesture. {WFJW}

September 8: Back pain returns and is alleviated with liquor and Seconal. Admitted to Gartley-Ramsay Hospital. {CR2}

September 9: Complains of "abdominal distress." {CR2}

September 10: Discharges himself from Gartley-Ramsay. Doctor's notes: "Patient left before treatment could be completed. Impossible to reason with him. Called family, but patient left. An acute and chronic alcoholic." {CR2}

September 20: Apologizes to Jill for his "dreadful behavior" (insobriety). {CR2}

September 26: Sends Joan Williams a happy birthday telegram. {B2}

September 28: *Life* publishes part 1 Robert Coughlan's profile, "The Private Life of William Faulkner," to the consternation of the subject and his family. {B2, CR2}

September 30: Phil Stone writes to Robert Coughlan: "The article is extremely good and has in it some splendid phrasing. . . . You emphasize too much that Bill occasionally, very occasionally, throws a drunk. . . . On the whole he drinks very little." {CR2}

October: Writes to Malcolm Franklin that he is feeling fine and working on his big book, which had run dry in August, but "going all right now." Mentions plan to do a film with Howard Hawks, editing of *The Faulkner Reader* for the Book-of-the-Month-Club, and conveys his regards to Malcolm's wife, Gloria. {SL}

Writes to Joan Williams declining the opportunity to see her in New York. "If this is the end, and I suppose, assume it is, I think the two people drawn together as we were and held together for four years by whatever it was we had, knew—love, sympathy, understanding, trust, belief—deserved a better period than a cup of coffee—not to end like two high school sweethearts breaking up over a Coca Cola in the corner drugstore." {BH2}

October 1: Phil Stone to Robert Coughlan: "Your article, I think, has the town stewing." Predicts a storm among the Faulkners about who supplied the family photographs. {BH2, CR2}

October 5: *Life* publishes part 2 of Robert Coughlan's profile, "The Man Behind the Faulkner Myth."

Responds to Phillip ("Moon") Mullen about the *Life* profile. "No, I haven't seen the piece in LIFE yet, but if you had anything to do with it, I know it is alright and I hope you make a nickel out of it." {SL, BH2}

Phil Stone to Robert Coughlan: "Almost all the grand old ladies around Oxford think your article is very fair and very accurate." {BH2}

October 6: Phil Stone writes to George A. Saucier, Mississippi Department of Public Safety, arranging to have Estelle's suspended license reinstated after she failed to report an accident. {BH2}

October 7: In Oxford, writes to Mullen he won't read the *Life* profile and mentions his mother is furious about it and canceled her subscription to the magazine. He tried to prevent the piece but regrets there is no "protection from journalism . . . There seems to be in this the same spirit which permits strangers to drive in my yard and pick up books or pipes I left in the chair where I had been sitting, as souvenirs." Honored abroad by Sweden and France, at home his privacy is invaded "over my protest and my plea. No wonder people in the rest of the world dont like us, since we seem to have neither taste nor courtesy, and know and believe in nothing but money and it doesn't much matter how you get it." {SL}

Mid-October: Drives with Joan Williams to New York. {JW}

October 16: Jill writes to Saxe Commins, asking him to confirm if Faulkner reached Egypt. "We've had no word from Pappy since hearing he was on his way to New York."[119] {SL}

c. October 17: From New York, writes Malcolm Franklin that he expects to be working with Hawks in December and will probably stay abroad until February, missing out on Christmas at home but also cutting down on the traveling back and forth. {SL}

October 19: From New York, writes his mother about his travel plans. He could not turn down Hawks's offer of $15,000 plus expenses. Believes his new book is a "good one. All the people here [at Random House] like what they have seen of it." {SL}

October 26: Robert Haas to Saxe Commins, calling *A Fable* "tremendous. To my mind it's one of the greatest novels that I've ever read . . ." But the "structure and sequences are sometimes harder to follow than need be," and he thinks the horse-thief section should be cut. {BH2}

October 27: Phil Stone to Henry Dalton: "When 'Sanctuary' was published I told Bill Faulkner that he didn't need any more help and that I was through reading manuscripts and fooling with writers." {BH2}

October 28: Phil Stone to Edwin R. Holmes, recalling how most people in Oxford ridiculed his "claims for Bill but now that he has become famous the same type of people and some of the same people have become his ardent friends and those people take particular pains to discredit my association with Bill." {BH2}

October 30: Donald Klopfer to Saxe Commins: Klopfer calls *A Fable* "great. Bill has promised to do a couple of pages summary, not for publication but for us, on what he is really trying to do in this book—the story line, the symbolism, what the characters stand for etc. By all means encourage him to do so because it will mean that a uniform story can go out of Random House." {BH2}

November: Gives his mother his address in Paris while he is working with Howard Hawks. "I don't want to go at all, dont want a movie job, but Mr Hawks has been too good to me." Expecting to spend three months with the director. "But it may not be as bad as I think. I will telephone home during this coming week end, will telegraph, and maybe you will be near the phone." {SL}

Dates foreword to *The Faulkner Reader*. Recalls a foreword written by Henryk Sienkiewicz: "This book was written . . . to uplift men's hearts . . ." {ESPL}

Last page of *A Fable Manuscript* dated "Oxford, December, 1944 / New York and Princeton, November 1953." {B2}

Estelle writes to Dorothy and Saxe Commins expressing her shock at arriving home from her travels in Mexico and discovering Saxe has been so sick. "Saxe was so very good to us in our trouble last fall." {BH2}

Early November: Staying with Saxe Commins in Princeton and working on the final pages of *A Fable*. Attends National Book Awards ceremony with Saxe Commins, where he stood, according to Mary Stahlman Douglas, "shy over in a corner with editor Commins and completely stole the show from the winners as the most distinguished writer present." {CWF}

Writes to Joan Williams assuring her that she can call on Robert Linscott if she ever requires assistance. In another letter expresses his hope she can attend a party hosted by Donald Klopfer. {WFJW}

November 4: Eliminates specific dates for headings of *A Fable*. At the end of the manuscript, page 654, writes: "December 1944 Oxford, New York Princeton November 1953." {B3}

November 5: Saxe Commins to Donald Klopfer announcing that WF will be bringing the final completed manuscript of *A Fable* to New York. He describes their work on the novel and other matters of presentation. {BH2}

November 7?: At the Colony for dinner, WF and Joan Williams are approached by Dylan Thomas, who speaks with them briefly and departs. {B3}

November 9: Dylan Thomas dies, and Faulkner and Joan Williams agree to attend his funeral.[120] {B3}

November 16: Agrees to request from Albert Camus's agent for permission to adapt *Requiem for a Nun* and stipulates that Ruth Ford should be consulted. {SL}

Howard Hawks to WF about arrangements to work on *Land of the Pharaohs* in Europe. Describes the nature of Egypt he plans to capture in the film and says "it ought to be fun." {BH2}

c. November 27: Warns Joan Williams about college friends who are "irresponsible parasites, who now dont even have to pass courses in order to stay there. They go through the motions of art—talking about what they are going to do over drinks, even defacing paper and canvas when necessary, in order to escape the responsibility of living." {SL}

November 30: Departs for Paris to begin work on *Land of the Pharaohs*, then on to Stresa and St. Moritz. {B3, JW, CR2}

To his mother: "On the way today. Will write you. I love you." {SL}

December: Writes to Joan Williams: "I think I was—am—the father which you never had—the one who never raised his hand against you, who desired, tried, to put always first your hopes and dreams and happiness." {B2, WFJW}

December–February 17, 1954: Works with Harry Kurnitz and Jack Bloom on screenplay of *Land of the Pharaohs*. {WFH}

December 1: Hawks and screenwriter Harry Kunitz await WF at Orly Airport, but Faulkner lands in Geneva and probably takes a train to Paris. {B3}

December 2: Arrives at Hawks's Paris hotel with a head wound and accompanied by two gendarmes. {B3, CR2}

December 3: Hawks, Kurnitz, and WF drive south. {B3}

December 4: The Hawks party crosses over into Switzerland. {B3}

December 9: Estelle to Saxe and Dorothy Commins, worried about her ailing mother and comforted that WF has such a good friend in Saxe. "Jill and I have the happy faculty of never becoming lonely even in this big untenanted house." {BH2}

December 12: Writes to his mother about Stresa, where he stayed in 1925. "We live in a 'palace' belonging to an Egyptian millionaire who turned it over to us. 3 servants. Elegant." {SL}

c. December 12: Writes to Joan Williams about his travel plans. {WFJW}

December 14: Phil Stone comments on *A Fable* to Carvel Collins: "I have not read the new book but he brought us part of the manuscript several years ago and it has some wonderful Faulkner writing in it." {BH2}

Writes to Joan Williams saying he thinks he is the father she never had and that the bond between them cannot be broken. Someday she will realize as much. {WFJW}

December 20: Addressing "Dear Moms" WF writes from St. Moritz in the Alps, a skiing and bob sledding paradise, "very beautiful," and the playground of the likes of King Farouk, Gregory Peck and other famous actors and agents. Still wishes he was home, the only place to spend Christmas. "I love you all and miss you all. . . . Will always let you know where I am. I love you. I have my camera, and will make pictures." {SL}

December 24: Meets Jean Stein in St. Moritz.

December 26: Meets Else Jonsson in Stockholm.

December 29–31: Stays with Harold Raymond at this estate in Kent, England.

1954

New England Journeys publishes "A Guest's Impression of New England, an account of a brief excursion with Malcolm Cowley. {ESPL}

WF writes a prefatory note for *A Fable*, which is not used. He declares he has not written a pacifist book, arguing that "to put an end war, man must find or invent something more powerful than war and man's aptitude for belligerence and his thirst for power at any cost, or use the fire itself to fight and destroy the fire with; that man may finally have to mobilize himself and arm himself with the implements of war to put an end to war." Ideological battles and national rivalries will not end war. {ESPL}

January 1–5: Continues his stay with Harold Raymond in Kent. {B2}

January 4: To Saxe and Dorothy Commins: "The job here [on *Land of the Pharaohs*] is going all right, but I was right about not wanting it. I am already sick to the teeth of rich American expatriates from income tax, who have moved intact their entire Hollywood lives to Europe. Got away from it Xmas, Stockholm and London & Paris." Asks for $2,500 to be transferred from his account. "*Don't notify anyone at Oxford.*" {BH2}

January 6: Returns to St. Moritz. {B2, CR2}

January 11: Writes Joan Williams about a pleasant Christmas in Stockholm. "I had forgot how in Europe the artist is like the athletic champion at home." Tries to remain out of sight in a small hotel but reporters have been following him with cameras. He is asked for autographs by "gangs of schoolchildren, and older people." A Swedish masseur has relieved him of back pain. In the same letter he speaks of his love for Williams in the past tense, of his loyalty to her, and pride in her development. Encourages her to keep working. Tells her about Jean Stein. {WFJW}

January 15: Thanks Harold Raymond for sending pipes to the Hotel Ambassador in Rome. Mentions his love of Kent. {SL}

Mid-January: A few days in Paris with Jean Stein and Monique Salomon, who reveres WF, who is her daughter's godfather. {B2}

January 19: Arrives in Rome and joins Howard Hawks, Humphrey Bogart, and Lauren Bacall. {B3}

January 23: Comments to Harold Raymond about the Chatto & Windus collection that includes *As I Lay Dying*, short stories (including "The Bear" and "Spotted Horses"), and the Nobel Prize speech. {SL}

January 24: Writes to Joan Williams from Rome: "I like this city. It is full of the sound of water, fountains everywhere, amazing and beautiful—big things full of marble figures—god and animal, naked girls wrestling with horses and swans with tons of water cascading over them." Happy to be out of snowy Switzerland. {SL}

January 29: Writes to Saxe Commins with some corrections to the galleys of *A Fable*. {SL}

Estelle writes to Saxe Commins for help in paying overdue bill from Levy's department store. "I have no authority to write checks on Bill's account." {BH2}

February 4: Provides details for Saxe Commins about how producer William Bacher pitched the idea for what became *A Fable*. Emphasizes that he has no legal obligation to Bacher, who does not hold film rights. He is willing, however, for there to be an agreement with Random House, Ober, and Bacher if that seems necessary. "Let it be so that no man alive will be sorry of the book, have any bad taste in the mouth because of it." The book "must not be blemished by a squabble over rights. I would take my own name off it first and give it to anyone who would defend it from that." {SL}

February 6: Estelle apologizes to Saxe Commins for supposing he could pay her account at Levy's department store. "Bill couldn't have a steadier hand or a better mind than yours, to steer the fable to completion." {BH2}

February 10: Howard Hawks and his crew fly to Egypt. {AB}

February 11: Flies to Paris. {B2}

Estelle tells Saxe Commins that Rowan Oak has suffered neglect while WF has been away. "I was just on the verge of writing Bill that I was suing for divorce—I still believe it is the only wise thing to do—on his account, as well as Jill's and mine," but Commins's letter to her has given her "pause." She notes that WF has been away from home frequently in the last four years and must be "very unhappy" in his "nightmare of drunkenness. . . . Jill (she will tell you this very frankly) and I are happier and *more at ease* when Bill is away—Since his unfortunate disclosure about his current affair [with Joan Williams]—she hasn't felt too secure around him. . . . Please believe that I'm only endeavoring to make everyone concerned, a little happier." {BH2}

Television adaptation of "Shall Not Perish" is broadcast. {WFH}

February 14: Joins Hawks on location near Cairo. {CR2}

February 17: Kurnitz, with WF's input, completes second draft of *Land of the Pharaohs*. {B2}

February 27: To Saxe Commins: "I am fairly well—working. I don't think very highly of Egypt." {BH2}

February 29: Estelle writes a long letter to Saxe Commins rehearsing the history of WF's involvement with Joan Williams and Estelle's own part in it and her feelings about it. She admits she is writing a "shocking letter," describing her husband's refusal to "face reality" and his need for a "*good* nurse. . . . Billy's continued drinking makes it most grave." {BH2}

March: In a long letter, Estelle thanks Saxe Commins for his "wonderfully spirit-lifting letter." She does not blame Joan Williams for the affair: "Had *I* been an aspiring writer and an elderly celebrity had fallen in love with me—I would have accepted him as avidly as Joan did Bill . . . He is in a mess, and I dare say is going to have a bad time of it . . . My one thought was *really* to get all three of us, Bill, Jill, and me, out of a tragic—and in some ways—comic—situation, in as dignified a manner as possible." She suggests that the article "Mississippi" explains the "two Bills." {BH2}

March 6: Joan Williams marries Ezra Bowen.

March 12: Estelle to Saxe Commins: "Joan's marriage, though, doesn't change the sad state Bill, Jill and I are in—It is well Bill is prolonging his stay in Egypt . . . Jill and I get along quite as well as things are." {BH2}

March 14: Has been working hard on the script for Hawks, WF reports to Jean Stein: "He can tear the script up again . . . But just maybe, maybe, he wont, by March 23rd I may, just may, be done with it." {SL}

Comments to Saxe Commins on Joan Willams's marriage: "I was not free to marry her, even if I had not been too old. So I—we—expected this." Goes on to describe his involvement with Jean Stein, who "has none of the emotional confusion which poor Joan had." {BH2}

March 22: Jill writes to her father announcing her intention to marry Paul Summers. {B3}

March 29: Departs on the night flight from Egypt for France and sees Monique Salomon, Jean Stein, and Else Jonsson. {B3}

March 30: Arrives at Orly Airport. {B2}

Estelle describes socializing with several friends and meeting Supreme Court Justice Felix Frankfurter, lecturing at the University of Mississippi: "I completely lost my heart to him. . . . Between entertaining, I've managed to make a few spring dresses for Jill and me, and really have done well with my gardening—Have always like to work out of doors. . . . Did you like Bill's Mississippi? [see next entry] The mother of the 'son-of-absconded-banker' cut me dead in our local super-market!!" {BH2}

April: *Holiday* publishes "Mississippi," which conflates state history, WF's biography, and his work. {ESPL}

Saxe Commins omits WF's prefatory note to *A Fable*. {CR2}

April 1: Random House publishes *The Faulkner Reader*.

New York Times review of *The Faulkner Reader*: "Anyone who can follow the punctuationless cadence of a telephone conversation can follow Faulkner." {WFC}

April 5–6: Else Jonsson accompanies WF to the American Hospital of Paris, where he is admitted as a patient. {CR2}

April 12: Wires Saxe Commins about rewriting one section of *A Fable*. {SL, B3, BH2}

April 13: Robert Coughlan writes to Phil Stone asking for several clarifications now that he is converting his *Life* articles into a book. "I was talking with his publisher[121] the other day, and he says he hasn't heard from Bill and doesn't know how soon he'll be coming back—he's over due now. Says also he has a hunch that Bill will never go back to live in Mississippi: that Bill believes he can't write there anymore." {BH2}

April 15: Phil Stone writes to Robert Coughlan supplying the comments and corrections Coughlan requested. "I also think that Bill is never coming back to Mississippi and, just between us, I don't care personally whether he does or not. I agree with you that it will be a great mistake, but I think the Nobel prize has ruined Bill and that what he writes anywhere from now on is not going to be worth much but there is no use in me trying to tell him because you can't tell a successful Falkner anything. . . . I think he is permanently getting rid of Estelle."[122]

Memphis Commercial Appeal reports Estelle's comment that WF, in Cairo, Egypt, is expected home around June 1. {BH2}

April 16: Phil Stone encloses *Memphis Commercial Appeal* article in note to Robert Coughlan, adding: "I am very doubtful that Estelle knows what she is talking about, but she may be right." {BH2}

April 19: Flies from Orly to New York and work at Random House on *A Fable*. {B2}

Estelle writes to Saxe Commins: "A Fable owes its completion to your untiring, loving work with Bill those last weeks in Princeton—I realize, only too well, that he was in no emotional nor physical condition to do it without *you*." {BH2}

April 22: Writes to Jean Stein about signing 1,000 autograph sheets of *A Fable:* "By now, I not only cant hold the pen anymore I hate Wmfaulkner almost as much as McCarthy." {SL}

April 24, 6:00 p.m.: Arrives in Roanoke, Virginia, from Princeton. {B3}

April 25, 10:30 p.m.: Arrives home after driving 703 miles from Roanoake, Virginia. {B3}

April 28: Writes to Saxe Commins about his record-setting drive, adding, "I dont intend to do it again." Sends photographs of the outline of *A Fable* that he made on the wall of his office, suggesting they might be reproduced in the book. Mentions that Jill is getting married in August and asks if Saxe and Dorothy can attend the wedding. "Still have the stomach, but hope it will improve here." {BH2}

April 29: Writes a $1000 check to Monique Salomon to cover any expenses she has incurred on his behalf.[123] {SL}

Checks with Saxe Commins about recipients of *A Fable*. {BH2}

c. May 2: Instructs Saxe Commins to give William Bacher the right of first refusal for screen rights to *A Fable*.[124] Mentions Jill's forthcoming wedding: "This business is going to cost, so I will need money, probably." {SL, BH2}

May 3: Commins marvels that WF drove 1133 miles in 36 hours [from Princeton to Virginia to Oxford]. "Are you sure you're all right and not suffering any consequences of the strain? How is your back? Affirms that he and Dorothy will attend Jill's wedding. "I saw Professor Einstein yesterday, and he asked particularly about you. He wanted to be remembered with all respect." {BH2}

May 10: Tells Jean Stein about his outdoor activities: farming, fencing, horse training. {SL}

May 29: Sends Jean Stein a snapshot of Jill's horse, Lady Go-Lightly. More outdoor work. {SL}

June 10: Jill's engagement to Paul D. Summers Jr. is announced. {B3}

In Oxford, signs and dates first edition of *A Fable*: "Phil, with love / Bill." {BH1}

June 11: Travels to Rockville, Maryland, to meet the parents of Paul Summers, Jill's intended. {B3, CR2}

June 12: Commins forwards invitation to speak at PEN[125] conference in New York, also, he has notified the PEN president that WF, engaged in writing the last volumes of the Snopes trilogy, would be unavailable. {BH2}

June 14: Attending a party at his in-laws in Maryland, WF describes Republicans as more reserved than Democrats because "to Republicans, politics is a mode of behavior instead of an activity." On race he comments: "Maybe the Negro is the best. He does more with less than anybody else." About Senator Joseph McCarthy's reputation in Mississippi, Faulkner says: "We feel shame down there just as you do here." {LG}

Mid-June: Writes to Commins: "No, cant attend PEN meeting. Work going along but slow, as I am busy getting Jill's horse ready to enter a horse show here last of July. Hot as bejesus but all well." Asks Commins to send wire pipe cleaners Faulkner saw in a Shirmer shop window. {BH2}

June 18: Acknowledges receipt of *A Fable* from Saxe Commins: "If we are right and it is my best and not the bust which I had considered it might be, I will ask nothing more." Expects Commins to show up at Jill's wedding and for a stay "long enough for a good visit and to see some of the country." Needs another $5000 by July 1 since "Jill and her mother seem bent on making a production out of this, and her trousseau wedding stuff, bridesmaid's dresses, champagne etc will run to quite a piece of jack I fear." Comments on the party at his son-in-law's: "damndest collection of prosperous concerned stuff-shirt Republican senators and military brass hats and their beupholsteed and becoiffed beldames as you ever saw. Fortunately hardly any of them ever heard of me, so I was let alone." {SL, BH2}

June 19: Rejects *Time* magazine cover story, telling Donald Klopfer that *Time* has done it once (for *The Wild Palms*) and *Life* as well, and since they want to send a reporter to him, he is sure it means prying into his private life. Does not want his family subjected to this attention, saying that "journalists as individuals are all right, they are just the victims of the system too, and can be fired by their bosses if they acquiesced to my feelings . . . One of the most fearful things in modern American life: the Freedom of the Press . . . when vast monied organizations such as the press or religion or political groups begin to federate under moral catchwords like democracy and freedom, in the structure of which the individual members or practitioners are absolved of all individual moral restraint, God help us all." {SL}

Telegram to Saxe Commins: "PLEASE CALL DON KLOPFER AT ONCE TO STOP REPORTER'S COMING DOWN NEXT WEEK."[126] {SL}

June 24: Telegram to Bennett Cerf: "LET ME WRITE THE BOOKS. LET SOMEONE WHO WANTS IT HAVE THE PUBLICITY. I PROTEST THE IDEA BUT WILL NEVER CONSENT TO MY PICTURE ON COVER. ESTIMATE WHAT REFUSAL WILL COST RANDOM HOUSE AND I WILL PAY IT." {SL}

June 24: William Faulkner and Estelle Oldham Faulkner sign a "Warranty deed": "In consideration of the love and affection we hold for our daughter, Jill Faulkner, and One dollar cash in hand paid, We convey and warrant to Jill Faulkner that land as described. . . . This is our homestead, known and comprised under the designation 'Rowan Oak.'" {CR2}

Kansas City Star review of *The Faulkner Reader*: "The harshness and evil Faulkner explores are no more harsh or evil than that of classic Greek or English tragedy." {WFC}

June 25: Faulkner's telegram to Bennett Cerf after he agrees not to cooperate with *Time*: "I LOVE YOU. I LOVE BOB AND DON. I LOVE PHYLLIS [CERF] TOO." {SL}

June 29: Writes to State Department official, a fellow southerner, about her invitation to a writers' conference in Brazil: "Can there be more than one Muna Lee? More than the one whose verse I have known since a long time?" He accepts the invitation and discusses travel arrangements. {SL}

Summer: "V. P. [Ferguson] says that Faulkner told him, "Dr. Busby, outside of Malcolm Cowley, is the greatest living jackass."[127] {CCP}

July 1: Telegram to Bennett Cerf: "I LOVE TIME TOO. ONLY MAG EVER CANCELLED PIECE ABOUT HIM ON SIMPLE PLEA OF ONE PRIVATE AND HENCE HELPLESS INDIVIDUAL." {SL}

c. July 2 or 9: Mentions to Saxe Commins the State Department visit to Brazil and asks for dinner jacket, coat and pants, in the closet of Saxe's son, Gene. Also needs a pair of dress shoes and provides specifications, including size, maker, and shop. {SL, BH2}

July 24: Estelle writes that she is looking forward to the Commins' visit for Jill's wedding. "Jill is radiantly happy—Bill is pleased over his coming trip to Brazil, and know we'll be prouder than ever of him—A Fable is a marvelous book—I feel so indebted to you, Saxe, for its beautiful completion." {BH2}

July 25: Invitation to Mr. and Mrs. Saxe Commins to Jill Faulkner's wedding and reception. {BH1}

Late July: Writes to Phil Mullen thanking him for the warning that a *Newsweek* reporter was arriving to write a profile. He does not blame the reporter but notes the "terrifying things in modern American life" that are justified as freedom of the press. "One individual can defend himself from another individual's freedom and liberty, but when big powerful monied organizations confederate under shibboleths and catchwords like liberty and democracy and religion, within the structure of which the individual practitioners are automatically freed of any moral responsibility whatever, then God help us; we damn sure need it." {BH2}

Writes to Saxe Commins, requesting that he send Jean Stein a copy of *A Fable*. {BH2}

August: Last will and testament. {BH1}

Early August: Sends telegram that he is willing to add Lima, Peru to his State Department itinerary, "SUBJECT LIMITATIONS OF PERSONAL IGNORANCE AND INEXPERIENCE." {SL}

August 1: Warren Beck in the *Milwaukee Journal* hails *A Fable* as a "tremendous venture in symbolic composition," demanding the attention given to a "fugue or symphony" that should be "viewed both closely and in perspective, like great architecture."

In the *New York Herald Tribune*, Malcolm Cowley deems *A Fable* "likely to stand above other novels of the year like a cathedral, if an imperfect and unfinished one, above a group of well built cottages."

In the *New York Times Book Review*, Carvel Collins suggests *A Fable* should be ranked with Kafka's parables—in this case about "opposition between nationalism and brotherhood, between force and love." {CR2}

August 2: Random House publishes *A Fable*. *Newsweek* publishes a photograph of WF on its cover and a review of *A Fable* but includes no profile since he refuses to cooperate with the reporter sent to interview him. {B2}

A Fable lacks WF's customary "demonic power," complains Orville Prescott in the *New York Times*. {WFC}

August 6: Departs for Lima, Peru, on State Department mission. {B2}

August 7: Arrives in Lima. {B2}

August 8: To São Paulo for International Writers' Conference. {B2}

August 9: Attended by physician after another drinking bout. {B2}

August 10: Recovered. {B2}

August 11: At a conference for the press, radio, and television, WF states: "Solidarity is imperative for men of all creeds, color and social conditions." {ESPL}

August 12: Visits a snake farm and a cathedral. Attends a working luncheon and dinner and answers questions, expressing his ambivalence about *A Fable*. {B2}

August 13: Visits an agricultural experimental station and a coffee plantation, with some remarks at a writers' congress in the evening. {B2}

August 14: After a brief and cheerful appearance in Caracas, Venezuela, returns home. {CR2}

August 15: At Rowan Oak, signs and dates first edition of *A Fable*: "For Victoria and Bill, with love / from Pappy." {BH1}

August 16: Writes to Harold E. Howland of the State Department, thanking him for the "unfailing courtesy and efficiency which expedited my whole trip, which gave me not only a wider knowledge of South America, but of the Foreign Service of my own country and the high type of men and women who run and represent it." He will respond to any questions about his impressions: "I became suddenly interested in what I was trying to do, once I reached the scene and learned exactly what was hoped from this plan of which I was a part . . . And can hold myself available to call on you to make a verbal report or discuss what further possibilities, situations, capacities, etc. in which I might do what I can to help give people of other countries a truer idea than they sometimes have, of what the U.S. actually is." {SL}

August. 21: Jill marries Paul D. Summers Jr. {B1, JW, CR2}

At Rowan Oak signs and dates first edition of *A Fable*: "To Ben [Wasson], with love / Bill." {BH1}

August 23: *Time* publishes a short account of WF speaking about *A Fable*, his reading, how he writes, and the loss of freedom in a mechanical civilization. {CWF}

August 24: Phil Stone responds to Carvel Collins's article about *The Sound and the Fury* and the significance of the dates in Easter week: "I think that if I had asked Bill what was the significance of the dates . . . he would have told me right off . . . I do not know why in the world I failed to ask him about these dates . . ." {BH2}

September 2: Harold Howland of the State Department writes an encouraging letter about WF's visits abroad: "The reports from Peru and Brazil have been most glowing accounts of your success there and the entire Department of State is indeed grateful that you took the time from your crowded schedule to assist us in our effort to gain respect and enhance our country's prestige abroad." {BH2}

Howland writes to WF about ensuring his reimbursements for travel. {BH2}

September 3: Apologizes to Harold Ober for the delay in acknowledging his letter lost in the "mess of my workshop." He wonders what else he will find, maybe "something with a check in it." {SL}

September 5: Expresses his doubts to Ober that he can write a piece about Vicksburg, even though *Holiday* has offered $2000 for it. Wants to discuss it when he is in New York. {SL}

September 10: Checks into the Algonquin. {B2}

September 15: Muna Lee of the State Department writes to Saxe Commins, enclosing reports of Faulkner's success in Peru and Brazil. {BH2}

September 20: Jill writes to her father about treating her mother properly now that she has married. "I want your help in making Mama happy. . . . I'm afraid she feels I'm more or less lost to her." {BH2, CR2}

Signs contract with Caedmon Publishers to record excerpts from *A Fable*, *Requiem for a Nun*, *As I Lay Dying*, *Old Man*, and *Light in August*.[128]

September 21: Presents Ober with "Race at Morning." {SL}

Congratulates Malcolm Franklin and his wife, Gloria, on the birth of their son, Mark. Mentions earning $100 for a television broadcast of "An Error in Chemistry." *The Saturday Evening Post* is going to purchase "Race at Morning." Estelle is planning a trip abroad to her daughter and son-in-law in Manila. {SL}

September 23: Ober sells "Race at Morning" to *The Saturday Evening Post* for $2,500. {B2}

September 27: Authorizes Jean-Louis Barrault to dramatize *As I Lay Dying* at the Theatre Maringy in Paris. Advises him to deal with Gallimard. {BH2}

September 30: Records the Nobel Prize speech, parts of *As I Lay Dying*, and "Old Man" for Caedmon Publishers. {B2}

October 4: Estelle visits Phil Stone's law office for help with a passport application for her trip to the Philippines to visit her daughter and son-in-law. {CR2}

October 6: Phil Stone to Robert Coughlan: "Estelle was in the office day before yesterday to get me to help her get a passport to visit 'Cho-cho' in the Philippines, and she told me that Bill was in New York and that she was going to try to get away before Bill got back. What this means I don't know, but it probably means nothing, as most of what Estelle says means." {BH2}

October 7: Attends the opening night of *Reclining Figure*, a play by fellow screenwriter Harry Kurnitz. WF offers to sit next to Brooks Atkinson, "so he can see how much I'm laughing." {B2}

October 11: From Maud Falkner, enclosing verse, with the comment: "This is a nice one": "May the wind be at your back, / May the road rise up to meet you, / And may God always hold you in / the palm of his hand." She signs herself: "I love you, Moms." {BH2}

Mid-October: Sends Ober "On Privacy: The American Dream: What Has Happened to It?" Mentions offers to lecture at colleges for a fee $1000 fee. He plans to use the piece as a lecture. {SL}

October 18: Returns to Oxford and angrily reads Robert Coughlan's profiles. {B3}

October 19: Submits "By the People" to Ober. {SL}

October 25: Mentions to Saxe Commins that he is getting more offers from colleges to lecture and his prices is now "up to $1000.00." Wants to write a book about what happened to the American Dream, "which at one time the whole earth looked up to, aspired to." {BH2}

c. October 26: Comments to Saxe Commins on Estelle's departure for Manila, even though she says she does not want to go, and the trip will cost "3000 bucks." Contemplates an expansion of his lecture/essay on freedom "American style—the sort of misused freedom and liberty which produced the McCarthys and from which people like Oppenheimer suffer."[129] {BH2}

October 31: Gloria Franklin, Malcolm's wife, writes to Dorothy and Saxe Commins with family news, noting, "Pappy is doing fine, so far, he has been in good spirits and I think utterly amazed that Mama really left him. Perhaps a taste of being alone in that house would serve him right and do him good—and I hope when he finds that no one is going to entertain him, he will return [to New York]—that would be just one more thing off of our mind to worry about." {BH2}

November 6: Phil Stone writes to Oscar Pimental explaining his role as WF's "only believer" for twelve years. "Now it is amusing to see how the idolators flock around him, some of the very same people who used to avoid him like he had the plague." {BH2}

c. Early November: Sends out several of his novels for leather binding. {BH2}

Asks Saxe Commins to send the blue suit hanging in his son Eugene's room. "I will probably continue to trouble you with jobs and errands for the rest of our lives." Wants to make sure that the name on the leather-bound books is Jill Faulkner not Jill Faulkner Summers. {BH2}

November 7: The *New York Times Book Review* publishes WF's one-paragraph letter about *No Time for Sergeants*, calling the "story of the bomber training flight . . . one of the funniest stories of war or peace either, of the functioning at its most efficient best, of man's invincible and immortal folly, that I ever read." {ESPL}

November 9: Tells Jean Stein he is reluctant to go on the annual deer hunt the last week of November, but he is now in charge of the club and has to be there. {SL}

Estelle writes to Dorothy and Saxe Commins about her departure for Manila, looking forward to visiting her daughter and son-in-law but already "plagued with home-sickness." {BH2}

November 11: Does not feel he can do justice to a piece about Vicksburg. It is not his town, WF tells Ober. Hopes to publish a story titled "Weekend Revisited," which is "about the man in the alcoholic retreat, which I think is not only funny but true: I mean, as summed up by the doctor friend's comment: 'So you tried to enter the human race, and found the place already occupied' and the protagonist's last cry of shocked and terrified illumination: 'You cant beat him (man)! You cannot! You never will!'"[130] {SL}

c. Mid-November: Annual deer hunt. Confesses to Jean Stein that he no longer wants to shoot a deer. He likes the pursuit but does not want to "kill anything anymore, and probably wont, give the guns and gear away. Because every time I see anything timeless and passionate with motion, speed, life, being alive, I see a young passionate beautiful living shape." {SL, CR2}

November 24: Phil Stone writes to James P. J. Murphy, noting that WF always presents him with autographed copies but does not like to do so for others. "I never ask him to do so. In fact, since he won the Nobel Prize he seldom comes to see me." {BH2}

November 27: Telegram to Finlay McDermid at Warner Brothers: "IN MY OPINION KURNITZ DID MOST OF JOB. WILL SUPPORT ANY CREDIT SUGGESTION HE MAKES PROVIDED HAWKS CONCURS. FAULKNER." {USC}

December: *Harper's Bazaar* publishes "Sepulture South: Gaslight."

Writes to Malcolm and Gloria Franklin about plans for Christmas, gifts for African American staff. {UVA}

c. Mid-December: In New York City, attends a party at Carl Van Vechten's and is photographed. {B2}

Writes to Muna Lee while in New York City mentioned two dozen copies of *A Fable* to be distributed to prominent Brazilians who welcomed him on his visit. {SL}

Writes to Henry F. Pommel confirming the professor's supposition of a misprint in a crucial sentence in *Light in August*, in which "Him" should be "Ham": "But the curse of the white race is the black man who will be forever God's chosen own because He once cursed Him." {SL}

December 22: Letter to the *New York Times* about the crash of an Italian airliner. {ESPL}

December 25: Saxe and Dorothy Commins host WF for Christmas in Princeton.

1955

n.d.: Editor Hiram Haydn meets WF at Random House and describes the setting and the author's manner of speaking and behaving. {CWF}

Winter: Delmore Schwartz's review of *A Fable* in *Perspectives* argues that the novel promotes the "cause of belief and nobility in other human beings." {WFC}

January 3: Ben Benjamin, Famous Artists to Harold Ober: "I spoke to Bill the other day because Jack Benny wanted him to appear on his television program, but Bill, in his inimitable way, said, 'It's not my cup of tea.'" {BH2}

January 10: Cables Chatto & Windus, giving them the option to place *As I Lay Dying* wherever the publisher wishes, although he does not think the novel should come first or last. {SL}

January 21: Signs a contract for *Big Woods*. {B2}

January 24: *Sports Illustrated* publishes "An Innocent at Rinkside," about hockey.

January 25, 3:30 pm.: With Saxe Commins, heads to the Hotel Commodore to receive National Book Award for Fiction for *A Fable*, cited "for its moments of powerful and profound insight, the bold scope of its imagination, and its creation of a varied, many-leveled background of human experience for the legend of Christian sacrifice which it undertakes to tell. Despite its imperfections, the heights it attains make it the most distinguished novel of 1954." In the presence of more than 700 writers, critics, and publishers, WF answers reporter's questions, pointing out, "There is too much success . . . Success is too easy. A young man can gain it with only a little industry" without learning the "humility to handle it with, or even to discover, realized, that he will need humility." {CWF}

January 27: Returns home to Oxford. {B3}

January 30: Harvey Breit walks with WF down Fifth Avenue discussing how his rating of contemporary writers has been misunderstood, and how artists are still viewed as court jesters. {B3}

January 31: *Richmond News Leader* publishes John Cook Wyllie's "off-the cuff impression of 57-year-old William Faulkner." Includes a question-and-answer session about writing, his service in World War I, and critical notices of his work. {CWF}

February: Works on dummy for *Big Woods*. {CR2}

February 3: Mentions to Harold Ober a commitment to give a lecture at the University of Oregon. Seems open to the possibility of working on a television project tentatively titled "The Era of Fear."[131] {SL}

February 6: *New York Times Book Review* prints text of National Book Award address. {ESPL}

February 10: Writes to the *Memphis Commercial Appeal* ridiculing a letter attacking "shiftless" Negroes. {ESPL}

To Herb Starr from Oxford: "Your letter finally caught up with me here. The trip to Europe sounds fine, but I have a job, reporting the Kentucky Derby for a mag. First week in May. I may go to Europe to do a job for the State Dept . . . If it comes through before you leave, I will get in touch with you. If not, and I come to Europe later this summer, will get in touch with you through Am. Express, Paris." {NYPL}

February 16: Wants Ober to put a stop to a proposed film shoot relating to a *Cosmopolitan* feature about him. {SL}

c. February 17 and 18: A long letter to Saxe Commins about Edward Shenton's drawings for *Big Woods*. WF makes suggestions but is also highly complimentary: "Mr. Shelton is doing so well, I am extremely timid about getting in the way." {SL}

Phil Stone writes to Judith S. Bond, curator of the Modern Poetry Library at the University of Chicago, telling her about lunching in Chicago with Harriet Monroe, editor of *Poetry*, and suggesting that the "literary star in America was passing from the Midwest to the South," and she should publish parts of *The Marble Faun*. Stone says she declined but later wrote a little editorial about what Stone told her.[132] {BH2}

February 19: Reports to Else Jonsson about his busy schedule of magazine work and travel for the State Department. "I had thought that perhaps with A FABLE, I would find myself empty of anything to say, do. But I was wrong." He has *Big Woods* and another book in mind.[133] {SL}

End of February: In New York, signs agreement permitting Albert Camus to adapt *Requiem for a Nun*. {CR2}

March: Mentions to Jean Stein some intestinal problem that may have resulted from his stay in Egypt, and he has crushed the end of his middle finger, the one he uses to type with, moving a concrete block. Announces he is getting his boat ready to sail. {SL}

March 2: Harold E. Howland of the State Department writes about an invitation to attend a seminar in Nagano with 30 Japanese scholars of English and American literature. {SL}

March 4: Robert Linscott to Leslie Fiedler: "As you can imagine, Bill doesn't like lecturing and does it, frankly, for the money . . . [H]e doesn't like crowds, receptions, and chit chat. You'd get along with him just fine and he'd love to see the Montana country but inquisitive females and fancy cocktail parties make him nervous." {UVA}

March 5: *The Saturday Evening Post* publishes "Race at Morning."

March 7: Attends the opening night performance of *Cat on a Hot Tin Roof*, dines with Jean Stein, Christoper Isherwood, Gore Vidal, and Carson McCullers. {B2}

March 11: Modern Library edition of *Go Down, Moses.*

March 16: Claims to Saxe Commins: "I have never learned how to write movies, nor even to take them very seriously." So the offer of a movie job does not interest him. Off to the hospital tomorrow to get his insides checked out. {SL}

March 17: Complains of stomach pains and enters hospital for tests, which prove negative. {B2}

March 19: Asks Ober to make one change in his American Dream essay, substituting "medieval witch-hunt" for "Vigilantes' Committee." {SL}

March 20: Writes to the *Memphis Commercial Appeal* pointing out that Mississippi schools are not "even good enough for white people," but instead of improving schools for everyone the state builds a second, inferior school system. {ESPL}

Estelle reports to Dorothy and Saxe Commins: "It is nice being at Rowan Oak again—Bill and I have worked in the grounds—trying to get the place looking lovely for Jill's first visit Home—and having no house servant, save Broadus!—I have been busy in the house too." {BH2}

March 21: Robert Linscott to Leslie Fiedler: "Bill likes a martini at lunch, one or two bourbons (preferably Old Grandad) and water before dinner . . . Bill is a good guy and a gentleman in the absolute sense of the word." {UVA}

March 25: The *New York Times* publishes WF's letter objecting to the US expulsion of the Metropolitan of the Roman Orthodox Church. {ESPL}

March 27: Letters responding to WF's March 20 letter to the *Memphis Commercial Appeal* {WC}

March 28: Phil Stone writes to Dave Womack, a Mississippi state representative, about WF as publicity seeker calling him "Mr. Greta Garbo." {BH2}

Spring: WF decides to help fund the college education of Earnest McEwen, Jr., an African American. {CR2}

April 3: Writes to the *Memphis Commercial Appeal*, reiterating the money wasted for two separate systems to educate whites and blacks. {ESPL}

April 4: Writes to a Mr. Green about his letter to the *Times* about the expulsion of the Metropolitan. "I have never been a Greek Orthodox

Metropolitan. When a young man I was closely enough associated with communists to learn quickly that I didn't like it, it is dangerous, and that it is a good deal more important to keep people talking freedom in communist countries than to keep people talking communism out of this one." Mentions that his experience with junior State Department staffers tells him that the "problems they have to cope with come not from foreign countries they are sent to, but from their Washington headquarters." {SL}

April 10: Writes to the *Memphis Commercial Appeal:* "Instead of holding the educational standard down to the lowest common denominator . . . let us raise it to that of the highest." {ESPL}

April 14: Delivers a lecture "Freedom American Style" at the University of Oregon. {CR2}

April 17: Delivers "Freedom American Style" at University of Montana. {CR2}

Writes to the *Memphis Commercial Appeal* endorsing the views of an anonymous young Mississippian in favor of integration: "and what a commentary that is on us: that in Mississippi communal adult opinion can reach such a general emotional pitch that your young sons and daughters dare not, from probably a very justified physical fear, sign their names to an opinion adverse to it." {ESPL}

April 20: Telegram to Saxe Commins, in whose house WF met Einstein: "ONE OF THE WISEST OF MEN AND ONE OF THE GENTLEST OF MEN, WHO CAN REPLACE HIM IN EITHER LET ALONE IN BOTH." {SL, BH2}

Early May: *A Fable* wins the Pulitzer Prize.

May 7: Attends the Kentucky Derby. {B3}

May 9: In New York to publicize *Land of the Pharaohs*. {B3}

May 10: Sends a telegram to James Geller, representing producer Jerry Wald at Columbia Pictures about screen rights to *Soldiers' Pay* and *The Sound and the Fury*, saying that Ober and Random House work together. {SL}

May 14: Submits to two interviews to promote *Land of the Pharaohs*. {B3}

May 16: Replies to Harold E. Howland of the State Department inquiring if he can be routed through Europe on his way to Japan. {SL}

Sports Illustrated publishes "Kentucky: May: Saturday, Three Days to the Afternoon."

May 23: Understands that the Japanese are a formal people and asks Harold E. Howland of the State Department if formal attire is required. Could he rent it there or bring black tie with him? {SL}

May 30: Estelle reports to Dorothy Commins that WF is "thoroughly engrossed now in re-conditioning his sail-boat." {BH2}

June 12: Tells Else Jonsson about his trips to Oregon and Montana, then Louisville, Kentucky, to cover the Kentucky Derby, and now home again, training his filly, getting his sailboard ready to launch, and preparing for an August State Department trip to Japan. Describes *Big Woods* as "a nice book, hunting stories, with drawings by a very fine man, I think." Asks her to write even if he does not answer promptly because of business. "I am nearing sixty, a writer, artist, at that age doesn't have much time left while the work will be good, sound; I wont live long enough to do all I have in mind even if I live to be 100." Predicts "much tragic trouble in Mississippi about Negroes." Worries about the Mississippi response to the Supreme Court's ruling against segregation. "I can see the possible time when I shall have to leave my native state, something as the Jew had to flee from Germany during Hitler . . . This is a depressing letter, I know. But human beings are terrible. One must believe well in man to endure him, wait out his folly and savagery and inhumanity." {SL}

June 13: Along with Jill, Estelle, Malcolm and Gloria Franklin, his brother Jack and wife Suzanne, and his Aunt Bama attends party promoting *Land of the Pharaohs*. {B2}

June 14: *Memphis Commercial Appeal* publishes an account of WF at a preview screening of *Land of the Pharaohs*. He observes that "studio process and dozens of hands" alter or even lose the author's "original story." Mentions his letters to the newspaper about segregation that have stimulated approving letters and calls, mainly from young people. {CWF}

Memphis Press-Scimitar publishes an account of a reception for WF, who calls *Land of the Pharaohs* "nothing new . . . It's the same movie Howard [Hawks] has been making for 35 years. It's *Red River* all over again. The Pharaoh is the cattle baron, his jewels are the cattle, and the Nile is the Red River. But the thing about Howard is, he knows it's the same movie, and he knows how to make it." {CWF}

June 23: Saxe Commins sends the galleys of *Big Woods* with some queries. {BH2}

Late June: Comments on whether "The Bear" should precede "The Old People" in *Big Woods*. He brings up the idea of switching the order of the two stories ["The Old People" first] but will abide by their original decision [which was to be "The Bear" first]. {SL}

July: *Harper's* publishes "On Privacy: The American Dream: What Happened to It," a version of the lecture delivered at the University of Oregon. "The point is that in America today any organization or group, simply by functioning under a phrase like Freedom of the Press or National Security or League Against Subversion, can postulate to itself complete immunity to violate the individualness—the individual privacy lacking which he cannot be an individual and lacking which individuality he is not anything at all worth the having or keeping—of anyone who is not himself a member of some organization or group numerous enough or rich enough to frighten them off." {ESPL}

July 2: *Land of the Pharaohs* is released.

July 5: Informs Harold E. Howland he is prepared to depart on the date the State Department sets. Will bring along a dinner jacket as Howland has suggested. He will also make himself available for other assignments should those materialize. {SL}

July 6: Requests $5000 from Saxe Commins to cover expenses for his wife and mother, plus a school year for the daughter of his dead brother, Dean. Plans to spend a month in Japan before going on to Europe. All is well. Sailing with Jill and her husband Paul. Gives his regards to Saxe's wife, adding, "Every night I compose in my mind the letter I intend to write her, which I dont ever do. My only poor excuse is, Dorothy already knows what I would say in it." {SL, BH2}

Writes to Ober saying he hopes something can be worked out for producer James Geller in gratitude for the "many times he saved all of us when we were all in Warner's saltmine." {SL}

July 8: Advises Harold E. Howland of the State Department that he is not a lecturer or a man of letters. He could deliver a version of his American Dream talk that has been published in *Harper's* and has another in preparation. {SL}

July 15: Signs agreement naming Saxe Commins as WF's "attorney-in-fact." {BH1}

July 23: Writes to Alberto Mondadori, his Italian publisher, that he expects to be in Rome in September and is looking forward to his visit since so many of the publisher's countrymen and women made his last visit "so pleasant and memorable." {SL}

July 29, 3:25 p.m.: Departs for Japan on State Department sponsored trip. {B3}

August 1, 8:45 a.m.: Arrives at Tokyo's Haneda Airport. {B3}

August 2: Complains of back pain after considerable drinking and refuses to attend a luncheon for 170 guests, and the ambassador directs his staff to send WF home. {SL}

5:30 p.m.: Arrives late at American Embassy for a reception. {B3}

August 3: Dr. Leon Picon, in charge of the embassy's book program, explains the ambassador's directive, and WF promises to be on his best behavior. {B3}

August 4: Conducts four 45-minute interviews mentioning his rudimentary understanding of Japanese literature and his relations with writers like Gide, Sartre, Dos Passos, and Fitzgerald. {B3}

In an interview with a Japanese editor and author, WF responds to questions about various writers, invoking his understanding of Edgar Allan Poe, T. S. Eliot and Theodore Dreiser. {LG}

2:00 p.m.: Meets hospitably with six Japanese writers from the PEN club. {B2}

Press release: "Impressions of Japan." {ESPL}

August 5: Arrives in Nagano city to attend a ten-day seminar with fifty Japanese scholars. {CR2}

Addresses the American literature seminar in Nagano, Japan. Calls America a "culture of successful generosity" and explains its development. {ESPL}

At a press conference, WF is asked about his impressions of Japanese culture, and he mentions his reading of Ezra Pound's translations, commenting as well on the differences and similarities of different cultures. He is asked about *A Fable* and his view of Christianity. Pays tribute to Sherwood Anderson. Asked his opinion about women, he demurs, although he adds: "I'm inclined to think that every young man should know one old woman, that they can talk more sense." {LG}

In several sessions of the Nagano seminar, he stresses the primacy of the individual, his understanding of God, the impact of race and environment, the role of the intellect in Japanese culture, the writer's quest for immortality, the role of style, the role of the artist, his favorite books, the importance of James Joyce, his reading of the Bible, his views of the younger generation, his reading of Somerset Maugham, his attitude toward the wilderness in "The Bear," his pipe smoking, his debt to Sherwood Anderson, his favorite poets, his ranking of modern American writers, how he came to write *Sanctuary*, the function of women and symbolism in his fiction, his commentary on "A Rose for Emily," the use of dialect in fiction, his impression of Japanese women and Japanese culture, the structure of *The Wild Palms*, why he decided to visit Japan, Mark Twain as the "first truly American writer," his training of horses and their appearance in his fiction, the confrontation with evil in *Intruder in the Dust*, his working practices as a writer, how he composed *The Sound and the Fury* and *As I Lay Dying*, the changes in a writer's work as he ages, his doubts about screenplays as art, and his attitude toward politics. {LG}

At the Zenkoji Temple, WF notes: "I'm interested in all religions as a form of man's behavior. {LG}

Meets with Nagano citizens, suggests they might begin with *Intruder in the Dust*. He describes the land of his fiction and is asked about American writers, saying he does not regard Hawthorne or Henry James as "truly American writers. Their tradition was from Europe." He is asked to discuss *Soldiers' Pay*, *Absalom, Absalom!*, *Sanctuary*, and *The Sound and the Fury*. He compares American and Japanese farming. {LG}

In an interview in *English Mainichi*, explains his reasons for visiting Japan, the clannish nature of the country life that formed his background, his role as farmer rather than literary man, the ramifications of the Nobel Prize speech, and the power of money and capital in the United States. In turn, WF asks certain questions about Japanese culture and writers. {LG}

August 14: Travels "up into the snow-topped mountains to Lake Nojiri, which was swept by strong winds." He sails blissfully on Lake Nojiri. {B3}

August 15: Before departure from Nagano, leaves a comment in host's guestbook praising Japanese "courtesy and generosity" that has "reached a height which I did not expect."[134] {B2}

August 16: Signs a photograph of himself at the inn in Nagano that hosted him. {B2}

Arrives in Kyoto for a four-day stay. {B3}

c. 5:00 p.m.: Attends reception given by president of Kyoto University. {B3}

August 17–19: Press conferences and interviews. Expresses his admiration of *Rashomon*. {B3}

August 20, 9:37 a.m.: Departs by train for Tokyo. {B2}

August 21: Meets with 150 Japanese teachers and students at the American Cultural Center, where he is asked questions about his style, what he plans to write, the influences on his writing, his reaction to the term "lost generation," how the writer uses his own background, his conviction that "man is tougher than any darkness," how he came to write *A Fable*, his ranking of modern American writers, his view of *The Sound and the Fury*, the best way to learn to write, his popularity in France, racial problems in the South, his opinion of Richard Wright, the differences between poets and novelists. {LG}

August 22: Asks Leon Picon, "Did I let you down? Or the State Department? Anything left undone?" Picon asks WF to leave something for the youth of Japan. {B3}

Writes 900-word message, "To the Youth of Japan." {ESPL}

Spends the day autographing books in a Tokyo bookstore. {B3}

After a party at the Picons, WF spends the night on their sofa. He tells Leon's wife, Lucy, "Leon is the son I never had." {B2}

August 23: Packs in preparation for leaving Japan. {B3}

6:10: To Manila on the way to Italy. {B2}

August 24, 2:00 a.m.: Reporters meet WF's plane arriving in Manila. He answers questions and then goes to the home of Bill and Victoria Fielden (Estelle's daughter by Cornell Franklin). {B2}

Afternoon: Delivers lecture on what happened to the American Dream to 4,000 at the University of the Philippines theater. {B3}

Reports to Leon Picon of the State Department about the flight from Manila, which included a good dinner of steak and champagne, although he already misses Japanese food and sake. Asks if Picon could arrange retrieval of clothing left behind in Japan to be sent on to Rome. He is scheduled to meet with some literary people and give a talk and will write from Rome. {SL}

Submits to interviews discoursing on the nature of freedom, the responsibilities of the writer, the role of local color in literature, his reading of Russian authors, his handling of violence and sex in fiction, the way national traditions shape literature, and the impact of war on the Philippines and its youth. {LG}

August 27: Departs for Rome.

August 28: Arrives in Rome and visits historic sites and the shops of the Via Veneto. {B3}

September 3: United Press calls for comment on the Emmett Till murder. {B3}

September 6: Issues 400-word statement about Emmett Till. Besides deploring the outrage of Till's death, WF predicts the white race cannot survive as long as such atrocities are committed. {ESPL}

September 9: *New York Herald Tribune* prints Faulkner's statement on the Emmett Till murder.

September 16: Takes the train from Italy to France via Munich. {B3}

September 18: Passes through Kehl (Germany) and Strasbourg and into France in the early morning hours. {B3}

September 19: Meets with French journalists and deftly handles political questions. Engages in playful interview with Cynthia Grenier, expressing his delight in being read all over the world and creating "a kind of keystone in the universe." {LG}

Reunites with Anita Loos at a party that includes Tennessee Williams, who describes WF as though he were a Williams character. But neither Williams nor Albert Camus seems able to penetrate WF's aloof facade. {CR2}

Writes to Alberto Mondadori, thanking him for his "kindness and courtesy" during a stay in Milan. He has left behind a part of himself and will not be complete until he returns to Milan. {SL}

September 29: Tells Piers Raymond he authorizes the United States Information Service to make use of his radio recording in Paris, which include excerpts from *A Fable*. He has no desire to request remuneration. {SL}

October: *Mademoiselle* publishes "By the People."

Requiem for a Nun opens in Zurich. {B3}

October 5: William E. Weld, a USIS official, hosts a party for WF and 42 literary figures. {B3}

October 6: In *Les Nouvelle Littéraires*, Annie Brierre publishes an account of WF's ancestry, his sojourn in Paris as a young man, his friendship with Sherwood Anderson, his youthful reading, and the themes of his fiction. {LG}

October 7: Flies to London for a four day stay at Brown's hotel. Visits Chatto & Windus, purchases English derby and other apparel. {B3}

October 12–17: Arrives in Reykjavík, Iceland, to begin five-day stay lecturing on the American Dream, and meeting informally with individuals and groups as well as giving interviews. Expresses his staunch support for NATO and the presence of American troops in Iceland as a guarantee of liberty. {CR2}

October 14: Random House publishes *Big Woods* with dedication to Saxe Commins: "we have never seen eye to eye but we have always looked toward the same thing." {CR2}

New York Herald Tribune review of *Big Woods*: "something new . . . Mr. Faulkner's fabulous Old Testament." {WFC}

October 20: He is well, WF tells Else Jonsson, repeating that he will never live long enough to write all he wants to about his imaginary county. {SL}

October 23: Departs from New York for Oxford after learning his mother has suffered a cerebral hemorrhage. {B3}

Louisville Courier-Journal review of *Big Woods*: stories that coalesce around the "theme of the passing of the wilderness, which for most Americans in our century is little more than a region of myth under the sunset, a symbol of man's lost happiness and freedom." {CR2}

October 29: *Nation* review of *Big Woods*: "Faulkner and his editor have achieved a real unity, both of theme and development." {WFC}

November: *Requiem for a Nun* opens in Berlin. {B3}

November 3: In the *Reporter*, Madeleine Chapsal publishes an account of WF's State Department visit to Paris, his behavior at a Gallimard cocktail party: "There is no use looking at Faulkner. You must read him. To someone who has read him, Faulkner has given all that he has, and he knows it. Then one can understand that when he keeps saying 'I am a farmer,' or 'I wrote that book so that I could buy a good horse,' it is only another way of putting first things first—what Faulkner wants one to be interested in are his books." {LG}

In Oxford, signs and dates first edition of *Big Woods*: "Phil Stone, with love / Bill." {BH1}

November 10: Addresses the annual meeting of the Southern Historical Association to discuss integration: "We speak now against the day when our Southern people who will resist to the last these inevitable changes in social relations, will, when they have been forced to accept what they at one time might have accepted with dignity and goodwill, will say, 'Why didn't someone tell us this before? Tell us this in time?'" {ESPL}

November 11: *Memphis Commercial Appeal* publishes address to the Southern Historical Association. {ESPL}

November 13: In New York, signs and dates first edition of *Big Woods*: "To Aunt Bama, with love." {BH1}

November 17: Attends a State Department debriefing in Washington. {B3}

November 18: Proposes unification of Germany, withdrawal of US troops and allowing the Germans to unify however they wish. He does not believe Russia could absorb or spread Communism in a unified Germany and thinks taking a "high moral plane" might be more effective than the current division of the country. {SL}

November 26: Departs by train for Charlottesville to spend an evening with Jill and her husband. {CR2}

November 27: Arrives by train in Washington, DC for a State Department briefing, answering questions about his travels abroad. {CR2}

November 28 or 29: Mentions to Jean Stein threatening mail and angry phone calls about his stance on civil rights. He does not know how seriously to take them and wishes he could endorse Ben Wasson's "complacent view that only sporadic incidents will happen in Mississippi." {SL}

Late November: Writes to Saxe Commins about his wife, a concert pianist: "Dorothy's concert went well, people still talk of it, she may have been a pioneer here for better music, familiarity with good music, etc., taking it out of the 'sissified' into the common, the dignified, the 'natural.'" {BH2}

December: In a telegram to Harold Ober, comments on a televised excerpt from *The Sound and the Fury*: "STORY CHANGED FROM ONE TO ANOTHER MEDIUM BOUND TO LOSE SOME MEANING THOUGH MAY GAIN COMPLETELY NEW SIGNIFICANCE. WHICH YOU LIKE DEPENDS ON WHERE YOU STAND."

Writes to Saxe Commins declining Carvel Collins's invitation to deliver a commencement address at Harvard. "All well here, Tempy, the horse, is jumping pretty well." Wears a polo player's girdle to help with his back, and "a little work on the next Snopes book. Have not taken fire in the old way yet, so it goes slow, but unless I am burned out, I will heat up soon and go right on with it. Miss. Such an unhappy state to live in now, that I need something like a book to get lost in." {SL, BH2}

December 2: Announces to Jean Stein that work on a second Snopes novel has commenced. {SL}

December 4: John Faulkner writes to the *Memphis Commercial Appeal* attacking the NAACP and the Supreme Court. {CR2}

December 5: WF drafts three replies to his brother John's letter to the *Memphis Commercial Appeal*, none of which are published and probably not sent. One draft begins: "All that's lacking of the old Hitler formula is the threat of Semitism." {CR2}

December 8: Writes to Bob Flatt, president of the Lions Club of Glendora, Mississippi, which passed a resolution condemning the murder of Clinton Melton, a black filling-station attendant. Mentions a letter he has received from a black woman saying his pro-integration position actually hurts her people, riling up the "bad ones in her race" when all blacks want is to be "let alone in segregation as it is." He suggests that the "best" blacks do not want integration any more than the best whites do. But he believes "the Negro" should be given a chance to prove his merit and whether he is "competent for educational and economic and political equality, before the Federal Government crams it down ours and the Negro's throat too." He also believes that there are "many more white people besides the members of your club, who are willing to see that the Negro is free from fear of violence and injustice and has freedom . . ." If he is correct, then the federal government should be told that "we dont need it in our home affairs." {SL}

Christmas: Joseph Blotner's notes: "On Christmas morning WF sent for young Bill Baker & made a formal presentation of an inscribed copy of Big Woods. He had just found a playmate, a Negro boy, and later said to his mother, 'I guess I'm about the luckiest boy in the world. I have William for a friend and Mr. Bill gave me his book.' When Kate told this to WF, he said, 'he placed them in the right order.'" {CFS}

1956

Sends a telegram to James W. Silver about equipment for the sailboat. {BH2}

Calvin Israel describes a chance meeting in New York City with WF in Washington Square Park. {CWF}

c. January: Reports to Commins that the "Snopes mss. is going pretty good. I still have the feeling that I am written out though and all remaining is the craftsmanship, no fire, force. My judgment might be extinct also, so I will go on with this until I know it is no good. I may even finish it without knowing it is bad, or admitting it at least." {BH2}

In an unfinished letter to the *Memphis Commercial Appeal*, WF makes a powerful argument for equality and dreads the consequences of not treating Negroes as equals. The letter breaks off just as he mentions: "In 1849, Senator John C. Calhoun made his address in favor of secession if the Wilmot Proviso was ever adopted." The next incomplete sentence begins with a reference to Jefferson Davis. {BH2)

January 5: Estelle reports to Dorothy and Saxe Commins that WF is "down on the Mississippi Gulf coast right now." Maud Falkner has been ill but recovering. {BH2}

January 12: Replies to W. C. Neill, who has attacked WF and others, including Congresswoman Edith Green, for their integrationist stance. "I doubt if we can afford to waste even on Congress, let alone on one another, that wit which we will sorely need when again for the second time in a hundred years, we Southerners will have destroyed our native land just because of [n----rs]." {SL, BH2}

January 13: Expresses his delight to Jean Stein that she likes his new work on the Snopeses. Worries that he no longer works with the intensity that once drove him to write. {SL}

January 18: Discusses with Harold Ober selling screen rights for *Pylon* to producer Jerry Wald. "Different people have been nibbling at this book for twenty years now. There must be something in it somewhere." Encloses a composite of talks he has given at the University of Montana, the Southern Historical Association, and in Japan and Manila. {SL}

In another letter to Ober, emphasizes he does not want his essays on race to appear in the slicks like *Life* and *Look*. Does not want a lot of fanfare. "I am not trying to sell a point of view, scratch anybody's back, NAACP or liberals or anybody else. I am simply trying to state, with compassion and grief, a condition, tragic, in the country where I was born and which I love, despite its faults." {SL}

January 20: Historian Bell I. Wiley writes to James W. Silver pointing out that lawyers for the Southern Historical Association suggest a comment on Richard Wright is "possibly libelous" and should be omitted.[135] {BH2}

January 30: Asks Ober to delete Richard Wright's name from the text of "On Fear" published in *Harper's*. {SL}

January 28: On the second volume of the Snopes trilogy to Jean Stein: "The book is going too good. I am afraid; my judgement may be dead and it is no good." {SL}

February: Elisabeth Linscott (wife of Random House editor, Robert Linscott) describes what it was like to have WF as a houseguest. {CWF}

Requiem for a Nun opens in Barcelona, Gothenburg, and Amsterdam.

February 5: To Ramon Magasaysay, president of the Philippines, introducing his son-in-law William Fielden, residing in Manila. Wishes that Fielden might be able to have the same privilege of meeting Magasaysay that WF has had. {SL}

February 15: WF's checkbook, held by Saxe Commins for WF's use in New York. Includes acknowledgment from Carl M. Love of Rhoades and Company of $5,000 check of February 14 credited to WF's stock account. {BH1}

February 20: Eleven receipts for WF's purchases and sales of stock, handled by Saxe Commins. {BH1}

February 21: In an interview with Russell Warren Howe of the *London Sunday Times*, a drunken WF expresses anxiety over the arming of southerners opposed to integration, calling for moderation but insisting that if necessary, he would go into the street and shoot Negroes, making the same choice Robert E. Lee made. {LG}

February 22: In a state of collapse, cancels luncheon with Joan Williams Bowen. {B3}

c. March: Offers producer Jerry Wald suggestions on how to improve a script for an adaptation of a novel, *A Stretch on the River*, by Richard Bissell. Supplies a 9-page story line with a "slightly new angle or a new theme." Does not mind acting as an advisor but is not available to write a full script since he is involved in his own project. Willing to make suggestions and do a polish, work on dialogue and new scenes. "Let the script writer have script credit if you like, use my name for story credit if it will help you." {SL}

March 1: Initials contract with Universal Pictures for $50,000 purchase of film rights to *Pylon*. Also signed by Estelle Faulkner. {BH1}

David Kirk, a University of Alabama student, writes to WF about his support of Autherine Lucy, an African American student attempting to enroll.[136] {CR2}

March 4: *London Sunday Times* publishes Russell Warren Howe's interview with the inflammatory comment: "If it came to fighting I'd fight for Mississippi against the United States even if it meant going out into the street and shooting Negroes."

March 5: A federal court orders the University of Alabama to admit Autherine Lucy, an African American. {B3}

"Letter to a Northern Editor": "I was against compulsory segregation. I am just as strongly against compulsory integration. Firstly of course from principle. Secondly because I dont believe it will work." {ESPL}

March 7: Declines Dr. Julius S. Bixler's conferral of an honorary degree, saying that his own inadequate education "would be an insult to those who have gained degrees by evidence of the long and arduous devotion commensurate with what any degree must be always worth." {SL}

March 8: Responds to David Kirk's request that WF join a group of prominent people offering their views on the admission of Autherine Lucy, a black woman, to the University of Alabama. Declares segregation will end, "whether we like it or not." The only question is how it is to be done and how the South will respond if desegregation is "forced on us." He prefers that the South voluntarily act to establish freedom and equality so that seventeen million Negroes are "on our side, rather than on that of

Russia." Advises Kirk to consult with editors of the school newspaper at the University of North Carolina at Chapel Hill. "A confederation of older men like me would not carry half this weight." He knows it is easier to be against than for something, but Kirk should remember he is dealing with "cowards. Most segregationists are afraid of something, possibly Negroes; I dont know. But they seem to function only as mobs, and mobs are always afraid of something, of something they doubt their ability to cope with singly and in daylight." {SL}

March 10: Lida Oldham, Estelle's mother, dies.

c. March 17: Relieved that the NAACP did not press for Autherine Lucy's admission to the University of Alabama, where "she would have been killed." Mentions sore ribs that prevent him from riding his horse Tempy. Redbuds are out and the dogwoods will soon blossom. {SL}

March 18: Vomits blood and collapses into unconsciousness. Taken to Baptist Hospital in Memphis and put into an oxygen tent. {CR2}

March 20: Writes a letter to the *Memphis Commercial Appeal* deploring the state of education for black and white in Mississippi. {ESPL}

March 22: Recovering, he sends a telegram to Jean Stein, to reassure her. {SL}

The *Reporter* publishes another version of the Russell Warren Howe interview, which is quoted in *Time*. {LG}

WF responds in the *Reporter*, repudiating the Howe interview "no sane man is going to choose one state against the Union today." {LG}

Howe responds insisting all of Faulkner's statements "were directly transcribed by me from verbatim shorthand notes of the interview." {LG}

March 23: X-rays show no ulcer. {CR2}

March 24: Mentions vomiting blood and that he passed out, was brought to the hospital for a transfusion and oxygen. Further tests to come. Will stop drinking for the next three months, cutting out coffee too and eating baby food. {SL}

March 26: Grandson Paul is born in Charlottesville.

Letter to *Life* about replies to "Letter to the North." While many take issue with his logic, they have not divined the reason for his piece, which was to intervene in such a way as to minimize the threat to Autherine Lucy's life. {ESPL}

March 29:

Leonard Wright Sanatorium, Byhalia, Mississippi.
Mr Wm Faulkner of Oxford
Hospital treatment and Med.Recd. 50.00
Nurse 12.50
Med . 2.50

L.D. phone calls. 2.21
67.21 {UVA}

March 27: W. C. Neill of North Carrollton, Mississippi, writes to the *Memphis Commercial Appeal* attacking WF's letters about the poor condition of Mississippi schools calling him "Weeping Willie." {CR2}

Dr. Richard B. Crowder photographs a recovering WF. {B2}

Spring: Jean Stein publishes her interview with WF in *The Paris Review*.[137] {LG} Explains why he does not like interviews, his view of his contemporaries, what makes a good novelist, the best environment for a writer, the compromises made in writing movies and his time in Hollywood, his attitude toward technique, the significance of *The Sound and the Fury*, *A Fable*, *The Wild Palms*, how he established himself as a writer and supported himself, his favorite characters, the function of critics, the role of fate in his work, his view of racial issues, ending with his summation: "Beginning with *Sartoris* I discovered that my own little postage stamp of native soil was worth writing about and that I would never live long enough to exhaust it, and by sublimating the actual into apocryphal I would have complete liberty to use whatever talent I might have to its absolute top." {LG}

April 3: Replies to W. C. Neill's attack on him in the *Memphis Commercial Appeal*. {SL}

April 15: Jill gives birth to Paul D. Summers III. {B3}

Mid-April: Visits Jill in Charlottesville and considers an appointment in January 1957 at the University of Virginia in a discussion with professors Floyd Stovall and Frederick L. Gwynn. {CR2}

April 16: W. E. B. Du Bois challenges WF to a debate on integration in front of the Sumner, Mississippi, courthouse, where Emmett Till's accused murderers will go on trial. {CR2}

April 17: Sends telegram to W. E. B. Du Bois declining to debate desegregation in Mississippi saying they are on the same side morally, legally, and ethically. If Du Bois does not endorse WF's plea for "moderation and patience" as the practical position, then they would be wasting their breaths in debate. {SL}

Writes to Harold Raymond at Chatto & Windus touting Jean Stein, *The Paris Review*, and her interview with him in the publication. He asks Raymond to provide Stein with a list of those he thinks should see the interview. She is hoping to entice subscribers. {SL}

In the first edition of *Rendezvous with America*, Melvin B. Tolson writes: "To William Faulkner—/ A rock in a weary land—." {BH1}

April 19: In a statement to the *Reporter*, Faulkner repudiates his inflammatory statements: "The statement that I or anyone else would choose any one state against the whole remaining Union of States, down to the ultimate price of shooting other human beings in the streets, is not only foolish but dangerous. Foolish because no sane man is going to choose one state against the Union today." Howe stands by his verbatim shorthand notes. {ESPL}

Not feeling so well, he reports to Jean Stein: "Am drinking milk every 2 hours, eating my infant rations, going to bed at 10 o'clock." {SL}

April 23: Repudiates inflammatory statements attributed to him, saying no one in his right mind would "choose any state against the whole Remaining Unions of States, down to the ultimate price of shooting other human beings in the streets," a statement which is "not only foolish but dangerous" because it might "inflame those few people in the South who might still believe such a situation possible." {SL}

April 27: In New York, at the National Broadcast Company, Carvel Collins arranges for a recording of Faulkner reading from the Modern Library edition of *Light in August*, pages 3–8, 421–30, and *The Bear* from the Dell edition of *Six Great Modern Novels*. {WC}

May 8: Returns home to work at Greenfield Farm and on his Snopes book. {CR2}

n.d: To Paul Flowers: "This time of year I'm a farmer. That's 17 miles from town. I dont have any regular schedule though so I suggest that the next time you are through Oxford, come out to my home in town and chance it. I can always spare a few minutes. Only please dont put my name in print. I dislike very much to see it." {UM}

May 20: Feels dull, he reports to Jean Stein. "Now I dont even want to work on my book, back is too painful to ride Tempy enough, so nothing to do but be a farmer while sitting in a car watching other people." {SL}

June: *Harper's* publishes "On Fear: The South in Labor": "To live anywhere in the world today and be against equality because of race or color, is like living in Alaska and being against snow." {ESPL}

In WF's living room at Rowan Oak P. D. East, James W. Silver, and WF discuss what to do about segregationists and decide on producing a satirical newspaper, distributing 10,000 copies on college campuses in Mississippi. WF contributes the headline about Mississippi's segregationist senator: "EASTLAND ELECTED BY NAACP AS OUTSTANDING MAN OF THE YEAR." {BH1}[138]

Early June: Sends the first third of *The Town* to Saxe Commins. "I still cant tell, it may be trash except for certain parts, though I think not. I still think it is fun, and at the end very moving; two women characters [Eula Varner Snopes and her daughter, Linda] I am proud of." {SL}

Letter from President Eisenhower inviting WF to take charge of the People-to-People Program enlisting other writers to create "understanding abroad" that will "contribute to lessening world tensions and to helping solve our problems." {BH2}

Mentions a trip to Washington to attend President Eisenhower's People-to-People Program, with WF heading a writers' group attempting to form cooperative activity with Soviet bloc writers. {SL, BH2}

Tells Saxe Commins he has spoken to a reporter at *Ebony*: "nothing about race: just a budding writer paying her respects to a veteran writer. That's all right with me." {SL, BH2}

June 19: Maud Falkner to Sallie Burns: "Billy has been remaking his sail boat. Every time he leaves it on the Reservoir, some one deliberately sinks it. The last time, it was a year before they located & raised it. You never saw such a hopeless wreck but he has practically made it over. Said the other day it was finished all but what Paul could do when he & Jill came. They came. Paul did." {CCP}

June 23: In a letter to Allan Morrison, an *Ebony* reporter, WF disavows the widely quoted statement about taking the side of Mississippi in a conflict with the United States. Recommends reading his "Letter to the Leaders in the Negro Race," later titled "If I Were a Negro." {SL}

Writes to Ober, mentioning Allan Morrison and their meeting in the street and what he wants published in *Ebony*. {SL}

June 27: Ober receives "If I Were a Negro" and submits it to *Ebony*.

June 29: *Ebony* purchases "If I Were a Negro" for $250.

July 20: Telegram to Hubert Starr from Bill and Estelle Faulkner: "WE BOTH CONGRATULATE YOU SIGHT UNSEEN. YOUR TASTE IN WOMEN HAS ALWAYS BEEN FIRST RATE." {NYPL}

August 8: Writes to the secretary of the Batesville Junior Chamber of Commerce about the case of Mrs. Kayo McClamroch fined $125 for violating the dry laws by importing a bottle of whiskey from Memphis. A group of citizens contributed funds to pay the fine, and WF encloses $1.00, noting he was too late to help with her fine but wanted to record his objection to secret police-like tactics—the very evil the nation opposed in the last war. He hopes his dollar is not too late for the "tar-and-feathers fund for the brave and honorable—and of course, naturally, nameless—patriot who reported her." {ESPL}

August 12: Tells Jean Stein that *The Town* is going "splendidly, too easy," which makes him realize he is not "written out" and that the "sickness" will probably kill him. {SL}

August 22: Finishing *The Town*, he confesses to Jean Stein that it "breaks my heart, I wrote one scene and almost cried. I thought it was just a funny book but I was wrong." {SL}

August 25: WF sends a telegram to Saxe Commins rejecting *Look* offer of $5,000 for a piece to accompany a photo layout. {SL, BH2}

September: *Ebony* publishes "If I Were a Negro": "I would say that all the Negroes in Montgomery should support the bus-line boycott, but never that all of them must, since by that must, we will descend to the same methods which those opposing us are using to oppress us, and our victory will be worth nothing until it is willed and not compelled." {ESPL}

September 11: To Washington, DC to chair meeting of writers in President Eisenhower's People-to-People Program. {CR2}

September 13: Writes to Harvey Breit, counting on him to get the People-to-People Program started, with a meeting in early September that WF will attend and that will take place at Random House. He encloses a letter that is to go out to writers invited to the meeting. {SL}

September 19: Working on revisions of *The Town*. {B3}

September 20: Albert Camus's adaptation of *Requiem for a Nun* is performed at the Théâtre de Mathurins in Paris.

Late September: WF's letter about the People-to-People Program is sent to writers emphasizing a desire to "organize American writers to see what we can do to give a true picture of our country to other people." He then lists a number of facetious suggestions, including anesthetizing American vocal chords for a year, abolishing for a year American passports, and other preposterous tongue-in-check comments. He proposes a program to host 10,000 young Communists to let them see America and enjoy its rights and privileges. Then he encloses "in a more serious vein," a one-page description of the program's purpose. {SL, BH}

c. October: Writes to Livio Garzanti, an Italian publisher, about a uniform edition of his work. Believes it would be a gesture reflecting his kinship with Italy and Italians "not just in spirit but in blood too."[139] {SL}

Sends a carbon copy of the letter to Alberto Mondadori with the message: "Let us pray that this may be successful." {SL}

October 4: Floyd Stovall, chair of the University of Virginia English Department sends a letter confirming the details of WF's appointment as a writer in residence. {B3}

Signs a Random House contract for *The Town*. {BH1}

October 10: Sends a telegram to Mme. R. Harr-Baur saying he is pleased with the reception of his play in Paris and sends his thanks to her and the company of performers. {SL}

Maud Falkner announces: "Billy & Estelle are going to Charlottesville in February where he will be writer in residence for the second semester—which means he will use the University as a peg to hang his baby-sittin' on. Jill lives there & her baby is precious & Billy is crazy about him." {CR2}

October 14: Poet Donald Hall writes to Faulkner about People-to-People Program: "There seems to be a general recalcitrance against joint action, some of which sounds vain, megalomaniac (imagine thinking that this committee would help Eisenhower be elected!) and exhibitionist to me. The man who says 'writers shouldn't be organized—must be free' is not reading your letter." {CR2}

Mid-October: Aunt Bama reports to Robert Daniel that "Jill had a baby a month or so ago—a boy—& Billie adores this grand-son . . ." {BH2}

October 18: WF answers Professor Floyd Stovall's letter ratifying his side of the agreement to become a writer in residence. He hopes the University of Virginia "will gain as much in benefit from the plan as I expect to gain in pleasure by sojourning in your country." {SL}

October 22: *The Town* is sent to the printer. {B3}

October 27: Issued a Mississippi hunting and fishing license with the following description: "hair: brown; eyes: gray: age: 59; height: 5'6". The space for occupation is left blank. {BH1}

October 30: Estelle writes to Saxe Commins about how busy she is at Rowan Oak inside and out. "Pappy is impatiently waiting for me to go downtown right now." {BH2}

November: *Requiem for a Nun* opens in Paris.

November 5: To Saxe Commins, Estelle describes her drinking as an escape from "unfortunate occurrences," but she has stopped—for good, she believes—and joined Alcoholics Anonymous. She mentions the strain over her mother's illness and death during Jill's pregnancy. "The week after Mama was buried, Bill started on his drinking bout that very nearly ended in disaster."[140] Then on a long drive, he told her about his affair with Jean Stein. She has been able to react with poise and dignity. "Bill feels some sort of compulsion to be attached to some young woman at all times—it's Bill—At long last I am sensible enough to concede him the right to do as he pleases, and without recrimination—It is not that I don't care—(I wish it were not so)—but all of a sudden feel sorry for him—wish he could know without words between us, that it's not very important after all." She fears the impact on Jill, who adores her father and is a "puritanical little monogamist. . . . Actually, Bill and I have lived more amicably, and with better understanding the past year than ever before—Perhaps it's because of my changed values, or because Bill feels better having seen that I'm not upset over Miss Stein." She wonders what Saxe thinks. {BH2}

November 8: Dates page 1 of *The Mansion* manuscript. {MC}

November 29, 4:00 p.m.: At Harvey's Breit's home for a meeting about the People-to-People Program attended by fourteen writers, two State Department officials, and three Random House editors. Transcript includes remarks by WF, Harvey Breit, Saul Bellow, Donald Hall, Edna Ferber, John Steinbeck, and others. {B2, BH1, BH5}

November 30: WF and Steinbeck meet in Random House offices for more talk about the People-to-People program, with WF supporting and Steinbeck opposing a proposal to urge releasing Ezra Pound from US custody. {B3}

December: *Requiem for a Nun* opens in Madrid.

December 2: James W. Silver writers to WF collector Linton Massey about the one WF manuscript he is loathe to part with and adds that he has thought about writing an objective account of WF, "but it would be something that could not be opened until after the principals were gone, and the size of that kind of job has scared me off. But I'm sure that no one will ever know the real Faulkner." {BH2}

December 3: Saxe Commins sends report of the People-to-People Program. {B3}

c. December 10: Responds to the Commins People-to-People report accepting it as it is, saying to change it would in effect be censoring it. {SL}

December 10: Writes to *Time* not exactly defending Britain's intervention in Egypt but supporting Britain and asking, "Do we critics always remember" that Britain has twice "held off the enemy and so given us time to realize at least that we could not buy our way through wars and would have to fight them?" {ESPL}

Confers with Saxe Commins about the People-to-People Program. {BH2}

December 11: Writes about the Suez crisis: "What this country needs right now is not a golf player but a poker player" to play the chips the British, French, and Israelis have given him to "probably settle not just the Middle East but the whole world too for the next fifty years." {ESPL}

December 13: Apologizes to Else Jonsson for not writing sooner, but when he is writing fiction, he does not write letters. Recounts the last four years finishing *A Fable* and the second volume of the Snopes trilogy and beginning the third. He supposes his talent will then have "burnt out and I can break the pencil and throw away the paper and rest, for I feel very tired." He writes "a little each day" while training a young jumping mare and sailing. {SL}

December 24: With Estelle, attends service at St. Peter's in Oxford. {B3}

December 25: Invites friends for homemade applejack punch. {B3}

December 26: Sends back galleys of *The Town* to Saxe Commins. {B3}

c. December 28: Informs Saxe Commins that he has signed and numbered 450 pages of *The Town* plus 25 extra ones. Describes Christmas as "pleasant" but does not "feel too good myself." He may have to return to his baby food diet. "I don't know what is wrong with me, but something is." {SL, BH2}

1957

Nancy Hale describes meeting Faulkner in Charlottesville and how the community responds to his and Estelle's presence. {CWF}

John Cullen to Floyd Watkins: "There's one thing about him that never entered our thoughts at that time. That this quiet dreamy eyed little boy with that far away look in his eyes, would remember every detail of all he heard or saw and would some day weave them into stories and become one of the world's greatest writers." {FW}

January: Estelle receives a call telling her about Faulkner's affair with Jean Stein. {CR2}

January 2: Completes corrections of galleys for *The Town*, which goes to the printer. {B3}

People-to-People Program report is sent out to participants. {BH2}

January 7: Sends copy of People-to-People Program report to Jean Ennis saying he will take care of his own expenses but would welcome secretarial support. Asks her to arrange a hotel for the February 4 meeting, preferably the Algonquin. Also suggests a briefing before the meeting with his fellow writers. {SL}

January 12: Explains why he could not meet earlier with Joan Williams. He has no excuse, but "a pretty young woman doesn't want to be scorned that cavalierly by anybody." In distress over the Autherine Lucy episode and worried that she would be killed, he had begun drinking and realized he was in no condition to have lunch with Williams. He wants to see her in February. {SL}

January 23: Writes to Saxe Commins about several calls to Estelle from someone telling her about Jean Stein and asking for money. "This is an outrage, persecution, not of me but of Estelle." {BH2}

February 1: Arrives with Estelle in Charlottesville to look for a home during his appointment at the University of Virginia. {B3}

February 2: Malcolm Franklin to Philip Duclos: "I know little of the Colonel as Pappy (William) has never told me & I probably spent more man hours with WF than anyone." {PD}

February 4: To New York for People-to-People Program. {B3}

February 5, 8:00 a.m.: Harvey Breit calls WF at Hotel Berkshire. {CR2}

8:30 a.m.: Breit finds WF in terrible condition, but WF manages to briefly attend a People-to-People Program meeting. {CR2}

Saxe Commins visits WF in his hotel room and finds him despondent about Jean Stein and the People-to-People Program. {CR2}

February 6, 9:00 p.m.: Falls into a doze after drinking most of a bottle of whiskey. Saxe Commins stays the night. {CR2}

10:40 p.m.: Falls out of bed waking up Saxe Commins, who has taken a Seconal pill. {CR2}

February 7: Continues drinking. {CR2}

February 9, 12:50 p.m.: After recuperating under a doctor's care, boards train for Charlottesville to begin semester as writer-in-residence. {CR2}

February 10: Makes the train trip from New York to Charlottesville. {CR2}

February 11: Writes to editor of *Time* comparing "our old foreign policy" to a casino covering all bets with a modest profit for the house to the new one that "seems to be the house manager's asking his syndicate to let the bouncer carry a pistol." {ESPL}

February 15: Photographed on the grounds of the University of Virginia. {B3}

Attends Frederick Gwynn's graduate class on American fiction to answer questions about *The Sound and the Fury*, "The Bear," *A Green Bough*, *Go Down, Moses*, *The Wild Palms*, "Red Leaves," *Sartoris*, *Sanctuary*. Joseph Blotner notices WF's "polite remoteness." {B2, FU}

At a one-hour press conference makes his famous statement about liking Virginians because they are snobs. {FU, CR2}

Tells the *Charlottesville Daily Progress*: "I'm terrified at first because I'm afraid it (class discussion) won't move." {CR2}

Estelle writes to Dorothy and Saxe Commins: "Bill admits he wants freedom, but evidently realized that he actually has it, for he will not even discuss divorce . . . *I* would like to be free, not from Bill, for once I love it's forever—but from the utterly false, undignified position I've occupied the past six years." Mentions the "unfortunate" phone calls about Jean Stein, but she won't tear herself to pieces over such trouble. {BH2}

February 18, 11:00–12:00 a.m.: Office hours in Room 505 of Cabell Hall for students who make appointments. Takes questions and asks some of his own about the students' interests.

February 19: Phil Stone writes to James B. Meriwether about various WF manuscripts in his possession and the history of the "Snopes idea," WF's reading and stolid behavior during a recent dinner at Rowan Oak and other examples of his "arrogance and egotism." {BH2}

February 20: Undergraduate course in American literature: discussion of *The Sound and the Fury*. {FU}

February 21, 11:00–12:00 a.m.: Office hours in Room 505 of Cabell Hall for students who make appointments. Takes questions and asks some of his own about the students' interests.

February 23: Does not want to be photographed for *The Saturday Evening Post* publication of "The Waifs," an excerpt from *The Town* but will have Ober submit one to the magazine for $1,000 cash in advance.[141] {SL}

February 25, 11:00–12:00 a.m.: Office hours in Room 505 of Cabell Hall for students who make appointments. Takes questions and asks some of his own about the students' interests.

Undergraduate course in writing: Discusses his method of writing, "The Bear," "That Evening Sun," living in New Orleans, "Carcassonne," "Red Leaves," "A Rose for Emily," and *A Fable*. {FU}

February 28, 11:00–12:00 a.m.: Office hours in Room 505 of Cabell Hall for students who make appointments. Takes questions and asks some of his own about the students' interests.

Requiem for a Nun opens in Athens.

March 2: Malcolm Cowley asks WF to present the Gold Medal for Fiction to John Dos Passos, saying it requires only 200 words and presence at the 90-minute ceremony. {FC}

Early March: Responds to Cowley's invitation to honor Dos Passos: "I hate like bejesus to face this sort of thing, but maybe when his vocation has been as kind to a bloke as this one has been to me, an obligation such as this is a part of the bloke's responsibility toward it, so, if you are sure I am the man, I will take on the job and do the best I know." {SL}

March 4, 11:00–12:00 a.m.: Office hours in Room 505 of Cabell Hall for students who make appointments. Takes questions and asks some of his own about the students' interests.

Retires to what comes to be called "the Squadron Room" (Fred Gwynn's office) for coffee with Gwynn and Blotner. {B2}

Writes to Joan Williams assuring her that the manuscript of *The Sound and the Fury* remains hers. {WFJW}

March 7, 11:00–12:00 a.m.: Office hours in Room 505 of Cabell Hall for students who make appointments. Takes questions and asks some of his own about the students' interests.

Retires to "the Squadron Room" for coffee with Gwynn and Blotner. {B2}

The English Club: Answers comments and questions about *The Hamlet*, "Spotted Horses," *The Sound and the Fury*, Snopeses, and *Absalom, Absalom!* {FU}

March 8: Phil Stone confirms for Carvel Collins that he did translate some Greek for WF. {BH2}

Writes to David Kirk at the University of Alabama with advice about how students should handle desegregation. {WC}

March 9: Undergraduate course in contemporary literature: Answers questions about "Was," "Red Leaves," *Light in August, The Unvanquished.* {FU}

March 11, 11:00–12:00 a.m.: Office hours in Room 505 of Cabell Hall for students who make appointments. Takes questions and asks some of his own about the students' interests.

Retires to "the Squadron Room" for coffee with Gwynn and Blotner. {B2}

Undergraduate course in contemporary literature: Discussion of *Light in August,* "Delta Autumn," "Was," "The Bear," "A Rose for Emily," "Death Drag," how he begins his stories, *Sanctuary,* his reading of the classics, his view of tragedy, and his view of Negroes. {FU}

March 12: Harold Ober reports earnings from options payments on novels and adds: "We could get $4000 for television rights to 'A Rose for Emily.'" {BH2}

Charlotte Kohler, editor of *Virginia Quarterly Review,* to Carvel Collins: "Mr. Faulkner seems to be enjoying himself here a great deal. He certainly adds a note of color to the community as he walks along Rugby Road in his amber-colored Bavarian hat and heavy tan walking gloves, with his pipe directly at a right angle to him. He has been very agreeable to the students here and I think they appreciate it." {CCP}

March 13: Undergraduate course in contemporary literature: On the sociological implications of his writing, "A Rose for Emily," "The Bear," *The Sound and the Fury, A Fable,* "Red Leaves," literary criticism, "Spotted Horses," Shakespeare, "Death Drag," "Was," and Hemingway. {FU}

March 14, 11:00–12:00 a.m.: Office hours in Room 505 of Cabell Hall for students who make appointments. Takes questions and asks some of his own about the students' interests.

Retires to "the Squadron Room" for coffee with Gwynn and Blotner. {B2}

March 17: Departs for Athens, Greece, on State Department tour. {B2}

March 18: Arrives in Athens on State Department sponsored visit; accepts Silver Medal of Greek Academy. {CR2}

Meets with members of the Athenian press and calls Greece the "cradle of civilized man." {B2}

Attends a formal dinner in his honor. {B2}

March 19: Visits Dimitri Myrat (playing Gavin Stevens in *Requiem for a Nun*) at the Kotopouli Theater. {B2}

Another dinner in WF's honor. {B2}

March 20: Calls on Panagiotis Poulitsas and Athanasiades Novas, presiding officers of the Athens Academy. {B2}

An unscheduled appearance at an unofficial reception at the Association of Traffic Police of Athens. {B2}

In the evening, a visit backstage during a special performance of *Requiem for a Nun* and a curtain speech to 1,200 members of the Workers Clubs of Athens. {B2}

March 21–22: Visits Delphi. {B2}

March 23–27: Sails to Aegina, Poros, Mycenae, Naupflion, and on to the Aegean, the island of Ermoupolis, to Tinos during some threatening weather and storms that do not fluster WF, who enjoys the ouzo and snacks and emerges from the end of the trip "fresh as a daisy." {B2}

March 28: Attends a formal dinner in his honor with diplomats from the United States, Sweden, France, Holland, South Africa, and Israel. Compliments his blond Greek hostess, Leto Catacouzinos: "Now I understand the Greeks better because yours is a face which might have launched a thousand ships." He says as much in a photograph he inscribes for her. {B2} Delivers a brief address accepting "this medal not alone as an American nor as a writer but as one choice by the Greek Academy to represent the principle that man shall be free." {ESPL}

March 29: Meets with 100 Greek students of American literature. {B2}

March 30: Attends a reception of the Association of Greek Men of Letters. {B2}

6:00: Escorted to the Athens Academy for a speech honoring him with the Silver Medal. Makes a brief speech once again lauding Greece's contributions to civilization. {B2}

Attends the gala performance of *Requiem for a Nun*. {B2}

March 31: Departs for Charlottesville. {B2}

April: Writes to Duncan Emrich at the Cultural Affairs Office in the American Embassy in Athens about the velvet box for his silver medal that has gone missing. Hopes to find a replacement for the box, so that it can be shown intact at the Princeton University exhibition of his work. {SL}

Signs the first edition of *The Town*: "To Phil Stone / With Love." {BH1}

April 2: At the Algonquin, Saxe Commins helps WF revive from his drinking and puts him on a train to Washington, DC, where he arrives, still drunk, unable to do a State Department briefing and is driven to Charlottesville. {B3}

April 4: Signs and dates the first edition of *The Town*: "To Dutch & Jim Silver." {BH1}

April 4–7: More drinking. {B3}

April 7: Hospitalized after too much drinking. {B3}

April 11, 11:00–12:00 a.m.: Office hours in Room 505 of Cabell Hall for students who make appointments. Takes questions and asks some of his own about the students' interests.

Retires to "the Squadron Room" for coffee with Gwynn and Blotner. {B2}

Attends a track meet between University of Virginia and Princeton. Joins Blotner in moving standards to the finish line for various races. {B2}

April 12: Meets John Dos Passos on the University of Virginia grounds and a brief conversation and drinks ensue. {CR2}

April 13: Graduate course in American fiction and undergraduate course in the novel: Questions about *Absalom, Absalom!*, *Light in August*, *The Wild Palms*, *Sanctuary*, "The Bear," and *Requiem for a Nun*. {FU}

April 15, 11:00–12:00 a.m.: Office hours in Room 505 of Cabell Hall for students who make appointments. Takes questions and asks some of his own about the students' interests.

Retires to "the Squadron Room" for coffee with Gwynn and Blotner.

Visitors from Virginia colleges: Questions about Faulkner's attitude toward the South, "Shingles for the Lord," Faulkner's style, *The Sound and the Fury*, *A Fable*, *Light in August*, *Requiem for a Nun*, *As I Lay Dying*, "A Rose for Emily." {FU}

April 17: To Joan Willams: "I haven't got over you yet, and you probably know it, women are usually quite aware of the men who love them, so I thought maybe you were dodging me." Promises to read her letters and comment on them. {BH2}

April 18, 11:00–12:00 a.m.: Office hours in Room 505 of Cabell Hall for students who make appointments. Takes questions and asks some of his own about the students' interests.

Retires to "the Squadron Room" for coffee with Gwynn and Blotner. {B2}

Phil Stone writes to William S. Dix at Princeton University regarding their WF exhibit. Stone mentions a "good deal of correspondence between him and myself . . . and some cancelled checks of bills I paid for him." {BH2}

April 19, 11:10 a.m.: Babysitting a grandchild, late for an interview in Charlottesville with Syed Ali Asraf. Expecting an aloof subject, the interviewer is surprised to find him sociable if shy and taciturn. He is not easy to draw out but admits he writes to "excel Balzac, Dostoevsky and Shakespeare." {CWF}

April 22, 11:00–12:00 a.m.: Office hours in Room 505 of Cabell Hall for students who make appointments. Takes questions and asks some of his own about the students' interests.

Retires to "the Squadron Room" for coffee with Gwynn and Blotner. {B2}

April 24: Estelle confides in Dorothy Commins about her troubles with her son, Malcolm. "When Bill finally came to his senses, Malcolm had already done some unfortunate things here, so Bill sensed immediately that medical aid was imperative, and *helped me no end* by persuading Malcolm to go to a hospital. . . . Malcolm adores Bill—always has—and has proven his devotion through the years, especially when Bill had been drinking . . . Sometimes I wonder whether or not I'll ever lead a sane, normal life." She mentions that Joan Williams is "bombarding" WF with manuscripts. {BH2}

April 25: Visits Mary Washington College, answering questions about his visit to Japan, *The Hamlet, Sanctuary*. A public reading of "Spotted Horses" and a visit to the Fredericksburg battlefield. {FU, B3}

April 27: Graduate course in American fiction and undergraduate course in the novel: Questions about *Light in August, Absalom, Absalom!, The Sound and the Fury, Requiem for a Nun, The Hamlet, The Town, The Mansion*, "The Bear." {FU}

April 28: *Jackson Clarion-Ledger* review of *The Town*: "one of Faulkner's strongest novels." {WFC}

April 29, 11:00–12:00 a.m.: Office hours in Room 505 of Cabell Hall for students who make appointments. Takes questions and asks some of his own about the students' interests.

Retires to "the Squadron Room" for coffee with Gwynn and Blotner. {B2}

April 30: The Jefferson Society: Questions about *The Town*, Communism, the position of the artist in the South, the role of imagination, observation, and experience, and the role of the artist in the United States. {FU}

May 1: Random House publishes *The Town*, dedicated to Phil Stone "who did half of the laughing for thirty years."

May 4: *The Saturday Evening Post* publishes "The Waifs," a chapter of *The Town*, receives $3,000.[142]

May 5: At a cocktail party mentions that he does not have to live in Mississippi to write about it. Estelle expresses an inclination to remain in Charlottesville with her daughter's family. {B2}

In Charlottesville, signs and dates the first edition of *The Town*: "To Saxe & Dorothy Commins," and to "M. A. Franklin / To Buddy, with love / Pappy" {BH1}

Alfred Kazin in the *New York Times Book Review* calls *The Town* "Tired, drummed-up, boring, often merely frivolous." {CR2}

May 6: Graduate course in American fiction and undergraduate course in American literature: Discusses a review of *The Town, As I Lay Dying, The Hamlet*, Christ symbolism in *Light in August, Requiem for a Nun*. {FU}

May 7: University Radio, English department language program: Discussion of dialect in WF's work. {FU}

May 8: The *Charlottesville Daily Progress* recounts WF's talk at the Albermarle High School during a Careers Day program. He describes his own brief experience with journalism in New Orleans and offers his opinion on various subjects, including education, style, and on what is necessary to write. {CWF}

Engineering students: Discusses his trip to Greece, *The Town*, "Was," his time at the university, *The Hamlet*. {FU}

May 10: Estelle writes to Dorothy and Saxe Commins about family news, noting that Malcolm is "in a very bad condition both mentally and physically though there is definite improvement." Malcolm's father, she notes, is "more than useless . . . thank God for Bill." {BH2}

May 10–August 30: Princeton University exhibition, "The Literary Career of William Faulkner."

May 11: Tells the *Charlottesville Daily Progress* that Virginia has to take the lead on improving race relations. {CR2}

May 13: Attends dress rehearsal of *Paterson*, produced by the Virginia Players, including Blotner's wife Yvonne. Blotner mentions enjoying a seance "when the mother and father were talking but sort of talking across each other. Each one was speaking his own thoughts without seeming to hear the other." WF agrees, calling the scene "an old trick. I used that in a movie script once. I had two characters on cotton bales on the levee talking across each other."[143] {SL}

Graduate course in the novel: discussion of Sir Walter Scott's influence, Southern writing and readers, WF's sense of time, *The Town*, *Knight's Gambit*, *Intruder in the Dust*, Joseph Conrad, Thomas Wolfe, Hemingway, his reading of poetry. {FU}

May 15: University and community public: Questions about *The Sound and the Fury*, integration, writing for film and television, Hemingway, WF's favorite books, T. S. Eliot, the American language. {FU}

May 16: The *Charlottesville Daily Progress* reports on a public reading of "Two Soldiers" that includes a question-and-answer session with comments on contemporary writers, the profession of writing, writing about the South and Negroes. {CWF}

Law school wives: Discussion of travel for the State Department, integration, getting information from motion pictures, the role of the writer in Europe, Faulkner's attitude toward other writers, the place of the writer in politics, America's reputation in Europe, racial problems in the South, the role of foreign aid, Communists, the Fulbright program, differences between the Old and New Testaments, his view of McCarthyism, government subsidization of artists, his support of Arthur Miller's moral objection to revealing the names of other writers in his testimony to Congress. {FU}

May 20: First-year English course: questions about *The Wild Palms*. {FU}

Press conference: Questions about his view of students, Virginia's leadership of the South, Southern Baptists, his view of Charlottesville and the university, advice to young writers. {FU}

May 21: Boards the train for New York City to present the Gold Medal for Fiction to John Dos Passos. {B2}

May 22: Tires of the Gold Medal ceremony, leaves the stage twice, and then gives a very short, abrupt speech, concluding, "No man deserves it more," while thrusting the medal into Dos Passos's hand. {CR2, ESPL}

Cavalier Daily publishes WF's denial that the English Department has "hampered his activities in Charlottesville": "I have them [Blotner and Gwynn] trained to fetch and carry." {CR2}

May 25: Phil Stone writes to James B. Meriwether that he "tried for years to drill into Bill's head the importance of dynamic design, but if he ever realized it or paid any attention to it I have no recollection of it." {BH2}

May 27: With Estelle, entertains the University of Virginia English Department, with the help of a butler and his wife. WF performs his duties as host with aplomb. {B2}

May 30: University and community public: questions about *The Town*, WF's writing habits, *Requiem for a Nun*, *The Sound and the Fury*, his attitude toward education, *Absalom, Absalom!*, *Light in August*, "A Rose for Emily." {FU}

June 5: University and community public: comments on *The Town*, women writers, Sherwood Anderson, his memory and ability to write anywhere, a writer's education, Thomas Wolfe, *The Sound and the Fury*, *As I Lay Dying*. {FU}

Summer: Responds to Norman Mailer's claim that the southern white man fears the black man's sexual potency and so resists integration. "I have heard this idea expressed several times during the last twenty years, though not before by a man. Usually it was women 40–50 from the North or Middle West. I dont know what a psychiatrist would find in this." {SL}

June 10: In New York helping his niece Dean prepare for her study-abroad year. {CR2}

June 11: In Princeton, signs and dates a first edition, second printing of *Go Down, Moses*: "Dorothy and Saxe, with love / Bill"[144] first edition, second printing of *Requiem for a Nun*: "For Saxe and Dorothy, with love," first edition of *A Fable*: "For Dorothy and Saxe, / with / love," and first edition of *Big Woods*: "For Saxe and Dorothy, with love." {BH1}

June 12: The *Washington Star* publishes an interview with a curt WF in Charlottesville saying he does not read reviews of his work and that Thomas Wolfe bores him. "I never tell the truth to reporters," he says to Betty Beale. {LG}

June 13: Attends a Little League baseball game and enjoys closely observing the action. {B2}

June 14, 5:30 a.m.: Sets off with Blotner, stepson, Malcolm, and son-in-law, Paul, to tour Civil War battlefields.[145] {B2}

June 26: Drives with Estelle from Charlottesville to Oxford. {B2}

June 27: Arrives in Oxford. {B2}

August 30: Phil Stone writes to O. B. Emerson explaining why WF dedicated *The Town* to him: "a recognition of the fact that I invented the idea of the book, a great many incidents and some of the characters. This was between 1925 and 1930 and we had a lot of fun laughing over these people and their doings. Believe me, they are very little exaggerated. We have people like that right around here now." {BH2}

September 9: WF accepts Professor Floyd Stovall's invitation to return in the following year as writer in residence at the University of Virginia, with conditions: He has to give his farm a little more time and could not resume work in Virginia until February for a stay of four to six weeks broken up in March for a return to his farm. He also needs to consider what the university can do for his living arrangements. {SL}

September 14: To Saxe Commins: "PLEASE SEND TWENTY THOUSAND ALL WELL HERE LOVE TO DOROTHY BILL." {SL}

September 15: Writes to the *Memphis Commercial Appeal* that so long as segregation persists, and the South resists integration, congressional action is likely to do more harm than good. {ESPL}

c. October: Tells Saxe Commins he still plans to visit Princeton and that Malcolm is "not doing at all well. He is listless and surly. "I personally think he has quite given up, will never be any better. Estelle is worried very much, it will be good for her to get away for a while." {BH2}

October 7: Writes to the *New York Times* about the "tragedy of Little Rock," which reveals "white people and Negroes do not like and trust each other, and perhaps never can." But liking and trusting may not be necessary if "we federate together, show a common unified front not for dull peace and amity, but for survival as a people and a nation." It could be too late, but he declines to accept that verdict. He urges dedication to the "proposition that a community of individual free man not merely must endure, but can endure." {ESPL, BH2}

October 30: Reports various travel arrangements to Dorothy Commins and asks Saxe to get him tickets to a Princeton football game.[146] {SL}

November: *Requiem for a Nun* opens in London.

November 13: Returns to Charlottesville with gifts of his mother's paintings for Blotner and Gwynn. {B2}

November 16: With Blotner attends the Virginia–South Carolina football game, favoring the amateurs of Virginia over the most polished players at Ole Miss. {B2}

November 23: Treats a severe sore throat with alcohol and is taken to a private hospital in Richmond. {B2}

December: Sends cable to Albert Camus after he wins the Nobel Prize: "ON SALLUT L'AME QUI CONSTAMMENT SE CHERCHE ET SE DEMANDE." {SL}

Early December: Writes to Johnette Tracy with more news about Malcolm's troubles. "He has been babied too much in his life. That's why he got himself into the mess he did."[147] {SL}

December 3: Estelle to Bennett Cerf: "Bill hasn't been too well lately—Bad throat and various aches—but like most men, sees a doctor & promptly disobeys orders. Nevertheless, rides every day, has bought some bird-dogs & is curiously waiting for quail season." {UVA}

December 13: James Silver writes a long letter to Johnette Tracy about Malcolm Franklin and relationships in the Faulkner family. {BH2}

1958

January: Premiere of *The Tarnished Angels*, a film adaptation of *Pylon*.

January 29: Works on chapter 3 of *The Mansion*. {B3}

President Darden of the University of Virginia rejects the proposal that WF be appointed a permanent member of the faculty.[148] {B3}

January 30: Returns to University of Virginia for another semester as writer-in-residence. {B3}

February 3, 10:30–12:00 a.m.: Office hours in Cabell Hall. Reads the *New York Times* or works on his fiction if no students appear.

February 4, 10:30–12:00 a.m.: Office hours in Cabell Hall. Reads the *New York Times* or works on his fiction if no students appear.

February 5, 10:30–12:00 a.m.: Office hours in Cabell Hall. Reads the *New York Times* or works on his fiction if no students appear.

Draws the insignia for "First Experimental Balch Hangar-Flying Squadron," a comic sendup of his drinking club with Frederick Gwynn and Joseph Blotner. {BH5}

February 6, 10:30–12:00 a.m.: Office hours in Cabell Hall. Reads the *New York Times* or works on his fiction if no students appear.

February 7, 10:30–12:00 a.m.: Office hours in Cabell Hall. Reads the *New York Times* or works on his fiction if no students appear.

February 10, 10:30–12:00 a.m.: Office hours in Cabell Hall. Reads the *New York Times* or works on his fiction if no students appear.

February 11, 10:30–12:00 a.m.: Office hours in Cabell Hall. Reads the *New York Times* or works on his fiction if no students appear.

February 12, 10:30–12:00 a.m.: Office hours in Cabell Hall. Reads the *New York Times* or works on his fiction if no students appear.

February 13, 10:30–12:00 a.m.: Office hours in Cabell Hall. Reads the *New York Times* or works on his fiction if no students appear.

February 14, 10:30–12:00 a.m.: Office hours in Cabell Hall. Reads the *New York Times* or works on his fiction if no students appear.

February 18: Consults with Blotner and Gwynn about his talk, "A Word to Virginians," exhorting Virginians to take the lead on civil rights and integration. {B3}

February 20: 350 people assemble in Peabody Hall to hear "A Word to Virginians." In the question-and-answer session, WF declares, "The Negro is not going to wait any longer." {ESPL, CWF, FU}

February 21: Graduate course in American fiction: comments on Sherwood Anderson, Dickens, Balzac, Dreiser. {FU}

February 26: Estelle writes to Dorothy Commins in excited anticipation of a visit with Saxe to Rowan Oak. {BH2}

Undergraduate course in writing: discussion of "Race at Morning." {FU}

March: *Requiem for a Nun* opens in Copenhagen.

March 1: Arrives in Princeton to attend University Council on Humanities. Stays with Saxe Commins. {B3}

March 3: Dan D. Coyle, head of the Department of Public Information at Princeton University, writes a memo indicating WF wants no publicity other than what is provided in the press release attached to Coyle's memo, announcing that WF will participate in several graduate seminars and conferences with undergraduates. {BH2}

March 4: Begins meeting with Princeton students. {CR2}

March 8: Harold Ober and Don Klopfer attend one of WF's seminars and dinner at the Comminses'. {B3}

March 11: Harold Ober writes to Phil Stone mentioning that WF will see him later in the month about adding codicil to his will. Ober includes the codicil, which has to do with moving picture rights to *The Hamlet*. {BH2}

March 12: Comments to James B. Meriwether on his unfinished novel *Elmer*: "funny, but not funny enough." {LC}

March 14: Saxe Commins writes to Ruth Ford, discussing her letter of March 7.[149] He reiterates that WF says he has given his word to Ford that the English version of *Requiem* "was for you and he will always abide by that word." He reports that WF's visit to Princeton "has been a great success so far as the students are concerned and certainly as far as Dorothy and I have had the great joy of his company in our house for two weeks. . . . We've never had a more considerate guest." {BH2}

March 15: Returns to Charlottesville briefly and then on to Oxford. {B3}

March 16: Howard Thompson of the *New York Times* interviews WF in a campus restaurant about his screenwriting career. "I made me some money, and I had me some fun." He mentions producer Jerry Wald with evident pleasure and claims: "I've never had much confidence in my capacity as a scenarist. It ain't my racket. I can't see things." {CWF}

March 19: The *Daily Princetonian* publishes an interview with WF about writing, saying it should be fun, not for money. For an income find another job. "Don't be a 'writer' but instead be *writing*." Recommends diligent reading. {CWF}

March 25: Accepts membership in the University of Virginia's Colonnade Club. {MC}

April 1: A document spoofing the drinking club formed by Faulkner, Gwyn, and Blotner, recording their actions and qualifications. {BH5}

April 9: To Leslie Aldridge: "I don't know what to say here: I am old enough to be your uncle but I don't feel much like it . . . What are your plans? I would like to see you . . ." {CR2}

April 14: Reports to Else Jonsson that he is about one third of the way through the final volume of the Snopes trilogy. "I am afraid I shall not have time to finish the work I want to do." Mentions a "very fine horse" he is raising for a horse show and will send her a photograph. {SL}

April 16: To Leslie Aldridge, commenting on a photograph of her: "Incidentally, your shoes are off again, like I remember before, which reveals character: you undress from the feet up: the last to come off will be the brassiere, unless you have on ear drops or a locket? Right?" {CR2}

April 24: Addresses the English Club of the University of Virginia in "A Word to Young Writers," discussing the "People-to-People" program and his impressions of young writers today. {ESPL}

April 28: First-year English course: memories of Confederate veterans, *The Unvanquished*, *Sartoris*, Hollywood. {FU}

April 30: Estelle writes to Dorothy Commins with family news. "I am hoping and *praying* that Bill *will* see his way clear to buy a place up here . . . We've found an ideal house and grounds that *I* already feel at home in . . . but of course I realized how serious a move it will be, for Billy—and say little—I've sort of trained myself to be reasonably satisfied anywhere—but to be near Jill and her little family means a great deal." {BH2}

May 1: Undergraduate course in contemporary American literature: *Mosquitoes*, Sherwood Anderson. {FU}

May 2: Undergraduate course in contemporary American literature: "A Courtship," "Red Leaves," Snopeses, *The Sound and the Fury*, *As I Lay Dying*. {FU}

May 6: Undergraduate course in language: *As I Lay Dying*, *The Portable Faulkner*, *Requiem for a Nun*. {FU}

Writing to John Cook Wyllie expresses his love for Charlottesville and Albemarle County. {MC}

May 7: Department of Psychiatry: Discusses irrational behavior, which he prefers to call unpredictable, the role of judgment in writing, and ideas about conformity. {FU}

May 8: Second-year course in types of literature and graduate course in American fiction: the meaning of the hunt, *Absalom, Absalom!*, "The Bear," "Delta Autumn." {FU}

May 12: Representatives of Virginia colleges: *Pylon*, "The Bear," James Joyce. {FU}

May 15: Washington and Lee University: *The Sound and the Fury*, Camus, his stay in Virginia, Snopses. {FU

May 23: M. Thomas Inge reports on WF's appearance at Randolph-Macon College answering questions about writing, including about style, other authors' influence on him, his "attitude toward the Negro," movie treatments of his book, and the fate of the South. {CWF}

University and community public: *Sartoris*, moviegoing, *The Hamlet*. {FU}

May 24: Holds a press conference in Richmond, Virginia, reads from *The Sound and the Fury*, and takes questions while expressing pleasure in his Virginia stay. {CWF}

May 26: WF is presented with the "Emily Clark Balch Pipe of American Literature" based on his drawn specifications earlier in the month. {BH5}

c. May 28: From Harold Ober Associates, a statement of earnings from November 12, 1957, to May 28, 1958. {BH1}

May 31: Rejects the idea of a trip to Russia, explaining to Frederick A. Colwell, chief of the American Specialists Branch, International Educational Exchange Service, US State Department: His refusal would be more valuable than an acceptance, since the Russia of the writers he admires (Dostoevsky, Tolstoy, Chekhov, Gogol, and others) no longer exists and is now a "police state." The writing inspired by them has gone underground. He would reconsider if he thought his visit would "free an Anna Karenina or *Cherry Orchard*. Visiting could be taken as condoning the current regime and a betrayal of those great writers. "If the Russians were free, they would probably conquer the earth." {SL}

June: Types chapter 6 of *The Mansion*. {B3}

July 16: Maud Brown writes to WF, expressing her wish to publish *The Wishing Tree*, which, she reminds him, he said "was mine to do with as I pleased." Although she has always considered the story her personal possession because it was written for her daughter Margaret, she now believes it should be published in view of its exhibition at Princeton University and the curiosity the story has aroused.[150] {BH2}

July 17: Saxe Commins succumbs to a heart attack. Estelle sends a telegram: "DEAREST DOROTHY WE ARE SHOCKED AND HEARTBROKEN." {BH2}

July 18: Telegram to Dorothy Commins: "THE FINEST EPITAPH EVERYONE WHO EVER KNEW SAXE WILL HAVE TO SUBSCRIBE TO WHETHER HE WILL OR NOT QUOTE HE LOVED ME UNQUOTE BILL FAULKNER." {BH2}

Early August: Asks Donald Klopfer to arrange for a few bottles of champagne and flowers to be sent to the ship the Blotners are sailing on to Denmark. {SL}

August 7: Faulkner does not want to make a financial claim ($750) for a collection of his interviews, *Faulkner at Nagano*. {SL}

August 11: Inquires about checks sent from the Authors League of America and whether Harold Ober has taken his commission. "We all miss Saxe. I will have to hunt up somebody else now who will stop anybody making the Wm Faulkner story the moment I have breathed my last. . . . I have had a belly full of Oxford. I cant keep tourists out of my front yard, rubbernecking at my house, and there is not one place in fifty miles that I have found yet where I can eat any food at all without having to listen to a juke box." Contemplates purchase of a Virginia residence. {SL}

August 12: Donald Klopfer receives a letter from Purdue University inviting WF to speak there in May of 1959. {SL}

WF'S undated reply to Klopfer: "Won't do it." He only visits Princeton and Virginia universities where he has kin and friends. He does not need $1,000 but $100,000. {SL}

August 13: James Silver writes to Ralph Graves at *Life* about the editor's interest in publishing *The Wishing Tree*. He thinks there is a "fifty-fifty chance" WF will agree to publish the story. Silver recounts the "story behind the story."[151]

September: *Requiem for a Nun* opens in Buenos Aires.

September 18: The Faulkners, including Jill, are guests at the home of WF collector Linton Massey. {B3}

September 25: Reporting to Klopfer on progress on *The Mansion*: "IN BACK STRETCH BUT WONT ETA UNTIL I CAN SEE THE WIRE." {SL}

October 2: Harold Ober reports interest in a television adaptation of "Turn About." Wants to know what agent represented WF for the *Today We Live* adaptation of the story. {SL}

October 9: Responds to Ober's query about film rights to "Turn About," saying it was either Selznick or George Volck, who formed an agency with Howard Hawks.[152] {SL}

October 10: Phil Stone informs Harold Ober that "Bill Faulkner at last came by and executed the Codicil [concerning movie rights to *The Hamlet*] in duplicate." {BH2}

Signs will originally drafted on April 1, 1957. {BH5}

October 21: Whitney Oates writes to Dorothy Commins, confirming a phone call with Faulkner about his arrival in Princeton on November 16 or 17 to participate in a humanities program at the university. {BH2}

November: *Requiem for a Nun* opens in Florence, other Italian cities, and Mexico City.

November 9: Attends the wedding of his niece Dean in Oxford. {B3}

November 16: Six days of meetings with Princeton students, fulfilling a promise to Saxe Commins. {B3}

November 28–30: Stays at the Algonquin. {BH5}

Works on *The Mansion* at Random House and then takes the train to Charlottesville. Begins chapter 13 of *The Mansion*. {B3}

December: *Esquire* publishes "Faulkner in Japan," excerpts from his interviews.

December 1: Maud Brown writes again concerning *The Wishing Tree* that "deserves a better fate than merely to have a place on my shelves. Besides, noting how Margaret loved it, I should like for other children to know it too."[153] {BH2}

December 2: Grandson William Cuthbert Summers born.

December 8: Writes to James Silver about an Australian history professor who wants to learn about the South, "economy, tenant framing, etc. I will appreciate what you can do." Expects to be home for bird shooting on January 2.[154] {BH2}

December 11: Purchases savings bonds for the children of his nephews Jimmy and Chooky Faulkner. {B3}

December 12: Discusses with Harold Ober how to handle Ruth Ford's adaptation of *Requiem for a Nun*, which Random House is to publish. {SL}

1959

January 1: Joins the Farmington New Year's Day Hunt in Charlottesville, Virginia. {B3}

January 2: Lets Ruth Ford know he is leaving for Mississippi for a quality shooting season. Estelle, Ella Somerville, and Vicky (Cho-Cho's daughter) plan to attend Ford's opening night in *Requiem for a Nun.* "I only wish this play could be what you deserve." {SL}

Sends a thank you note to Mrs. Julio S. Galban for giving him the opportunity to ride with the Farmington Hunt Club, "a pleasure and an honor too." Will sign a copy of one of his books for her when he returns in February. {SL}

January 4: Returns to Oxford for quail-hunting season.

c. Early January: To John Cullen: "Have been hoping to see you in town . . . The $15.00 received. Am sorry you returned it, since I had pleasure in thinking I had helped in camp one of our best hunters and woodsmen and a good friend besides." Mentions that after his return from Virginia in mid-April they should "see about getting back to the old ways, just our crowd. I would like that better even if we never saw a deer." {FWP}

January 7: Sends telegram to Ruth Ford at the Schubert Theatre opening of *Requiem for a Nun:* "MY WORDS OF PRAISE I WILL NOT HOARD / WHEN CHEERING THE VERSATILE TALENTS OF FORD / BRAVOS AND LOVE" {BH2}

Mid-January: Plans to send Donald Klopfer the first section of *The Mansion* as soon as he does a months' worth of cleanup on it. Mentions his "good runs" with the Farmington and Keswick Hunt Clubs during Christmas. He has been shooting birds since New Year's, although it is "cold as bejesus outdoors today." Considering the purchase of a $95,000 farm in Charlottesville. Expects to draw money on his Random House account. {SL}

January 23: Wires from Oxford to Estelle in Charlottesville: FINISHED FIRST DRAFT AND AM HOMESICK FOR EVERYBODY. REPORT ON PLAY WHEN I ARRIVE. VALENTINE'S LOVE. PAPPY." {SL, B3}

January 30: American debut of *Requiem for a Nun* on Broadway.

February 1: Happy to hear from his son-in-law William Fielden. Says he does not want the principal he loaned to Fielden, and will ask for it only when his own affairs require it. Plans to return to Virginia February 14 and stay through Easter (March 29). Mentions riding a horse named Powerhouse, who can take "4 foot walls and fences all day long. Good fun, also pleases my vanity to still be able for it at 61 years old." {SL}

February 4: Writes to editor Albert Erskine at Random House about discrepancies between *The Mansion* and the two other volumes in the Snopes trilogy. Encloses "Mink," the first part of *The Mansion.* {SL}

Expresses his shock that Mrs. Brown wishes to profit from *The Wishing Story,* a tale he wrote for her daughter dying of cancer. If she needs the money that badly, he consents to publication. "By now I would certainly have got used to the fact that most of my erstwhile friends and acquaintances here believe I am rich from sheer blind chance, and are determined to have a little of it. I learned last week (he [Phil Stone] did not tell me himself) that another one gathered up all the odds and ends of mine he had in his possession and sold it to a Texas university; he needed money too evidently. So do I—the $6000.00 of my cancelled life insurance which paid a mortgage on his property 20 years ago which I'll never see again." {SL}

February 6: Albert Erskine writes about the Mink section of *The Mansion* in a long letter about discrepancies in the Snopes trilogy. {BH2}

February 8: Writes from Oxford to Mrs. Julio S. Galban in gratitude for her including him in the Farmington Hunt Club activities. He mentions he will be in Charlottesville in a week and is "looking forward to seeing all the Virginians who have made us so welcome." {SL}

February 9: While he agrees with Albert Erskine about dealing with discrepancies, he adds: "The essential truth of these people and their doing, is the thing; the facts are not too important." {SL}

Newsweek reports an interview with WF sipping bourbon and commenting on Mississippi politics, daughter Jill, hunting, Virginia, segregationists," and his play now on Broadway. {CWF}

c. February 10: Detailed instructions to Albert Erskine about changes in the trilogy to avoid discrepancies. Looks forward to someday printing the trilogy with "same binding, imprints etc." Encloses "Linda," the second section of *The Mansion*, with the third, "Flem," to come. {SL}

February 19: Lawrence Langner of the Theater Guild writes to attorney Arnold Weissberger, thanking WF for waiving his royalties for two weeks commencing February 23, which will "insure the play running for a longer period of time." {BH2}

c. February 24: Expects the last section of *The Mansion* to be delivered in about two weeks. He will bring it with him so they can go over it. Asks Albert Erskine to book a room at the Algonquin for March 23. {SL}

February 25: The *Richmond Times* reports the death of Cornell Franklin, Estelle's first husband.

March 4: Jerry Wald's production of *The Sound and the Fury* premiers in Jackson, Mississippi.

Writes to Muna Lee of the State Department, saying he does not think a speech from him at a UNESCO conference would have much value as an "officially delegated mouthpiece." He is willing to attend as himself, and that might do some good. Mentions going through a thicket in "high gear" scraping his left eye, which is watering and affecting his typing. {SL}

Early March: Clearing up some details about chapters of *The Town* for Albert Erskine at Random House. {SL}

March 9: Signs and dates the last completed typescript page of *The Mansion*. {MC}

March 12: Albert Erskine, WF's new editor at Random House, receives the last two chapters of *The Mansion*. He is willing to work with James B. Meriwether on the novel. "I'm no prima Donna." Asks for a room at the Algonquin. {SL}

March 14: Fractures right collarbone in fall from horse in Charlottesville. {B2, FK}

March 16: To Leslie Aldridge: "So you remember me at last. What happened? It will be nice if you come to VA. If I were president of the university or had any weight with him, I would certainly recommend and insist on you coming here . . . I have had a fine hunting season with one of the hunts here and ended the season yesterday with the customary broken collar bone when I finally fell off. Threw the horse down turning him too fast on wet ground . . . I want to see you . . ." {CR2}

March 18: X-rayed and cast is removed. {B3}

March 22: Collarbone pain prevents a trip to New York with WF collector Linton Massey. {B3}

More drinking to alleviate pain. {B3, CR2}

March 23: Renews contract with Loew's, Inc. for "Turnabout." {BH1}

March 26: In Faulkner's absence, Albert Erskine and James B. Meriwether meet to work on the discrepancies in the Snopes trilogy. {B3}

March 27: Philip Alston Stone (Phil's son) signs a copy of his novel, *No Place to Run:* "To Mr. Bill and Mrs. Bill from Philip." {B2}

Ober sends check for $14,228.40, first installment of movie rights for *Requiem for a Nun*. {UVA}

April 3: In Charlottesville, Dr. Twyman gives WF a physical exam. Detects a urinary tract infection treated with a sulfa drug, an enlarged prostate but typical for a man his age, but X-rays does not show an enlarged liver. {CFS}

April 4: Carbon typescript of *The Town* with the inscription: "To Linton Massey / Mary Massey / Connie Massey / In recognition of the many favors they have done my family, favors / which we will probably repay in the simple human fashion of increasing them / William Faulkner / Charlottesville, VA." {MC}

April 6: Feeling better on return to Rowan Oak but is told not to ride horses for two months. {FK}

Writes to Joan Williams that he would like to sit under a tree and drink a beer with her. {WFJW}

April 7: Writes to Dr. Nicole, who treated him for bone pain in Charlottesville. Still stiff from bruising but feels "pretty good." His strength is coming back. Wonders how soon he can ride again. "I dont want to break self up for good at a mere 61." {SL}

Informs Albert Erskine he is at home in Oxford "sore but sober." Mentions Estelle. Says calls from Erskine have left the impression that the manuscript of the novel is in "good shape." Reaffirms the book should be dedicated to Phil Stone as was in the case for *The Hamlet* and *The Town*. {SL}

Mid-April: Does not expect to get to New York before June 1. Explains the accident: "I was going too fast in wet ground and turned the horse too quick to face a fence and threw him down myself. I broke the collar bone twisting out from under him when he fell. I wont turn one that fast in treacherous ground anymore." {SL}

April 28: Reporter Joe Hyams visits Oxford but is unable to elicit much from a recalcitrant WF, who is roused only at the mention of producer Jerry Wald and fellow screenwriter Harry Kurnitz. WF asks Hyams to say hello to them, "They're nice fellows." {CWF, CR2}

May 2: Albert Erskine writes to say he prefers not making any changes in *The Mansion* until they can go over the novel together. {SL}

c. May 7: Wants what he writes in 1958 to be the standard by which his work is measured rather than correcting it to conform with what has gone before in the trilogy. Still hard to ride: "stiff and painful." {SL}

May 19: Bennett Cerf writes to invite WF to Mount Kisko. "And I do hope that this will be one of my letters that you will actually read—even though there is no check enclosed therein!" {RHR}

Late spring: Counsels Joan Williams not to worry about someone saying she was influenced by WF. Writers are influenced by everything that makes an impression on them. {WFJW}

June: Transfer of manuscripts and typescripts from Princeton University Library to Alderman Library at the University of Virginia. {B3}

June 2: Phil Stone writes a long letter to Hal Smith about his and WF's efforts to get published in the *New Republic*. {BH2}

June 8–13: At the Algonquin for a week's work on *The Mansion* with Albert Erskine at Random House. {B3}

June 12: Writes to Joan Williams, saying he has decided he cannot see her because it is too painful. {WFJW}

June 13–14: In Charlottesville. {B3}

June 15: Asks Ruth Ford and Zachary Scott to make payments to Harold Ober for the motion pictures rights to *Light in August*. {BH2}

June 15–22: Returns to the Algonquin and another week of work on *The Mansion* at Random House. {B3}

June 22: Returns to Charlottesville. Supplies the title for Linton Massey's exhibition, the most comprehensive display thus far of WF's work: "William Faulkner Man Working 1919–1959." {B3}

June 24: Deeds Rowan Oak and Greenfield Farm to Jill on her twenty-first birthday. {B3}

June 27: Christening of grandson, "Little Will." {B2, B3}

June 28: Returns to Oxford. {B3}

June 29: Phil Stone writes to Howard C. Will Jr. that Gavin Stevens and Horace Benbow "were partly drawn from me." {BH2}

Bennett Cerf writes: "To my horror, I discovered we don't have a contract for THE MANSION. I am, therefore, enclosing two copies of a contract, made out identical to the one for THE TOWN. I hope they are satisfactory to you." {RHR}

June 29–July 2: Dated galleys of *The Mansion.*

July 4: To Leslie Aldridge in Germany: "Do come on home. In 2 and 1/2 years more my white beard may be so long I shant be able to find you through it . . ." {CR2}

Mid-July: Finishes correcting the galleys of *The Mansion.* {B3}

Returns to horseback riding in the mornings and some afternoons with his niece Dean, her mother, Louise, neighbors Kate Baker and Jane Coers. {CR2}

July 21: Reports to Erskine that he has gone over the galleys. Does not see any bad inconsistencies but he can go through *The Hamlet* and *The Town* before the next printing and make everything match. {SL}

July 24: Mentions to Albert Erskine that Saxe Commins opposed publication of *Faulkner in the University* interviews because it would be taken as "definitive." WF did not agree, and Commins relented. Does he mind if Ober sells some of it to magazines? "It was done impromptu, off the cuff ad lib, no rehearsal; I just answered what sounded right and interesting to the best of my recollection after elapsed years at the moment." {SL}

July 26: Wants to accept $2500 from *Esquire* for a part of *The Mansion* before book publication. Discusses how to avoid inheritance taxes. Mentions deeding his property to his daughter, Jill. {SL}

July 27: Professor Floyd Watkins writes to Albert Erskine about his collaboration with John Cullen on *Old Times in Faulkner Country.* Watkins calls the book favorable to WF but containing some material concerning WF's drinking that WF or Erskine might not like. He wishes to proceed with publication if WF and Erskine do not object. {FWP}

c. August 6, 9:00 a.m.: Refers to *Old Times in Faulkner Country* as belonging to the "scavenger school of literature." Not a book for Random House, but "he should not have too much trouble placing it, and we hope he enjoys the profits." Riding in the late afternoon when it is cooler and looking forward to fall fox hunting. {SL}

6:00 p.m.: Reports that his sister-in-law tells him that Floyd Watkins has been in Oxford off and on for a year collecting material for the book with John Cullen, whom WF likes and finds "innocent enough. . . . I think this explains the whole thing. This man is telling what he has heard from others, fired up by his own imagination and his desire to be literary, with no desire to harm or be inaccurate . . . In the last few years, the woods down here have been full of people like Watkins. I dont know what can be done about it, or if it really deserves having anything done. . . . I believe the man [Cullen] likes me, and if he had of his own accord got up a mss. about me, he would have told me about it himself." Expects Cullen would want his opinion, "like the sandlot boy might as Babe Ruth what's wrong with my swing, if he had the chance." {SL}

August 10: Informs Joan Williams that the manuscript of *The Sound and the Fury* has moved from Princeton University to the University of Virginia. After the Virginia exhibition, he will send it to her.[155] {WFJW}

August 21: Purchases house at 917 Rugby Road, Charlottesville. {B3}

September 10: Accepts his study room in Alderman Library as his official headquarters. {MC}

September 13: Harold Ober writes that David Selznick wants to produce *The Mansion* first as a Broadway play and then a film. Ober draws up contracts but advises to wait until the novel's publication and reviews. {SL}

c. September 18: Tells Ober he has purchased a house in Charlottesville and consults his agent about how to handle his tax situation. He is also looking at a country place as well. {SL}

September 24: In the *Oxford Eagle*: Thanks the mayor and the city engineers for removing the commercial sign at the front gate of Rowan Oak. {ESPL}

September 29: To Denver for UNESCO conference. {B3}

October 1–December 23: Linton Massey's exhibition at Alderman Library, University of Virginia: "William Faulkner: 'Man Working,' 1919–1959."

October 2: Delivers a two-minute speech to the UNESCO conference in Denver, Colorado, emphasizing the ephemeral nature of governments and ideologies and the eternal fortitude of human beings. {ESPL}

October 5: In Oxford, signs and dates the first edition of *The Mansion*: "To Phil Stone / from Bill." {BH1}

October 7: Thanks his son-in-law, William Fielden, for interest payment on the loan. Explains he is putting his affairs in order in case he breaks his neck fox hunting. Hopes that someday Fielden and Sister (his nickname for his stepdaughter) will live at Rowan Oak. "Sister and Jill will be co-owners; there will never be trouble there I think. Malcolm [his stepson] has already been taken care of by his Franklin kin which Sister was not, and I dont like that." Mentions that "this is all tentative yet." {SL}

October 15: Humanities Research Center, University of Texas at Austin, opens a WF exhibition.

c. October 15: Sends Albert Erskine his new address, 917 Rugby Road, Charlottesville, Virginia. Asks the Random House editor to send *The Bedside Book of Famous British Stories* and ten copies of *The Mansion*. He wants the novel to be bound in blue leather to match the set he has given to Jill. He also asks for Modern Giant editions of *War and Peace*, *The Life of Samuel Johnson*, *Les Misérables*, *The Complete Poetical Works of Keats and Shelley*, *The Decline and Fall of the Roman Empire*, *Don Quixote*, *The Complete Works of Homer*, *Anna Karenina*, *Tom Sawyer & Huckleberry Finn*, *Moby-Dick*, *The Complete Poetry and Selected Prose of John Donne*, and *The Poetry of William Blake*. Thanks Erskine for invitation to his wedding: "After having seen her [Marisa] once, anyone congratulates you; after knowing you as many years as I have, I can even risk congratulating her." {SL}

In *Oxford Eagle*: Announcing the squirrels are fair game in Bailey's Woods, not his horses and cow.

October 22: Takes possession of new home on Rugby Road. {B3}

October 24: With Blotner, attends the Virginia-Vanderbilt football game, and afterwards they retire for drinks at Rugby Road. {B3}

October 25: Sociable dinner at the Blotner's with Jill and Paul Summers. {B3}

October 29: Inscription: "To Linton Massey / personally, sincerely & God bless / William Faulkner / Charlottesville" {MC}

October 31: Harold Ober dies of a heart attack. {CR2}

November 1: *Shreveport Times* review of *The Mansion*: "Mr. Faulkner, as it has become painfully evident in recent years, is not the writer he once was." {WFC}

November 4: "Harold will be missed, may be by not too many people, but by the sort of people I hope will miss me; there are not too many like that." Enjoying the fine hunting and "nice country." Invites Robert Haas and his wife, Merle, whom Jill would like to see. "She—Jill—has 2 little demon boys now, the youngest named William C. F. Summers, for me." {SL}

November 6: To Joan Williams: mentions hunting four or five times a week in Charlottesville. Likes his "tremendous big strong horse. . . . Even at 62, I can still go harder and further and longer than some of the others. That is, I seem to have reached the point where all I have to risk is just my bones." Plans to return to Mississippi in January to shoot quail. {SL}

November 8: The *Memphis Commercial Appeal* publishes photographs of "The Flying Faulkners" alongside the Waco plane in which Dean Faulkner died. Another photograph is of Faulkner's nephew, Jimmy, in front of a jet plane.

November 9: Enclosed payment for Dorothy Oldham's black handyman.[156] {BH2}

November 11: Bennett Cerf writes to James Silver reporting he has written to WF asking permission to publish *The Wishing Tree* in a limited edition of 2000 copies. {BH2}

November 13: Random House publishes *The Mansion.*

New York Times review of *The Mansion*: "An intolerable bore." {WFC}

November 17: Bennett Cerf writes to James Silver quoting WF's letter, stating he would never authorize publication of *The Wishing Tree.* Cerf adds he will discuss the matter with WF in person. {BH2}

November 19: Estelle writes to Dorothy Commins about her new home in Charlottesville: "At long last, we've gotten it furnished in at least a livable fashion, and want you to come down to see us when you can." {BH2}

December 9: Albert Erskine sends a copy of *The Mansion* to be autographed to present to Boris Pasternak, whom editor Robert Loomis is going to interview in Russia. {SL}

Phil Stone writes to WF thanking him for the copy of *The Mansion.* He is busy with legal work and hopes to read the novel during the holidays. {BH2}

December 14: In Charlottesville, two x-rays, "antero posterior and lateral, shows vertebra no. 6 squashed, a fracture of D6, anterior compression fracture could cause intense pain no 4 involved." {CFS}

Mid-December: Replies to Erskine's request for an autographed copy of *The Mansion* to be presented to Boris Pasternak: "Nonsense. Pasternak is a good writer, of the 1st class, and no first-rate writer wants strangers scribbling and scrawling on his books. I wouldn't want Pasternak or Shakespeare either writing on mine, and I believe he feels the same way." Wants Erskine to send him a box of small cigars. {SL}

December 18: Blotner's notes: Enters University Hospital "for acute respiratory infection and alcoholism. Given "gamma globulin because of Jill's hepatitis." {CFS}

December 19: Blotner's notes: "Admitted to University hospital, acute alcoholic intoxication. Pain from falls off horses. More x-rays no special orthopedic treatment was advised." {CFS}

December 21: Blotner's notes: "went home [from hospital] (too soon)" {CFS}

Christmas, 10:30 a.m.: Presents guests with their "Santy Claus," a bottle of Jack Daniels. Signs copies of *The Mansion* for friends. {B3}

1960

January 3: Blotner drives WF to the train station for the trip to Mississippi. {B2}

January 6: Writes to Mary W. Chapman, Secretary of the Longreen Hunt, Germantown, Tennessee explaining he cannot join the hunt this time. {BH2}

c. January 20: A very long letter to Estelle, sent from Oxford to Charlottesville. In effect, a tall tale about his mother's mistaken belief she can cover her medical expenses with a cheap insurance policy, a belief fostered by his brother John, who then becomes the subject of a story about how John tried to take care of brother Bill during a bout of pleurisy, made worse by WF's resort to drinking, that ended up with both of them in a clinic, with WF winning $35 from a young doctor. Assures Estelle he feels "pretty fair, nothing to brag about but well enough." He asks Estelle to share the letter with Jill and her husband, Paul, as well as Linton Massey [a friend and WF collector] and to Blotner as well, if Jill and Estelle wish to do so. "Evidently John has sold another book or something, and is going to be a nuisance and a menace until he has drunk it up." {SL, CR2}

January 21: Dorothy Olding of the Harold Ober Associates writes that *Esquire* has offered $1,500 for a 3,000-word article about New York. {SL}

January 26: Dorothy Olding receives WF's response to her report of the offer from *Esquire* to write about New York: "Tell them anything I wrote about New York would have to be fiction, and my fiction rates are now higher than 50¢ a word." {SL}

January 28: Phil Stone writes to WF that he can drop by the office if he wants a copy of *La New Orleans e la Louisiana del Faulkner*. {BH2}

February 4: Writes to Joan Williams implying that even after sixty and seventy he won't quit the desire to bed her, and that perhaps even at ninety he will feel the same. {WFJW}

February 8: Writes to Anne Louise Davis at Ober Associates about his short homage to Albert Camus and where it might be printed in the United States. "I wrote it of course without any commercial thought at all: a private salute farewell from one bloke to another doomed in the same anguish." {SL}

February 12: Sets out by automobile in the snow from Oxford to Charlottesville. {JP}

February 13: Still on the road to Charlottesville.

February 14: Arrives in Charlottesville after several delays due to snow and ice and takes care of Estelle at home with influenza. {JP}

February 24: Writes to Paul Pollard, who worked for him in Charlottesville, hoping they can resume their friendship but explaining why he cannot grant Pollard's request to contribute to the NAACP. Initially sympathetic to the organization, he has concluded that it is making mistakes, pushing whites to extremes that work against the goals of the NAACP. He does not believe justice can be sustained by force. "As I see it, your people must earn by being individually responsible to bear it [social justice and equality] they want and should have. As Dr. Carver said, 'We must make the white people need us, want us to be in equality with them." He has set aside money, "in individual cases," to help Pollard's people: "Since they are a minority, they must behave better than white people. They must be *more* responsible, more honest more moral, more industrious, more literate and educated. They, not the law, have got to compel the white people to say, Please come and be equal with us." {SL}

March: Ruth Ford, Zachary Scott, and Harvey Breit pay $5000 for film rights to *Light in August*, with $45,000 more to be paid over four years. {SL}

Early March: Meets with a dozen Uruguayans, part of a State Department program, and greets them with a short welcome in Spanish. {B3}

Mid-March: Returns to Oxford to be with an ailing Maud Falkner. {B3}

March 18: Anne Louise Davis of Ober Associates writes to WF about importing 1,500 copies of *Faulkner at Nagano* for a US sale. {SL}

March 24: Anne Louise Davis receives WF's letter saying distribution of *Faulkner at Nagano* should be handled by his agents and publisher. He sees no reason why the book should be published in the US but will consent to an agreement between Random House and Davis. {SL}

Early May: Returns to Charlottesville. {B3}

Early June: Returns to Oxford, sails his boat, *The Ring Dove*, on Sardis Lake, spending time at Greenfield Farm and visiting his mother, who is periodically hospitalized. {B3}

June 9: Joan Williams writes thanking WF for his letter and asking where she should send a copy of her new novel to him. {WFJW}

June 17: Dorothy Olding of Ober Associates writes that *Life* has offered $5000 for a Civil War Centennial series. {SL}

June 19: Assures Joan Williams he wants to read her novel and blurb it. Nothing wrong with friendship he comments, but he wants much more. He still loves her and wants to make love to her. He treasures his feeling for her and would never want to feel nothing. {WFJW}

June 23: Turns down *Life* offer to write about the Civil War, saying he never has been a made "to order" writer. {SL}

July: Jimmy Faulkner to Joseph Blotner about telling his uncle about his promotion to colonel: "I told him about it the day I heard and I believe he was prouder of that than anything else I've ever done. I think . . . because of The Old Colonel, and he thought somebody else in the family had to do it. Every time he had a chance after that he introduced me as Col. Falkner." {CFS}

July 7: Phil Stone writes to James B. Meriwether pointing out errors in the *Princeton University Library Chronicle* article about the WF exhibition. Claims the title *The Sound and the Fury* was his invention and relates a conversation with WF about how he should not be discouraged and just "write what he damn pleased, and see whether they took it or not that even if he could not make money out of it he would probably get some literary recognition which might help." Adds that he made WF read every page of *The Sound and the Fury* to him in the "old Delta Psi chapter house." {BH2}

July 9: Shows three chapters of *The Horse Stealers* [*The Reivers*] to Joseph Blotner. {CR2}

August 21: Finishes a draft of *The Reivers*. {CR2}

August 22: Accepts Muna Lee's invitation to make a State Department sponsored visit to Venezuela and proposes possible dates. Asks for advice about clothes to wear. {SL}

August 25: Accepts appointment to University of Virginia faculty, saying he does not want to accept the $250 for a public talk. He expects to be in Virginia for the fox hunting season. {SL}

August 26: Writes to Anne Louise Davis of Ober Associates about various checks for a television script and magazine publications. {SL}

August 28: Writes to the *New York Times* about U-2 pilot Francis Gary Powers and his trial, which will become part of Russian propaganda. {ESPL}

September 4: Thanks Gerald Maxfield of the North American Association of Venezuela for his invitation to visit proposing dates of arrival. "I am grateful that you thought of me, and I hope I can meet the requirements of a share in supporting relations between our country and our neighbors." {SL}

September 23: Wants to make sure that Ruth Ford can be reimbursed by selling her rights to *Light in August* to another producer since she has not been able to mount a production of her own. He is amenable to postponing for a year her second payment on film rights. {SL}

September 30: To Anne Louise Davis of Ober Associates, WF reiterates his refusal to participate in publicity for television script, *The Graduation Dress*. Wants to make sure Joan Williams is credited as coauthor. {SL}

October 10: Accepts appointment as Balch Lecturer in American Literature. {MC}

October 18: Maud Falkner dies.

October 21: Phil Stone describes funeral services for Maud Falkner. "I was one of the pallbearers and a few people only were there because they knew the Faulkners didn't want a big crowd." {BH2}

October 27: Albert Erskine informs WF that Random House expects to put *The Town* into paperback in the spring and inquires about making certain changes to avoid discrepancies in the trilogy. {SL}

Late October: Returns to Charlottesville. {B3}

Farmington, Virginia Hunt Club asks WF to wear its colors. {B3}

Writes to Albert Erskine, agreeing to work on list of corrections the editor deems necessary for the paperback edition of *The Town*. "Fox hunting is fine here, country is beautiful. I have been awarded a pink coat, a splendor worthy of being photographed in." {SL}

Early November: At the Rugby Road home, WF joins Blotner in singing the Tex Ritter song from *High Noon*: "Do not forsake me, oh my darling." {B2}

Writes to his nephew, Jimmy Faulkner: "I have been given my colors by the Master of the Farmington Hunt." Wants his top boots which are in the Rowan Oak room called the "office" where he writes. {SL}

December 3: Signs second edition of *The Hamlet*: "To Buddy, with love / Pappy" and first edition of *The Mansion*: "To Buddy, with love / Pappy." {BH1}

December 12: To Joan Williams: "I wrote you a letter about a month ago then decided not to send it for a while, if at all maybe." {BH2}

December 20: Blotner is greeted at the front door of the Rugby Home by WF's traditional holiday greeting: "Here's your Santy Claus!"

December 25: Serves his homemade punch to the Blotners.

Poses in his full hunting regalia for photographer J. R. Cofield. {FK}

Christmas dinners with the Summerses, Fieldens, and Masseys.

December 28: William Faulkner Foundation is named in will as recipient of WF manuscripts to be deposited at Alderman Library at the University of Virginia.

December 31: New Year's celebration at Rowan Oak. J. R. Cofield photographs WF in full hunting outfit.

1961

January 3: J. R. Cofield takes the "best character shot of my career"—the famous "Riding Habit" portrait: "When I was making this special pink-coat shot, he said, 'I suppose you wonder at the vivid hue of this garment. Well, it is purposely colored: in case one should topple off his hoss, he can be found easily.'" {WFO}

January 4: Writes to Joan Williams saying little about her first novel and more about expectations for her second one: "It's a good first book and will be a bad last one." {SL}

Early January: Sends a mixed response to Joan Williams's novel calling it "hopeful" but expecting she will write "a better one." To her editor, Hiram Haydn, he angrily objects to the request for a blurb. To her, concludes with expressing his love for her and suggesting a renewal of their physical intimacy. {WFJW}

January 17: Writes to Richard I. Phillips, Bureau of Inter-American Affairs asking for instructions concerning his visit to Venezuela and the climate. {SL}

February 14: Tells Ivan von Auw, Jr. that he is flattered by a proposal from producer/director Raoul Levy to work on a script for $50,000: "I am too rusty now; I dont know that I could cope with it in French." But he is pleased and honored that the filmmaker has thought of him, and he would like to see the story, although he doubts he could "do anything to advance it." {SL}

February 15: Autographs the riding habit portrait: "To J. R. Cofield, from his friend William Faulkner." {WFO}

February 16: Accepts an invitation from General William Westmoreland to visit West Point. {B3}

February 24: Critic John Crosby walks up Broadway and sees that WF's name is listed above both stars and the title of the adaptation of *Sanctuary*. {B2}

March 2: Asks Muna Lee of the State Department if he has to fly to Venezuela. "As I get older, I get more and more frightened of aeroplanes." Mentions that his stepdaughter and husband live in Caracas, but "they stay up too late at night for me. I'd prefer a hotel. In fact, I insist, not with them. I have enough kinfolks at home." {SL}

c. March 8: Wants to assure Muna Lee that he treats the Venezuelan trip as a job, not a "pleasure trip . . . I am still afraid I am the wrong bloke for this. Even while I was still writing, I was merely a writer and never at all a literary man; since I ran dry three years ago, I am not even interested in writing anymore: only in reading for pleasure in the old books I discovered when I was 18 years old." Does not want to sign autographs for Americans, "since the addition of my signature to a book is part of my daily bread. I intend, and want, to sign any and all from Venezuelans and other Latin Americans who ask." {SL}

March 14: Estelle's kidney infection worsens. {B3}

March 21: Confides to son-in-law William Fielden that he has no confidence in the trip to Venezuela because it is for Americans in the country who can make more money living there than anywhere else. He is only going at the importunity of the State Department. Plans to spend time with the Fieldens. Mentions Estelle's hospitalization and bed rest, which has altered his travel plans. {SL}

Spring: *Transatlantic Review* publishes "Albert Camus." {ESPL}

Christopher Paddock meets WF at the University of Virginia and puts several questions to him about his favorite contemporary authors, his own favorite work, his reaction to the Nobel Prize, and to a woman at a Charlottesville party who asked him what he did. "I write," WF replied. {CWF}

April 1: Departs for Venezuela via New Orleans and Miami. {B2}

April 2: Arrives in Venezuela on State Department sponsored trip. Rests with his step-daughter, Victoria Fielden and her husband. {B2}

April 3, 10:00 a.m.: Press conference in which WF deftly fields questions about race. {B2}

April 6: Welcomed to the Venezuelan Ministry of Education and presented with several gifts and the Order of Andrés Bello, the highest award given to a civilian. Reads his one-page acceptance speech in Spanish describing the artist's conception of immortality, followed by a formal dinner. {B2, ESPL}

Address at the Teatro Municipal, Caracas, thanking the dancers of "Danzas Venezuela." {ESPL}

April 8: Speaks briefly at the Museo de Bellas Artest and answers questions. {B2}

April 9: Attends a night concert in his honor by the Venezuelan Symphony. {B2}

April 10–14: Tours Venezuela up the northern coast toward Columbia. {B2}

April 11: An hour of horseback riding in Maracay. {B2}

April 12–13: In Zulia, holds a press conference, meets with students, and engages in a roundtable discussion with faculty members at the Universidad de Zulia. {B2}

April 14: More school visits. {B2}

Noon: Flies back to Caracas. {B2}

Evening: American Embassy hosts cocktail party for WF. {B2}

April 15–16: A weekend with the Fieldens. Signs copies of his books for Venezuelans at another cocktail party. {B2}

Signs and dates in Caracas the first edition of *Big Woods*: "To Sister and Bill, with love/ Pappy." {BH1}

April 17: WF flies home. {B2}

State department reports are glowing about his warm reception, his patriotic performance of his duties that contributed to a "personal success" and "rendered a high service to the United States." {B2}

April 22: Tells Joan Williams he has received a copy of her first novel *The Morning and the Evening*: "Beautiful. I am proud of you. Dont stop now. I believe, hope you are already working on the next one. Love" {BH2}

May 2: Writes part of a letter in Spanish to his Venezuelan interpreter, Hugh Jencks, thanking him for his services and declaring, "I intend to know the language next time." {SL}

May 6: Writes to Mary Winslow Chapman, secretary of the Longreen Hunt, Germantown, Tennessee, saying he would subscribe even if he did not hunt. Encloses a check and says he hopes she will "bring the hounds and mounts down here. We can do some night hill-topping with cars and see how the fox will run, and ride the country by day and see where to open it up." {BH2}

May 9: Returns to Charlottesville. {B2}

May 30: Grandson A. Burks Summers is born. {B3}

May or June: Provides his nephew, Jimmy Faulkner, with details about tombstones for his mother and father, stating only the facts, but adding he will agree to whatever the family wants. Still enjoys morning rides on several different horses, some for jumping, some for hunting. Mentions becoming a member of the Longreen Hunt at Germantown, Tennessee. "We will go up this fall and hunt with them. I can get us horses." {SL}

June: Joseph Blotner's notes: WF & E, Jill & Paul, Sally & Ted. Immensely successful. Best evening with . . . WF & E. WF expansive, story-telling. In dining room, when men are having port & cigars he does changing of guard step, half-step, stamp & turn." {CFS}

June 11: The *New York Times* reports that the William Faulkner Foundation has plans to promote Latin American writers and the education of blacks in Mississippi.

Summer: Jack Cheatman, an Ole Miss student and horse fancier, manages to strike up a friendship with WF. {B2}

July 2: Ernest Hemingway shoots himself with a shotgun and WF immediately deems it a suicide. {JP, CR2}

July 9: Joseph Blotner's notes: "6:00 go to WF's for drink. E knocked downstairs by Will—3 stitches in scalp. WF gives me 3 chs of typed ms to read: 'The Horse Stealers: A Reminiscence.' Strikes me as mellow & funny." {CFS}

July 14: Elliott Chaze describes WF answering the door of his Charlottesville home, "absolutely composed and motionless as a photograph." In spite of the interruption, WF invites Chaze in even while expressing his disgust with interviewers who want WF to say something for their readers. But he explains his own attitude toward writing and accepts Chaze's gift of a pipe. {CWF}

July 18: Joseph Blotner's notes: "Ronnie & MJ phone that they're in town & we phone E, who says bring them to the cocktail party. WF says he has more pages to me to read. Most laughing & eye contact I can remember with him ever. He says he's going to write the jacket blurb himself: 'A very important statement—the book will become the Western World's Bible of Free Will and Private Enterprise.' E.V. True blood, Oxford Eagle, Miss. He gives me bottle of Pouilly-Fuisse, too. WF convulsed & red with his silent laughter. 'This book gets funnier all the time,' he says." {CFS}

Late July: Returns to Rowan Oak. {B2}

August 2: Tells Albert Erskine he believes he has gone through the list of changes in *The Mansion*. Mentions his new job of writing, with the preliminary title *The Horse Stealers*. {SL}

August 21: In Oxford, completes and dates the typescript of *The Horse Stealers*. {B3}

James W. Silver in a letter "To Whom It May Concern" describes the circumstances of WF's invitation to speak at the Southern Historical Association. {BH2}

August 28: Writes to Albert Erskine about *The Horse Stealers*: "I suddenly got hot and finished the first draft of this work last week." Describes the plot and characters. Asks for the $35,000 he has accrued in royalties. {SL}

September 1: James W. Silver explains to John Cook Wyllie what he knows about the circumstances in which *The Wishing Tree* was written and WF's attitude toward it. {BH2}

September 16: Linton Massey tells James W. Silver that WF read *The Wishing Tree* "to a group of children a few years ago." {BH2}

September 19: Considering a title change of *The Horse Stealers* to The Stealers or The Reavers, "maybe Reivers." He wants something more "swashbuckling" than the original, he tells Albert Erskine. Inquires about an edition of his selected short stories.[157] {SL}

October 4: Phil Stone answers scholar Richard P. Adams's queries about WF's reading. {BH2}

October 6: Signs Farmer-District Cooperative Agreement. {B2}

October 10: Dr. Chester McLarty administers a flu shot in his Oxford office. {B2}

October 11: Discusses his tax situation and royalty reports with Albert Erskine. He is pleased that Erskine likes *The Reivers*. "I thought it was funny myself. I would still like to use that blurb on the jacket I wrote you about, like this: 'An extremely important statement . . . Eminently qualified to be the Western World's bible of freedom of choice and Private enterprise.' Ernest V. Trueblood, Literary & Dramatic Critic, *Oxford (Miss.) Eagle*." {SL}

October 21: With Estelle, arrives in a red Rambler at their Rugby Road home, which is put up for sale pending possession of Knole Farm. The Faulkners temporarily reside at 2027 Minor Road. {B2}

October 22: Mentions his Charlottesville house has been burgled. Requests certain changes in characters' names, include Butch Lovemaiden instead of Butch Lovelass. Agrees to an editorial meeting on November 6. "But I live up to my arse in delightful family, and I may want a holiday, at the Algonquin." {SL}

October 23: John Cullen to Floyd Watkins: "I met William Faulkner on the street some time ago. He stopped and shook hands with me in a very friendly manner. We had a few friendly words and he continued on up the street. I was talking with another friend at the time. So nothing can be made out of it, only that he has no resentment over our book."[158] {FW}

October 30: Bennett Cerf wires to say the Book-of-the-Month Club has chosen *The Reivers* as a future selection. {SL}

November 3: Pleased with the Book-of-the-Month Club selection of *The Reivers*. Horses and fox hunting are his main occupation, he reports to Bennett Cerf. "I wont work until I get hot on something; too many writing blokes think they have to show something on book stalls. I will wait until the stuff is ready, until I can follow instead of trying to drive it." {SL}

November 27: Checks into the Algonquin for more work on *The Reivers* at Random House. {B3}

Princeton University Press publishes James B. Meriwether's *The Literary Career of Faulkner: A Bibliographical Study*.

December 1: Blotner visits Knole Farm and learns that Estelle is to be hospitalized to treat her ulcer. {B2}

December 14: Reads "Christmas Night in the Quarters" by Irwin Russell for radio station WELK. {B2, B3}

December 18: Suffering from a painful back and bad cold treated with more bourbon. Admitted to University of Virginia Hospital, receives an injection of gamma globulin to protect from hepatitis Jill had contracted. {B2}

December 20, 10:30 a.m.: Released from hospital in a state of exhaustion. {B2}

December 24: Relapses. Admitted to Tucker Neurological and Psychiatric Hospital in Richmond. Vital signs are good but much pain in the lower back. Treated with mild sedation and cold medication, diet, and rest. {CR2}

Dr. Asa Shield's report: Blood pressure 126/70, "which is extremely good for a man of his age. So was the rest of the inventory: lungs clear, heart normal, abdomen negative. No indication of enlarged liver." Explains to Joseph Blotner: "WF was an excellent patient, most cooperative. He would tell you about his pain if you asked about it, but he didn't complain about it and didn't ask for a lot of medicine." {CFS}

Christmas: At Knole Farm "the Summer" estate. {JP}

December 29: Released from hospital. Takes the 5:45 bus to Charlottesville. {CFS}

1962

January 1: Declares himself recovered. {B2, B3}

January 3: Injures left eye and forehead in fall from horse in Charlottesville. {B2, B3}

January 4: Treated with Demerol for back pain and told not to ride horses. {B2, B3}

January 6: Coughing spells and chest pain. Drinking again. {B2, B3}

January 8: Readmitted to Tucker Neurological and Psychiatric Hospital in Richmond. Dr. Asa Shield's report: Electrocardiogram normal, heart not enlarged. WF tells Dr. Shield: "I'm going to stop being a damn fool and acting like a 45-year-old and start living as a 65-year-old and perhaps live to be 85 years old." {CFS}

January 10: Running a fever with chest pain and contracts pleurisy. Given penicillin and streptomycin every eight hours. {B2}

January 12: Weak but free of fever. {B2}

January 15: Released from hospital. {B2}

January 20: In Oxford, obtains a new hunting and fishing license. Purchases two hunting dogs for $500. {B2}

Judge J. W. T. Falkner dies. {B2, B3}

January 21, 7:29 p.m.: Owner of neither a radio nor television, shows up at the home of Jim and Dutch Silver to watch *Car 54, Where Are You?* {B2}

January 28, 7:29 p.m.: Shows up at the home of Jim and Dutch Silver to watch *Car 54, Where are You?* {B2}

January 29: Quail shooting and working with horses is the report to Joseph Blotner from Oxford. Plans to return to Charlottesville around April 10. Planned visits to West Point and New York for Gold Medal ceremony and then granddaughter's graduation in Charlottesville in May. Relies on Blotner to arrange public appearances. Estelle is doing well, but his horse stepped in a groundhog hole and he broke a tooth and has to have a new bridge made. "I feel now I've got a mouse trap in my mouth. It dont hurt Jack Daniel though thank God." {SL}

February 2: Three broken teeth extracted and replaced with a partial plate. {B2}

February 4: Shows up at the home of Jim and Dutch Silver to watch *Car 54, Where Are You?* {B2}

February 9: Ivan von Auw Jr. of Ober Associates writes to ask Faulkner if he wishes to consent to a Polish production of Camus's translation of *Requiem for a Nun*, with a 5 percent royalty to be split between Camus's wife and Faulkner. {SL}

February 11: Shows up at the home of Jim and Dutch Silver to watch *Car 54, Where Are You?* {B2}

February 15: Tells Ivan von Auw Jr. of Ober Associates that Camus's dramatic version of *Requiem for a Nun* was "mostly Camus" and that he will agree to "whatever Mme Camus wants." {SL}

February 18: Shows up at the home of Jim and Dutch Silver to watch *Car 54, Where Are You?* {B2}

February 25: Shows up at the home of Jim and Dutch Silver to watch *Car 54, Where Are You?* {B2}

March 4: Shows up at the home of Jim and Dutch Silver to watch *Car 54, Where Are You?* {B2}

March 11: Shows up at the home of Jim and Dutch Silver to watch *Car 54, Where Are You?* {B2}

March 18: Shows up at the home of Jim and Dutch Silver to watch *Car 54, Where Are You?* {B2}

March 19: Meets to discuss a commissioned portrait for the University of Mississippi. Prefers to be photographed in his tweed jacket rather than in cap and gown. It is decided that WF's favorite chair would be included and that photographs would be taken in J. R. Cofield's studio for use by painter Murry Goldsborough. {B2}

Ivan von Auw of Ober Associates transmits producer Elliot Kastner's offer to option *Light in August.*

March 22: Photographed at Rowan Oak with pipe in hand, Quiet Birdman pin in his lapel, looking straight at the camera, without a smile. {B2}

March 23: Ivan von Auw Jr. of Ober Associates receives WF's agreement to refund Ruth Ford's option money for *Light in August* out of what he will receive from another producer. {B2}

Simon Claxton knocks on WF's front door in Charlottesville after having received no answer to his letter saying that as an English boy in America he wanted to meet and talk with WF. He describes approaching the house, spotting WF in a wicker chair, who says no to Claxton's inquiry if WF received his letter. But WF agrees to answer "any questions you have." He describes WF's physical presence: "enormous strength of character, dressed in scruffy clothes, fondling a pipe in his hand, and answering questions about his work tersely insisting he is just a 'story-teller.' He advises this young student to read "a lot, and of everything—fiction, biography, history, law." He leaves believing WF is susceptible to a "man-to-man discussion." {LG}

March 25: Shows up at the home of Jim and Dutch Silver to watch *Car 54, Where Are You?* {B2}

March 31: *Esquire* publishes "Hell Creek Crossing," an excerpt from *The Reivers.*

April: Writes to Joan Williams he has one more book to write. {WFJW}

April 2: Ivan von Auw Jr. of Ober Associates writes Faulkner that he is not legally obligated to return Ruth Ford's option money for *Light in August.* He also questions an agreement WF apparently made over the phone to allow Ford to have right of first refusal for others' rights to *Absalom, Absalom!*, "The Bear," and *As I Lay Dying.* {SL}

Signs and dates portrait photograph by Jack Cofield: "For Professor Silver / William Faulkner." {BH1}

April 3: Signs contract with MGM for films rights to "Ambuscade," "Retreat," and "Raid." {BH1}

April 4: Writes to James W. Silver asking him to tell photographer Martin Dain not to take any more pictures of the Rowan Oak property. "Please impress on him that I dont want photographs of myself and home and animals etc. in newspapers or magazine or books or in the possession of strangers." {BH2}

April 5: Returns to Charlottesville and Knole Farm. {B2}

April 6: Linton and Mary Massey visit Knole. {B2}

Bennett Cerf: "I am enclosing herewith a contract for THE REIVERS, which Manny Harper is getting agitated about, since we now have bound books." {RHR}

April 8: Blotner visits and is told WF has fully recovered from his January mishaps. {B2}

April 10: Does not remember the phone calls about rights to *Absalom, Absalom!*, "The Bear," and *As I Lay Dying* claimed by Ruth Ford, which Ivan von Auw Jr. of Ober Associates mentions in a letter. But if she says Ober gave her those rights, then WF will take her word for it. But if there are other bidders, she must notify Ober Associates within 24 hours that she is going to exercise her option. {SL}

April 19, noon: Arrives at Stewart Air Force Base and is driven to Hotel Thayer and installed in the presidential suite in preparation for a visit and lecture at US Military Academy at West Point. {B2}

Tours West Point and then attends black-tie dinner in the superintendent's quarters. {B2}

Delivers a public reading of *The Reivers*, selecting "one of the funniest horse races I ever heard of." He bows to applause and takes questions about his Nobel Prize, his own favorite of his novels, his reaction to Hemingway's death, his purpose in *Absalom, Absalom!*, his view of modern literature, his favorite author, his outlook on the human race, his creation of the Snopes and Sartoris families, and his understanding of naturalism. He receives a standing ovation. {B2}

At a press conference, he is asked for his impressions of West Point and its cadets, what delights him, what he reads now, and his attitude toward *The Reivers*. {B2}

April 20, 5:45 a.m.: An early breakfast, afterwards meeting two West Point classes, commenting: "War is a shabby, really impractical thing." {CWF}

7:55–8:50 a.m.: A discussion of "Turnabout," his Nobel Prize speech, his understanding of Hemingway's *The Old Man and the Sea*, his view of literature and of his characters, his attitude toward youth, the South, and segregation, his view of war, the role of the United States in the world. {CWF}

9:30–10:25 a.m.: A discussion of WF's admiration of *Don Quixote*, Faulkner's style, his biography, *As I Lay Dying*, his view of writing as a profession, integration, his view of World War I and expatriates, questions about "Beyond" and "The Bear," *Uncle Tom's Cabin*, what inspired him to become a writer, *The Reivers*, *The Sound and the Fury*, characteristics of Southern society, *Knight's Gambit*, the Depression, the primacy of poetry, on confronting discouragement with his writing, and his relationship with his characters. {CWF}

April 20: President Kennedy invites WF to a White House dinner for Nobel Prize winners. WF remarks: "I'm too old at my age to travel that far to eat with strangers." {B2, CR2}

April 22: Linton Massey writes to James W. Silver that Estelle has given him a copy of WF's "Beer Broadside." {BH2}

April 23: Estelle writes to James W. Silver about West Point visit: "fun, but exhausting—Anyway Bill and I were housed in the Presidential Suite in the post hotel—and I had generals in plenty to squire me around." Mentions that WF rejected invitation to White House dinner: "said he wouldn't go to Washington just to eat." {BH2}

May: *Esquire* publishes "Education of Lucius Priest," an excerpt from *The Reivers*.

May 5: Attends, as one of the patrons, the 37th running of the Virginia Gold Cup at the Broadview Course at Warrenton. {B3}

May 6: Vida Marković interviews Faulkner and questions him about his liking of animals, fox hunting, and horses, his view of human nature, farming, his reluctance to talk about his books, his favorite reading, his characterization of the French and Italians, but ends by saying "I am not a conversationalist. I can write; I cannot talk." {LG, CR2}

May 17: Reads from *The Reivers* at the Rotunda on the grounds of the University of Virginia. {B2}

May 24: In New York for award of Gold Medal for Fiction of National Institute of Arts and Letters. {ESPL}

Reminisces with Lillian Hellman about their good times with Dashiell Hammett. {CR2}

May 27: *Denver Post* review of *The Reivers*: "Faulkner's Tall Tale Tops Mark Twain's." {CR2}

May 29: A picnic at which Faulkner teaches a four-year-old boy how to fish. {B2}

May 30: Departs Charlottesville for Oxford. {B2}

June 1: Phil Stone answers scholar Richard P. Adams's queries about Faulkner's reading.[159] {BH2}

At Rowan Oak, signs and dates first edition of *The Reivers*: "For Sister and Bill, with love/ Pappy." {BH1}

June 3: Winfield Townley Scott's review of *The Reivers* in the *Santa Fe New Mexican*: "I can only, however awkwardly, record my curious sensation that I was reading a book which had long been classic American literature. I dare say that's what's going to happen to it." {WFC}

Miami Herald and *Atlanta Journal* reviews of *The Reivers*: "truly fine" and "a small, fresh masterpiece." {CR2}

June 4: Random House publishes *The Reivers.*

June 6: Goes to vote for Congressman Frank E. Smith, whom WF regards as a moderate like himself. Smith loses. {B2}

June 8: Phil Stone to Richard P. Adams: "Bill has been home for a few days and I saw him on the street the other day. I have never seen him look so old before; it is not his eyes, but the skin around his eyes; looks like that of an old man, and he looks to me like he has aged about five years since I saw him a few months ago." {BH2}

June 12: In Oxford, signs and dates *The Reivers* "To Emily and Phil / from Bill." {SS}

June 13: Phil Stone thanks Faulkner for leaving at the office an autographed copy of *The Reivers*. Expects it will take some time to read the novel since he spends all his time reading law books. {BH2}

June 15: Phil Stone reports to James B. Meriwether: "Bill got thrown by another horse and is having trouble with his back again. I told him he was going to break his neck one of these days." {BH2}

June 17: Injured in fall from horse in Oxford. {B3}

June 19: Faulkner rejects Dr. McLarty's advice to go to the Campbell Clinic in Memphis for treatment of his back. {B3}

June 24: Dr. McLarty observes a pale Faulkner at the post office. Faulkner again rejects advice to check into the Campbell Clinic. {B3} Meta Carpenter writes to Faulkner, and he responds, saying he expects to be in California in September. {CR2}

June 25: Writes to Major General W. C. Westmoreland about the visit to West Point, saying it was "memorable for the honor it conferred on me, but for the many and unfailing courtesies with which the four of us—Mrs. Faulkner, myself, and our son[160] and daughter—were surrounded." Sends the "grateful thanks of Mrs. Faulkner and myself and Mr and Mrs Summers for the pleasure of our visit to the Point, and to Mrs Westmoreland and yourself mine and Mrs. Faulkner's kindest personal regards."

June 28: In Oxford, Jane Coers meets WF on the street and asks him how he is feeling: "If I sit down I'm not comfortable. If I lie down, I can't stand it." {B3}

June 29–30: Slight improvement in painful back. {B3}

June 29: Asks friend and Faulkner collector Linton Massey for $50,000, which WF can return by September 1. He is making an offer on a 250-acre farm, nine miles out of Charlottesville, and he will be broke if the offer is accepted. Will supply more details if needed and will understand if Massey says no.[161]

June 30: A letter in French to Ginette Strickland, wife of the chairman of the Department of Modern Languages at the University of Virginia concerning joining a faculty-student trip to France and to Aubigny, Ginette's original home.[162]

July 2: Sends Massey a telegram saying he just wanted to make sure he could have the $50,000 for Red Acres, if that became necessary. "COULD SOLO BUT THIS ABOLISHES RISK OF POSSIBLE SACRIFICE IN PRESENT HOLDINGS TO MEET DEADLINE. BLESS YOU. BILL."[163]

J. Aubrey Seay accompanies Faulkner to an outing on Sardis Lake and finds his friend looking "healthy and in good spirits." {B2}

Signs and dates a copy of *The Reivers* "To Else and Helen, with love / Bill."[164] {Patrik Andersson catalogue, http://patrikandersson.net/en/\}

July 3: Mails a copy of *The Reivers* to Else Jonsson. Complains to Mac Reed about his painful back. {B3}

8:30: Out to dinner with Estelle at the Mansion in Oxford. WF tells Estelle his food does not taste right. {WFO, B2}

July 4: Drinking and taking prescription pain killers for acute back pain. Estelle considers taking WF to Wright's Sanitarium in Byhalia. {B2}

July 5, 6:00 p.m.: Admitted to Wright's Sanitarium. {B2}

6:00–10:45 p.m.: Vitamin injections followed with a half-ounce of alcohol every hour. {CR2}

10:00 p.m.: Two egg flips (an antinausea medication). {CR2}

July 6, 1:30 a.m.: Groans, sits up on the side of his bed, and falls over dead. Forty-five-minute heart massage and mouth-to-mouth resuscitation produces no effect. {CR2}

c. 2:00 a.m.: Estelle receives the call about her husband's death. {CR2}

Estelle Faulkner telegram to Dorothy Commins: "BILL DIED HEART ATTACK. SERVICES SATURDAY AFTERNOON." {B2}

July 7: Buried in St. Peter's Cemetery, Oxford.

NOTES

1. These were not the same slaves recorded by the census in 1850–see JW.

2. Aspects of the colonel's Civil War experiences filter into *Flags in the Dust*, *The Unvanquished*, and *Requiem for a Nun*.

3. J. W. T. Falkner, shrewd and ambitious but not as histrionic as his father, is reminiscent of old Bayard in *Flags in the Dust*.

4. JW speculates that Lena may be William C. Falkner's black daughter by Emeline Falkner.

5. Set aboard a steamboat during an elaborate masquerade, this picaresque and melodramatic novel reflects a penchant for violence and romance and hidden identities. If *The White Rose of Memphis* bears little resemblance to the plots, styles, and characters of WF's fiction, it nevertheless works out the protocols of the gentleman's code that WF embodied in his own life and work.

6. Later, his grandson will think of doing the same on his European sojourn.

7. This incident is later transformed into Colonel Sartoris's similar avowal in *The Unvanquished*.

8. The pipe is crucial in the depiction of Colonel Sartoris in *Flags in the Dust*.

9. The statue is transmogrified into Colonel Sartoris's statue in *Flags in the Dust*, depicting him standing on a stone pedestal with his head "lifted a little in that gesture of haughty pride which repeated itself generation after generation with a fateful fidelity, his back to the world and his carven eyes gazing out across the valley where his railroad ran, and the blue changeless hills beyond, and beyond that, the ramparts of infinity itself." Like Bayard Sartoris in *The Unvanquished*, J. W. T. Falkner decides not to avenge his father's murder. He now takes on the services of Ned Barnett, the colonel's man who wears the colonel's clothes and becomes a fixture in the colonel's great-grandson's life.

10. *Southern Sentinel*, October 27: "Our town was thrown into a fever of excitement and suspense last Thursday evening by the news over the telephone that conductor Murry Falkner had been dangerously if not fatally shot by Mr Elias Walker at Pontotoc. The shooting occurred in a Mitchell and Barringers' Drugstore, where young Falkner had gone for some medicine. Reports of all such affairs of course are a little conflicting, but the most reliable information we get is about as follows: Falkner had called for the medicine and was standing at the counter to receive it his side to the door and apparently without thought of danger, when Walker appeared at the door with a shot gun, told Falkner that he 'had to take back what he said' and immediately fired."

11. Phil Stone to Hudson Strode, April 23, 1951: "Bill's mother says that Bill was born about 11:00 o'clock on a Saturday night." {BH2}

12. A rare disease now, but then a terror, resulting in fever with aches and pains, sometimes leading to severe liver disease with bleeding and yellowing skin (jaundice). In *Absalom, Absalom!* Charles Etienne Saint-Valery Bon and Judith Sutpen die of yellow fever in 1884.

13. JW infers that Emeline was the mother of black Falkners, sired by William Clark Falkner. "At some point between mid-1864 and April, 1866, she gave birth to a baby girl, Fannie Forrest Falkner. Emeline's descendants have always maintained that Colonel Falkner—not Ben Harris [a former owner]—was Fannie's father."

14. Years later he would write about the visit in a letter, remembering, "I was suddenly taken with one of those spells of loneliness and nameless sorrow that children suffer, for what or because of what they did not know." {SL}

15. A bacterial illness, which presents as a bright red rash over much of the body accompanied by a sore throat and fever treated now with antibiotics. Untreated, this serious childhood disease can damage the heart, kidneys, and other parts of the body.

16. Grounded in the classics by her grandfather, Judge Henry C. Niles, Estelle gravitates to the artistically inclined Billy.

17. Events based on the lynching will appear in "Dry September" and *Light in August*," although what WF witnessed of this event has not been determined. That he heard about it is beyond question. See CR1 and JW.

18. Horse auctions and races fascinate Billy and become a feature of his earliest prose, beginning with "Father Abraham" in 1925 but also continuing in the Snopes trilogy and *A Fable.*

19. Reminiscent of the scenes with the MacCallums in *Flags in the Dust.*

20. Featured in Jason Compson's ridicule of the business in *The Sound and the Fury.*

21. WF later put his bank work to use in the opening scenes of his screenplay for *Sutter's Gold.*

22. A possible source for scenes in "Dry September" and *Light in August.*

23. Mass-produced Greek figurines.

24. WF never actually flew a plane during his RAF training.

25. WF did not, in fact, get a pilot's license.

26. WF refers to four hours flying, which, in fact, he never did during his training in Toronto.

27. This is apparently the excuse WF used in returning home without a license to fly.

28. Returning veterans could enroll in college even though, in WF's case, he had not completed high school.

29. A village on the Scottish border famous as a wedding destination.

30. The first prose presentation of the topography of Yoknapatawpha. Decades later, WF will return to this perspective in *The Town.*

31. WF thought he had left behind a muffler and his pipe, he apparently did not. Throughout his life he seemed to misplace his pipes and wrote letters asking about their whereabouts.

32. Other writers besides Anderson were paid cash for their work.

33. Most likely the Al Jackson letters, some of which are incorporated into *Mosquitoes.* The book with Anderson is never completed.

34. WF received a $10 first prize for the essay.

35. The genesis of *Mosquitoes.*

36. A negative review.

37. WF gave Percy a mixed review in the *Mississippian.* See entry for November 10, 1920.

38. A precursor of Benjy Compson.

39. Modeled in some respects on WF.

40. Howard Mumford Jones, ed., *The Letters of Sherwood Anderson.*

41. Jimmy was a lifelong favorite of WF. Jimmy called him "Brother Will."

42. From *Mayday* to *Soldiers' Pay.*

43. Evidently referring to "Elmer," which WF never finished.

44. William Odiorne, who took photographs of WF in Paris.

45. No record of how this demand was resolved is extant.

46. WF later tells the story in *Old Man.*

47. Did WF have in mind that $200 check from Liveright that he could not cash in France?

48. Most likely *The Sound and the Fury.*

49. WF seems to be referring to Estelle Oldham, although it has been pointed out that Aunt Bama would probably have known her. But no other woman has so far been identified as a likely source of Faulkner's sentiments, and Aunt Bama, after all, lived in Memphis, not Oxford.

50. Memorializing their frequenting of the Prohibition-era saloons.

51. WF did not lease or purchase this property.

52. LC reproduces WF's sending schedule.

53. One of the stories WF amalgamates into *Absalom, Absalom!*

54. No such story is extant, but James B. Meriwether suggests it might be the original title of "Spotted Horses." See LC.

55. On Native Americans as slaveholders: "https://www.smithsonianmag.com/smithsonian-institution/how-native-american-slaveholders-complicate-trail-tears-narrative-180968339/.

56. WF writes the date "31 October 1820."

57. One of precursors of *Absalom, Absalom!*

58. In an undated reply, Will Bryant preferred adhering to the original contract but agreed with WF's proposition to $500 as the total of annual payments, September 1 to September 1 of each year. {RO}

59. BH2 includes Stone's letter attempting to sell copies of *The Marble Faun.*

60. See entry for July 10, 1931.

61. A screenwriter (1896–1940). There is no record of Conselman working with WF on a film.

62. Kawin (MGM) sees some evidence of WF's work on the screenplay.

63. Byron Sage (1915–1974), an actor in silent and talking films.

64. Joel Sayre worked with WF on this adaptation of a French novel, *Wooden Crosses*, which was also made into a French film. The script includes other dates on substituted pages of revisions, but it is not clear if this is still the work of WF and Sayre.

65. Refers to *Absalom, Absalom!*

66. Neither party took additional action.

67. A screenwriter (1896–1940). There is no record of his working with WF on a film.

68. "He kept me alive," she later said.

69. "Bill liked to come home. He never felt quite himself away from Oxford or Rowan Oak."—John Faulkner. {JP}

70. ESPL.

71. Faulkner draws a map of the properties in question. {RO}

72. Probably *Intruder in the Dust.*

73. The first extant mention of what was to become *The Reivers.*

74. The story was not sold and instead took its place as "Was" in *Go Down, Moses.*

75. Brennan would later write about his visit in the *University of Kansas Review*, included in LG.

76. An early presentiment of *The Reivers.*

77. Published by Harcourt, Brace in 1941.

78. Ober wired the money.

79. A cousin, nephew of Aunt Bama (Alabama Leroy Falkner).

80. WF had made a personal loan to Stone.

81. "Snow" is published USWF and "Knight's Gambit" is included in a book by that title.

82. More than a little. Stone is not always reliable.

83. Faulkner did not respond.

84. (1910–1991), composer whose *Lincoln Cantata* is used as a refrain throughout *Battle Cry*.

85. WF could have his time off, the studio is telling him, but that time off will be tacked on to the length of his original contract.

86. (1880–1960). Hollywood screenwriter.

87. Nothing worked out.

88. The screenplay, "Angel's Flight," is in the Academy of Motion Pictures Arts and Sciences. For a discussion of the work, see CR2. It was never produced.

89. Bart H. Welling, "William Faulkner's Library Revisited," *Mississippi Quarterly* (Summer 1999): 365–420.

90. "The Garter Principal King of Arms (also Garter King of Arms or simply Garter) is the senior King of Arms, and the senior Officer of Arms of the College of Arms, the heraldic authority with jurisdiction over England, Wales and Northern Ireland. The position has existed since 1415." https://en.wikipedia.org/wiki/Garter_Principal_King_of_Arms.

91. A replacement copy for the one destroyed in 1942 when Phil Stone's home burned.

92. Carvel Collins interview on March 29, 1963, with an unidentified liquor salesman.

93. This may be *Dreadful Hollow*, a script Howard Hawks purchased in 1944. See CR2.

94. Perhaps this is Hawks's payment for work on *Dreadful Hollow*, a complete script all done by WF alone.

95. Trilling rejected McDermid's suggestion and wrote on the memo: "Definitely No! We will exercise and keep suspended." {BH2}

96. Actually, *The Little Review*.

97. Malcolm Franklin.

98. Dorothy Commins was a concert pianist.

99. See BH1, p. 147 for a slightly different version of the insertion.

100. Refers to an incident when he went missing and returned to write several unproduced screen treatments.

101. WF often called Malcolm Franklin "Buddy."

102. The meeting never occurred.

103. The meeting never occurred.

104. An apparent reference to his liaison with Else Jonsson.

105. I haven't found any evidence that Sherwood looked at the play.

106. WF liked to draw pipes and seems to have been keenly attracted to their shapes.

107. For work on *A Fable*, much of which is set in France.

108. Faulkner sent a postcard: "All Right. Bill."

109. In SL, Joseph Blotner included this letter in those for 1951, while admitting that "it is impossible to date this letter precisely. It might have been written at almost any time after the purchase of Greenfield Farm in 1938 when Faulkner was not preoccupied with other material." Blotner compares WF's statement about the semi-fictional aspect of the memoirs to the essay "Mississippi," which *Holiday* published in April 1954. Another reason why the letter may have been written in 1951 is that it may have been WF's way of blunting, if not stopping, Coughlan's projected biographical profile.

110. Williams did not visit Rowan Oak.

111. Ella Somerville, an Oxford friend.

112. Her father owned a dynamite business.

113. Not sent until September 28. See entry for that date.

114. Presumably, Estelle expected to be addressed as Mrs. William Faulkner.

115. He later changed his mind and in a codicil to his will (December 28, 1960) bequeathed all his manuscripts to the William Faulkner Foundation.

116. Never produced.

117. WF had dropped the notes on his way to the post office. {BH2}

118. She declined.

119. WF was working on *Land of the Pharaohs* for Howard Hawks.

120. They did not attend the funeral.

121. It is not clear if Coughlan is referring to Bennett Cerf, his partner, Donald Klopfer, or someone else in the firm.

122. It is noticeable that Stone spells the family name "Falkner" since he usually adds the u, even though many members of the family did not. Stone had written about the history of the Falkners, and his characterization of family men who will not listen to others is reminiscent of what was said about the old colonel, Faulkner's great-grandfather. Stone's animus toward Estelle appears in several letters and began when he took Faulkner away to Yale while Estelle married Cornell Franklin. Stone disapproved of the marriage to Estelle to begin with and never changed his mind about her.

123. She did not cash the check.

124. See entry for February 4.

125. Poets, playwrights, editors, essayists, and novelists.

126. *Time* wanted to do a cover story on *A Fable.*

127. V. P. Ferguson authored *Days of Yoknapatawpha* and befriended Faulkner in the 1950s. I have not been able to identify Dr. Busby.

128. The actual recording did not include *Light in August* and *Requiem for a Nun.*

129. WF was an outspoken opponent of Senator Joseph McCarthy's rabid anti-Communism and investigations of government officials. Physicist Robert Oppenheimer, organizer of the atomic bomb project at Los Alamos, lost his appointment to the Atomic Energy Commission because of his association with Communists.

130. Eventually published as "Mr. Acarius" in *The Saturday Evening Post,* October 9, 1965.

131. The project was never produced.

132. I have not been able to locate the editorial.

133. Apparently the second volume of the Snopes trilogy.

134. Gay Wilson Allen later published his account of the Nagano period. {CWF}

135. Faulkner omitted the comment.

136. Kirk was beaten for setting up a barricade to protect Lucy.

137. It has often been called the "most important and most influential of all WF's interviews."

138. See BH1 for a reproduction of the front page with Faulkner's headline.

139. The uniform edition has never been completed.

140. See entry for March 18, 1956.

141. The magazine did not take WF up on his offer.

142. The highest he had ever been paid for a periodical publication.

143. WF is alluding to his screen treatment of *Banjo on my Knee.*

144. "And Other Stories," was dropped from the title since WF considered *Go Down, Moses* a novel.

145. WF "knew the battles in considerable detail, far better than any of the rest of us," Blotner recalled.

146. WF's plans changed, and he did not visit Princeton.

147. WF was writing to a close friend of Malcolm to explain he did not write the harsh letter that upset Malcolm. It was Malcolm's aunt, Dorothy Oldham. See Tracy's letter in BH2.

148. Apparently WF's opposition to segregation offended Darden, who had not been enthusiastic about WF's presence on campus because of his earlier drunken performance there in 1931. But Darden also said he did not want other writers to think they might become permanent members of the English Department.

149. Ford wrote to Commins about her concerns that others would produce *Requiem for a Nun* before she had her own opportunity to mount productions. See BH2 for her letter.

150. WF does not seem to have responded.

151. WF presented three copies of the story to Margaret Brown, Estelle's stepdaughter, Cho-Cho (Victoria), and Ruth Ford's daughter, Shelley. He never seems to have thought of the story as publishable.

152. In fact, the agent was Leland Hayward of the American Play Company. WF's friend Ben Wasson worked for the agency.

153. WF does not seem to have answered the letter, and Random House did not publish the story until 1967.

154. Perhaps the same person referred to only as a "gentleman" in a letter in early December and December 8 to Phil Mullen asking him to help out. {BH2}

155. WF never returned the manuscript to Joan Williams.

156. Estelle's sister managed Rowan Oak while the Faulkners were away.

157. Random House published the *Selected Stories of William Faulkner* in 1962.

158. *Old Times in the Faulkner Country.*

159. See also Stone's long July 19, 1962, letter to Elizabeth Yeager Grosch about his involvement in WF's development as a writer. {BH2}

160. Son-in-law Paul Summers, West Point, class of 1951.

161. Massey said yes.

162. He died before sending the letter.

163. WF had put down $15,000 in his offer for Red Acres.

164. Helen was Else Jonsson's daughter.

INDEX

ABOUT THE AUTHOR

Self-portrait courtesy of the author

Carl Rollyson, professor emeritus of journalism, at Baruch College, CUNY, has published twelve biographies: *A Real American Character: The Life of Walter Brennan*; *A Private Life of Michael Foot*; *To Be A Woman: The Life of Jill Craigie*; *Amy Lowell Anew: A Biography*; *American Isis: The Life and Art of Sylvia Plath*; *Hollywood Enigma: Dana Andrews*; *Marilyn Monroe: A Life of the Actress*; *Lillian Hellman: Her Life and Legend*; *Beautiful Exile: The Life of Martha Gellhorn*; *Norman Mailer: The Last Romantic*; *Rebecca West: A Modern Sibyl*; *Susan Sontag: The Making of an Icon*. He has also published three studies of biography: *A Higher Form of Cannibalism? Adventures in the Art and Politics of Biography*; *Biography: A User's Guide*; and *Confessions of a Serial Biographer*. His reviews of biography have appeared in *Reading Biography*, *American Biography*, *Lives of the Novelists*, *Essays in Biography*, the *Wall Street Journal*, the *Weekly Standard*, the *New Criterion*, and other newspapers and periodicals. He has published four biographies for young adults on Pablo Picasso, Marie Curie, Emily Dickinson, and Thurgood Marshall. *The Life of William Faulkner* and *The Last Days of Sylvia Plath* were published in the spring and fall of 2020.